Multi-Ethnic Canada
Identities and Inequalities

Multi-Ethnic Canada
Identities and Inequalities

Leo Driedger

Toronto Oxford New York
OXFORD UNIVERSITY PRESS
1996

Oxford University Press
70 Wynford Drive, Don Mills, Ontario M3C 1J9

Oxford New York
Athens Auckland Bangkok Bombay
Calcutta Cape Town Dar es Salaam Delhi
Florence Hong Kong Istanbul Karachi
Kuala Lumpur Madras Madrid Melbourne
Mexico City Nairobi Paris Singapore
Taipei Tokyo Toronto

and associated companies in
Berlin Ibadan

Oxford is a trademark of Oxford University Press

Canadian Cataloguing in Publication Data

Driedger, Leo
    Multi-ethnic Canada : identities and inequalities

Includes bibliographical references and index.

ISBN 0–19–541161–7

1. Multiculturalism – Canada.*   I. Title.

FC104.D75   1996   305.8'00971   C96–931217–2
F1035.A1D75   1996

Design: Max Gabriel Izod

Composition: IBEX Graphic Communications

Cartography: Free & Creative

TABLE OF CONTENTS

PART IV: STRATIFICATION: POWER, STATUS, INEQUALITIES

LIST OF FIGURES

LIST OF TABLES

PREFACE

The focus of this book is unabashedly multi-ethnic and pluralist. I agree with William McNeill that polyethnicity is the trend in industrial urban societies, and the unitary nation-state with its yearning for a homogeneous ethnic society is both misguided and out of date.

The challenge is to provide a theoretical and conceptual frame of the field, which is still quite diverse and proliferated. Unfortunately, the classical theorists such as Karl Marx, Emile Durkheim, and Max Weber provide little guidance in ethnic relations. Only Weber wrote briefly on ethnicity. While American social science research has existed much longer, Park and the Chicago School focused so heavily on race relations and assimilation that research in ethnic pluralism was neglected. Thus, in a more multicultural Canada, we are faced with hoeing new theoretical rows, adapting and adjusting what research there is as best we can to fit our more polyethnic society. Such theoretical pioneering is both difficult and fraught with problems.

But the 1995 Quebec Referendum, where we almost lost Canada as we knew it; the fighting and negotiations between the Serbs, Bosnians, and Croatians; the violent turmoil in Somalia; the holocaust in Rwanda; and the assassination of Yitzak Rabin in the Middle East, all remind us that polyethnic societies do not come easily. Alas, mediation and murder too often seem to be bedfellows.

The last challenge is to find what empirical research we can, and fit it with conceptual frames for enlightenment and explanation. Much empirical research has been done, and especially during the thirty years following the studies launched by both John Porter and the Bilingual and Bicultural Commission in the 1960s. Canadian publications on race and racism have escalated particularly in the last ten years. Having studied in the interdisciplinary program at Chicago, I wanted to blend the sociological, anthropological, psychological, economic, political, and historical contributions to give ethnicity a rich conceptual frame, as well as a broad context for understanding this complex phenomenon. While this volume is focused on sociology, I hope the reader will detect other disciplinary uses and appreciations as well. This complexity, of course, makes the whole enterprise of definition and careful thought even more difficult.

In addition to the many people whose writings stimulated me and who are listed in the references, I convey special thanks to the anonymous reader who helped improve this work. I also wish to thank Darlene Driedger, who processed many drafts faithfully.

Leo Driedger
University of Manitoba
1996

PART I

Finding a Theoretical Focus

CHAPTER 1

Ethnic Pluralism and Industrialization

Canada is a multiethnic nation with a variety of ethnic, racial, religious, and political identities. Some societies have more diverse populations than others; Canada is among the most polyethnic. But except for Weber, the classical theorists were little concerned with ethnic minorities. However, early American scholars such as Park and Thomas of the Chicago School were intensely interested in race and ethnic relations. Let us review their contributions to gain some perspective on ethnic pluralism and industrialization.

Chicago historian William McNeill (1985) addressed scholars at the University of Toronto saying that 'polyethnicity is normal in civilized societies, whereas the ideal of one ethnically unitary state was exceptional in theory and rarely approached in practice. Marginality and pluralism were and are the norm of civilized existence' (1986: 4, 6). He claims that 'the idea that a government rightfully should rule only over citizens of a single ethnos took root haltingly in western Europe, beginning in the late middle ages; it got into full gear and became fully conscious in the late eighteenth century and flourished vigorously until about 1920' (1986: 7). Since then it has weakened in the West, but it still finds fertile ground in the ex-colonial lands of Africa and Asia.

McNeill (1986) shows that before 1750, conquest, disease, and trade all contributed to the reinforcement of polyethnicity, but between 1750 and 1920, especially in western Europe, the triumph of nationalism introduced the contrasting ideal of ethnic homogeneity, or monoethnicity, within a geographic or sovereign boundary. Ironically, this nationalism—particularly in England and France—fed the monoethnic ideal while overseas wars and the expansion of world commerce were mixing peoples more vigorously than ever before. In Latin America, people of mixed American, African, and European heritage constitute a large proportion of the populations. In North America, English and French nationalism greatly influenced the United States and Canada, but the different histories of the two countries require separate analysis.

McNeill (1986: 59–85) argues that since 1920 the multiethnic norm has reasserted itself, so that we are now back to recognizing the factors which

promote ethnic mixing and which are the norm of civilized societies. Industrialization, urbanization, and modern communication all encourage polyethnicity, whereas the earlier practice of encasing each ethnic group within its
own separate state fell painfully short of expectations for the reduction of ethnic and class frictions. Since World War II Western Europe has been reorganized into transnational affiliations within the United Nations, NATO, the
former Warsaw Pact, and the European Common Market. McNeill (1986:
70) suggests that new ideas, demographic changes, military organization, and
the intensification of communication and transport have all helped to undermine the recent past's ideal of ethnic unity. Hitler's passion for racial unity
and his genocidal campaign to accomplish homogeneity have shown where
such ideals of monoethnicity can lead. Sharp declines in birthrates in Europe
after the war led to the recruitment of workers under the *gastarbeiter* policy,
which brought many south Europeans into the north. The two world wars
scattered Caucasians around the world, and to this day peace-keeping and
jockeying for political power bring many of them together through military
operations. The recent North American Free Trade Agreement (NAFTA) will
add to interchange. Modern communications and transportation make it relatively easy for immigrants to continue to stay in touch with their kin by telephone and air travel. Thus, ethnic communities are becoming somewhat more
detached from geographical territory. Ethnic ties and religious networks have
become more portable, just as the world religions of Buddhism, Confucian-
ism, Christianity, and Islam did.

Joan Nagel (1984) sounds a similar theme, pointing out the modern ethnic
revolution in many parts of the world with its 'secession, organization, devolu-
tion and genocide representing the many faces of ethnicity'. Nagel (1984: 418)
sees 'the pervasive presence of ethnicity underlying such political issues as
East–West relations, North–South inequalities, human rights abuses, and
short- and long-term political stability'. Quebec's passing Bill 101 making the
French language official in Quebec in 1977; the long-standing conflict
between Protestants and Catholics in Northern Ireland; the fighting among
warlords in Mozambique; massacres in Rwanda; and the attempts of Aboriginals to entrench land claim rights in the Canadian constitution are but a few of
the ethno-religious conflicts in the news today.

In this volume we shall focus on polyethnicity in North America, specifically in Canada. We agree with McNeill and Nagel that our societies have
always been multiethnic, that the drive of North Europeans for monoethnicity does not bode well in a global village of the future, and that we should
now concentrate on Canadian ethnic pluralism and see what we can learn
from it in the quest for a more just and humane society.

In the first part of this chapter we want to find a theoretical focus by first
looking at what the classical theorists such as Weber, Durkheim, and Marx

had to say about ethnicity. Max Weber is most helpful because he wrote about race, and the role of culture, language, nationality, and religion in industrial society. Weber's analysis of the characteristics of ethnic groups and identity will naturally lead into an examination of what is meant by ethnicity. In the second part of this chapter we shall discuss the influence that European scholars had on American sociologists, especially those of the Chicago School (Persons, 1987). Ethnic and racial studies were central to the research at the University of Chicago, and the Chicago perspective in turn influenced early Canadian sociologists (Shore, 1987).

Scholars have not sufficiently linked the study of ethnic relations to classical theorists such as Weber, Durkheim, and Marx. One reason is that very few of the classical theorists dealt with the category of ethnicity at all, so there is little natural, ready-made material that can be easily used. Max Weber is one of the few scholars who explicitly addressed the issue, and he discussed it only briefly. The writings of Weber and Marx were left unfinished, but even if they had completed the larger studies which they planned, it is doubtful that ethnicity would have had an important place. When nationalism in northern Europe was on the rise, ethnicity did not seem to be the most pressing among the many issues which required research.

However, the classical social theorists dealt with many issues of identity, solidarity, conflict, and social inequalities of concern to scholars of ethnic relations today. We shall begin by using important material which Weber wrote about ethnic relations, and we shall use Durkheim's and Marx's contributions on how industrial change affects ethnicity. These theorists lived in England, France, and Germany, the most industrialized countries of the day, and sought to understand the dehumanizing effects of industry. They help us to understand industrialization as one of the major factors influencing changes in all aspects of life, including ethnicity.

MAX WEBER AND ETHNIC IDENTITY

Max Weber (1864–1920) spent most of his life in Germany, one of the most highly industrial northern European countries. Germany had only recently emerged as a national power from the multiethnic Austro-Hungarian empire with its variety of languages, cultures, and ideas, so we would expect Weber to be aware of the benefits of diversity. He examined values, leadership, religion, ethnicity, and other non-economic factors which he felt were crucial in the rise of industrialization because he wanted to understand the role and importance of values, ideology, and symbols in shaping the industrialization process.

While Weber did not research ethnicity extensively, he had plans to do so and left us an outline on 'Ethnic Groups' which is useful in providing a conceptual frame (Weber, 1978: 379–98). A careful study of his outline shows that Weber saw race, culture, tribe, nationality, and religion as the central foci that define ethnic identity. In his treatise on ethnic groups, he mentioned the need to develop a more careful analysis of the complex phenomenon of ethnicity, but he died before he could do so. Let us use his five points to define and clarify the concept of ethnic identity.

RACE AND BIOLOGICAL INHERITANCE

Race, Weber's first ethnic identity factor, is based on heredity and endogamous conjugal groups. Whether or not racial heredity becomes an important feature for delineating social circles depends largely upon social and regional settings and values. All kinds of visible differences can serve as sources of repulsion and contempt, or affection and appreciation. Biological physical differences can be the focus of consciousness of kind:

> Strikingly different racial types, bred in isolation, may live in sharply segregated proximity to one another either because of monopolistic closure or because of migration. . . . Almost any kind of similarity or contrast of physical type and of habits can induce the belief that affinity or disaffinity exists between groups that attract or repel each other. (Weber, 1978: 386)

There is a biological unity of humankind, in that no other species of the genus *Homo* now exists, and our species is restricted to its own members (Kallen, 1995: 13). But there is the all-too-human tendency to emphasize and exaggerate differences.

There is no such thing as a 'pure race'. Since the discoveries of Gregor Mendel (1822–1884), the science of genetics shows that there are variations within the species *Homo*:

> It is clear from these genetic data that primary divisions of humankind are distinguishable from one another. The evidence of physical features, skeletal features, and many genetic markers combine to indicate clearly that there are differences among populations of the same human species that are drawn from the three major geographical breeding grounds of human populations: Africa, Asia, Europe. These biogeographical divisions (races) are commonly identified as Negroid ('Black'), Mongoloid ('Yellow'), and Caucasoid ('White'). (Kallen, 1995: 15)

Within any human society, the social construction of the concept of race can reflect ideological, political, economic, and cultural biases of those who have authority because they have the power to define. Thus, racial categories often do not remain neutral. Their social relevance then lies not in themselves, but the use to which they are put by those in power to differentiate. Ideologies of racism may develop where, in a system of dominance which socializes and communicates differences based on biological features, minorities become less valued (Henry et al., 1995: 14).

Intermarriage becomes a factor, depending on how important physical racial features are to a group, and whether they encourage physical attraction or segregation. When racial features become important in distinguishing groups, then the offspring of intermarriage by individuals from different races may not be fully accepted by one or both groups. This does not sanction intermarriage and the resultant mixed offspring as fully in social circles as endogamous marriages would. In Chapter Ten we will expand on the whole concept of race and its relevance in the discussion of ethnic identity.

CULTURE AND CONSCIOUSNESS OF KIND

Although racial differences are based on heredity, Weber (1978: 387) says social circles 'may be linked to the most superficial features of historically accidental habits just as much as to inherited racial characteristics'. Cultural differences in clothing styles and grooming, food and eating habits, and the division of labour between sexes can all be the focus of a consciousness of kind that can become either shared characteristics of identity or barriers between groups.

> Any cultural trait, no matter how superficial, can serve as a starting point for the familiar tendency to monopolistic closure. . . .
>
> But if there are sharp boundaries between areas of observable styles of life, they are due to conscious monopolistic closure, which started from small differences that were then cultivated and intensified; or they are due to the peaceful or warlike migrations of groups that previously lived far from each other and had accommodated themselves to their heterogeneous conditions of existence. . . .
>
> Such a belief can exist and can develop group-forming powers when it is buttressed by a memory of an actual migration, be it colonization or individual migration. The persistent effect of the old ways and of childhood reminiscences continues as a source of native-country sentiment (*Heimatsgefühl*) among emigrants even when they have become so thoroughly adjusted to the new country that return to their homeland would be intolerable. (Weber, 1978: 388)

Heimatsgefühl, or feeling at home in a culture, is a key factor because humans want to live by habit rather than decide constantly what to do next. It is comfortable to sense a 'consciousness of kind' where you are accepted as you are.

After having discussed race and culture as major foci for ethnic identity, Weber presents his definition of ethnic groups:

> We shall call 'ethnic groups' those human groups that entertain a subjective belief in their common descent because of similarities of physical type or of customs or both, or because of memories of colonization and migration;

this belief must be important for the propagation of group formation; conversely, it does not matter whether or not an objective blood relationship exists. Ethnic membership (*Gemeinsamkeit*) differs from the kinship group precisely by being a presumed identity, not a group with concrete social action, like the latter. (Weber, 1978: 389)

Weber stresses the importance of a belief in a common ethnicity, no matter how artificial the origin of this belief may be. This belief in common ethnicity often delimits social circles where shared sentiments of likeness emerge and are groomed. When the memory of group experiences remains alive, there is the potential for a powerful sense of ethnic identity, involving 'persistent ties with the old cult, or the strengthening of kinship and other groups, both in the old and the new community' (Weber, 1978: 390).

In the process of group identification, a sense of ethnic honour can develop as a part of the subjectively believed community of descent: 'Behind all ethnic diversities there is somehow naturally the notion of the "chosen people", which is merely a counterpart of status differentiation . . .' (Weber, 1978: 391). The idea of a chosen people permits anyone to claim this right, no matter what the quality of his or her identity may be. Being one of 'the chosen' encourages differentiation into ingroup and outgroup categories. Any cultural traits—including beards, hats, hairdos, etc.—can then become differentiating symbols of the ingroup. Hutterites, Lubavitcher Jews, and the Amish are but a few examples of groups who use clothing as symbols of identity. These distinguishing features are often used as blood disaffinity (*Blutsfremdheit*) symbols, regardless of their importance in objective reality. Thus, it is common to think of *Kulturgemeinschaft*, a cultural *gemeinschaft*, a shared culture, as a central feature of ethnic group identity. In Chapter Eight we provide specific Canadian examples of typical ethnic cultural communities.

TRIBE: EMERGENCE OF 'A PEOPLE'

Many tribal groups simply refer to themselves as The People, and the Inuit are our best Canadian example. It is no wonder that the Inuit preferred their own name to the European nickname 'Eskimo', taken from a native Indian word meaning 'eaters of raw meat'. Isolated in the Arctic, far away from other humans, they were The People; there were no others until the Europeans came. Tribe implies the emergence of political organization on a small scale, usually a subdivision of a larger whole. The twelve tribes of Israel became subparts of The People of Israel. This subdivision is similar to that which occurred in the Classic world: 'The three Doric *phylai* and the various *phylai* of the other Hellenes' in Greece were similar tribal subdivisions (Weber, 1978: 393). Such divisions can soon be symbolized as analogous to blood relationships, political artifacts which create feelings of affinity akin to blood relationships.

Tribes have been formed by families banding together in the past, to engage in common political action, to defend themselves, or to get some work done. Thus, the memory of their Tribe having lived through common political experiences becomes a social construct, or a memory of cohesion and solidarity which they identify with. In such political actions, they develop a sense of moral duty to other members of their People. The tribe represents an elementary stage of organization around symbols and memory which is more diverse than family blood relationships. When the Europeans came to North America, native Indians had formed many tribes, many of which still perpetuate their memory and organization in most parts of Canada. They feel special obligations toward each other because of a feeling of affinity that began in the past.

Stories, a form of oral history usually told by the tribal elders, where written language has not yet been developed, are an important part of perpetuating the shared memory of their origins. Stories of the origins of cults that were central to the tribe's beginning, shared places that symbolize these beginnings, and leaders who were central to preserving these memories are all part of the collective memory of The People as a tribe. Religion and shared religious beliefs are important because questions of origin—where they began, why they began, and what sustained their cohesion as The People—are difficult to answer, so that beliefs in being a chosen People show belief in oracles, gods, or cults as a logical progression of symbolism. Memories, epic tales, and legends often become religious beliefs. Studies show that religion is an important part of tribal consciousness. In Chapter Seven we deal more deeply with the development of the sense of the sacred.

NATIONALITY: THE NOTION OF 'VOLK'

Lest we think that only food-gathering tribal peoples are preoccupied with common descent, we must recognize that urban industrial humans share the same need for nationality and cohesion on a larger scale, which likewise perpetuates the symbols of common descent. People living in modern nations have even less claim to blood relations, but according to Weber (1978: 395), they also promote the 'vague connotation that whatever is felt to be distinctly common must derive from common descent'. They perpetuate the concept of 'Volk', or People, on a much larger national scale. Why do Canadian youth travelling abroad often carry the maple leaf flag on their backpacks?

'Today, in the age of language conflicts, a shared common language is pre-eminently considered the normal basis of nationality. . . . Indeed, "nation-state" has become conceptually identical with "state" based on common language' (Weber, 1978: 395). In reality, modern states usually have different language groups within them, so that often nationalism is seen to include an insistence on one common language so that a national identity (*Nationalsgefühl*) can be perpetuated. In Canada, French Canadians are a problem for nationalists, even though Canada is now officially a bilingual country. Many Ukrainians, Germans, Italians, Chinese, and aboriginals still speak their own languages at home; thus in most modern nations today multilinguistic tendencies survive. The various languages then take on their own prestige rankings, so that for many, the English language has higher prestige than does French (especially outside Quebec), while the French language has higher prestige in the province of Quebec.

Weber defines nationality as being oriented toward a common language and culture, which is a problem when applied to multiethnic societies like Canada and the United States. He admits that feelings of identity subsumed under the term 'national' are not uniform but may derive from diverse sources including customs, shared political memories, religion, language, and race. Nations have political power, which makes them unique, but how this power is used in moulding ethnicity in a country varies enormously. In Canada we can no longer assume, as they did in Europe, that people of one nation share a common language, religion, or customs. Canada does not have a state religion, but allows freedom of religious expression in many forms. Politically, Canada is not subject to a king, as were many Europeans in the past, but is only symbolically related to the British crown. Canadians choose between many political philosophies, parties, and leaders who change frequently. French Canadians have also retained their distinctive identity, as have the Indian peoples and many other ethnic and visible minorities. This is why Canada has wrestled and continues to wrestle with how to govern such a pluralistic people. What does 'The People' mean in Canada, or is it still possible to think in such terms? What is Canadian national identity, and how can this diversity be ordered? A monoethnic ideal does not seem possible, so Pierre Trudeau called for a bilingual and multicultural Canada. While the Meech Lake accord seemed to include French Quebeckers in the Canadian constitution, they could not agree to such an accord. In Chapter Five we focus on the importance of language and a bilingual Canada and Quebec's insistence on special status in Canada as a nation within a nation. Quebec separatists, of course, want Quebec to separate as a distinct nation.

RELIGION: AN IDEOLOGICAL SYMBOL SYSTEM
In his ethnic identity discussion, Weber included religion under culture and tribe, where we have also included it in our review. However, Weber wrote a half dozen volumes on the role of religion in society; it deserves special discussion as a fifth focus in his characterization of ethnic identity. It is especially important to see the place of religion not only in tribal folk societies, but in the industrial urban setting which he dealt with extensively.

Reinhard Bendix (1977: 43) suggests that 'Weber emphasized both the importance of ideas for an understanding of the economic behavior and the social foundation of such ideas if they were to have an effect upon human conduct.' Weber's emphasis on ideas had already become apparent in his early studies of the Junkers in eastern Germany. Ideas and actions were not simply the product of their economic interests, as the Marxists had maintained, but a part of a larger social value system.

> We want to cultivate and support what appear to us as valuable in man: his personal responsibility, his basic drive toward higher things, toward the spiritual and moral values of mankind, even where this drive confronts us in its most primitive form. Insofar as it is in our power we want to create the external conditions which will help to preserve—in the face of the inevitable struggle for existence with its suffering—the best that is in man, those physical and emotional qualities which we would like to maintain for the nation. (Weber, 1894: 159)

It is clear, however, that Weber wanted both lines of inquiry—values and materialism—examined, as he clearly stated later in *The Protestant Ethic and the Spirit of Capitalism* (1904):

> It is of course, not my aim to substitute for a one-sided materialism an equally one-sided spiritualistic causal interpretation of culture and history. Each is equally possible, but each, if it does not serve as the preparation, but as the conclusion of an investigation, accomplishes equally little in the interest of historical truth. (Weber, 1904: 183)

This double emphasis was the guiding consideration of Weber's work on the sociology of religion, and it is well expressed by Otto Hintze (1931: 252):

> . . . man develops his capacities to the highest extent only if he believes that in so doing he serves a higher rather than a purely egoistic purpose. Interests without such 'spiritual wings' are lame; on the other hand, ideas can win out in history only if and insofar as they are associated with real interests . . . Wherever interests are vigorously pursued, an ideology tends to be developed also to give meaning, reinforcement and justification to these interests. And the ideology is as 'real' as the real interests themselves, for ideology is an indispensable part of the life process which is expressed in action . . .

Weber spent enormous time and energy writing *The Protestant Ethic and the Spirit of Capitalism*, as well as his volumes on religion in China, India, and Palestine, and a general sociology of religion. Like Durkheim, he sensed that religion played an important part in society; unlike Marx, who dismissed religion as 'an opiate of the people', Weber set ideology—whether religious or political—in an important place. In his discussion of ethnicity, Weber included religion along with language, race, tribe, and culture as one of five important characteristics in the formation of ethnic identity. In Chapter Seven we discuss how the sacred is perpetuated by groups such as the aboriginals, Hutterites, and Jews. We expect that similar patterns of perpetuation occur among many minorities where both religion and ethnicity act as foci for solidarity and identification.

Weber clearly recognized ethnicity as an important social category and phenomenon which he wanted to expand and develop later. Race, culture, and religion have been used extensively as characteristics of ethnicity in the literature. Most ethnic writers have in mind the concept of 'tribe' which involves consciousness of kind when they refer to folk or rural groups that have not yet been greatly influenced by industrialization and urbanization. The concept of 'Volk', or the nation-state, is a more recent urban and industrial sense of peoplehood based on somewhat secondary factors, while the sense of tribe is more based on primary relations. Most scholars grant that pre-industrial societies recognize smaller groupings of tribes and ethnic groups, and that these tribes and groups are able to retain a separate solidarity and identity by spatial segregation, kinship ties, and close primary friendship networks. When industrialization and urbanization set in, however, these ethnic boundaries are subject to extensive change. Of the process of industrialization, the classical theorists, Marx and Durkheim, had much more to say than they did about ethnicity.

INDUSTRIAL CHANGE: A MAJOR CLASSICAL CONCERN

The classical theorists, while less interested in ethnicity than industrialization, were deeply concerned with the impact of industry on society. They thought it promoted mechanical materialism and undermined social solidarity. These foci are relevant in our discussion of ethnicity because stratification and secularization affect ethnic values such as culture, religion, consciousness of kind, a sense of being a People, and how we relate as racial groups. Marx was concerned with stratification, power, and the potential for alienation; Durkheim probed the role of secularization and what this does to social cohesion and sacred values. Stratification and secularization affect ethnic identity, which is the point of discussing industrialization here.

Over the past century, most Western countries have increasingly modified laissez-faire industrial capitalism by a greater emphasis on the social needs of all citizens. There are at least five basic tenets of early capitalism: 1) individual enterprise, 2) the profit motive, 3) private property, 4) competition, and 5) inheritance, all of which have since been greatly modified. Industrial capitalism, in the days of Marx, was designed to give individuals freedom to do business without government interference. Making a margin of profit was most important to the industrialist, so that often factory workers became mere tools in making money. The profits belonged to the owner, and he could pass them on as an inheritance to whomever he wished. Those individuals could freely compete in the marketplace, seeking to gain an advantage over others.

In the fray of competition there was a tendency to focus on private gains so extensively that workers and other people often were of secondary importance. This excessive individualism was of great concern to the classical theorists. It is relevant to our study because we propose that ethnicity is, for many people, a way to nurture a consciousness of kind and a distinctive identity which focuses not on material but on human needs.

MARX: MATERIALISM AND STRATIFICATION

Let us briefly focus on materialism and stratification, two concerns of Karl Marx in the industrial process. Marx spent his early years in Germany, and the latter part of his life in Britain. Marx (1818–1883) was among the first to be concerned with the capitalist industrial scene in England, Germany, and France. Industrialization was greatly enhanced by steam power: the exploration of new lands had resulted in the emergence of numerous colonial powers in Europe, and raw materials from these colonies were increasingly processed in north European factories. More and more peasants were moving off their lands into urban areas where factories gobbled up their labour skills. Both Marx and Durkheim were profoundly influenced by industrial change, and both were greatly preoccupied with analyzing what was happening to the human factor during this social upheaval. The various social theorists turned to different parts of the problem. Marx was preoccupied with the effects of economic materialism and its resulting human alienation; he saw a solution only in a complete restructuring of the political economy.

> Marx was profoundly opposed to mechanical materialism . . . Marx's main criticism of capitalism was precisely that it makes man a prisoner of material interests. Socialism was for him that social order which would liberate man from slavery to greed as well as to blind economic forces. For him, man should become a being who is much, rather than one who has much. (Fromm, 1956: xv)

According to Fromm, the often-mistaken interpretation of Marx's works— that he was a materialist interested in promoting satisfaction in material goods—is opposite to Marx's concerns.

Marx viewed not only the product, but the process of production under the capitalist system as alienating. Workers who had only their labour to sell tended not to identify with the end result; in the process of producing the product, they took little pride in their work because, aside from their wages, the profits they generated benefited only the bourgeoisie, the owners of the capitalist process. Industry also tends to focus attention on machines, schedules, and the mechanical process, distracting from concerns of human fulfilment, creativity, and pride in the product of individuals' skills. As a result the worker feels homeless, work becomes external to him, and he does not fulfil himself in his work. 'His work is not voluntary, but imposed, forced labour. It is not the satifaction of a need, but only a means for satisfying other needs' (Marx, 1844: 85–6).

This work for someone else does not belong to the worker but to the owner. Spontaneity is lost. Marx thought that as the person becomes poorer in himself, he feels he belongs less to himself than to someone else, or he is dependent on machines which are not emotionally satisfying. In the process, money becomes the object of all work because it alone will buy the necessities of life. As a result of the worker's alienation from his work, money tends to have more and more power over him. Thus, Marx concludes that 'all human servitude is involved in the relation of the worker to production, and all types of servitude are only modifications or consequences of this relation' (Marx, 1844: 92–3).

While Marx was concerned that industrial materialism not become an alienating factor for humans, he was also concerned with the way in which industrial capitalism stratified humans into the rich and the poor, the powerful and the powerless, the bourgeoisie and the working proletariat. While Hegel used this dialectic in philosophical terms, Marx gave it a concrete empirical context in which the economic classes of the bourgeoisie were pitted again the proletariat masses. The owners of capital, whose major interest was a margin of profit, the accumulation of capital, and investment in more industry, came into conflict with the labourers, who needed to labour in order to earn wages to subsist. Thus, Marx thought, struggle between the two opposites, the two classes, was inevitable. The process promoted 'the mass of misery, oppression, slavery, degradation, and exploitation; but with this too grew the revolt of the working-class, a class always increasing in numbers' (Marx, 1867: 801–4).

Marx concluded that capitalism and its alienating processes were the villains. Thus, it must be exterminated by a structural overthrow of the bourgeoisie, the proponents of capital. Through the ages, the economically and politically powerful had often enslaved the masses, and capitalists enslaved the proletariat in his day. There was but one way to root out this cancerous plague, and that was to overthrow the bourgeoisie by the revolt of the masses. Ironically, communist experiments in eastern European countries, which were designed to replace oppressive capitalist systems, also became oppressive and have been toppled recently. Marx spent much time analyzing the failures of capitalism, but too little time developing effective alternatives.

Since the capitalist structure could not be reformed, Marx proposed that we begin afresh. What his new society would be like, and how it would operate, he addressed only in general communal terms:

> . . . the empirical world should be arranged in such a way that man experiences and assimilates there what is really human, that he experiences himself as man. If the enlightened self interest is the principle of all morality it is

necessary for the private interest of each man to coincide with the general interest of humanity. (Marx, 1845: 307–8)

Communism is the positive abolition of private property, of human self-alienation, and thus the real appropriation of human nature through, and for man. It is therefore the return of man itself as a social, that is really human being . . . Religion, the family, the State, law, morality, science, art, etc., are only particular forms of production and come under its general law. (Marx, 1844: 114–5)

Industrialization affects the maintenance of ethnic identity enormously. We agree with Marx that materialism and stratification, the results of industrialization, tend to undermine community and social relations. Ethnicity remains an important part of industrial modern societies. Many people find ethnic identity an important way of fighting alienation because it enhances consciousness of kind, a sense of belonging to 'a people' who care; it promotes meaningful communities and networks which provide support; and it stimulates a vision and hope for ideology and symbolic interaction.

DURKHEIM: COHESION AND SACRALIZATION

It is not surprising that, in the midst of the European industrial revolution, scholars would also search for the factors which provide cohesion and solidarity during periods of social change. While Marx focused on the macro economic industrial trends toward materialism and stratification, Emile Durkheim (1857–1917) devoted himself to looking at elements of social cohesion and sacralization. What are the sustaining ties of community during the decline of the religious dogma of the old Catholic world, and where will new guides for the future lie?

Durkheim spent most of his time in France. 'The third Republic was the eighth regime since 1789. There had been three monarchies, two empires, and three republics in the period between 1779 and 1870, and these eight regimes had produced fourteen constitutions' (Bellah, 1973: xvi). French society had for a long time been enfeebled by an excessive spirit of individualism which influenced Durkheim to seek the sources of social cohesion and solidarity.

The social milieu and the industrial and political revolutions of Durkheim's time tended to weaken the structures of belief, authority, and community within which human beings had lived for centuries, even millennia (Nisbet, 1974: 14). Durkheim was deeply concerned with the effects of the increasing emphasis on individualism. Individuals everywhere were dislocated from traditional associations and communities. Durkheim rejected this extreme individualism and saw it as leading to the destruction of community, values, and the social order. He focused on the coherence of society and the factors of collective solidarity. Alienation, anomie, and disintegration spelled non-society.

Durkheim saw the crises of the modern age basically in terms of a disintegration of the roots of stability and authority (Nisbet, 1974 :9). The marks of conservatism are clear in Durkheim's life and work and may likely have sprung from his own Jewish heritage where the sense of community was strong. While scholars such as Gabriel Tarde and Herbert Spencer focused on individuals, Durkheim, in contrast, saw society as the most important centre of attention.

Ferdinand Toennies's *Gemeinschaft und Gesellschaft*, which Durkheim reviewed, was published in Germany in 1889. Toennies's discussion of community surely influenced Durkheim's thinking. Four years later (1893), Durkheim introduced the concepts of mechanical and organic solidarity in his first published work, *The Division of Labor in Society*. These two polarities tend to convey the evolutionary trend of the time, and he did not use them again in his later works. He labelled labour in folk and rural societies *mechanical* solidarity, because adherents of such communities tend not to think about their structures very much, but follow tradition mechanically and without much evaluation. However, as industrial change sets in, societies are forced to develop new forms of social structures such as associations, which depend more on *organic* or cohesive values and norms more rationally agreed upon and adhered to in free association. His later books such as *Suicide* (1897) and *Elementary Forms of Religious Life* (1912) continue the search for factors which support social solidarity.

Durkheim advocated intermediate associations that would act as a buffer between the traditional folk norms and values which had formerly been adhered to mechanically and the emerging rational bureaucratic institutions which were a result of the industrial revolution. These associations, often centring on occupation, would permit human beings to 'regain the reinforcing sense of membership in society—lost, as Durkheim so forcefully stated in *Suicide*, through the acids of modernity' (Nisbet, 1974: 138). If Durkheim's argument holds, then 'the crowning need of contemporary society is for centres of authority and solidarity in which the present anomie and egoism leading to suicide and other forms of deviant behavior will be checked' (Nisbet, 1974: 139).

Durkheim 'traces the idea of contract back to the aboriginal relationship between a people and its god, back to the overriding, overpowering condition Durkheim calls the Sacred' (Nisbet, 1974: 78). He focuses on some god or sacred things that are deemed antecedent to—and in control of—the contradictory parties. Solidarity becomes a contract between humans and the sacred realm. As humans later turned to agriculture, they added land and a sacred trust to their concept of sacred *descent*. Patriarchs eventually became trustees of the people, charged with perpetuating their sacred history.

Our first human notion of force was expressed in religious terms, which are social terms in Durkheim's view:

Our analysis of the facts has already enabled us to see that the prototype of the idea of force was the *mana, orenda,* the totemic principle or any of the various names given to the collective force objectified and projected into things. The first power which men have thought of as such seems to have been that exercised by humanity over its members. (Durkheim, 1912: 363)

Primitive people began to feel the awesome force of the entire community to create and hold a sense of loyalty and obligation, a sense which in turn developed rituals and rites as an expression of their relationships.

Robert Nisbet (1974: 164–5) succinctly summarizes Durkheim's treatment of religion and its function in society: 1) religion is necessary to society as a vital mechanism of integration for human beings and as a means to unify symbols; 2) religion is a seedbed for social change, which both Durkheim and Weber say in their discussions of Protestantism; 3) more important than creed or belief, religion's most enduring elements are in ritual, ceremony, hierarchy, and community; 4) there is a link between religion and the origins of human thought and reason. Religion stimulates the search for knowledge and answers deep questions. Durkheim saw religion as a consecration of community, a respect for society.

While some scholars saw religion as a crutch for primitives who had not yet separated empirical reality from myth, Durkheim thought that the sacred would remain for all time, that it would vary from age to age, and that it would manifest itself differently among different peoples. It is in this larger sense of the sacred that ethnicity can be viewed as 'sacred' in modern society. Religion may be an important distinctive element, as being Anglican can be for Anglo-Saxons, or it may be a more pervasive, undifferentiated whole linking religion as the defining factor of community, as it is for Hutterites. But ethnicity for secular Jews, non-religious Ukrainians, or other groups may still carry many non-religious elements of sacredness: their attachments to a heritage, a culture, a myth, a set of norms, a consciousness of kind, or values with a particular cultural, social, and communal focal point.

For both the religious and the non-religious, Durkheim suggests that morality based on a system of rules of conduct is crucial. The mechanical rules of the past cannot be forgotten as traditional baggage enslaving the individual, as some proponents of individualism such as Spencer have advocated. Rather, norms of obligation and duty must always be present, albeit often in changed and sometimes new forms. The preeminent attribute of morality is its capacity to inspire the individual to a sense of obligation. Here we shall see to what extent ethnicity has played, and still plays, such a role of obligation and sense of morality. Is it disappearing in the rise of industrialization? Is it adapting and changing? To what extent is it, and will it remain, a driving force in Canadian society?

Durkheim sees the family, religion, and socialization as integrating forms of solidarity. In this volume we propose that ethnicity, especially in North America, can also be a form of identification with a heritage, culture, language, religion, or race. Such solidarity is evident in French rural Quebec, in the northlands where the aboriginal people are a majority, and in many rural or agricultural areas where Ukrainians, Germans, Scandinavians, and others seek to maintain ethnic enclaves. For Durkheim, the attachment to meaningful groups is crucial to an integrated society.

Both Marx and Durkheim were concerned with the effects of industrialization on the quality of human existence. Marx observed increased stratification, alienation, and misuse of power, and suggested that the power relationships and the social structure must be totally changed. Durkheim observed the decline of social solidarity and cohesion when the sacred became profane, and how the threat of anomie increased with industrialization. While they did not apply their findings to ethnicity, their relevance to modern ethnicity is quite obvious. While Marx proposed communism, Durkheim and Weber explored the roles of religion, social cohesion, and identity. Only Weber briefly examined the role of ethnicity in the industrialization process. However, American scholars in Chicago applied many of these European principles and theories to their multiethnic society.

ETHNICITY AND THE CHICAGO SCHOOL

While European sociologists did not focus extensively on ethnicity, early American sociologists fortunately did; they also took the changes in industrialization and urbanization into account. The first Department of Sociology in North America was established in 1892 at the University of Chicago, where the *Journal of American Sociology* has been published since 1895. Extensive immigration to the United States from southeastern Europe began in the 1880s and continued until restrictive legislation occurred in the 1920s. Anglo-Americans became increasingly apprehensive about the ability of these immigrants to be assimilated, and about their effect on the American identity. Large influxes of Germans into Pennsylvania, earlier, had fostered similar apprehensions. Pressures toward Anglo-Americanization began to mount, especially during World War I. These immigrants from Europe also came to Chicago and the mid-West, and soon southern Blacks also arrived.

While the early Chicago sociologists, sometimes referred to as 'The Chicago School', are best known for their studies in urban sociology, a number of them also did extensive research in race and ethnic relations. They were among the first scholars to try to study these many immigrants in the city objectively and in a climate of goodwill. Those particularly concerned with ethnic studies included faculty members William Isaac Thomas, Robert Ezra

Park, and Louis Wirth,' and their students Edward Reuter, Franklin Frazier, Emory Bogardus, Everett Stonequist, and Everett and Helen Hughes (Persons, 1987: 33). Because Thomas and Park emphasized quite different interests in ethnic studies, we will review their respective pluralist and assimilationist contributions and will also discuss the contributions of two of their students: Charles Dawson and Everett Hughes, who were located at McGill University and who influenced Canadian ethnic studies.

THOMAS AND IMMIGRANT REORGANIZATION
While Park has often been considered the central figure in the Chicago School of sociology, W.I. Thomas was a dominant influence in introducing ethnic and racial studies (Persons, 1987). Thomas studied sociology in Germany before he finished his Ph.D. in sociology at Chicago in 1896. He was a member of the Chicago faculty for twenty-two years, until a scandal forced his resignation. This early resignation was unfortunate, because he would likely have moved ethnic studies much more in the direction of ethnic identity and pluralism.

Thomas's and Florian Znaniecki's major five-volume study, *The Polish Peasant in Europe and America*, published between 1918 and 1920, was to be the first of a series of studies on ethnic groups, a project abandoned after Thomas left the University of Chicago in 1922. The work traced the experience of immigrating peasants when they left Poland and arrived in American cities such as Chicago. Ferdinand Toennies's *gemeinschaft-gesellschaft* continuum was of considerable interest to these Chicago scholars, and Thomas and Znaniecki wanted to plot the changes which occurred when Polish peasants moved from a closed peasant *gemeinschaft* to a more open urban Chicago *gesellschaft*.

Thomas and Znaniecki assumed that there would be a change from a *gemeinschaft* to more *gesellschaft* forms of ethnic organization if Toennies's theory was correct. This change they called ethnic reorganization, in which traditional Polish culture and values would be blended with the new American experience into a reorganized Polish-American *gemeinschaft*. They found that the Polish family was the main primary group with strong social bonds and mutual obligations and respect. Families rallied to help each other in case of trouble. When family solidarity waned, community unity was exposed to social disorganization, which today we would see as secondary relations in a *gesellschaft* society. Thomas and Znaniecki found that peasant family solidarity suffered as individualism increased, when these families moved to cities. They also found that in succeeding generations family structures changed into smaller units which provided less support.

The enormous influx of immigrants into America left many Americans uneasy about the extent to which the United States would change culturally, religiously, economically, and politically. By the twenties, there was a great

Americanization movement to force assimilation on new immigrants. This movement grew so strong that by the end of the 1920s laws were passed to severely restrict further immigration into the United States. At the same time, an Americanization research program was launched. Americanization Studies produced ten volumes on immigrant schooling, predominantly immigrant neighbourhoods, transplanted traits, land ownership by immigrants, health, their aged, the immigrant press, the law as it applied to immigrants, and adjustments to industry to accommodate the immigrants. W.I. Thomas was asked to write the volume which was to become *Old World Traits Transplanted* (1921).

In this volume Thomas resists the Americanization pressures for immigrants to give up their 'alien' values and patterns of life, but he clearly takes a modified pluralist approach. He refutes the demand for immigrant cultural extinction and tries to show that this demand would lead only to disorganization and problems. Although the term 'cultural pluralism' is not found in it, the book strongly supports a multiethnic policy of forbearance, rather than suppression, of cultural differences (Young, 1971: xiv). Thomas again deals with modified pluralism when he discusses immigrant heritages, ethnic types, the potential for demoralization, immigrant institutions and communities, and the need for reconciliation of heritages. In Part III of our text we devote three chapters (Five through Seven) to ethnic solidarity and identity.

Had Thomas been able to remain at the University of Chicago, his influence in pluralism and modified forms of ethnic change might have been more clearly developed to modify Robert Park's assimilation theory. Thomas rejected the Americanization forces and thought it imperative that continuity between the immigrant's former and present lives should be integrated into a new identity. He insisted that continued use of the native language, participation in immigrant organizations, and an active immigrant press during the transition period helped maintain stable personalities and avoid demoralization (Persons, 1987: 55). Thomas's focus on social psychology was also important because he might have been able to develop further attitudinal and symbolic features of ethnic change, especially in the city.

ROBERT PARK AND RACE RELATIONS

While Thomas and Znaniecki studied the adjustment of foreign immigrants, Robert Park focused more on race relations based on his experiences in the American deep South. Park had studied philosophy in Europe and was also greatly influenced by Georg Simmel and studies of social conflict. He was particularly interested in urban ecology and change, including superordination and subordination, and had spent considerable time at Alabama's Tuskegee Institute, working with Blacks in the southern United States.

As a former newspaper writer, Park saw social relations as a dynamic process of society. In this process the social relations cycle of interaction involved a sequence of stages from the initial social contact (which often resulted in conflict) to competition, accommodation, and, finally, the fusion or assimilation of ideas, cultures, or populations. Like Simmel, Park thought that this competition often took the form of relationships of superiority and subordination which he had observed between Blacks and whites in the South. Slavery and caste systems were extreme forms of human stratification. Although Thomas and Park worked together, their interests were quite different. Thomas focused on the extent of ethnic solidarity maintained by immigrants, while Park examined the industrial urban process of change whereby ethnic and racial groups would assimilate into the mainstream.

Park wrote the seventh volume in the Americanization Studies series, titled *The Immigrant Press and Its Control* (1922); it is still one of the best of its kind. He traced the history of the foreign-language press in the United States, describing its contents and range of material, and assessing its function in preserving the cultural heritage of groups. It is interesting that, although he found 1,052 periodicals published by the foreign-language press in 1920, he nevertheless chose to discuss immigrants in assimilationist terms, and the ethnic press as a means of preventing assimilation. His figures for the period between 1884 and 1897 show a steady increase in the number of foreign-language newspapers and periodicals: well over 1,000 until 1920, and involving thirty-one different ethnic groups (Park, 1922: 310, 318).

During the decade of the First World War (1910–20), there was a shortage of white labour, and a large influx of Blacks into Chicago from the rural South posed another problem. This time it was not foreign immigrants but Blacks that sparked research in race relations. In 1919, one of the most destructive American race riots erupted in Chicago; there had also been race riots in 1917 and 1918 (Raushenbush, 1979: 94). 'Thirty-eight individuals were killed, hundreds injured, and some thousand rendered homeless. Order was restored by the state militia' (Persons, 1987: 64). The governor commissioned Charles S. Johnson to investigate. The outcome was the publication of *The Negro in Chicago*, one of the most important studies by the Chicago School (Raushenbush, 1979: 95), in which Johnson applied Park's social relations cycle to race relations.

In 1923, racial tensions involving Japanese on the West Coast also required study, and Park was asked to make a survey so that the race relations cycle could again be tested. Although Blacks, and to some extent Japanese as well, had assimilated culturally, they did not fuse or assimilate as the race relations cycle predicted. They tended to remain in various states of conflict or competition because their racial visibility became a barrier to assimilation and whites often did not allow them free access to jobs and equality. It was Emory Bogardus, a student of the Chicago School, who substantially modified the cycle in an attempt to measure degrees of nearness and farness in what became the well-known Bogardus Social Distance Scale. This scale was designed to measure the degree of acceptance and rejection of minorities by others. It became evident that, while white Poles studied by Thomas had a better chance of integrating, Blacks—who were physically visible—had more difficulties even though they might want to integrate and were already culturally assimilated.

'By 1937, Park had so far modified his theory of the ethnic cycle as to concede that any of three configurations could prevail when the cycle was concluded: a caste system as in India; complete assimilation as in China; or a permanent unassimilated racial minority as with the Jews of Europe' (Persons, 1987: 73). His training in philosophy at Heidelberg and the models he observed in European nation-states were related more or less to assimilated populations, which led him to look for homogeneous ethnic populations. American Blacks had been stripped of their cultures as slaves, so they were wholly assimilated culturally. Many Black Chicago students were also questioning the applicability of the race relations cycle to American Blacks, so that by 1930 Park increasingly left more room for pluralist options; by 1937 he had abandoned the theory of inevitable fusion or assimilation, although he did not go as far as Horace Kallen in the direction of pluralism.

STUDENTS OF THE CHICAGO SCHOOL

Park influenced large numbers of students, many of whom are still well known in sociology.

> The forty-two theses or books written about race, culture and ethnic relations by students while Park was teaching at Chicago constitute a special chapter in the history of American sociology. . . . Park wrote an introduction or a foreword for Jesse F. Steiner, *The Japanese Invasion*, 1917; Maurice T. Price, *Protestant Missions as Culture Contact*, 1924; Louis Wirth, *The Ghetto: A Study in Isolation*, 1926; Pauline V. Young, *The Pilgrims of a Russian Town*, 1932; Charles S. Johnson, *Shadow of the Plantation*, 1934; Romanzo Adams, *Interracial Marriage in Hawaii*, 1937; Bertram Doyle, *Etiquette of Race Relations*, 1937; Everett Stonequist, *The Marginal Man*, 1937; Donald Pierson, *The Negro in Brazil*, 1938; and Andrew Lind, *Island Community*, 1939. (Raushenbush, 1979: 99)

Some of Park's Black students (such as Franklin Frazier) did not, however, share Park's initial assumption that the ethnic cycle would culminate in assimilation. Frazier's major work, *The Negro in the United States* (1949), emphasized much more the first stages of conflict and competition, including exploitation. Frazier's last stage was characterized by a bi-racial system of social organization, with each race involved in its own set of social relations. This was really a form of pluralism. Frazier also distinguished acculturation from assimilation, which was more like Thomas's modified pluralism

(Persons, 1987: 74). He saw that race relations had stopped short of the full assimilation projected by Park, and made a distinction between ethnic and race relations. Frazier worked more with Bogardus's last stages in his scale of rejection of racial groups by the majority white society.

Of Park's Chicago students who did important work in ethnic and race relations, Charles Dawson and Everett Hughes both came to Montreal to begin sociology in Canada.

Charles Dawson, a graduate of Chicago, came to McGill University in Montreal in 1922 to found what later became the Department of Sociology. Dawson had studied with Park when Park and Roderick McKenzie formulated their theories on human ecology. Dawson began his research related to ethnicity in Montreal and later turned to research of ethnic groups on the western prairies.

> By 1931 the proportion of Montreal's residents who were neither British nor French extraction had risen to 135,262 (13.5 per cent) from a percentage of 4.5 in 1901. Despite the change in racial composition, very few studies of how immigrants had adapted to life in the city existed . . . Dawson was eager to use Rockefeller funds to study immigrant groups and their assimilation . . . following the same lines as Park's program in Chicago. (Shore, 1987: 233)

In Canada, too, there were fears of cultural disunity, especially as large numbers of immigrants entered eastern cities and the West. The British, who were the majority in Canada at that time, pushed hard for restricting immigration to groups from Britain and the countries of northern Europe. Thus, some studies made by McGill researchers were quite controversial because Dawson and his associates were seen as being too sympathetic to a variety of immigrants.

Like the ten Americanization studies made in the United States, a 'Canadian Frontiers of Settlement' series of nine volumes was launched in the 1930s. Dawson wrote two volumes in the series and is best known for his *Group Settlement: Ethnic Communities in Western Canada* (1936). It includes a study of five groups in the West, including the Doukhobors, Mennonites, Mormons, German Catholics, and French Canadians, a study in which he tried to apply Park's assimilation race relations cycle, but which seemed to make Dawson aware that although many of these groups changed considerably over time, their distinctiveness did not seem to disappear. One of the great laboratories for examining the natural history of group interaction was the Canadian West, with its distinctive bloc settlements which enabled the immigrants to maintain their language, culture, and institutions. These settlements were cultural islands, segregated from each other.

At McGill during the 1920s, 25% of the faculty of arts, 40% of the law students, and 15% of the students in medicine were Jewish so that McGill began to make restrictions on the number of Jews admitted. In Montreal Jews were adapting, but not necessarily assimilating (Shore, 1987: 247, 248). The British, of course, were a minority in Montreal; they, too, kept distinct boundaries between themselves and the larger majority of French Canadians. Some of Dawson's students began to use sources and metaphors like 'mosaic' and 'patchwork quilt', when they referred to ethnic and racial groups in Montreal.

It was to this Montreal setting that Everett Hughes came in 1927 to join Dawson at McGill after finishing his Ph.D. at Chicago in 1928. While Dawson never learned French, Hughes did; the two divided their research, with Hughes studying Quebec, and Dawson studying the West. In his eleven years at McGill (he returned to teach at Chicago in 1938), Hughes quickly discovered that the Chicago theories did not fit well into the study of the French-Canadian experience. Hughes broke decisively with the Chicago ethnic assimilation doctrines. In their study of the small city of Cantonville, Helen and Everett Hughes were impressed with how the French and English remained segregated and how industrialization did not change that segregation. Since then, Hughes's *French Canada in Transition: The Effects of Anglo-American Industrialization Upon a French-Canadian Town* (1943) has become a classic. Horace Miner, a student of Hughes at McGill, studied St Denis, a rural parish, as a village counterpart which was not influenced by industry. He published his findings in 1939 as *St Denis: A French-Canadian Parish*.

The studies of Hughes and Miner broke new ground in that they did not follow the Parkian race relations cycle, but rather followed the ethnographic methods of Robert Redfield (anthropologist at Chicago) and his study of villages in Mexico. Ethnic communities were studied in their own right, without the imposition of a deterministic assimilation process. These studies were more akin to some of the interests of Thomas and Znaniecki in Polish communities. 'When near the end of his life Robert Park remarked that the United States was becoming a nation of federated ethnic groups rather than of geographical territories, he both repudiated the thrust of his own work and forecast a new uncertain age of ethnic relations politics' (Persons, 1987: 150). Perhaps he did not repudiate the assimilation cycle, but he did leave room for modified pluralism.

SUMMARY

According to McNeill (1986) polyethnicity is normal in urban industrial civilization and ethnic pluralism seems to be on the rise.

While the classical sociologists did not focus explicitly on ethnicity, Max Weber does provide a concise outline, which may serve as our conceptual frame to introduce the field. Weber defines the area in five categories: inheritance, culture and consciousness of kind, the emergence of tribe and 'a

People', the notion of 'Volk' and nationality, and religion as an ideological symbol system. In our study of ethnicity, some of these characteristics will apply more to a particular group or country than will others. Ethnicity is a complex phenomenon which requires a multidimensional approach. Indeed, Weber himself wanted to analyze the concept more thoroughly, but never returned to it.

While Durkheim and Marx said little about ethnicity, they were highly interested in the effects of industrialization and sought to find alternative means of counteracting its dehumanizing influences. As industrialization increases, so does specialization and bureaucratization. This increase leads to more involved stratification of groups. Majorities tend to dominate over minorities, resulting in conflict. While Marx was concerned with industrial conflict, Durkheim wanted to find the sources of solidarity and cohesion: religion, culture, and social institutions seemed important.

The Chicago School produced some of the leading early sociologists in North America, and race and ethnic relations were an important part of their studies. While Thomas focused on immigrant pluralism, Park introduced the race relations cycle of assimilation. These two foci of ethnic interests were continued by the graduates of Chicago who came to Canada. Dawson tended to follow the Parkian assimilation interests, while Hughes followed the interests of Thomas and Redfield, focusing on pluralism. McGill, like Chicago in the United States, was at the forefront of early sociology in Canada, and ethnicity was an important emphasis from the beginning of formal studies in each country.

CHAPTER 2

Theories of Ethnic Change and Persistence

While Weber elaborated the potential racial, cultural, religious, tribal, and national diversities of our modern age, he and other classical theorists were also concerned with the impact of industrialization on humanity. Powerful economic and political forces beckon the many groups into the mainstream; for many, these temptations are irresistible. Early sociologists of the Chicago School worked to understand these forces. W.I. Thomas focused on the adjustments of Polish immigrants in Chicago and found that changes to language, culture, and institutions occurred, causing reorganization. Robert Park focused more on the forces of industrialization and urbanization and tried to understand these dynamic forces of change (Persons, 1987). In this chapter, we want to explore what happens to immigrants who enter North America, and the changes that they undergo.

Many theories have been developed to explain what will happen to ethnic groups in an industrial-technological society. The first two theories to be discussed, assimilation and amalgamation, assume that the urban industrial forces of technology and majority power will cause loss of ethnic identity. The third and fourth theories, modified assimilation and modified pluralism, admit that the technological forces will change ethnic minorities, but predict that minorities will retain ethnic characteristics partially or in changed forms. The remaining two theories, ethnic pluralism and ethnic conflict, emphasize that ethnic solidarity and identity can be maintained despite industrialization in both rural and urban environments.

SORTING THEORIES OF ETHNIC CHANGE

While the classical social theorists were relatively unconcerned with ethnicity in Europe, early sociologists in America and Canada have been greatly interested in ethnic change because most residents in North America are the descendants of immigrants who came relatively recently. They have faced enormous ethnic changes in a relatively short period. Fortunately, early sociologists of the Chicago School like Robert Park, Louis Wirth, W.I. Thomas, Florian Znaniecki, Robert Redfield, and others did considerable research on immigrants during the industrial boom in Chicago (Persons, 1987). The logical question was, what will happen to these newcomers, and how will they change as a result?

These Chicago scholars of the 1920s and 1930s, influenced by writings of European sociologists, sought to systematize the insights of Europeans and thus establish a more rigorous investigation of their own contemporary urban community (Persons, 1987). Studies of race and ethnicity were at the centre of their interests. 'The rapid influx of immigrants, as well as the increasing expansion of the metropolitan area, had precipitated the emergence of a type of community the understanding of which was critical for grasping the structural transformation that modern civilization was undergoing' (McGahan, 1994: 16). Park and his associates, like Durkheim and Toennies, were also concerned with the disintegrating influences of city life and its related problems:

> Transportation and communication have affected what I have called the 'mobilization of the individual man'. They have multiplied the opportunities of the individual man for contact and for association with his fellows, but they have made these contacts and associations more transitory and less stable. (Park, 1967: 40)

Park saw a decline in the neighbourhood as a socially significant unit and the weakening of the family as an important support group. The rise of delinquency and crime, he thought, was a result of the breakdown of social networks and the traditional ethnic community. He also thought that increased freedom of movement in the industrial arena encouraged weaker ties to primary group values. Park therefore encouraged urban empirical research, and as a result many scholars who came out of the Chicago School fanned out into the rest of North America seeking to better understand the many changes taking place (Driedger, 1989). As indicated in Chapter One, many Chicago sociologists assumed that there would be assimilation, but they were not sure of what these European minorities would assimilate into. The melting pot and Anglo-conformity are two potential outcomes.

ASSIMILATION: THE MELTING POT

Weber, Durkheim, and Marx all agreed that the pervasive force of industrialization tends to attract workers and capitalists alike into the economic work arena, where making a living becomes a primary goal. All three agreed that industry was a major force of change, but they proposed different solutions as to what should be done about it. At the same time, the theory of evolution was becoming more popular so there was the tendency to think, like Darwin and Spencer, that mankind was evolving. Liberalism and the enlightenment, with its stress on freedom, added to the buoyant hope that the goodness of humans would triumph and that Utopia might be close at hand.

It is not surprising that, for theorists of assimilation, all humans of whatever culture, language, or belief would be drawn into the industrial fray by the promise of better things for the well-being of all. The arrival of immigrants to the shores of America provided the opportunity for a new beginning; it offered new freedoms to experiment and let the human spirit be creative. The immigrants did not wish to be dominated by a majority group, as many had already been, so they were similar to the Americans who had fought to become independent from the British. Unlike these earlier Americans, however, they were wary of domination by their fellow Americans. Thus, the tenets of free enterprise, individual initiative, competition, private property, and the profit motive fitted well into a laissez-faire style of capitalism. According to the melting-pot theory, many immigrants would no longer wish to continue the traditions of the restricted old world, but would opt for the opportunities of the new. Openness to abandoning the restrictive past for future opportunities is common in the melting-pot theory of ethnic change.

Americans often refer to their country as a melting pot. They broke free of British dominance more than 200 years ago and created a nation ostensibly dominated by no one group. All groups contributed to the American dream, with its new constitution, multitude of cultures from many parts of the world, and system of free enterprise. Independence and freedom were popular watchwords. It was a new nation, a new culture, a new continent: a pot to which all might contribute. Assimilation theory suggests that immigrant groups will be synthesized into a new group. This evolutionary process results in a melting pot different from any of the groups involved and different from the original melting pot.

FIGURE 2-1   PARK'S ASSIMILATION CYCLE

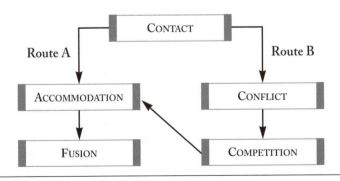

A chief advocate of this process was Robert Park. He suggested that immigrants came into contact with the new society and either took the route of least resistance (contact, accommodation, and fusion) or a more circuitous route (contact, conflict, competition, accommodation, and fusion) (Shore, 1987). Whereas the latter route could take longer and could entail considerable resistance on the part of the immigrant, the end result would be the same—the loss of a distinctive ethnic identity. The new culture and values would emerge.

There were a sufficient number of minorities who did assimilate, as Park predicted, to keep American researchers preoccupied with documenting the progress of their assimilation. For fifty years, these scholars tended to ignore groups which retained a separate identity and to regard their separateness as a relatively insignificant factor in the total pattern of minority-majority relations. The assimilational theory was so influential when combined with the evolutionary thinking of the day, that it was forgotten that such well-known pluralist studies as Thomas and Znaniecki's *The Polish Peasant in Europe and America* (1918), Louis Wirth's *The Ghetto* (1928), and Harvey Zorbaugh's *The Gold Coast and the Slum* (1929) illustrated considerable resistance to assimilation.

The theory of assimilation was, and is, attractive because it is dynamic. It takes into account the enormous technological change which dominates our North American societies. Furthermore, numerous studies show that many north European groups such as the Dutch, the Scandinavians, and the Germans fairly quickly lose many of their distinctive cultural traits such as ethnic language use. However, in the eyes of some, melting-pot assimilation is too deterministic. That is, as a macro theory it may explain a general process for some groups, but it does not take into account the many dimensions of cultural change. Not all of these forces may be changing in the same direction; the targets of change may be quite different. Nor does it sufficiently take into account the fact that the distinctiveness of all groups may not disappear; Park's cycle does allow for some groups not to follow to the end of fusion, but it implies that industrial momentum will eventually sweep everyone into fusion with the general society. Park and his associates did not focus very much on what was meant by fusion.

Herberg (1955) contends, however, that in America the Protestants, Catholics, and Jews have never 'melted'. Nor have they in Canada. Certainly the French in Quebec are a bulwark against assimilation, whose prophesied synthesis is not happening in Canada. The racial component, well represented in Canada by our Aboriginal peoples and in America by Blacks, Aboriginals, and Asians, is not melting very noticeably either. To what extent other ethnic groups such as the French, Chinese, and Italians are melting is the subject of much research, and it is as yet incomplete. Even in the United States where the melting pot theory is often applied, more and more scholars are having doubts about its application to all ethnic groups (Kallen, 1924; Nagel, 1984; Reitz and Breton, 1994).

Canada's relatively open immigration policy has proved the potential for many peoples to contribute to a melting pot. At the time of Confederation, however, the two founding peoples represented most of the population; their historical influence has been much stronger than any of the other groups that followed. Early British and French influences have tended to dominate early Canadian history and the lives of more recent immigrants. The two charter groups have fought hard not to assimilate either culturally or linguistically; from the beginning, the Canadian melting pot has contained ingredients that don't melt easily.

The synthesis of British, French, Germans, Ukrainians, Italians, Canadian Aboriginals, and others into a recognizable national character has been slow. Some scholars think it is this melting process, more than any other, which is needed to develop a spirited Canadian nationalism. Americans, on the other hand, have stressed assimilation more than have Canadians, and have evolved a stronger feeling of nationalism than Canadians have been able to achieve.

AMALGAMATION: CONFORMITY TO A DOMINANT GROUP

A second possibility in the process of minorities losing their traditional identity is joining or amalgamating with a dominant group. In Canada, the British represent the largest group, so we could call this process Anglo-conformity. While industrialization has escalated during the past several centuries, nationalism has greatly influenced North American ethnic development as well. McNeill (1986) shows that nationalism rose in western Europe between 1750 and 1920, especially in the most successful capitalist countries of Britain and France who were also the most influential European players in the development of Canada and America. The American revolution culminated in a new nation in 1776, severing colonial ties with Europe and freeing the Americans to follow a melting-pot policy. In Canada, however, the French—largely in Acadia and Quebec—and the British—especially after the war of 1759—considered Canada in colonial terms (Breton, 1984). The influence of British nationalism and colonialism was greatly strengthened with the coming of the British Empire Loyalists to Canada.

McNeill (1986) suggests that the triumph of nationalism in Europe introduced the ideal of ethnic homogeneity within a geographic boundary; this rising emphasis on national sovereignty sought to bring about monoethnicity within its boundaries. McNeill (1986) sees this as an intrusion into the polyethnicity that we would normally expect in civilized industrialized countries. The British and French, driven by the capitalist need for profits and colonization, greatly influenced North America. They fought many wars in an attempt to gain world dominance over resources. These wars had strong

repercussions for Canada, especially in 1759, when the British finally conquered the French in Canada. Later the British and French again sought to
gain a monoethnic dominance in western Canada, where the British gained
strong footholds after the Riel rebellions of 1870 and 1885.

While monoethnic nationalism may be the most efficient way for economic capitalism to flourish with its motives of individual enterprise, competition, and profit, it is often directly contradictory to philosophies of political
democracy and Christian religion—also important in western civilization.
Democracy emphasizes universal suffrage and cooperation, not the competition of individuals for profit. Christianity emphasizes brotherhood and sister-
hood, human equality, and the welfare of all. While laissez-faire capitalism
may allow monoethnic dominance, political and religious values make such
dominance unjust.

The emphasis on immigrants amalgamating into a monoethnic culture has
influenced Canadian thinking greatly during the past. It is the product of an
evolutionary perspective that assumes that ethnic groups are constantly changing from their present minority cultural and structural status to join the majority culture, which in Canada is represented by the British. This theory tends to
be deterministic and assumes that the temptation to join the majority will be
too much for any minority group to resist. Even if they resist, minorities may
still have to live and compete by the rules set up and enforced by the majority.
This practice indoctrinates them into the ethos of the majority, and assimilationists predict that minorities will disappear into the dominant group.

There is a great deal of evidence in Canadian history that many British
leaders had an Anglo-conformity model in mind when they thought of the
Aboriginal people, the French, and other immigrants (Breton, 1984). Lord
Durham assumed that others would assimilate to a British legal, political,
economic, and cultural system (Stanley, 1960). Leaders like Durham seem to
have hoped that somehow even the French would finally amalgamate into
the dominant culture, although not without conflict and competition. They
assumed the desirability of British social institutions and expected all others
to learn the English language. For them, the core of nationalism was to
remain English while French institutions, language, and history had to take
a lesser role (McNeill, 1986). This attitude was also dominant in western
Canada, where the French and British developed their cultures, both having
approximately equal numbers in early Manitoba. Soon, however, the languages and schools of other immigrants on the prairies took second place to
the English. Canada did not sever its ties with the British as the Americans
did, so the British colonial influence lasted longer and helped mould Anglo-
conformity to a much greater extent than occurred in the United States.

Berry, Kalin, and Taylor's (1976: 36–8) national sample shows that 81% of
their respondents of British origin identified themselves as Canadian. They

also found that 'Canadian' was the most popular response in the most easterly Atlantic provinces where the population is mainly of British origin. The use of the term 'Canadian' varies by subgroups. This suggests that respondents of British origin chose to relabel their loyalties by adopting the 'Canadian' label. As the largest and most powerful group, the British can afford to abandon the 'ethnic' label, hoping that others will join them under a new national label strongly influenced by British history, culture, and language. This is an interesting modification of Anglo-conformity, which nevertheless would favour a new Anglo-conformist Canadian identity. Other groups would be encouraged to join or unite with the British to merge into a single 'Canadian' amalgam structured and shaped by British values.

MODIFIED ASSIMILATION

The two theories of ethnic adjustment discussed so far are essentially ideal types of assimilation in which ethnic groups give up their identity. Weber liked to work with ideal types because they allowed him to delineate and distinguish complexes of social action so that research could proceed in an orderly way. As we all know, however, ideal types rarely exist in real life because social behaviour is usually more difficult to classify in practice than in the ideal. Thus, two modified versions (Modified Assimilation and Modified Pluralism) have been developed by Milton Gordon, in *Assimilation in American Life* (1964), and by Nathan Glazer and Daniel P. Moynihan, in *Beyond the Melting Pot* (1963). These versions lean to the assimilationist and pluralist sides respectively, but take numerous modifications into account. These modified versions can be applied very usefully to real ethnic group studies in North America.

Gordon suggests that assimilation is not a single social process, but a number of subprocesses which he classifies under the headings 'cultural' and 'structural'. Cultural assimilation includes the incoming group's acceptance of the modes of dress, language, and other cultural characteristics of the host society. Structural assimilation concerns the degree to which immigrants enter the social institutions of the society (e.g., political leadership) and the degree to which they are accepted into these institutions by the majority. Gordon suggests that assimilation may occur more readily in economic, political, and educational institutions than in the areas of religion, family, structure, and recreation. As Newman (1973: 85) points out, however, 'Gordon contends (that) once structural assimilation is far advanced, all other types of assimilation will naturally follow.'

Gordon's multivariate approach forced scholars out of their unilinear rut. Each of the seven stages or types of assimilation he established, however, tended to be oriented toward either an assimilationist or an amalgamationist target. He saw seven distinctive forms of assimilation for ethnic groups in the

TABLE 2-1   THE SEVEN ASSIMILATION VARIABLES DEVELOPED BY GORDON

Subprocess or Condition	Type of Assimilation
Change of cultural patterns to those of host society	Cultural or behavioural assimilation
Large-scale entrance into primary group level of cliques, clubs, and institutions of host society	Structural assimilation
Large-scale intermarriage with host society	Marital assimilation
Development of sense of peoplehood based exclusively on host society	Identificational assimilation
Absence of prejudice from host society	Attitudinal assimilation society
Absence of discrimination from host society	Behaviour receptional assimilation
Absence of value and power conflict	Civic assimilation

Adapted from *Assimilation in American Life: The Role of Race, Religion and National Origins* by Milton M. Gordon, p. 71. Copyright by Oxford University Press, Inc.

process of decline: cultural, structural, marital, identificational, civic, attitudinal, and behaviour receptional.

Gordon's major contribution is his complex multilinear, multidimensional view of the assimilation process. It has been seen as a considerable improvement on Park's assimilation cycle. Although Gordon was primarily concerned with assimilation as such, and though he did not dwell on pluralism, he did not negate pluralist expressions in religion, the family, and recreation.

Application of the seven assimilation variables to such ethnic groups as Blacks, Aboriginals, French Canadians, and Scandinavians results in varied patterns that are most interesting. Most Blacks in Toronto and Halifax and most Blacks in America, for example, have undergone complete cultural assimilation: their former African languages, customs, and religion have been lost. They have not, however, assimilated with respect to the last five variables: intermarriage with whites is limited; they are identifiable racially; there is considerable prejudice and discrimination against them; and they have limited access to civic power (Henry et al., 1995). Aboriginals in northern Canada have hardly assimilated with respect to any of the seven variables, but this situation changes somewhat when they migrate into southern cities (Frideres, 1993).

One group, the Icelanders in Manitoba, has assimilated a great deal. Few Icelandic cultural and ethnic institutions remain; they intermarry freely; they attract little prejudice and discrimination; and some are entering positions of civic influence (Driedger, 1975). Most French Canadians in Quebec, in contrast, have not assimilated according to Gordon's criteria. They retain their language, culture, and French institutions. Most marry within the group. They have even achieved considerable civic power. Gordon's variables are useful, because they show that individuals of some groups assimilate more than others. The degree of variation depends on the ethnic group and its location, and varies considerably (Guindon, 1988; Gagnon, 1993). We see that the process is complex, varied, and multilinear; it adds interest to multiethnic comparative research, as Weber advocated.

MODIFIED PLURALISM

Glazer and Moynihan (1963) distinguish four major events in New York's history that they think structured a series of ethnic patterns which reflected modified pluralism rather than modified assimilation in that city. The first was the shaping of the Jewish community under the impact of the Nazi persecution of Jews in Europe and the establishment of the state of Israel. The second was a parallel, if less marked, shaping of a Catholic community by the re-emergence of the Catholic school controversy. The third was the migration of southern Blacks to New York following World War I and continuing after the fifties. The fourth was the influx of Puerto Ricans following World War II. These migrations introduced the element of race.

Glazer and Moynihan claim that the melting pot did not function in New York. They further claim that, throughout America's history, the various streams of population separated from one another by origin, religion, and outlook seemed always to be on the verge of merging, but that the anticipated comingling was always deferred.

Glazer and Moynihan suggest that the Blacks are often discriminated against, and that their assimilation is not tolerated by the majority. The Jews, with their distinct religion, do not wish to assimilate because they are proud of their distinct identity. The Puerto Ricans and Irish Catholics represent combinations of these voluntary and involuntary pluralist variations. Over time they change, but they remain distinct ethnic groups. Modified pluralism takes account of this process of change, as do the assimilationist and amalgamation theories, but it also provides for degrees of pluralism often demonstrated in North American groups such as Aboriginals, Italians, French Québécois, Jews, Asiatics, and many others.

This fourth theoretical summary focuses on Glazer and Moynihan's theory that, while all groups change, those that are able to shift from traditional cultural identities to new interest foci may maintain their distinctive identities. This formulation recognizes change and maintains that identification can be shifted. It also suggests that some groups may change more than others and implies that the outcome may be a pluralist mixture differing from the Anglo-conformist target. Indeed, Glazer and Moynihan contend that traumatic experiences such as conflict encourage the development of a sense of identity among minorities and may form the basis of a viable Canadian pluralist theory. Although their theory is very general and its dimensions require expansion, it does focus on the dynamics of change that influence the development of group identities.

The French in Quebec are an example of selected change, a form of Glazer and Moynihan's modified pluralism. They are changing from a dominantly rural, religion-oriented population to an increasingly urban, industrial people (Guindon, 1988). Nevertheless, this enormous shift in value orientations does not seem to have affected their determination to survive culturally and structurally in North America. This modified pluralism takes account of change, which the assimilationist and amalgamationist theories stress, but it also provides for degrees of pluralism often demonstrated in Canadian groups such as the Japanese, Chinese, Mormons, Mennonites, and many others.

While French Québécois in Quebec rely on linguistic, cultural, and institutional completeness for their territorial solidarity, the Jews—who are almost exclusively urban—fortify their identity with a distinctive religion, symbolic means of identification, and strong family ties. Many Jews readily change cultural distinctivness, but often change to ideological, symbolic, and institutional means of modified identity.

THE ETHNIC MOSAIC: MULTICULTURAL PLURALISM

Whereas proponents of the melting pot and Anglo-conformity assume that minorities will assimilate and lose their separate identities, scholars of pluralism and conflict focus on the alternative options of solidarity and identity that are available to minorities (Berry and Laponce, 1994: 3–16). Like Max Weber, advocates of these theories assume that there are alternatives to losing oneself in the industrial arena, and that many individuals and groups have the creativity and resources to fight modern alienation, by maintaining their ethnic *gemeinschaft*. In particular, Durkheim worked at questions of social cohesion and solidarity, which many ethnic scholars have also explored.

Ideal cultural pluralism may represent different ethnic groups that over time maintain their own unique identities. Cultural pluralism is often viewed as an arrangement in which distinct groups live side by side in relatively harmonious coexistence. 'The author of this view of pluralism was a Harvard educated philosopher of Jewish immigrant stock named Horace Kallen,' who espoused pluralism for three main reasons (Newman, 1973: 67). He argued that there are many kinds of social relationships and identities that can be chosen voluntarily, but that no one may choose his ancestry. Further, each of the minority groups has something of value to contribute to a country, and that the American constitution carried with it an implicit assumption that all people were created equal, even though there might be many distinct differences. Kallen wished to refute the ideas of assimilation and the melting pot which had gained considerable contemporary influence. Since then numerous sociologists have proposed plural theories of ethnic and religious identity (Dashefsky, 1975; Mol, 1985). Part III (Chapters Four through Seven) will discuss multiethnic identity and solidarity.

Dashefsky (1975) developed a fourfold model of ethnic identity that included two sociological perspectives—the sociocultural and interactionist—and two psychological approaches—group dynamicist and psychoanalytic—in the study of ethnic identity. The sociocultural perspective is especially important in the study of recent immigrants, Indian and Inuit aboriginals, northern Europeans on the prairies, French Québécois in Quebec, and smaller groups like the Hutterites. The symbolic interactionist focus is more useful in exploring the identity of urbanites such as the Jews, Chinese, and Japanese: racial and visible minorities who have come to Canada more recently. Hans Mol (1985) has posited that the role of religion and the process of sacralization are ideological and symbolic interactionist forms of identity.

Whereas the preceding discussion of assimilation tends to emphasize the overwhelming influence of technology and urbanization, sweeping away all forms of ethnic differentiation before it, cultural pluralism tends to focus on countervailing forces such as democracy and human justice which presuppose that all people are of equal worth and all should have the freedom to choose their distinct quality of life. Assimilation theories envision the disappearance of immigrant and racial groups; identity theories, in contrast, suggest that there may be greater resistance to assimilation and amalgamation than had formerly been thought. In fact, the trend toward permissive differentiation seems to be set. In North America we have accepted pluralist religious expressions, which were hardly tolerated in Reformation Europe. The same is now true of the political scene, where a diversity of political parties and ideologies exist and are accepted by society. Multiculturalism in Canada is now also recognized federally, albeit ambiguously and not without some resistance.

CONFLICT: THE DIALECTIC OF INCOMPATIBLES
Assimilation and amalgamation theories perceive society as changing toward melting-pot or Anglo-conformist goals. They view group conflict as a temporary phenomenon which will improve after minorities have had sufficient time to adjust to the new situation and the new order. Both theories treat social change and conflict as a temporary dislocation in the normal ordered state of a uniform nation-state (Driedger, 1989). The theories of modified assimilation and modified pluralism allow for a greater measure of inherent conflict in the social system. Gordon's modified assimilation allows for different rates of assimilation which can bring about disjuncture and stress; Glazer and Moynihan's modified pluralism suggests that the minority becomes very much a part

of the industrial urban process of change which involves conflict and turmoil as new forms of identity emerge. The counterculture in pluralism becomes a sub-cultural antithesis to the larger society. Simmel (1955) contended that both conflict and consensus are ever-present in society, and Coser (1956) and Dahrendorf (1959) tended to follow this view. In general, these theorists assume that all social phenomena reflect a combination of opposed tendencies. In western countries race is certainly a factor. The nature of this conflict varies, however, depending on the group's aspirations.

Theories of ethnic conflict also have many dimensions and components related to change which need to be explored. The conflict focus, although concerned with structure and institutions, also focuses on the processes of ethnic group relations. Since conflict suggests the meeting of people with dis-similar or opposite values and norms, it includes the processes of competition, confrontation, and a dialectic of opposites. Dahrendorf defines social conflict as consisting of 'all relations between sets of individuals that involve an incompatible difference of objectives with regard to positions, resources or values' (1959: 135).

Our discussion of the assimilationist-pluralist range of options suggests that the two opposite ideal poles are seldom if ever present in reality. The majority of activity occurs between these two extremes and shows varying degrees of conformity to the majority or separation into a distinctive identity. In the mid-dle we find considerable conflict between the two tendencies; as a result we have a range of outcomes depending on which pole is stronger and more influ-ential. Examples of the entire range of ethnic identity, or the lack of it, can be found in Canada. In this volume we focus on ethnic identity and solidarity to explore what forms of pluralism and multiculturalism exist in Canada.

The various theories of conflict are too many, and too complex, to discuss here in detail. However, we wish to touch on at least three aspects that are useful in our discussion of ethnic conflict. First, John Jackson (1975) suggests that, contrary to Park's assumption that minorities tend to move through his race relations cycle, some might remain very much in a state of conflict with-out advancing to competition, accommodation, and eventual fusion. Jackson tried to show in his study of French-English relations in an Ontario commu-nity that conflict was a normal and natural outcome of structural processes—of the interplay of power and position, and of boundary maintenance activity. It was not a pathological phenomenon to him. Other examples also suggest that the separatist revolution in Quebec, the Aboriginal quest for land rights, and the race relations between whites and visible minorities demonstrate a constant potential for conflict. Examples of such ethnic countercultural con-flicts include Hutterite expansion into Alberta farmlands and the province's subsequent restrictive legislation, the conflict of French and other ethnic groups over language rights and education during the Manitoba School question (Clark, 1968), Bill 22 and the conflicts of Italians and recent immigrants with the Quebec government over English education in Montreal, and conflict between Blacks, Asians, and those of European ancestry.

A second way is to view conflict as Marx did in *The Communist Manifesto* (1848) in which he saw 'the history of all hitherto existing society as the history of class struggles'. This was an adaptation of the Hegelian dialectic's emphasis on the struggle of opposites; the dialectical movement of conflict between a thesis and an antithesis would result in a form of synthesis. Marx saw the struggle for control over the economic and political institutions of a society as a pervasive conflict; it could involve revolution and the overthrow of existing structures so that those who are powerless might gain greater participation in their destiny. Most ethnic groups in Canada do not aspire to such an extensive power struggle, although the Separatist movement led by Lucien Bouchard and Jacques Parizeau is the more recent form of institutional conflict which seeks to gain sovereign control of Quebec's structure and economic, political, and social institutions by a referendum to secede.

Third, Edna Bonacich (1972) has expanded the Marxian argument and has applied it directly to ethnic relations and the 'cultural division of labour' approach. She claims that ethnic solidarity is a derivative of the dual labour market exploitation that arises when immigrants enter lower-paying jobs that others are reluctant to do and, as a result, have little opportunity for advancement. Hechter (1978) suggests that minorities tend to be at the periphery of the industrial power centre and tend to be exploited by those in power; thus class distinctions emerge, and polarities for conflict develop. Norbert Wiley (1967) attempts to separate the structural, cultural, and social-psychological dimensions of the social class issues and suggests that minorities who remain within the ethnic sub-culture will have limited opportunities to achieve socio-economic mobility (Isajiw, Sev'er, Driedger, 1993). John Porter (1965: 73–103) was also concerned that a preoccupation with ethnic identity would restrict mobility and opportunity. Most of these scholars see ethnic identity in stratification terms and expect that class and ethnic strata will inevitably be in conflict.

FINDING A CONCEPTUAL MODEL

In discussing the six theories of ethnic change and persistence our focus is on ethnic identities, inequalities, and varieties of modifications. Let us begin by developing the theories' opposite tendencies on a continuum, and then offering a more complex model using more dimensions and variations as pattern variables. We shall use two continua, each with opposite polarities. In this model we will combine a conformity-pluralism continuum with a voluntary-involuntary continuum (Driedger, 1989).

The assimilation and amalgamation theories are located at the conformity end of the first continuum, where ethnic groups lose their distinctive identity and become part of a melting pot by conforming to a dominant group. The pluralism theory is at the opposite end of the continuum, where ethnic groups voluntarily retain their separate identity or are forced to remain separate. Modified assimilation and modified pluralism theories both fall in the middle: the first representing modification of assimilation; and the second, modifications of pluralism due to change.

In many respects a continuum with two polarities is simplistic and unidimensional because it does not take into account numerous other dimensions that should be added. Furthermore, it is difficult to include conflict theories unless additional dimensions are added to provide more contrast. Talcott Parsons is well known for his elaboration of numerous continua and his development of them into pattern variables or cells. Such elaborate patterns can become too rigid, locking us into social structures which do not include change and conflict sufficiently. Nevertheless, we shall use a second voluntary-involuntary continuum, which does illustrate interesting pattern variables when contrasted with the conformity-identity continuum. The resulting four-cell model is shown in Figure 2-2. Other axes could also be added, but handling two at a time is complex enough, and the model does permit us to include conflict points as a third dimension, making it much more dynamic and interesting.

CONFORMITY-PLURALIST MODEL

Wsevolod Isajiw (1978) has suggested that the centre of Canadian society is the market-place where all groups, including the various ethnic groups, must meet to make a living. Everett Hughes (1952) says that indigenous people cannot always supply the whole working force in any industrial society, so immigrants are usually brought in to augment the labour pool. In the industrial process, the many peoples in a country mix with each other. Some, however, will be closer to the centre of power and have more influence than others, while these others will find themselves in layers or concentric zones of less power and influence and farther removed from the centre (Driedger, 1989). In the centre of Figure 2-2 we have placed the melting pot as Cell A, the place where Park's assimilation is most influential. Various ethnic groups try to influence control over the industrial cell while others seek to separate themselves from it. Still others try to enter the industrial fray, but are often repelled or rebuffed. Of the six theories discussed earlier, at least one fits into each part of the model.

Weber, Durkheim, and Marx were all concerned with the pervasive influence of industrialization in western society, which we have plotted as the central Cell A in the middle of Figure 2-2. We agree with the classical theorists

FIGURE 2-2   A CONFORMITY-PLURALIST CONCEPTUAL MODEL

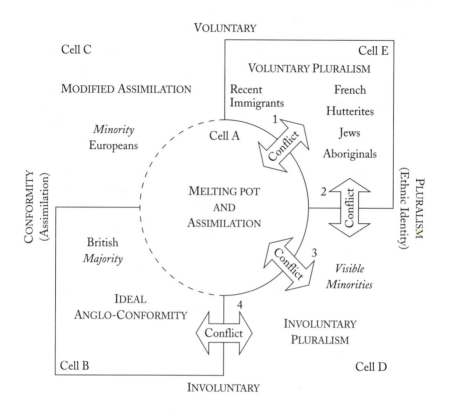

and the assimilationists that the capitalist political economy tends to draw all citizens into the middle of the economic arena because they need to earn a living in the economic fray. This sphere seeks to attract the majority and minorities alike, seeking to plot a new goal or target of assimilation where the outcome will be a melting pot. The many groups will become not British, French, and German, etc., but Canadians: a new entity different from any one of the ethnic contributors. Industry provides the crucible in which the many peoples meet to forge a living.

Thus, industrial changes to both societal structures and values tend to create a free-for-all where new needs for *gemeinschaft* are created. The four cells (B,C,D,E) created by the intersection of our conformity-pluralism and voluntary-involuntary axes show that various means are used by different groups to preserve values important to them within new structures. Let us think of the four corners of the model (B,C,D, and E) as four ways in which different groups attempt to create new means of dealing with industrial alienation.

As illustrated in Cell B, the largest (British) or most powerful group will try to shape society by leavening the whole (Cell A) so that its own language, culture, morality, and institutions are dominant, and often may force such conformity upon other minorities. Thus, the line between their goals (Cell B) and national economic and political values (Cell A) tends to be blurred (perforated line between Cells A and B). It is a nationalistic attempt at getting others to conform or assimilate or skew into the dominant form (Cell B of the model). Like all ethnic groups, the dominant majority wants to preserve and perpetuate its own cultural ethos; as the majority, it has the power to dominate. The French were in such a position in early Acadia, but with their defeat in 1759, the British became both the numerically and politically dominant group in Canada. At the turn of the century, the British represented almost two-thirds of the population of Canada, but by 1995 they had declined to 28% of the total population; they remain the largest group, but not a majority.

In Cell C are located the older, mostly northern European groups such as the Scandinavians, Dutch, and Germans who have lived in Canada for a number of generations. Most of them have adopted the English language and are now beginning to conform and accommodate themselves voluntarily to an assimilationist goal in the centre (Cell A) where they compete quite well economically. Using Gordon's seven indicators, northern Europeans are losing some of their cultural and structural accommodation to the forces in Cell A. Being Caucasian like the two largest groups, the British and French, they are subject to little prejudice and discrimination, and some are beginning to enter civic positions of power. With some exceptions, these Canadians follow the line of least resistance as assimilationists would predict. They are modified assimilators because Gordon's seven factors of assimilation are hard at work. Depending on the group, some ethnic features are more in the process of assimilation into Cell A or amalgamation with the British in Cell B than others. Studies show that the Scandinavians in particular are assimilating into Cell A and amalgamating into Cell B quickly (Driedger, 1975; Isajiw, 1981).

VOLUNTARY AND INVOLUNTARY PLURALISM

The minorities in Cells D and E deal with voluntary and involuntary forms of pluralist identity, the focus of this volume. In Part III, we focus on the various dimensions of voluntary ethnic identity and solidarity located in Cell E. In Part IV, dealing with ethnic and racial stratification, we concentrate on social distance, the focus of Cell D.

Whereas Cell C represents intermediary forms of modified assimilation achieved by conforming voluntarily to modified assimilation, Cell D is an intermediary process closer to the pluralism pole. In this cell, individuals and groups remain pluralist involuntarily because they are forced to remain iso-lated because of race. Many visible minorities like Asians, South Asians, and Blacks would like to participate more in the centre of the industrialization process but are often prevented from doing so fully because of racial prejudice and discrimination. They are likewise kept in their place by the majority groups of Cell B, as well as by other Caucasian pluralists of Cell E. It is this group that faces the greatest potential for conflict because Canadian and American charters grant them equal rights ideologically, but in real life this is often not the case. Democracy and Christianity also say they are equal, yet visible minorities find themselves discriminated against in the market-place for reasons which are contradictory to these principles of equality. Social and economic reality does not necessarily match national ideals. We shall enlarge on these three points of conflict later.

Cell E represents Ideal Pluralism, in which individuals and groups volun-tarily withdraw into their pluralist corner, seeking to remain separate from industrial amalgamation into the national melting pot, and the French Québécois 'nation', are the best example. In many ways these people are tradi-tionalists, but their traditionalism takes a number of pluralist forms. We shall discuss four distinct forms of pluralist groups: rural French habitants, reli-gious minorities like Hutterites and Jews, first-generation immigrants like the Italians and Greeks, and non-urban Aboriginals.

First, the large French population (25%) highly concentrated in Quebec has always made up a very substantial sociocultural tile in the mosaic; it has not melted, nor has it assimilated into the larger industrial pot (Cell A). The rural French habitants of the nineteenth and early twentieth centuries in Quebec isolated and segregated themselves in rural Catholic parishes away from the industrial fray. One of the reasons that multiculturalism has been established in Canada is because of the preponderance of the French Québé-cois in Quebec. They were the first European settlers and have from the beginning insisted on another option besides Anglo-conformity. They sup-port Franco-conformity.

Second, religious minorities such as the Hutterites and the Jews are also placed in Cell E. The Hutterites on the prairies are a rural example of tradi-tional pluralism focused clearly on a separate Protestant religious ideology. Their case is characterized by extensive boundary maintenance and social control in segregated areas. This form of pluralism has lasted for 470 years, since the Protestant Reformation of which the Hutterites are a remnant.

The orthodox Lubavitcher Chassidim Jews in Montreal are an excellent example of urban pluralism (Shaffir, 1993). Jews in general represent a dis-tinct religious tradition different from the large Christian majority in North America. Lubavitcher Chassidim Jews are careful to delineate ritual, cultural, and scriptural boundaries to separate them from Gentiles as well as other Jews of less traditional practice. Religion is an important second factor important to the maintenance of ethnic identity and solidarity in the pluralist Cell E.

Recent first-generation immigrants are a third example of a pluralist group. Portuguese and Greeks have come to urban centres recently. Southern and eastern Europeans such as Italians and Ukrainians with their distinct languages and cultures use cultural residential segregation as a spatial means of boundaried separation in both rural and urban areas. The Ukrainians have the advantages of a separate orthodox religion, which Italians—who are mostly Roman Catholic—do not have. Rural ethnic bloc settlements, especially in western Canada, are common where the Ukrainians settled in the Aspen Belt, stretching from Manitoba's Inter-Lake region to Edmonton. Rural hinterlands often supply migrants to the city; these migrants tend to perpetuate the urban village way of life. An example of this may be seen in the north end of Winnipeg, until recently the stronghold of Ukrainians, Poles, and Jews (Driedger and Church, 1974). Kalbach (1990) found historical Jewish and Italian settlement patterns in Toronto and traced how they shifted over time. Balakrishnan and Kralt (1987) have documented such residential segregation in Toronto, Montreal and Vancouver. Institutional completeness (Breton, 1964; Driedger, 1982) is important so that ethnic schools, churches, and associations can support identity. The maintenance of a separate language and culture is difficult and unlikely without a sufficiently large ethnic concentration in a given area. Minorities need territory, and they need to control this territory so their offspring can perpetuate their heritage within it. This can best be done in tightly knit communities. Community space thus becomes an arena in which ethnic activities occur and are shared. We have placed recent immigrants in Cell E, but close to Cell B, because some will most likely enter modified forms of assimilation as the generations remain in Canada.

Fourth, rural Indian reserves also demonstrate ethnic territorial segregation. Many Aboriginals live in the Canadian northlands, isolated from other Canadians. Some of them are still in a food-gathering economy and wish to retain a sacred way of life. We have placed these Aboriginals in Cell E, but near Cell D, because they are to some extent also a visible minority. Rural and reserve Indians, however, usually wish to retain their distinct ethnic identity by staying close to the land. Increasingly, Aboriginals enter southern Canadian cities, and many of these could be placed in Cell D, where their visible distinctiveness keeps them from entering the industrial workplace in Cell A as freely as they would like.

RACIAL AND ETHNIC CONFLICT

Our model clearly demonstrates at least four points of conflict (1,2,3, and 4). The major point of conflict is between those in Cell E and Cell A; three points of conflict also involve Cell D as visible racial minorities in this cell come into contact with those in Cells A, B, and E.

When ideal pluralists such as the French, Hutterites, Jews, recent immigrants, and Aboriginals (Cell E) seek to retain their culture and ethnic institutions, while earning a living in the melting-pot economy (Cell A), there is bound to be a variety of conflict which we have labelled as our first point of stress. Now that the Constitution has declared Canada a bilingual country, French language rights are guaranteed. While such rights are easier to maintain in the province of Quebec, where French Québécois are a majority and have control over their provincial government, these language rights raise much conflict elsewhere, where the French represent only a small portion of the population. The Hutterites and Jews seek to retain their distinctive religious traditions in a sea of increased secularization in the larger society. Their youth do not find it easy to identify with their family traditions when those of their peers are different. First-generation immigrants often have severe conflict with the main stream, and their children are seduced away from their language, culture, and traditions. The Aboriginal land claims represent but one point of conflict with the rest of Canada; constitutional guarantees are slow in coming, and untreatied land is increasingly being invaded without legal settlement. There is a dialectic between those in Cell E, who voluntarily wish to retain a separate ethnic identity, and the assimilatory influences of the melting pot in Cell A.

In Cell D, visible minorities such as Blacks, Asians, South Asians, and urban Indians are in conflict at three different points (2, 3, and 4). With some exceptions, these non-Caucasians would likely be in closer contact and integration with those in Cells E, A, and B, but they are often unable to do so because of prejudice and discrimination. The voluntary pluralists in Cell E want to retain a separate identity, unlike the visible minorities in Cell D, who often do not, so their goals of relating to the melting pot are very different. These voluntary pluralists are also mainly Caucasians, while most visible minorities are distinguishable by their Mongoloid or Negroid skin colour. Most Jews, Hutterites, French, and recent immigrants want their children to marry their own kind so they can perpetuate their distinctive identities, while many visible minorities do not share this desire. In fact, most of the groups in Cell D want to get rid of such barriers and often see the protectiveness of ideal pluralists as racist. They have different goals; voluntary pluralists don't want to melt, while visible minorities usually do (although there are always exceptions). According to Jackson (1966), these voluntary Cell E pluralists remain in a position of conflict in Park's assimilation cycle and do not proceed toward fusion and the melting pot because they are committed to distinctive sociocultural and/or religious values incompatible with others.

One of the greatest points of conflict is at point 3, between visible minorities in Cell D and those assimilated visible minorities in Cell A of the melting pot. Most Marxists and neo-Marxists see access to the labour market as the major form of conflict in society in general and see the plight of visible and racial minorities who are unable to compete for jobs in the melting pot as but one version of this class conflict. As we will demonstrate, there is always the potential for racial prejudice and discrimination as visible minorities try to enter the industrial melting pot to earn a living in a market of scarce resources and positions. As Bonacich (1972) suggests, these visible minorities are part of a cultural division of labour; they are in a dual labour market that exploits those who have to take lesser jobs because of their visibility and provides them with less opportunity for advancement. Since Blacks are such a large part of the American population, such racial conflicts have been common with them. In Canada, however, visible minorities represent only about 5–10 per cent of all Canadians, so such conflict has been less prominent. Many recent immigrants, however, are visible minorities; this fact is leading to increased conflict in cities especially. We have placed these visible minorities in Cell D because they are involuntarily kept from assimilating into the melting pot as quickly as many of them would like. They are on the pluralist end of the continuum because of their racial visibility; others keep them from accommodating.

The fourth point of conflict is between visible minorities in Cell D and the largest, most powerful ethnic group in Cell B, who generally try to persuade others into amalgamating their British culture, institutions, and values. The conflict between these two cells is clearly a point of class conflict. Hechter (1978) suggests that minorities generally are at the periphery of the industrial power centre and tend to be exploited by those in power. Visible minorities, therefore, will tend to see their relations with the British as a class struggle with the largest, most influential group in power. They see themselves as an exploited minority that finds it hard to enter civic, political, and economic arenas where they can have more influence. Norbert Wiley (1967) suggests that such minorities are forced into ethnic and racial sub-cultures with limited opportunities to escape the socio-economic mobility trap. John Porter (1965: 73–103) was concerned with similar stratification problems that would limit mobility for some ethnic groups more than others. Racial stereotypes remain with us, making these forms of stratification difficult to combat (Henry et al., 1995).

The conceptual model we have just discussed is one way of trying to order some of the dimensions into a logical whole so that various relationships can be compared and observed. It is not without its limitations but it can generate additional insights that are not so easily apparent when the individual parts remain separate. Such a model has limitations because we can never include all of the factors which operate. In this model we dealt with only two axes, leaving out others which also play a part. We do try to include conflict as a third dimension to make it more dynamic. Models can be useful, but they can also become restrictive, and for some they are too static.

IDEAL ETHNIC TYPES

Many traits and features can be wrapped into symbolic characters which can be used as prototypes. Many sociologists have developed individual types which can be fitted into our model, especially into the pluralist and modified pluralist cells to illustrate additional information and insights. Let us discuss three ideal ethnic types to enrich our *Verstehen* or in-depth understanding of some of the more subtle aspects of being ethnic. It is interesting to see how many scholars used this device, and the material of some sociologists can easily be adapted to create other individual types, even though these sociologists did not do so themselves. Georg Simmel and W.I. Thomas were adept at creating individual types and many sociologists followed their lead.

THE TRADITION-DIRECTED ETHNIC

In *The Lonely Crowd*, David Riesman (1950) developed three types: tradition-directed, inner-directed, and other-directed persons. The tradition-directed person represents the majority of the people from those parts of the world where industrialization has not yet become a major factor. This includes non-urban people in Africa and Asia, where birth and death rates are high and where spatial and social mobility is low. In industrialized countries, it includes many rural people. As these people are introduced to the industrial environment, they move through an inner-directed phase in which they become conscious of their traditional state and begin to become aware of other non-traditional forms of existence. Their rising awareness causes them much inner turmoil and evaluation. Riesman's other-directed third type is one who has become urbanized, lives in an industrial environment, and is oriented toward secondary others who have entered his social arena and influenced his values (Driedger, 1989). Rural French Québécois, the Hutterites, and northern Aboriginals in the pluralist Cell E of our model are clearly tradition-directed types. Orthodox Jews and many recent rural immigrants are also urban tradition-directed types.

In his discussion of the tradition-directed person or society, Riesman (1950: 26–8) describes it as a type of social order which is relatively unchanging: 'The conformity of the individual tends to be dictated to a very large degree by power relations among the various age and sex groups, the clans, castes, professions and so forth, relations which have endured for centuries and are modified but slightly, if at all, by successive generations.' The ingroup culture controls behaviour minutely: there is intensive socialization and a careful and fairly rigid etiquette. Little energy is directed toward finding new solutions for age-old problems or toward developing new agricultural techniques or the like. Usually the tradition-directed ethnic is found in a rural, agriculture, or food-gathering society, although these values are also brought to the city by ethnic villagers (Gans, 1962). The tradition-directed society is in many ways similar to Redfield's (1953) folk society and Toennies's (1957) *gemeinschaft* community.

Perhaps the best example of the tradition-directed ethnic in Canada is the Quebec rural habitant whose ancestors lived in the area for 400 years. This person faces limited geographical mobility, a traditional French culture and language which has not changed greatly, a conservative Roman Catholic religion, slowly changing agricultural methods, and a general orientation to the local values of the community (Miner, 1939). Although change takes place slowly, it is at a pace which can be integrated fairly readily into the traditional lifestyle.

Numerous other tradition-directed ethnic communities in Canada include the Hutterites on the prairies (Hostetler, 1974; Hofer, 1988; Driedger, 1997); the northern food-gathering Inuit and Indians (Dickason, 1992); and numerous rural bloc settlements of the Ukrainians, French, Mennonites, Doukhobors, and others. These communities have not yet been greatly influenced by industrial, urban technological change; instead the changes have been accepted into a context of traditional values which have integrated the new trends into stable, slowly changing structures.

Herbert Gans (1962) shows how some tradition-directed persons migrated to the city and transplanted their values, culture, and institutions by forming urban ethnic villages. Often these enclaves show their origins through names like 'Little Sicily' or 'Little Italy'. Such tradition-directed urbanites may be recent immigrants who came to Toronto, for instance, from rural areas such as those of Italy, Greece, Turkey, or Portugal.

The tradition-directed ethnic type, as Riesman suggests, is oriented to traditional ethnic and cultural values; he is reluctant to change, and his major reference group is his traditional ethnic heritage. He is located most often in isolated and rural areas, but may also reside in the city as an ethnic villager. The tradition-directed type is clearly located in the pluralist Cell E of our model.

THE MARGINAL

Park's (1950: 348) ideal marginal person is typical of many people in the involuntary modified pluralist Cell D. While teaching in Chicago in the 1920s, Park observed the migration of Blacks from the rural American tenant farms of the south into northern cities. This change of residence and the concomitant breaking of home ties with traditional rural values and norms resulted in great cultural upheavals which led to change and sometimes to disorganization and conflict. 'It is in the cities', he writes, 'that the old clan and kinship groups are broken up and replaced by social organizations based on rational interests and temperamental predilections' (Park, 1950: 353).

There are no doubt periods of transition and crises in the lives of most of us that are comparable with those the immigrant experiences when he leaves home to seek his fortune in a strange country. But in the case of the marginal person the period of crises and marginality tends to become a permanent personality characteristic. Ordinarily the marginal person is a mixed blood, like the Mulatto in the United States or the Eurasian in Asia, but that is apparently because persons of mixed blood live in two worlds, in both of which they are more or less a stranger. (Park, 1950: 356–7)

It is in the mind of the man that the moral turmoil which new cultural contacts occasion, manifests itself in the most obvious forms. It is in the mind of the marginal man—where the changes and fusions of culture are going on—that we can best study the processes of civilization and of progress. (Park, 1950: 356)

In his earlier essay, 'Human Migration and the Marginal Man' (1928), Park thinks of the marginal person as a racial or cultural hybrid: one who lives in two worlds, in both of which he is more or less a stranger; one who aspires to, but is excluded from, full membership in a new group. The marginal person is between two cultures, and not fully a part of either. 'Park's excluded marginal man was depicted as suffering from spiritual instability, intensified self-consciousness, restlessness, and in a state of malaise' (Levine et al., 1976: 830). He thought of him as a person who could not cope in the new situation, a potential deviant who might look for outlets of expression in unacceptable ways. This type grew largely out of Park's concern with Blacks in the rural American south as well as the urban north, especially Chicago.

Canada is now in the midst of an enormous influx of migrants who are bringing tremendous changes to cities like Toronto. As Asians and West and East Indians of diverse races, cultures, and religions enter, there is much potential for conflict and marginality. The dynamics within Cell D add to marginalization; Isajiw (1978) and Hechter (1978) consign many racial minorities to the periphery of industrial power and opportunities. Because of their visibility and race, many of these minorities find it difficult to compete for jobs in the centre (Cell A), which again places them near the margins (Driedger, 1989). The stratification system clearly places the British at the top of the order, and visible minorities tend to fall toward the bottom.

THE BROKER OR MIDDLEMAN

Having established clear ethnic types in the two pluralist and modified plural-ist cells of our model, we can find changed types who emerge out of these two cells in contact with the industrial melting pot in Cell A.

A broker or middleman is one who enters the industrial fray in Cell A from Cell E. The Jews are the best example of North America's middlemen. Pierre van den Berghe claims that every country has its middlemen: 'Turkey has Armenians and Greeks; West Africa has Lebanese; East Africa has Indians and Pakistanis; Egypt has Copts; Indonesia, the Philippines, Malaysia, Vietnam and Thailand have the Chinese' (van den Berghe, 1981: 137). These are minorities who compete well economically and therefore also are fairly well-to-do socio-economically. When they compete in the melting pot economically, they seem to be able to separate their economic and social lives, and retain their separate ethnic identity.

Van den Berghe (1981: 138) suggests that there is a cluster of characteristics of middlemen minorities (MM) which are remarkably uniform from society to society. He discusses the ideal type in three categories: the characteristics of these groups themselves, the nature of the larger society in which they live, and the particular economic niche they fill. According to van den Berghe, MMs arise from voluntary immigrants who enter a country without having been enslaved previously, but who are often propelled by difficult economic or political situations in their previous homeland to pursue brighter economic prospects in the country of destination. MMs usually maintain strong extended families, perpetuate endogamy, and try to perpetuate their own cultural, institutional, and spatial identity so that they acculturate more slowly than most other groups.

Van den Berghe (1981: 138) classified MMs as an urban petty bourgeoisie social class, better off than the majority of the population but often far from wealthy. This better-than-average socio-economic status often provides them with many advantages in competition with their neighbours. MMs often hold ethnic values such as thrift, frugality, lack of ostentation, and postponement of gratification. Jews, Chinese, Japanese, East Indians, and Mennonites come readily to mind, and most of these can be recognized by their distinctive religion or visibility.

Van den Berghe (1981: 139) makes it clear that the host societies in which MMs survive are often complex stratified agrarian societies with mercantile capitalist economies. Existing and potential markets, trade, and supporting agencies provide opportunities for exchange and expansion for those who have the skills and drive to exploit them. The special characteristics of MMs are usually visibly successful; they tend also to become the targets of discrimination when economic times are difficult.

Georg Simmel's 'the stranger' is similar to the middleman. The concept of 'the stranger' unifies the two characteristics of fixity and transience (Simmel, 1950: 402). Simmel thought that the stranger could retain a separate identity by controlling his behaviour with others, often by being physically near them to perform economic functions, for example, but distant with respect to their values. On the other hand, the stranger could often be far away from his reference ingroup when performing his duties in urban society, but could still retain a symbolic feeling of nearness and belonging to his ingroup.

Simmel's stranger is a rich concept because it raises major questions such as how can a person retain a 'ground' of identification, as Lewin (1948) would put it, within his own social psychological world and at the same time relate securely to others. We would expect that when the stranger or middleman enters the strange environment of others, he is secure only if he is grounded in a reference group or if he is socially and psychologically motivated by the norms and networks of such a group. This raises many related questions; what must be the nature of such a reference group; how often and how much must an individual contact the reference group to sustain his/her separate identity; what must be the quality of such sustenance; and can an individual make only occasional forays into the strange world on business or can he work outside his group consistently, with occasional refresher periods with his own reference group through telephone, mail, and modern communication networks? How important is spatial proximity for ongoing ties, or can *gemeinschaft* networks be maintained through modern communication networks?

It is important to see identity and distance in the total context of Simmel's view of social phenomena, as Levine et al. suggest:

> Simmel's formulation that the stranger represents a combination of nearness and distance, far from being a logical flaw, aptly illustrates his more general assumption that all social phenomena reflect a combination of opposed tendencies. (Levine et al., 1976: 839)
>
> The various ways in which Simmel employs the symbolism of simultaneous closeness and remoteness in 'The Stranger' in fact provide a basic insight about strangerhood which is of great use in developing a more rigorous and systematic sociology of the stranger or modified forms of identity. (Levine et al., 1976)

It must be remembered, of course, that these three images of the ethnic individual are all ideal types; as Max Weber (1946) pointed out, the degree to which they are reflected in any society may be partial and never complete. The task then is to examine Canadian society to find which of these ideal types may be most applicable. Indeed, depending on which ethnic group we examine, it may well be that each of the ideal types is applicable to some of the groups within Canada. Our analysis suggests that the rural Québécois habitant and the prairie Hutterite are represented best by the tradition-directed ethnic type; on the other hand, the urban Jew in Montreal and Toronto seems to be typical of the middleman or stranger type. Visible minorities can often be seen as marginals when they find it more difficult to compete in the industrial marketplace where status and prestige are important to finding acceptance and jobs.

SUMMARY

In this chapter we have addressed the extent to which ethnic groups persist and maintain their solidarity, and the changes which occur in the process of industrialization. We discussed six theories of change, developed a conceptual model seeking to integrate some of the ideas, and dealt with three ideal types that characterize individual prospects for survival.

Proponents of two of the six theories of change (assimilation and amalgamation) assume that the industrial magnet is irresistible, requiring minorities either to assimilate with others into a melting pot, or to amalgamate into Anglo-conformity. Proponents of two other theories (pluralism and conflict), however, propose that minorities can retain their identity through a variety of traditional and ideological means to build a pluralist society in which they remain in conflict either voluntarily or involuntarily. Scholars of two other theories claim that there are modified means of survival between the assimilationist and pluralist poles. Cultural and structural dimensions do not change at the same pace, nor do the various groups hold to or aspire to the same ends and goals. As a result a variety of differentiations must be considered.

To illustrate the complexity of the processes and the diversity of factors operating, we showed what could be done when just the two conformity-pluralism and voluntary-involuntary axes were plotted together in one diagram. Five cells were created, each representing one of five theories discussed; conflict theory was also accommodated at the boundaries of each. Furthermore, we found that ethnic groups could be placed into each of the cells to illustrate that Canadian ethnic groups fit all of the theories and cells.

To summarize, we presented three social psychological plural ideal ethnic types. The tradition-directed ethnic is an example of ideal pluralism. The marginal person is often typical among visible minorities who are involuntarily kept from free upward mobility. Jewish and Chinese middlemen have become upwardly mobile types who retain their identity as ethnic strangers. In Parts III, IV, and V we will elaborate on these many forms of pluralism.

PART II

Providing an Empirical Context

—————————————— CHAPTER 3 ——————————————

A Demographic History

In Part II we present general empirical evidence of the diversity of the Canadian population. We have the opportunity to use more than one hundred years of census data, the best general longitudinal comparable statistics available. Our plan is first to present a demographic history of the many peoples who entered Canada, tracing immigration patterns over time. We present factors which influenced ethnic groups in Chapter Three. In Chapter Four we explore the various regions of Canada, showing that linguistic and cultural patterns vary considerably. Canada is made up of many ethnic regions, forming a multiethnic Canadian mosaic.

IMMIGRATION AND DEMOGRAPHY

It is important to trace the components, trends, selection, and origin of Canada's immigrants over time. We can then explore rural-urban and demographic types such as Aboriginals, charter Europeans and other immigrant and racial groups.

Births have been the most important population growth factor shaping Canadian demography. In Figure 3-1 we show the indicators of population increase through natural increase (births minus deaths) and net migration (immigration minus emigration) between 1871 and 1991. We expect natural increase to rise with some modifications, such as a dip downward during the Depression of the 1930s, when economic and social hardships resulted in fewer births. Figure 3-1 shows the baby boom and a sharp rise in births after World War II. The birthrate has turned downward since the 1970s, with birthrates decreasing dramatically so that the natural population increase is not as great as in the past (Krotki and Reid, 1994; Grindstaff and Trovato, 1994).

The migration factor is considerably less predictable than natural increase, but it is important to ethnic population growth. Figure 3-1 shows two periods of net emigration before the turn of the century; more people left Canada, especially for the United States, than entered Canada through immigration. The second brief net emigration period occurred in the 1930s, which,

FIGURE 3-1 COMPONENTS OF POPULATION CHANGE

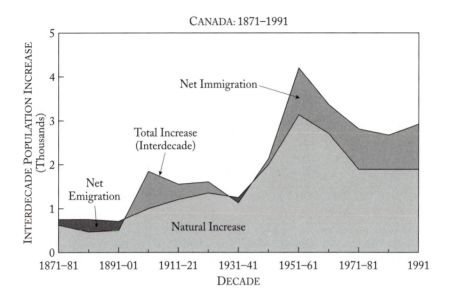

CANADA: 1871–1991

SOURCES: Dept. of Employment and Immigration. *Immigration, 1984.* Ottawa: Minister of Supply and Services Canada. Warren E. Kalbach, 'Growth and Distribution of Canada's Ethnic Populations, 1971–1981', in Leo Driedger (ed.), *Ethnic Canada.* Toronto: Copp Clark Pitman, 1987, p. 90. *Quarterly Demographic Statistics*, Vol. 6, No. 4. Ottawa: Statistics Canada, 1992.

together with a decline in birthrates, brought a sharp dip in the total population growth pattern during the economic depression.

There were also two peak immigration growth periods in 1901–11 and 1951–61, when immigrants into Canada affected total population growth substantially. The second growth period, the 1950s, occurred during the baby boom, so that net immigration and natural increase combined to escalate growth during a very dynamic period of economic expansion and ensuing, considerable social change. In Figure 3-2 we present the extent of immigrant arrivals in more detail.

CANADIAN IMMIGRATION TRENDS

Immigration exceeded the natural population increase during the two decades, 1901–11 and 1911–21. The 1,759,000 immigrants who came to Canada during the decade of 1901–11 increased the population by 28 per cent. This is an enormous increase when we consider that almost two million new immigrants had to be integrated into the Canadian population, which in 1901 was only 5,371,000, in one decade. Almost as many (1,612,000) entered during the decade of 1911–21, increasing the Canadian population by another 21.2 per cent (Kalbach, 1987: 84). During the peak year of 1913, just before the First

FIGURE 3-2 NUMBER OF IMMIGRANT ARRIVALS, CANADA, 1867–1995

SOURCES: Canada Censuses, Department of Manpower and Immigration Annual Reports. *The Effect of Immigration on Population.* Ottawa: Information Canada, 1974, p. 6. Jane Badets and Tina Chui, Canada's *Changing Immigrant Population,* Catalogue No 96–311E. Ottawa: Statistics Canada, 1994, p. 6. Citizenship and Immigration Canada, *Immigration Statistics 1992,* Catalogue MP22–1/1992. Ottawa: Public Works and Government Services Canada. Sergio Marchi, *A Broader Vision: Immigration Plan,* Annual Report to Parliament, 1996. Ottawa: Citizenship and Immigration Canada, 1996, pp. 22 and 23.

World War, more than 400,000 immigrants arrived in a single year. The First World War, however, brought immigration into Canada down sharply. This mass migration—mostly from Europe—was possible when the Canadian West was opened up to agriculture. Lands freed through treaties with the Aboriginals and the building of the railroad during the 1880s opened up opportunities for agricultural homesteaders. Another 1,203,000 immigrants entered Canada after World War I (during the decade from 1921–1931), but since the Canadian population had grown to 8,788,000 in 1921, these immigrants increased the population by only 12.6 per cent.

As shown in Figure 3-2, similar large numbers of immigrants again entered Canada after World War II, with 1,543,000 immigrants arriving from 1951 to 1961; 1,429,000 from 1961 to 1971; 1,447,000 from 1961 to 1971; and also a million and a half from 1971 to 1981 and from 1981 to 1991. The total number of immigrants admitted into the country fell from 129,000 in 1981 to 84,000 in 1985. Since 1986, however, levels have risen to 253,000 in 1992 and then dropped again to 218,000 in 1994. Since the Canadian population had reached twenty-seven million in 1991, these substantial immigrant numbers still increased the total Canadian population only by 5 to 10 per cent per decade (Badets and Chiu, 1994). In the past, most of these immigrants came from Europe, but since the sixties many more have come from other parts of the world such as Asia. These immigrants have tended to enter metropolitan cities, and since many represent visible minorities we need to examine this trend as well.

SELECTION OF IMMIGRANTS

Canadian immigration policy has evolved over more than one hundred years. Between 1867 and 1895 there was a free-entry period of laissez-faire, on the assumption that the forces of supply and demand for population would spontaneously produce equilibrium. From time to time Orders-in-Council excluded the destitute or restricted Chinese immigrants. Clifford Sifton changed this policy between 1896 and 1914, when he aggressively promoted immigration, especially to western Canada, to provide an opportunity for the development of primary resources (Department of Manpower and Immigration, 1974: 3–16). Free land was offered first to northern European immigrants and, when this did not produce enough response, to eastern and southern Europeans as well. Group immigration was also encouraged, making possible the entrance of substantial numbers of non-English and non-French immigrants. Between the two world wars (1914–45), a period of uncertainty developed and was exacerbated by the Depression. The First World War had virtually cut off immigration, and the 1930s Depression and the Second World War also discouraged immigration greatly. Both wars created sharp sentiments against Germans such as the Hutterites and Mennonites who were briefly restricted as immigrants. Also during the Second World War, the Japanese deportation and relocation took place.

The second great flowering of immigration began after the Second World War; from 1946 to 1961, many Canadians wished to rescue their relatives from the chaos in Europe. As a result, two categories of immigrants became major concerns: those who were sponsored by relatives, and those who were resettled displaced persons or refugees. Restrictions on German, Japanese, and Asian entries were increasingly lifted. Two million immigrants came to Canada during these years, an average of 130,000 a year (Department of Manpower and Immigration, 1974: 27). After such a large influx of immigrants, and as socio-economic needs left by the Second World War waned, there were again sentiments after 1961 favouring a more rational policy for selecting immigrants. This train of events persuaded the government to begin a policy review in a White Paper on immigration in 1966. As a result a point system was developed.

When Prime Minister Pierre Trudeau announced the federal multiculturalism policy of 1971, he also linked it with bilingualism. The need to accommodate Quebec nationalism and the separatists was actually first priority, so that the French language could be legally raised to equal status with English. To maintain French in Quebec its government was also concerned about francophonizing newcomers to the province (Richmond, 1994: 180). When federal multiculturalism programs began in the 1970s, they focused primarily on the needs and interests of European immigrants who wanted to preserve their cultural traditions, ethnic organizations, and heritage languages, and to boost historical and cultural activities which governmental funding assisted. By the 1980s, there was growing evidence of racism with extremist anti-Semitic, anti-Asian, and White supremacist groups on the rise. By 1985 Bill C-85 was passed to deal with employment equity and affirmative action, and by 1988 this came into force (Richmond, 1994: 181). Affirmative action is designed to help those who are less able to upgrade their education and job skills, the better to compete in the marketplace. Bill C-93 was passed in 1988, with new programs to combat racism, and by 1990 Bill C-63 was introduced to establish the Canadian Race Relations Foundation. Implementation, however, has been postponed because of budget cuts. The shift in policy, from European to visible minority immigrants and their needs, was originally brought about with the introduction of the point system for the selection of immigrants to Canada, which allowed people from around the world to apply. Since then many non-European, non-white immigrants have come to Canada in the eighties and nineties.

As Table 3-1 shows, three categories for the selection of immigrants were developed (Independent, Nominated, and Sponsored). Citizens of Canada may sponsor close relatives such as parents, brothers, or sisters to come to Canada if the sponsor guarantees to take care of their maintenance for at least a year. (It was felt that newly sponsored immigrants should not become an economic burden to Canada.)

Applicants who have no relatives in Canada may apply for entry as Independents, subject to competition under a point system. As Table 3-1 shows, a total of one hundred points can be earned through education, personal qualities, occupational demand, occupational skill, age, arranged employment, and knowledge of the official languages. The number of points required to gain entry varies, depending on the government's desired control over immigrants. Fifty or sixty points are usually required for entry.

Nominated immigrants, the third category of selection, are judged on characteristics from both the Independent and the Sponsored categories. A Nominated applicant can earn up to seventy points under the Independent point system and can also earn up to thirty points if he or she has a Canadian relative not as closely related as those required for sponsorship.

Figure 3-3 shows how this new selection process has affected entry into Canada and what the immigrant trends have been. The number of immigrants has varied annually from just under 75,000 in 1961 to 250,000 in 1992. The number of immigrants who were sponsored and nominated (Family Class) during these decades has fluctuated between 30,000 and 110,000. Immigrants in the Independent category have fluctuated the most in number, ranging from a low of 35,000 in 1961 to a high of 150,000 in 1967. The

TABLE 3-1 SUMMARY OF FACTORS USED FOR THE SELECTION OF IMMIGRANTS TO CANADA

INDEPENDENT APPLICATIONS

Factors	Range of Units of Assessment That May Be Awarded
Education	0–12
Personal Suitability	0–10
Occupation	0–10
Specific Vocational Preparation	0–15
Age	0–10
Experience	0–8
Arranged Employment	0–10
Knowledge of English and/or French	0–15
Levels of Control	0–10
Potential Maximum	100

NOMINATED RELATIVES

Long-Term Factors (as for independent application)	1–70
Short-Term Settlement Arrangements Provided by Relative in Canada	0–30
Potential Maximum	100

SPONSORED DEPENDANTS

Close Relative in Canada Willing to Take Responsibility for Care and Maintenance	Units of Assessment Not Required

Note: Independent Applicants and Nominated Relatives, to qualify for selection, must normally earn 70 or more of the potential 100 units of assessment.

SOURCE: *The Revised Selection Criteria for Immigrants.* Ottawa: Canada Employment and Immigration Commission, 1985.

Canadian government can control the Independent immigrant category by raising or lowering the number of points required to enter, depending on the country's economic and social needs.

Of the 218,000 immigrants who entered Canada in 1994 almost half, or 111,000, were in the Family Class including sponsored and nominated persons. Refugees in 1994 were down to 28,000 from 1991 when there were twice as many (53,000), so this category also fluctuates depending on world conditions. The Independent class has recently included an economic class of 16,000 entrepreneurs in 1992, 35,000 in 1993 and 24,000 in 1994. In 1992 the 15,697 entrepreneurs included 8,000 from Hong Kong which will soon become a part of China, 1,900 from Korea, and 1,400 from Taiwan, all of which are part of the

FIGURE 3-3   IMMIGRANT ARRIVALS BY ENTRY CLASS, 1961–1995

Thousands

Year of Arrival

SOURCES: *Immigration to Canada: A Statistical Overview*, Ottawa, Employment and Immigration Canada, 1989, pp. 8, 25, 31, 47. Citizenship and Immigration Canada, *Immigration Statistics*, 1992, Catalogue MP22–1/1992. Ottawa: Public Works and Governmental Services Canada. Sergio Marchi, *A Broader Vision: Immigration Plan*, Annual Report to Parliament, 1996. Ottawa: Citizenship and Immigration Canada, 1996, pp. 22 and 23.

emerging industrial Pacific Rim countries increasingly competing in the world market. These entrepreneur immigrants with capital flowed predominantly into Quebec (5,661), British Columbia (3,908), and Ontario (3,557).

The new selection policy was designed to give applicants from all countries of the world a chance to compete for entry into Canada. Formerly, northern Europeans were strongly encouraged to come, and others were often discouraged through Orders-in-Council or other restrictions. Since the implementation of the new policy, the selection process has increasingly encouraged immigrants from the Third World. The Sponsored category still favours northern Europeans—the bulk of Canada's present population who encourage relatives to come. The Independent category provides opportunities for all immigrants.

ORIGIN OF IMMIGRANTS, 1926–80

Prior to the Depression, immigrants were largely from northern European countries, especially Britain, Germany, the Netherlands, and the Scandinavian countries. Ninety per cent of immigrants who arrived in Canada before 1961 were born in Europe. This proportion fell to 69% for those who arrived between 1961 and 1970 to 36% for those who immigrated between 1971 and 1980, and to one-fourth for those who arrived in 1981–1991. Since then, however, the origins of immigrants have become more varied. Almost one-half (47.8%) of the immigrants between 1926 and 1945 came from the British Isles but this proportion has declined since then; between 1976 and 1980, only 14.1% came from the same source, and by 1981–1991 the British proportion dropped to 7.5% (Badets and Chiu, 1994: 20). From 1926 to 1945, approximately three-fourths (72.2%) of all immigrants were from northern Europe, but by 1981 to 1991, this proportion had declined drastically to only 12.4%.

A basic shift in immigration patterns has taken place during the last fifty years. Central and East European immigrants had already begun to arrive in Canada during the great influx just before the First World War, and represented approximately one-fifth (19.1%) of the immigrants in 1926 to 1945. However, this proportion declined drastically after the Second World War. Southeastern and southern Europe became an important source of immigrants immediately after the Second World War, representing about one-fourth of all immigrants during 1955 to 1970 and declining again to 8.8% by 1976 to 1980. The most recent source of large immigrant groups has been Asia. Almost none (.8%) came from Asia between 1926 and 1945, but by 1976 to 1980, almost one-third (31.7%) of all immigrants came from the Far East and by 1991 this had grown to half (49.7%) (Badets and Chiu, 1994: 20). This dramatic increase in immigrants of another race, usually of different religions and very different cultures, marks a major shift from the large proportions of northern European immigrants in the past. Why has this major shift occurred, and what will be the consequences for the Canadian population?

RECENT LEADING SOURCE COUNTRIES 1980–93
Since the changes to the Immigration Act in 1976 (proclaimed in 1978), immigrant patterns based on the country of origin have changed substantially. As seen in Table 3-2, in 1951 nine of the top ten source countries were European; six of these nine were northern European. Immigrants from the tenth country, the United States, were largely of original European stock as well. This trend remained roughly the same during the 1960s, although Hong Kong ranked in the top five in 1968. The order changed considerably in 1976, when six of the top ten countries of origin were non-European. Immigrants from Britain were still most numerous, followed by American immigrants in second place. By 1984, six years after the new Immigration Act had been proclaimed, two Asian countries—Vietnam and Hong Kong—ranked first and second; Britain had dropped to fifth place, and seven of the ten leading countries of origin were in the Third World. This continued into the nineties when Britain dropped to ninth. By 1993, the seven top donor countries were Asian and were sending visible minorities to Canada. Many immigrants from all over the world were now able to compete with Europeans in gaining entrance through the point system.

In 1995 the population of twenty-seven million Canadians was still mainly Christian Caucasians of European ethnic stock representing several European languages and cultures. More recent immigrants of Mongoloid and Negroid races, whose religions are primarily Buddhist, Muslim, or otherwise non-Christian, brought with them quite different languages and cultures, which is making the Canadian population more heterogeneous. Since the accumulated European ethnic stock is so large, however, the proportion of

TABLE 3-2   THE LEADING SOURCE COUNTRIES OF IMMIGRANTS, SELECTED
            YEARS

1951	1960	1968
Britain	Italy	Britain
Germany	Britain	United States
Italy	United States	Italy
Netherlands	Germany	Germany
Poland	Netherlands	Hong Kong
France	Portugal	France
United States	Greece	Austria
Belgium	France	Greece
Yugoslavia	Poland	Portugal
Denmark	Austria	Yugoslavia

SOURCES: Department of Manpower and Immigration, *The Immigration Program*, Vol. 2, *A Report of the Canadian Immigration and Population Study* (Ottawa: Information Canada, 1974) p. 84; *1976 Immigration Statistics*, Table 3; and Employment and Immigration Canada, *Annual Report to Parliament on Future Immigration Levels*, 1985. Ottawa: Minister of Supply and Services Canada, 1985. Statistical Appendix; Immigration Statistics Employment and Immigrant Canada, 1986-90; *Facts and Figures: Overview of Immigration*. Hull: Citizenship and Immigration, 1994, p. 3.

immigration from Third World countries will increase only modestly in the general population. With the economic downturn in the 1980s, the government's immigration quotas dropped to about 70,000, tending to restrict opportunities for large increments in immigrant growth. In the nineties with an economic upturn, immigration quotas have increased again.

THE CANADIAN ETHNIC POPULATION

Having discussed general Canadian demographic trends, let us now focus on 110 years of ethnic population growth, the foreign-born population in Canada over time, and rural-urban distribution.

ETHNIC POPULATION, 1871–1991

In Table 3-3 we see that the 1871 census reported that Canada had a population of 3,486,000, comprised largely of the British (60.0%) and the French (31.1%), the two charter groups who together represented 91.7% of the population. This census was taken in five of the provinces in confederation at that time, representing a small part of what is now eastern Canada. It did not include the majority of Aboriginals in the Northwest, and most of the existing provinces have been enlarged since. This population grew by about one million per decade, and the ethnic proportions remained roughly the same until the beginning of the great immigrant influx after 1901.

TABLE 3-2 (CONTINUED)

1976	1984	1993
Britain	Vietnam	Hong Kong
United States	Hong Kong	India
Hong Kong	United States	Philippines
Jamaica	India	Taiwan
Lebanon	Britain	China
India	Poland	Sri Lanka
Philippines	Philippines	Vietnam
Portugal	El Salvador	United States
Italy	Jamaica	Britain
Guyana	China	Poland

Since the turn of the century ethnic proportions have changed considerably, largely due to new immigration patterns. In 1901 the British population was still in the majority at 57.0%, and the French population remained at 30.7%. By 1991, the single response (those who reported a single ethnic origin) population of the British had declined to 28.1% and the French population had dropped to 22.8%, so that the two charter groups now represent just over one-half of the Canadian population. Other ethnic populations grew from 22.3% in 1901 to 27.5% in 1991. Twenty-two per cent chose multiple responses. None of the ethnic groups now represents a majority, and the diversity of others is clearly on the rise. It is not surprising that thoughts of multicultural-ism now make more sense than they did much earlier (Krotki and Reid, 1994).

THE FOREIGN-BORN POPULATION

We expect that the foreign-born population, immigrants who have spent at least some of their formative years outside Canada, and who are first genera-tion Canadians, will be most eager to continue the linguistic and cultural pat-terns of their mother countries. In Table 3-4 we see that there were 700,000 foreign-born immigrants in Canada in 1901, representing 13.0% of the pop-ulation before the great immigrant influx. By 1921 there were almost two mil-lion (1,956,000) foreign-born immigrants who represented almost one-fourth (22.3%) of the population in Canada after the great immigrant influx of 1911 to 1920. By 1991, the Canadian foreign-born population had grown to over four million (4,420,000), but the proportion had declined to 16.5%, largely since immigration rates have declined proportionately.

The foreign-born population is not, however, evenly distributed across Canada. Almost half (46.3%) of the foreign-born immigrants resided in

TABLE 3-3   POPULATION[a] OF BRITISH ISLES, FRENCH, AND OTHER SELECTED ORIGINS, CANADA, SELECTED YEARS: 1871–1991

Ethnic Group	1871[b]	1881	1901	1921	1941	1961	1981[f]	1991[f]
Total[c]	3,486	4,325	5,371	8,788	11,507	18,238	24,084	26,994
British Isles	2,111	2,549	3,063	4,869	5,716	7,997	9,674	7,595
English	706	881	1,261	2,545	2,968	4,195		3,958
Irish	846	957	989	1,108	1,268	1,753		726
Scottish	550	700	800	1,174	1,404	1,902		893
Other	8	10	13	42	76	146		2,018
French	1,083	1,299	1,649	2,453	3,483	5,540	6,439	6,147
Other European	240	299	454	1,247	2,044	4,117	4,627	4,146
Dutch	30	30	34	118	213	430	408	358
German	203	254	311	295	465	1,050	1,142	912
Greek				6	12	56	154	151
Hungarian[d]			2	13	55	126	116	101
Italian	1	2	11	67	113	450	748	750
Jewish	1	16	126		170	173	264	246
Polish			6	53	167	324	254	273
Portuguese								245
Scandinavian	2	5	31	167	245	387	283	174
Ukrainian			6	107	306	473	530	407
Other	4	7	37	18	10	88	452	278
Asian/ African		4	24	66	74	122	533	1,634
African								26
Arab								144
Chinese		4	17	40	35	58	289	587
East Indian							121	325
Japanese			5	16	23	29	41	49
Other			2	10	16	34	82	421
Aboriginal		40	105	114	126	220	413	471
Other[e]	52	84	72	39	64	242	559	1,191
Black				18	22	32	45	225
Other				21	42	210	514	966
Multiple Groups[f]							1,839	5,806

SOURCES: Dominion Bureau of Statistics, 1961 *Census of Canada, Bulletin* 7:1–6, Ottawa: The Queen's Printer, 1966, Table 1; Statistics Canada, 1971 *Census of Canada*, Bulletin 1.3–2. Ottawa: Information Canada, 1973, Table 1; D. Kubat and D. Thornton, *A Statistical Profile of Canadian Society*. Toronto: McGraw-Hill Ryerson, Ltd, 1974, Table f–10. Reprinted from Warren E. Kalbach, 'Growth and Distribution of Canada's Ethnic Population, 1871–1081' in Leo Driedger (ed.) *Ethnic Canada*. Toronto: Copp Clark Pitman, 1987, p. 87; *Ethnic Origin: The Nation*, Census 91, Catalogue 93–315. Ottawa: Statistics Canada, 1993.

Notes:
[a] Numbers rounded to the nearest 1,000.
[b] Four original provinces only.
[c] Excludes Newfoundland prior to 1951.
[d] Includes Lithuanian and Moravian in 1901 and 1911 and Magyar in 1981.
[e] Includes 'not stated' prior to 1971. In 1971 'not stated' cases were computer-assigned.
[f] Somewhat different ethnic divisions where multiple origins have been separated into special categories.

TABLE 3-4 PER CENT OF FOREIGN-BORN POPULATION IN CANADA'S REGIONS,
SELECTED YEARS: 1901–1991

Region	1901	1911	1921	1931	1941	1951[a]	1961	1971	1981	1991
	(Per cent Foreign Born)									
Atlantic Provinces	6.7	3.6	3.4	3.0	3.2	2.7	2.3	2.2	2.1	1.8
Quebec	12.7	9.2	9.7	10.9	11.1	11.1	13.6	14.2	13.6	13.6
Ontario	46.3	32.0	32.8	34.9	36.3	41.2	47.6	51.8	52.4	54.3
Prairie Provinces	20.3	40.8	40.7	37.3	34.2	28.4	21.4	16.5	15.4	13.0
British Columbia	11.3	14.1	13.3	13.8	15.1	16.5	14.9	15.1	16.3	16.6
Yukon and Northwest Territories	2.7	0.3	0.1	0.1	0.1	0.1	0.2	0.1	0.2	0.1
Total: Per cent	100.0	100.0	100.0	100.0	100.0	100.0	100.0	99.9	100.0	100.0
Number (in hundreds)	700	1,587	1,956	2,308	2,019	2,060	2,844	3,296	3,919[b]	4,420

SOURCE: Censuses of Canada, 1901–1991.
Reprinted from Warren E. Kalbach, 'Growth and Distribution of Canada's Ethnic Population, 1871–1981' in Leo Driedger (ed.), *Ethnic Canada*. Toronto: Copp Clark Pitman, 1987, p. 97. *Immigration and Citzenship: The Nation*, Catalogue no. 93–316, 1991 Census. Ottawa: Statistics Canada, 1992, pp. 8, 9, 12, 13.

Notes

[a] Newfoundland not included prior to 1951.

[b] Estimates of total and foreign-born population, from the 20% sample, reported as 24,083,500 and 3,867,160 respectively.

Ontario in 1901; this proportion fell to close to one-third (32.0%) in 1911. By 1991, it had grown to over one-half (54.3%). This shows that new immigrants have been disproportionately attracted to the industrial heartland of Canada, except from 1911 to 1931 when the Sifton immigration policy funnelled immigrants to the agricultural West. The prairie provinces received the largest proportion of immigrants during this period. While the Ontario foreign-born population curve is U-shaped, the prairie curve is more bell-shaped. As the figures for 1951–91 show, immigrants after the Second World War have clearly gone to the cities of the industrial belt in Ontario.

The proportion of foreign-born immigrants in the Atlantic provinces and the Yukon and Northwest Territories is negligible. Quebec, the second largest province, has been able to attract only a small portion of immigrants ranging between 9.2 and 14.2%: considerably less than half of the 26% share they would normally be expected to attract. Compared to Ontario, Quebec's inability to attract new immigrants has continued to erode the Quebec proportion of the Canadian foreign-born population. Because about 82% of the population in Quebec is French, this does not bode well for Quebec's political future in Canada. Earlier, Quebec was able to make up for lack of new immigrants by much higher birth rates, but recently births have declined dramatically as more Quebeckers become urban.

RURAL–URBAN ETHNIC DISTRIBUTIONS
Our discussion of the foreign-born suggests that many immigrants have moved to industrial areas recently; we should, therefore, examine the rural–urban ethnic distribution. In Table 3-5 we see that only about one-fifth (19.6%) of the Canadian population was urban in 1871; by 1991 the trend had reversed to three-fourths (76.9%) of the population being urban. The British and French charter populations have remained very close to the rural–urban national average with the British somewhat above and the French somewhat below it.

The Aboriginal peoples have always been a much more rural population, first as food-gathering people, and more recently living on reserves. The Aboriginals are among Canada's most rural population, although many have moved off the reserves and into the cities during the past three decades, so that by 1991 more than one-third (42.3%) of them were urban. In the next section of this chapter, we shall discuss the Aboriginals as a distinctive ethnic type in many respects.

The Germans, along with the Dutch and Scandinavians, were part of the European immigration to the prairies after the turn of the century. They too have remained more rural than the national average, but not as rural as the Aboriginals.

The Italians, along with others like the Greeks and Portuguese who moved mostly into the city, represent more recent immigration after World War Two; by 1961 almost all of them (94.7 to 96.6%) were urban. The Chinese are almost all urban. The Jews arrived earlier and have always been the most urban ethnic group in Canada, with almost all of them (94.0 to 98.8%) living in cities as early as 1901. Both the Italians and the Jews have always been much more urban than the national average, and both groups have also been most heavily located in the largest cities of Montreal and Toronto. Urbanization has increased for all groups, but the differences between rural Aboriginals and urban Jews are very great. We expect that this range of differences will also be found with respect to other characteristics.

DEMOGRAPHIC ETHNIC TYPES

The general demographic data we have examined so far suggest that some groups can best be understood as ethnic types when attempting to summarize

TABLE 3-5 PER CENT URBAN[a] FOR SELECTED ETHNIC-ORIGIN POPULATIONS IN CANADA, 1871–1991

ETHNIC ORIGIN

Year	Total	Aboriginal Peoples	German	French	British	Italian	Chinese	Jewish
				(Per cent)				
1871	19.6	1.7	11.1	18.8	22.3	53.5		67.2
1881	25.7	0.6	16.4	23.1	28.8	61.3		79.5
1901	37.5	5.1	28.0	33.7	41.8	65.4		94.2
1911	45.4	3.7	33.5	40.9	50.4	69.8		94.0
1921	49.5	3.7	33.2	47.7	53.7	79.3		95.7
1931	53.7	3.9	36.9	54.0	57.5	81.6		96.5
1941	54.3	3.6	36.4	54.9	58.3	80.9		96.0
1951	61.6	6.7	44.2	59.9	65.7	88.1		98.7
1961	69.6	12.9	61.8	68.2	71.2	94.7		98.8
1971	76.2	30.1	68.8	75.9	75.9	96.6		98.8
1981	75.6	36.4	68.3	73.3	74.5	94.9		98.5
1991	76.5	42.3	68.2	72.8	72.6	93.9	97.9	98.5

SOURCES: Censuses of Canada, 1871–1991.

Reprinted from Warren E. Kalbach, 'Growth and Distribution of Canada's Ethnic Population, 1981' in Leo Driedger (ed.), *Ethnic Canada Identities and Inequalities.* Toronto: Copp Clark Pitman, 1987, p. 93. *Profile of Urban and Rural Areas,* Part B, Canada, Provinces and Territories. Ottawa: 1991 Statistics Canada, 1994.

Note
[a] Definition of 'urban' is that in effect at the time of the particular census.

some of the population's diversity. We begin with the earliest native Indians and Inuit and move on to the French and British who later traded and settled in this vast territory. Many other Europeans eventually followed; recently, Third World immigrants have entered the mosaic. The Aboriginals, the charter Europeans, the non-charter Europeans, and the more recent visible minorities provide ethnic foci.

THE ABORIGINALS
Anthropologists tell us that the earliest *Homo sapiens* came to the two Americas at least 12,000 years ago, probably via the Bering Strait. The native Indians were here when our European ancestors were still barbarians roaming the European continent. Some Aboriginals remained food gatherers, but others turned to agriculture; by the early 1500s, the Spanish conquistadores found the great civilizations among the Maya, the Aztec, and the Inca in Central and South America.

FIGURE 3-4   PERCENTAGE OF ABORIGINALS IN CANADA BY TYPE, 1991

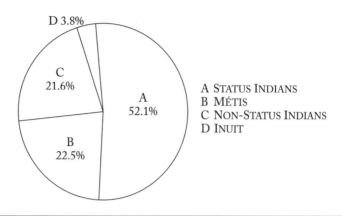

A STATUS INDIANS
B MÉTIS
C NON-STATUS INDIANS
D INUIT

Note: Status Indians are sometimes referred to as registered or legal Indians.

SOURCES: Department of Indian Affairs and Native Development, *Indian Register*, 1961-87, Ottawa: Minister of Supply and Services, 1987; DIAND, *Basic Departmental Data*, 1991. Ottawa: Minister of Supply and Services Canada, 1992.

The French and the British did not find such great civilizations among the Aboriginals of the territory that is now Canada. The Hurons and Iroquois had begun farming (Price, 1979: 1–20) and the Aboriginals of the West Coast were engaged in large-scale fishing (Frideres, 1993) but neither had advanced to the state of their South American counterparts. Aboriginals of the central plains and the northlands were food gatherers, the image often perpetuated in Canadian history. Canadians tend to see a very limited part of the many diversified Aboriginal groupings throughout the two Americas. Too often, we tend to forget that the first Aboriginal *Homo sapiens* lived in the region of what is now Canada twenty-five times as long as any Europeans have lived there.

Although the Aboriginals were the majority until the Europeans arrived, they had declined to 470,615 in 1991, representing less than two per cent of the total population of Canada. The 1991 census found that half of the Aboriginal people (52.1%) were status Indians—Aboriginals with whom the government had made treaties, and 23% were Métis, representing a mixture of Indian and French or British ancestry. Figure 3-4 also shows that non-status Indians, who have not entered into treaties with Canada, ranked third at 21.6%. The Inuit (3.8%), who came to Canada later than the Indians and who live in the most northerly parts of Canada, represent only a very small proportion of the Aboriginal category.

The census in 1991 counted Aboriginals in each of the ten provinces and two territories, but over one-half live in the four most westerly provinces. Only four per cent of Aboriginals live in the Atlantic provinces, and only six per cent live in the territories. About one-fourth live in Ontario, and about one-tenth

FIGURE 3-5   ABORIGINAL PERCENTAGE OF TOTAL POPULATION LOCATED IN
PROVINCES AND TERRITORIES, 1991

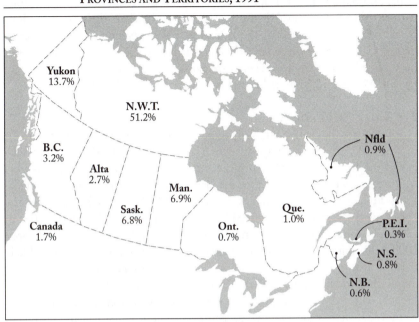

SOURCE: *Ethnic Origin: The Nation*, Catalogue 93–315, 1991 Cenus. Ottawa: Statistics Canada, 1993, pp. 40–1.

in Quebec. Aboriginal peoples are one of the most rural ethnic groups in Canada: six in ten Aboriginals live in rural areas, and only about one-fourth (24%) live in cities larger than 100,000. The 1991 census shows that 70% of non-status Indians live in urban areas and 60% of Métis are urban; in contrast only 20% of Inuit and 30% of status Indians are city dwellers.

The 292,705 status Indians in the 1991 census represent over half of all Aboriginals, and they are most heavily located on the prairies (38.6%). Of the 75,110 non-status Indians, 34.7% are located in Ontario, presumably drawn to industrial work opportunities; approximately one-fourth (25.4%) are in British Columbia, where few treaties have been signed; and nearly another fourth (24.7%) live on the prairies. The 98,260 Métis represent 15.3% of all Aboriginals; two-thirds (66.2%) live on the prairies, where the British and French first opened up the West to the fur trade. About two-thirds (63.0%) of the 25,300 Inuit reside in the Yukon and Northwest Territories, and nearly one-fifth (19.2%) live in northern Quebec, which was their original hunting grounds and still is for many. The Inuit represent only 5.2% of all Aboriginals.

Figure 3-5 shows the proportions of Aboriginals in the total population of the provinces and territories. Aboriginals represent 51% of the population in the Northwest Territories; this is the only region in which they are a majority.

They still represent 14%, 7%, and 7% of the total population in Yukon, Manitoba, and Saskatchewan respectively. There are relatively few (less than one per cent) located in the Atlantic provinces and Quebec, the eastern regions which were first occupied by the Europeans. We conclude that the Aboriginals of Canada represent a special demographic type because they have lived here much longer than anyone else, are closer to a food-gathering lifestyle, are racially Mongoloid, and are located largely in the Canadian Northwest.

THE CHARTER EUROPEANS

One year after the British established the first permanent European settlement in North America at Jamestown (now Maryland) in 1607, the French established the first permanent European settlement in Canada at what is now Montreal, some 150 years before the British settled permanently in Canada. Early French explorers, such as Cartier in the 1530s and Champlain in the 1600s, were the first European explorers to come to what is now Quebec in eastern Canada. The Vikings came to explore and settle Newfoundland about 1000 A.D., but our knowledge of these settlements is limited and it is unlikely that the historical European continuity of these Scandinavians is evident in our population today. Thus, the first Europeans to settle in Canada were the French, who today are recognized as one of the two charter group partners.

In 1871, shortly after Canadian confederation, the first census was taken. We see in Table 3-4 that of the approximately 3.5 million people who lived in Canada, almost all (92%) were either of British (61%) or French (31%) origin. A further six per cent of the population was German. The 1871 census did not include the estimated one-half million native Indians scattered over the northwestern territories because the census included only the four original provinces of the East, a fraction of the territory which is now Canada.

Thus, it seemed logical that the Canadian confederation in 1867 would be a union between two peoples of European origin, the British and the French. The British North America Act of 1867 legalized the claims of the two original European migrating groups for such historically established privileges as the perpetuation of their separate languages and cultures. The 1960s Royal Commission on Bilingualism and Biculturalism continued to support and encourage the charter group status of the French, even though immigrants of other ethnic origins comprised one-third of the Canadian population by 1991.

During the 125 years following 1871, a considerable demographic shift occurred, with a decline in the British charter majority proportion from 61% to 28% by 1991. Now none of the ethnic groups is a majority. Immigration from Britain after the turn of the century has continued to add to the British charter group, but considerable numbers of immigrants from other countries have diminished the British total proportion by 1991. Although the British majority tried very hard to make Canada a unilingual and unicultural society,

FIGURE 3-6   PERCENTAGE OF CANADIAN POPULATION BRITISH, FRENCH, AND OTHER IN 1871 AND 1991

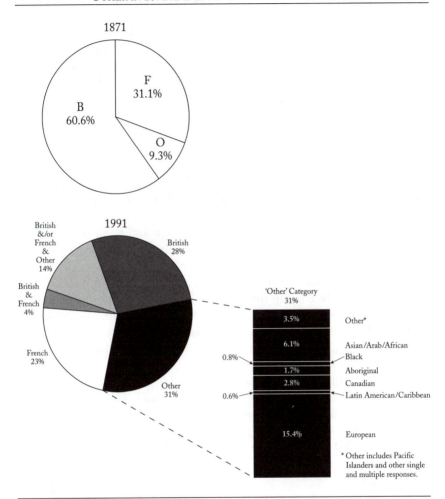

SOURCE: Statistics Canada, 1871 and 1991. Reproduced with permission of the Minister of Supply and Services Canada.

the country was bilingual and bicultural in 1871. However, since no ethnic group was a demographic majority in the 1990s, suggestions of building a multicultural society have become a more viable option, especially since Canada is now legally and officially bilingual and multicultural.

When we consider that the British group comprises the English, Scottish, Irish, and Welsh, the category of British ethnicity becomes more diverse. The English population in Canada has usually been twice as large as the Scottish, Irish, and Welsh combined. The mixed British-French category of 1,522,075 shows that intermarriage is also taking place between individuals of the two charter populations. In 1991 Canadians who intermarried represented 6.3% of the total Canadian population.

While the smaller French charter group maintained roughly one-third of the Canadian population since 1871, their proportion has begun to drop: by 1991 they represented closer to one-fourth (23%) of the total. Caldwell and Fournier (1987: 12) clearly show the recent decline of Quebec's population growth rate. During the 1921–31 decade, the Quebec population growth rate was greater than Canada's (21.8 to 18.1%); during 1941–51 the two were even (21.7 and 21.8%); during 1971–81 Quebec was falling behind dramatically (12.9 to 6.8%). Quebec has had difficulty getting its share of immigrants in the past, and recently the birth rate has dropped much more than in the rest of Canada (Caldwell and Fournier, 1987: 22–35). Since a large majority of those with French origins reside in Quebec, indications are that the proportion of the French charter minority will continue to decline. This decline in the French population in Canada will result in a decline in their political power as well, although their proportionate population has not declined for as many years as that of the British.

In Table 3-6 we see that the British still represent a majority in only the three most easterly Atlantic provinces. However, their proportions have declined in each of these provinces since 1901, most dramatically in Ontario (from 79.3% in 1901 to 30.0% in 1991. The French are a very large majority in Quebec (80.2%) and have held this majority over time with a slight drop.

THE MULTI-EUROPEAN ENTRANCE

While non-charter Europeans represented only about seven per cent of the Canadian population in 1871, they have immigrated in increasing numbers. Table 3-7 shows that the charter groups were still a dominant majority in 1901, but by 1991 they dropped to one-half (50.9%). While the French population had declined to 22.8% by 1991, the proportion of British origin dropped to 28.1%.

The other European groups entered Canada well after the coming of the charter groups. Many of the Germans came to Ontario about 150 years ago, but the majority of the others came to open up the West and encountered a country where the charter groups had earlier established the political and economic patterns. The position to which ethnic groups are admitted and the level at which they are allowed to function in the power structure of a society is described as entrance status by Porter (1965). This non-charter group presence mushroomed after the turn of the century and before the First World War into one of the largest world migrations from northern, and later eastern, Europe to North America. These European groups, who numbered 4,146,601 in 1991, represent 15.4% of the Canadian population (Table 3-7).

While the large French population has always tended to resist a national

TABLE 3-6 COMPOSITION OF THE POPULATION OF CANADA BY ETHNIC ORIGIN, 1901 AND 1991

Ethnic Origin	Total	B.C.	Alta.	Sask.	Man.	Ont.	Que.	NB	NS	PEI	Nfld
					(Per cent)						
1901											
British	57.0	59.6	47.8	43.9	64.4	79.3	17.6	71.7	78.1	85.1	
French	30.7	2.6	6.2	2.9	6.3	7.3	80.2	24.2	9.8	13.4	
Other	12.3	37.9	46.0	53.2	29.4	13.4	2.2	4.1	12.0	1.5	
Total	100.0	100.0	100.0	100.0	100.0	100.0	100.0	100.0	100.0	100.0	
1991											
British	28.1	35.3	28.1	23.4	25.0	30.0	5.1	44.3	58.4	64.0	88.0
French	22.8	2.1	3.0	3.1	5.0	5.3	74.6	33.8	6.2	9.2	1.7
Other	37.5	33.0	35.0	36.9	40.0	36.7	12.3	4.5	9.6	3.7	2.1
Multiple	21.6	29.6	33.9	36.6	30.0	28.0	8.0	18.3	25.8	23.1	8.2
Total	100.0	100.0	100.0	100.0	100.0	100.0	100.0	100.0	100.0	100.0	100.0

SOURCES: Dominion Bureau of Statistics, *1921 Census of Canada*, Vol. 1, 1924, Table 23; Statistics Canada, *Ethnic Origin, The Nation*, catalogue no. 93–315, 1993.

unilingual and unicultural Canada, these large migrations of Europeans into Canada, especially into western Canada, have created other non-charter majorities in some of the western provinces. Thus, in western Canada, the non-charter European entrance may be seen as another ethnic type of milieu, especially on the prairies where wheat has replaced fur as the dominant focus of commerce. Certainly, Sifton's immigration policy in the early 1900s was a major factor in the creation of this European non-charter majority in the West. Later we shall examine in more detail how this has contributed to much alienation in the West and has led to western attempts at raising new political parties to counter the eastern Canadian dominance of the charter groups in Ontario and Quebec. Although these non-charter European entrants are too diverse to be considered a 'Third Force' as Paul Yuzyk (1975) suggests, ethnic factors often combine with economic and political issues, making it difficult to see which of the factors, including the ethnic one, is most salient.

VISIBLE THIRD WORLD MINORITIES

Earlier, immigrants from northern Europe were encouraged to come to Canada, but recently more immigrants from southern Europe, South America, Asia, Africa, and the Caribbean have come as well. Table 3-3 shows that

TABLE 3-7   ETHNIC ORIGINS IN CANADA, 1991

	Single Response			Multiple Response
	N	%		N
Total Canadian	21,183,910			5,810,130
European	17,888,365		59.0	
British	*7,595,120*	*28.1*		6,436,870
English	3,958,405	14.7		4,646,720
Irish	725,660	2.7		3,057,695
Scottish	893,125	3.3		3,355,240
Other	33,860	.1		
French	*6,146,601*	*22.8*		242,580
Other European	*4,146,065*	*15.4*		4,229,675
Dutch	358,180	1.3		603,415
German	911,560	3.4		1,882,220
Scandinavian	174,373	.6		542,825
Hungarian	100,725	.4		112,975
Polish	272,805	1.0		467,905
Ukrainian	406,645	1.5		647,650
Balkans	131,440	.5		67,210
Greek	151,150	.6		40,330
Italian	750,055	2.8		397,720
Portuguese	246,890	.9		45,295
Jewish	245,840	.9		123,725
Other	396,400	1.5		
Asian/African	1,633,660		6.1	
Arab	144,050	.5		50,830
West Asian	81,660	.3		16,315
South Asian	420,295	1.6		68,080
East Indian	324,845	1.2		54,435
East and S.E. Asian	961,225	3.6		105,840
Chinese	586,645	2.2		66,000
Filipino	157,250	.6		17,725
Indo-Chinese	116,535	.4		14,355
African	26,430	.1		13,160
Pacific Islands	7,210	.0		4,605
Latin American	177,930		.7	
South and Central	85,535	.3		34,445
Caribbean	94,395	.4		72,225
Aboriginal	470,615		1.7	532,060
Native Indian	361,375	1.3		418,605
Other	109,240	.4		113,455
Other	989,715		3.6	
Black	224,620	.8		127,045
Canadian	765,095	2.8		267,935
Multiple Origins	5,810,130		21.5	
			100.0	

Note: This table includes all specific groups for whom single responses exceeded 100,000. There is double counting of groups in the multiple-response category.

SOURCE: Statistics Canada, *'Ethnic Origin', The Nation*, 1991 Census of Canada, Catalogue no. 93–315, February 1993.

in 1951, shortly after the war, the leading source countries of immigrants were in Europe, but by 1993 northern European immigrants had been replaced by immigrants of other racial, cultural, and religious backgrounds from the Third World. The change in Canadian immigration policy to a point system was designed to provide these immigrants a better chance to enter Canada. In Table 3-3 we saw that seven immigrant source countries in 1993 were Asian.

Closer examination of Table 3-7 shows that the category of non-charter and multiple region Canadians had grown to almost half (49.1%) in 1991; of these 1,633,660 (6.1%) came from Asian backgrounds. The Chinese (586,645 [2.2%]) represent the largest group, followed by East Indians (1.2%). These immigrants stand out among the predominantly northern European Canadian population as visible minorities whose Asian ancestry is physically apparent. Their racial, religious, linguistic, and cultural diversity is readily apparent. These Canadians are still a relatively small proportion of our population, but their numbers and percentages are growing, so that Canada is becoming more heterogeneous ethnically and racially.

Most of these recent immigrants settle in urban centres, especially Toronto, Vancouver, and Montreal. In Table 3-8 we present a selection of ethnic groups to illustrate the extent of the urbanization of these recent arrivals. More than 90% of the Asians are urban; 95.4% of the Chinese live in urban centres of 100,000 or more. Only the Jews, who have lived in Canada for a longer period of time, are more urban than these recent visible arrivals. In contrast, Germans are only 68.2% urban, and only half live in larger urban

TABLE 3-8   SELECTED ETHNIC ORIGIN POPULATIONS BY URBAN SIZE GROUPS, CANADA, 1991

Ethnic Origin	Rural	SIZE OF COMMUNITY 1,000- 99,999	100,000 Plus	Total Urban
		(Per cent)		
Aboriginal	57.7	16.7	25.9	42.6
German	31.8	16.8	51.4	68.2
British	27.4	18.9	53.7	72.6
French	27.2	17.7	55.1	72.8
Canadian	19.5	10.5	70.0	80.5
Italian	6.1	3.4	90.5	93.9
Portuguese	3.4	10.8	85.8	96.6
Chinese	2.6	2.0	95.4	97.4
Jewish	1.5	2.8	95.7	98.5

SOURCE: Statistics Canada, 1991 Census, Catalogue 93–340. Ottawa: Statistics Canada, 1994, p. 8.

centres. Again we see a considerable difference between early northern European immigrants and more recent Asian arrivals, so that we shall consider them as distinctive Canadian ethnic types.

After the Second World War, large numbers of southern Europeans such as the Italians, Greeks, Portuguese, and Spanish arrived. These Canadians are also mostly urban, and they also reside in larger metropolitan centres, especially Toronto and Montreal. Although southern and northern Europeans are all Caucasians, southern Europeans are to some extent more visible because of their darker physical features and distinctive Mediterranean cultures. Many of them arrived from countries less industrialized than northern Europe and they tend on average to be of lower socio-economic status.

SUMMARY

The purpose of this chapter is to prepare an empirical demographic context so that the reader may get a sense of how the general Canadian population has grown during the past century. We trace natural increase and immigration, as well as the origin of immigrants. We find that the recent selection system has resulted in many more immigrants from the Third World, in contrast to the earlier predominance of northern European immigrants.

While in 1871 Canada was made up largely of the British and French charter groups, by 1991 others represented one-third of the population. Since immigrants have come to Canada each year, a considerable foreign-born population has continued to replenish existing ethnic diversity. Ontario has always attracted the largest percentage of the foreign-born, with over half of all immigrants residing there in 1991. Whereas at the turn of the century large numbers of European immigrants helped to open the West to agriculture, since the Second World War south Europeans and Third World immigrants have been more drawn to the metropolitan centres.

Four ethnic types clearly emerged: the Aboriginals, the charter Europeans, the non-charter Europeans, and the visible Third World minorities. Aboriginals represent only two per cent of all Canadians now, and over half of them have signed treaties and live mostly in the Northwest. The British and French, who represent the original European charter groups, now comprise only half of the Canadian population and hold the most political and economic power. Other Europeans who came to pioneer in the West continued to strengthen the European presence in Canada. Since the advent of the new immigration policy, many Third World visible minorities have arrived from Asia, bringing greater ethnic diversity racially, religiously, culturally, and linguistically. These new visible minorities have entered the larger metropolitan centres of Toronto, Montreal, and Vancouver, and have changed the ethnic makeup of these cities considerably.

CHAPTER 4

Multicultural Regionalism

Our discussion of Canada's population patterns over time illustrates that the Aboriginals possessed the land first, followed by the French, the British, other European groups, and Third World immigrants. The proportions of various groups increased at different times; by 1991 the many ethnic groups were not evenly distributed throughout Canada. The British, for example, dominate in the Atlantic provinces but are a small minority in Quebec, while the French dominate in Quebec and, except for New Brunswick, are a small minority elsewhere. Other Canadians tend to be the majority on the prairies and in southern British Columbia, but are very sparsely represented in the five most easterly provinces. Ethnically, the various Canadian regions are very different, and we need to examine these regional differences.

REGIONALISM: A SENSE OF PLACE

In 1936 Howard W. Odum (1936: 8) proposed using 'region as a tool for analysis' because it can be used as 'a gestalt in which all factors are sought out and interpreted in their proper perspective and in a framework for social planning'. Samuel E. Wallace (1981: 431), in his presidential address to the Mid-South Sociological Society, suggested that the conception of the American South as a distinctive region was well established by 1800. Wallace (1981: 432) claims that each section of the country has different needs, interests, ambitions, even different theories and forms of government, and in the South ethnicity and race relations play an important part. He goes on to say that 'the South is a region, a society, a set of institutions, an attitudinal stance, a people, a symbol, an idea' (Wallace, 1981: 438).

Wallace laments that sociological theories and models of the last two or three decades have been devoid of any sense of place, and he wonders whether that is why they downplay the importance of regions. Regionalism persists because 'to be identified with space means to treat space as part of the self—not simply something to use, abuse, destroy, deface, or pollute' (Wallace,

1981: 438). In America's deep South, the sentiment toward the land and symbolism of the land are still important; I suggest in many Canadian regions this sense of sanctified and hallowed ground is also emerging. Wallace claims that 'we lose explanatory power and we also lose history when we abandon the concept of regionalism. . . . Functionalists occupied no space, so they also included neither past nor future in their models. Regionalism, however, can develop only over time' (1981: 439).

Ralph Matthews (1980: 43–61) follows the same argument: 'There has been virtually no sustained attempt to develop a "regional sociology".' He is impressed with the overriding concern of Canadian sociologists for the nature of Canadian unity and identity. John Porter, in *The Vertical Mosaic*, provides no analysis of the regional basis of the Canadian élite; indeed, he declares, 'it has never struck me that regions provide basic group identities in Canada' (1975: 6). In his view, modernization tends to obscure a sense of place. Matthews (1980) tries to outline the significance of regional considerations and to prepare the ground for an explanation of regional differences in an attempt to develop a theoretical and analytical framework capable of providing insight into the various divisions in Canada.

For sociologists, however, regions are mostly containers in which important social, political, and economic interaction and structure may be found. Richard Simeon (1979: 293) says, 'We must first recognize that in no sense is region an explanatory variable; by itself it doesn't explain anything; nothing happens because of regionalism. If we find differences of any sort among regions, it remains for us to find out why they exist; regionalism is not an answer.' Matthews adds, 'We must delve more deeply into their nature and causes' (Matthews, 1980: 50). Some studies (Driedger, 1977) have focused on language and ethnicity in the various Canadian regions. Ralph Matthews, in his call for a Canadian sociology of regionalism, talks about 'distinctive regional cultures', (1981: 49, 51) and suggests that at least socio-economic, political, and cultural or group identity factors must be considered. Simeon and Elkins (1979) have formed a four-fold typology based on efficacy and trust in politics with significant differences in various regions of Canada. They controlled separately for social class, education, party identification, sex, age, and size of community, and found that substantial regional differences remained after the controls had been introduced (Simeon and Elkins, 1979: 43). They conclude that there are 'distinctive regional cultures'.

Many social factors contribute to distinctive Canadian regions, but here we will briefly discuss the original cultural ethos which differentiates regions and the linguistic worlds created by migrants who occupy these regions. Tracing these two factors in at least six regions of Canada, we find very different ethnic combinations which indeed form quite different Canadian ethnic regions.

LINGUISTIC DEMOGRAPHY

Sapir (1949) suggests that language is a structural symbol system into which children are socialized. He uses the Whorf hypothesis which goes further, to say that this structure of symbols provides an entry into a world of symbols. Language also becomes restrictive because the organization of these symbols directs our thinking toward some ways and not others. Language thus becomes a window through which we look at the universe in a certain way, a form of *Weltanschauung*, or conditioning to see the world in a distinctive way (Shibutani and Kwan, 1965: 61). While most European languages have grown out of a similar language pool, other language complexes in Asia, Africa, and the aboriginal Americas are quite different structurally and in their origins. According to Sapir, immigrants who come to North America from the Third World will see the world in quite different ways. Indeed, when the Europeans came to the Americas, they contacted aboriginals who had very different world views.

Scholars have devoted considerable attention to the relationship between language and the ethnic identity of immigrant groups in multilingual settings. They have frequently claimed that preservation and continued use of the traditional mother tongue is an important—if not the most important—component of ethnic identity. Factors such as urbanization, secularization, internal migration, widespread exogamy, industrialization, and others are cited as influential in this general process of linguistic change.

In the 1960s and early 1970s in Canada, it was mostly social psychologists and psycholinguists who began to study the context and dynamics of language groups. They concentrated mainly on English and French as official languages, dealing with questions of bilingualism, second language learning, and the like (see, for example, Clement, 1994; Cummins, 1994; Bouhris, 1994; Taylor and Gardner, 1970; Berry and Wilde, 1972). Similarly, demographic studies based on census data concentrated on the official languages with some reference to non-official language groups which were frequently lumped into the category 'Others' (Lieberson, 1970; Henripin, 1974).

The 1975 study conference, The Individual, Language and Society in Canada (Coons et al., 1977), was an early interdisciplinary effort by psychologists, sociologists, and sociolinguists to deal with different aspects of the languages-in-contact situation, including non-official languages. While psychologists mainly brought to the meeting their research on official languages (Gardner, 1977; Berry, 1977), sociologists stressed the broader multilingual and regional dimensions of linguistic research in Canada (Driedger, 1977a, Jackson, 1977). They saw competence in the traditional mother tongue and its continued use as one of a number of ethnic identity factors including religion, endogamy, parochial education, participation in voluntary associations, etc. (Driedger, 1978; Isajiw, 1981; Reitz, 1980). Later sociological studies have increasingly focused on language as one important variable related to ethnic identity (deVries and Vallee, 1980; Isajiw, 1981; Edwards, 1985; Bouhris, 1994; Cummins, 1994; Berry and Laponce, 1994).

Several Canadian studies have demonstrated the importance of controlling for immigrant generation and community size in the analysis of language maintenance. For the urban context, O'Bryan et al. (1976) sampled ten groups of adult speakers of non-official languages in five Canadian metropolitan centres and found a fairly rapid decline in traditional mother tongue competence from first- to third-generation Canadians. Fluency in the respective languages was fairly high for the first generation (between 56.0 and 80.7%), but had virtually disappeared by the third generation. These ethnic groups were able to maintain 'some knowledge' (38.7%) of their ethnic language only into the third generation (O'Bryan et al., 1976: 45–6). DeVries and Vallee amply describe this phenomenon as 'the levelling effect of the third generation' (1980: 132).

Breton, Isajiw, Kalbach, and Reitz (1990) found the same decline when they studied three generations of six groups in Toronto. Those studies in Toronto reveal a similar pattern of progressive linguistic assimilation with succeeding generations, although the patterns of shift differ significantly among the ethnic groups surveyed. Whereas there is still some ethnic language knowledge in the third generation (mostly skills in reading and writing), verbal interaction has virtually disappeared. Breton et al. (1990: 34–91) concur with Gans (1979), and suggest a progressive change in language function from instrumental to expressive or symbolic use.

Comparable studies for rural environments have shown that ethnolinguistic or ethnoreligious groups in more segregated rural enclaves have been somewhat more successful in maintaining ethnic languages (Anderson, 1980; Anderson and Driedger, 1980). While an extremely high proportion of all respondents were still competent in an ethnic mother tongue (though most of them were bilingual), the actual use and the desire to speak it was consistently lower and varied significantly among the different groups—most markedly among the three German groups (Hutterites: 100%; Mennonites: 68.9%; Catholics: 29.0%) (Driedger and Hengstenberg, 1986: 90–109).

Macro-level surveys of the type discussed in the preceding paragraphs include questions on ethnic origin and aspects of traditional mother tongue competence and use: they are a powerful instrument for determining the linguistic condition of large groups (Lieberson, 1966; Lieberson and Waters, 1990). A number of the previously mentioned sociological studies of specific groups and geographic locations in Canada, as well as studies which are based on census data (deVries and Vallee, 1980; Henripin, 1974) have yielded valuable insights into the relationship between ethnic identity and language maintenance. However, inherent constraints on form, number, and content of questions on language and the resulting need for categorization and standard-ization tend to obscure the fact that language is 'a highly complex phenomenon comprised of many physiological, psychological, social and other attributes' (Khubchandoni, 1976: 97). Consequently, macro-level data need to be interpreted in a socio-psychological context, taking into account the historical tradition and the language-specific peculiarities of the different ethnic groups.

In 1971, Prime Minister Trudeau proclaimed Canada a bilingual and mul-ticultural nation. How do Canadian demographics conform to governmental policy? In the 1991 census 16,311,200 Canadians (60.4%) reported their mother tongue to be English; 6,562,100 (24.3%) reported it to be French; and 4,120,800 (15.3%) claimed a non-official mother tongue. Thus, 85% of the Canadian population reported one of the two official languages as their mother tongue.

These official-language Canadians are not, however, distributed evenly across the country. Figure 4-1 shows that, in the three most easterly provinces (Newfoundland, Nova Scotia, and Prince Edward Island), more than 90% of Canadians learned English as their mother tongue. In the three most westerly provinces (British Columbia, Alberta, Saskatchewan) and the Yukon roughly 80% or more of Canadians learned English as their mother tongue. In the interior provinces (Manitoba and Ontario) more than 70% claim English as their mother tongue. Two-thirds (65%) of the population of New Brunswick, more than half (55%) of the population of the Northwest Territories, and only 9% of the population of Quebec report an English mother tongue. Thus, in each of the twelve regions (except Quebec) more than half of the population had learned English first.

French, the second official language, was the mother tongue of 82% of the people in Quebec. One-third (34%) of the population learned French first in New Brunswick, but five per cent or less learned French first in each of the other provinces and regions (Harrison and Marmen, 1994). French ranks first in Quebec and second in three other provinces (New Brunswick, Prince Edward Island, and Nova Scotia).

The greatest concentration of Canadians who learned a non-official mother tongue first is in the Northwest Territories, where 42% of the population learned a non-official language first. Most of these people had learned an abo-riginal language first. Non-official mother tongues rank second in the seven most westerly provinces and regions: the Northwest Territories (42%), Mani-toba (22%), Ontario (20%), British Columbia (19%), Saskatchewan (15%), and the Yukon (8%). After English, the aboriginal languages rank second in the northern territories, and German ranks second in the prairies and British Columbia. Ukrainian ranks third in the prairies and Chinese ranks third in British Columbia. French ranks fourth in the prairies (Harrison and Marmen,

FIGURE 4-1   PERCENTAGE OF ENGLISH, FRENCH, AND OTHER MOTHER
              TONGUES BY PROVINCES, 1991

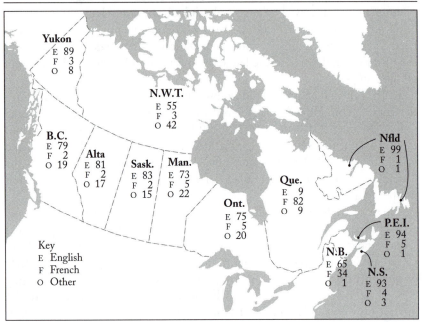

SOURCE: Brian Harrison and Louise Marmen, *Languages in Canada*, Catalogue No. 96–313E. Scarborough, ON: Prentice Hall and Statistics Canada, 1994, pp. 8, 15, 24.

1994). It is clear that the two official languages dominate in the six most easterly regions; in the six most westerly regions, however, English dominates, followed by other non-official languages.

The extent to which Canadians actually use their mother tongues at home shows even more clearly that Canada is a bilingual country. In Quebec the match between the French mother tongue and the use of French at home is identical (82%). However, in each of the other eleven regions, there is more use of English and less use of French and other languages than their mother tongues suggest. Except for New Brunswick, where one-third (31%) of the population speaks French at home, French is hardly used at all outside Quebec. Only three per cent of the population of Ontario and less than three per cent of the population elsewhere use it in the home. Those who speak non-official other tongues at home represent 32% of the population of the Northwest Territories, 10% in Manitoba and British Columbia, 5–8% in Alberta, 12% in Ontario, Saskatchewan, and Quebec, and less than 2% elsewhere. French is the dominant language used in Quebec, and English is used in the rest of Canada. The ethnic linguistic demographics tend to conform quite well to official bilingual national policy.

FIGURE 4-2 ETHNIC ORIGIN OF CANADIAN POPULATION BY PROVINCES AND
REGIONS, 1991

SOURCE: *Ethnic Origin: The Nation*, Catalogue 93–315. Ottawa: Statistics Canada, 1993. 1991 Census, pp. 12–27.

ORIGINAL CULTURAL ETHOS

While the linguistic demographics confirm that Canada is largely bilingual, we find that culturally the nation is much more ethnically diverse. While immigrants came to Canada largely from northern Europe before the First World War, and from eastern and southern Europe between the two world wars, many others have entered since the Second World War, making the population more culturally diverse.

Comparing Figures 4-1 and 4-2, we see the proportion of British descendants is lower in Figure 4-2 in each of the twelve regions of Canada. On the other hand, the proportion of French, non-charter, and multiple-response descendants is higher in Figure 4-2. This comparison shows that the country is moving increasingly toward bilingualism (Figure 4-1), but remains much more differentiated and multicultural in its ethnic origins (Figure 4-2). Let us look at the general regional picture before we discuss ethnic regions.

The first observation in Figure 4-2 is that the Aboriginals are a majority in the Northwest Territories and the French are a huge majority in Quebec. The British are a majority in the three most easterly provinces. Multiple-response and non-charter Canadians are a majority in the five most westerly provinces and the Yukon. These regional tendencies are not surprising when we consider that the Aboriginals still dominate the Northwest Territories, their original lands. The prairies are dominated by European agriculturalists who were part of the great immigration in the 1910–20s, and the eastern regions are occupied by the two charter peoples in Quebec and the Maritimes. Figure 4-2 includes Asians and Africans as Visible Minorities (VM).

Our task later in this chapter is to examine these six regions of Canada, which we suggest are ethnically distinct because of their historically unique demographic and ecological features brought about by immigration and other factors over the past. We also suggest that ethnicity, as a major factor in distinguishing these regions, affects the nation politically, economically, and socially.

CANADIAN ETHNIC REGIONS

Our analysis of the various regions plots the northlands, the Atlantic region, Quebec, the bilingual belt, Upper Canada, and the West as shown in Figure 4-3. The regions vary from unicultural and monolingual in the East, to multicultural and multilingual in the Northwest. High concentrations of the Aboriginals in the North, the 'other' ethnic groups in the West, the French in Quebec, and the British in the East represent an interesting mix of cultural values and linguistic patterns.

In sketching the historical, ecological, demographic, political, and economic macro-structures within each region, our underlying assumption is that these six regional ethnic structures in Canada will be quite different, and that they will have different languages, cultural needs, abilities, and aspirations because of these variations. We begin with the Aboriginals who still occupy 80% of Canada in the northerly parts. The Europeans began to invade in the southeast and moved westward to occupy all of the Canadian south, increasingly displacing the Aboriginals toward the north. We shall trace these patterns of invasion and succession historically in the six ethnic regions.

THE NORTHLANDS: MULTILINGUAL AND MULTICULTURAL

The Northlands constitute about four-fifths of Canada's territory, a staggering 3,000,000 square miles. Its boreal forests, tundra, and Arctic desert stretch from the Yukon through the vast Northwest Territories to Labrador, and include the northerly two-thirds of British Columbia, the prairie provinces, Ontario, and Quebec. Relatively few people inhabit this space, which has a population density of about 0.23 persons per square mile. Of this population, a majority (51%) are of Native Indian or Inuit origin. Their ancestors arrived here some 14,000 or more years ago, having come over the Siberian land bridge from Asia after the last ice age. The proportion of people of Aboriginal origin increases as we move northward. However, more non-Aboriginal

FIGURE 4-3 CULTURAL AND LINGUISTIC REGIONS CANADA

SOURCE: Leo Driedger and Neena Chappell, *Aging and Ethnicity: Toward an Interface*. Toronto: Butterworths, 1987, p. 49. Reproduced by permission.

people are eroding this northern Aboriginal majority as industry seeks to exploit renewable and non-renewable resources.

The population of this region has a very high proportion of rural, non-farm residents. Of this group, the Native Indian and Inuit component far outnumbers the non-Aboriginal one. Most people of non-Aboriginal ancestry, on the other hand, live mostly in the region's few small cities and towns and on work sites connected with construction, metal mining, or oil exploration and extraction. Even in the towns and settlements where Aboriginal people share space with non-Aboriginals, the two groups are clearly segregated.

Politically, a large portion of the Northwest Territories is not formally organized, possibly because the way of life in the North does not require it. Nunavut became an organized territory in the eastern half of the Northwest Territories, where the Inuit are a majority. The northern parts that belong to the six most westerly provincial political jurisdictions are largely neglected and ignored. As industry and the southern economic system extends into the north, even more need for political and economic organization will likely develop. The development of a northern oil pipeline is a good example of how the ecology and demography of the region is changing as a result of political and economic decisions to develop an oil industry in the north. The language of communication used in this economic extension is mostly English. If Aboriginals wish to benefit from this economic development, they will need to learn one of the two official languages, probably English, in order to get a job.

The issues which attract the most attention and concern for Aboriginals in the Northlands have to do with Aboriginal rights, the settlement of land claims, and a voice in deciding their own fate. Roughly three in ten claimed a native language (most commonly Cree, Ojibway, and Inuktitut), as their mother tongue in 1991; 86% of those used their mother tongues at home most often (Harrison and Marmen, 1994: 29). The Inuit and status Indians use theirs most; the non-status Indians use theirs least. Less than half of the status Indians living off reserves used their mother tongues at home. Their substantial numbers and isolation in the Northlands have made it possible for the Aboriginal peoples to maintain their languages to a greater degree than have the Aboriginal peoples in other regions.

In Figure 4-4, Price (1979: 52–3) shows the original cultural areas of the Aboriginals with the Inuit still located in the northerly Arctic cultural area, and the Native Indians still heavily concentrated in the western and eastern subarctic areas. Price (1979: 34–5) also shows that the Eskimo-Aleut language families were located roughly in the Arctic, the Athapascan language families in the western subarctic, and the Algonquian language families in the eastern subarctic cultural areas. The area designated as the Northlands in Figure 4-4 includes the three Arctic, western, and eastern subarctic cultural and linguistic Aboriginal areas.

'The Arctic is an unusual cultural area in that it has such a severe climate for humans that it was occupied very late in human history and by only one society, the Inuit, who are relatively homogeneous. Inuit culture extends along the coastlines from the eastern tip of Siberia through northern Alaska and Canada to Greenland' (Price, 1979: 41). The population of the Inuit in the Canadian Arctic is zero to ten persons per hundred square kilometres. They have traditionally lived in igloos in winter and hide tents in summer, used stone lamps to toast their food and used kayaks and sleds for transportation. Many still live in this fashion, although others have moved to villages near industrial developments.

The subarctic is the largest cultural area in the Northlands, stretching from the interior of Alaska, across the Yukon and the Northwest Territories, through northern Ontario and Quebec, and into the Atlantic provinces. It is an area of boreal forests with long, cold winters. Population densities range from zero to sixty persons per hundred square kilometres. They used to hunt in semi-nomadic bands, are members of the Athapascan and Algonquian language families, roast their meats, live in earth lodges in winter and in bark

FIGURE 4-4   EARLY CULTURAL AREAS OF ABORIGINALS IN CANADA

SOURCE: John Price, *Indians of Canada, Cultural Dynamics*. Toronto: Prentice-Hall Canada Limited, 1979, pp. 52–3.

and hide wigwams in summer, and use the canoe in summer and toboggan in winter for transportation (Price, 1979: 42). While some Indians still live in this fashion, most now live in villages near urban and mining projects operated by southern Canadians.

The Aboriginal residents were the people who lived here first, and they occupy the majority of our land area. Treaties have not yet been made in many areas. They are, however, a very small percentage of our population and are economically and politically powerless. They are also multilingual and multicultural. The trend seems to be for the Aboriginals to come south into more urban settings, and there is strong evidence that they adopt English very quickly; only 33% of the Aboriginal people in urban areas use their mother tongues (Vallee and deVries, 1975). The Northlands could best be described as multicultural and multilingual.

THE QUÉBÉCOIS HEARTLAND: FRANCOPHONE AND MULTICULTURAL

Although Jacques Cartier explored the St Lawrence River as early as 1534, it was Samuel de Champlain who established the first permanent European settlement in Canada on the north shores of the St Lawrence at Montreal in 1608 (Trudel, 1985: 315). While this first settlement was originally designed to control the French fur trade, it later developed into the settled French Quebec Heartland, a French colony which Champlain had dreamed about. This French settlement in Canada occurred sixty years before the founding of the Hudson's Bay Company by the British in 1670, and 150 years before the British settled in Upper Canada in the 1700s (Guindon, 1988).

For our purposes the discussion of the modern French Heartland comprises all the parts of Quebec that we have not included in the Northlands. It encompasses much of the area on both sides of the St Lawrence and the Gaspé. Hundreds of thousands of people in the region east of Montreal trace their ancestry to settlers in the seventeenth and eighteenth centuries. A very high proportion (95.5%) are of French ethnic origin, and 84% speak French exclusively (Henripin, 1993). Small enclaves of people of non-French ethnic origin and language live in the region, but it is one of the most culturally and linguistically homogeneous parts of Canada.

The social and cultural worlds which people experience directly are French and Québécois. Even in urban places like Quebec City, Chicoutimi, and Trois-Rivières, a person could live out his life in a virtually exclusively French-speaking milieu without hearing or using English. Most stimuli which come from the broader North American context are conveyed in the French language (Guindon, 1988). For instance, football and baseball games, late-night movies, and other American, British, and Canadian media offerings either originate in the French language or have it dubbed in.

A measure of French dominance in this region is seen in the fact that the population of the eastern parts of Quebec shows a net shift from English to French (deVries and Vallee, 1980). Because much of this region is economically underdeveloped, it receives very few immigrants. The language support system for the French is very strong in all sectors—with one exception: the economy. Much of the economic sector is bilingual or English at the upper levels of management, although this is changing (Gagnon, 1993). With its high degree of *de facto* French unilingualism and uniculturalism, it would appear that *within the region* itself, language is not a burning issue for the majority of French speakers, although some express concern for the French language in the Bilingual Belt or for the over-representation of English in the economic sector (Guindon, 1988).

In the Québécois Heartland, 82% of the population report French as their mother tongue and 83% also speak French in their homes (Harrison and Marmen, 1994). English is declining as the home language in Quebec, falling from 13% in 1971 to 8% in 1991. The number who are bilingual rose from 2,065,100 in 1981 to 2,413,000 in 1991: more than half (55%) of the bilinguals in Canada, their largest concentration is in Montreal (Harrison and Marmen, 1994: 36). The numerical increase in bilingualism among the Québécois French mother tongue group was much greater, totalling more than one-quarter of a million. However, the proportion of Quebeckers who are bilingual increased from 29% in 1981 to 35% in 1991 (Harrison and Marmen, 1994: 36).

One of the reasons the English language has persisted in Quebec is that the economic élite were English and tended to use English in their industrial connections with the larger North American scene. However, Toronto is increasingly becoming Canada's dominant financial and industrial base, which means that business headquarters and offices are gradually shifting to Ontario. Therefore, the power of the English business élite in the province has declined. The use of the French language is a second factor which has encouraged greater French linguistic and cultural influence in Quebec, including provincial legislation which favours the French language. The influence of the Parti Québécois and French nationalists has resulted in some English interests leaving Quebec, which is increasingly adding to an emphasis on French language and culture.

The six million French Québécois living in Quebec represent the largest ethnic regional block in Canada. With their long history in Canada, their renewed emphasis on French identity, the new emphasis to promote French in Canada, and provincial legislation to promote French language and culture, this will remain the strongest single ethnic region if Quebec remains a part of Canada.

With increasing urbanization, multiculturalism with a strong French emphasis is also emerging in Quebec. This is because Montreal will most likely continue to flourish and draw some immigrants who, together with the British minority, will push for multiculturalism. The influences of American investment will likely keep the city multicultural, as will the influence from the rest of Canada.

It is interesting to note the aspiration of French Québécois. They created an early, rural, French Catholic community life in this region; as they became more urban, however, they lost their rural and religious community ties. They seem to have transferred their allegiance from religion to language. Whether language is sufficient ground for a claim to distinctiveness remains a question. At the same time that French Québécois dominate the region, they seem to resort increasingly to provincial legislation to restrict other languages in favour of French. In this practice, they are similar to the British in the past, who relied on language legislation in the West. Quebec's language legislation may help the provincial French majority, but it does little for the others who may desire multiculturalism. This raises the suspicion that neither the British nor the French are interested in multiculturalism, and that both want linguistic dominance (Dion, 1975). The reluctance of leaders in Quebec and of many French-speaking federal cabinet ministers to support multiculturalism furthers the suspicion that they desire French dominance in the region and might want to limit other cultural and linguistic identities, a form of Franco-conformity.

ATLANTIC CANADA: ANGLOPHONE AND ANGLOCULTURAL
As far as we know, the Viking Norsemen were the first Europeans to touch North America in about A.D. 1000 in the Newfoundland area. There is some evidence that they may have settled briefly, but the probability that their progeny is now part of the Canadian population is remote. In 1497, John Cabot left Bristol and landed somewhere on the coast of what is now Newfoundland, claiming it for England. In 1534 Jacques Cartier charted the St Lawrence, bringing Indians back with him to France (Parsons, 1985: 253). In 1604, Samuel de Champlain sailed to Acadia with a plan to establish a French colony in the Annapolis valley of what is now Nova Scotia. Atlantic Canada was visited early by many European explorers; conflict and some evictions took place, especially as the British and French sought to gain control over the new territory.

The most easterly three Atlantic provinces (Newfoundland, Nova Scotia, and Prince Edward Island) exhibit British unilingualism and uniculturalism, with a few small French enclaves. Atlantic Canada is anchored in the east by Newfoundland, which was a British colony until it entered the confederation of Canada in 1949. Eighty-two per cent of Newfoundlanders are of British origin, and ninety-nine per cent reported English as their mother tongue in 1991 (Harrison and Marmen, 1994: 10). Over half of the population of Prince Edward Island (54%) and Nova Scotia (58%) claimed to be British in 1991, and almost all (93–94%) reported their mother tongue to be English (see Figures 4-1 and 4-2).

Their long history is largely British and demographically they are English. Very few immigrants enter these provinces, leaving the population mainly of British origin. This region represents only six or seven per cent of the Canadian population, so its impact on the total mosaic is small. It is highly unlikely that residents of this region will push for a heterogeneous mosaic. Their Aboriginal population is very small. Their Black population is English-speaking and small, and multiple responses are growing.

In many ways this region resembles the French Heartland. First, it is underdeveloped economically and has attracted comparatively small numbers of immigrants. Second, apart from the native Aboriginals who were here when the Europeans arrived, scores of thousands of people in Atlantic Canada are descended from ancestors who settled the region several hundred years ago. As in the French Heartland, some of these ancestors—the Acadians—were French-speaking; the great majority, however, were from England, Ireland, Scotland, and Wales. Thus the British-Canadian character is even more dominant here than it is in parts of Upper Canada.

Survey results suggest that the majority of the people in this region favour two official languages for Canada, certainly more so than in Upper Canada and the West (Vallee and deVries, 1978: 762). Multiculturalism and official language policies must seem rather remote to the great majority of people in this eastern area, where the British-Canadian culture and the English language are so dominant. This is the most unilingual and one of the most unicultural regions in Canada; because they are located in the extreme east with its British history, we expect that these Canadians will tend to see Canada very much from an early British perspective.

THE BILINGUAL AND MULTICULTURAL BELT

While the British in the Atlantic provinces are segregated from the French in the heartland of Quebec, these two charter peoples have come into contact frequently ever since they invaded this land from the east. The Hudson's Bay Company, founded by the British, and the Northwest Trading Company, founded by the French, frequently fought to control trading territories as they moved west into the Aboriginal lands in pursuit of trade. The remnants of these contacts are still evident in what Joy (1972) calls a bilingual belt which stretches from Moncton, New Brunswick, to Sault Ste Marie on Lake Huron in Ontario. This belt does not conform neatly to any of the provincial territories we have today, but we shall follow it westward from New Brunswick.

New Brunswick is really the only region which approaches the bilingual and bicultural model. In Figure 4-2 we see that 44% of the population of New Brunswick are of British origin, and one-third (34%) are French; one-fourth (22%) claim other origins. As seen in Figure 4-1, two-thirds (65%) of the population claim English as their mother tongue, and one-third reported French (34%). Only one per cent learned a non-offical tongue first. The French live in the northern half of the province, adjacent to Quebec, and the British live in the southern half in a fairly segregated fashion similar to Atlantic Canada. This province represents only two to three per cent of the population of Canada.

This bilingual and bicultural region in New Brunswick is the remnant of the earlier Acadian settlements in eastern Canada, and the result of subsequent contacts and invasions which have followed. According to Joy (1972) the likelihood that the French in northern New Brunswick will retain their French language and culture is high; the region hugs the under-belly of the French Quebec Heartland, from which it can continue to receive sustenance from the much larger viable French language and culture in the north. Joy (1972: 6) designates Moncton, located in the middle and on the east side of New Brunswick, as the most easterly pole of his Soo-Moncton bilingual line. Joy claims:

four regions make up an area 1,000 miles long, bounded on the West by a line drawn from Sault Ste Marie through Ottawa to Cornwall, and on the East by a line from Edmundston to Moncton. Within these limits French is a language in general use; outside this area, it is rarely heard. (1972: 23)

We have plotted this Soo-Moncton bilingual belt in Figure 4-5 to illustrate the thrust of French exploration and settlement into the West. The early French drive into the West reached into St Boniface and other parts of Manitoba first by trade, and then by settlement. However, the French settlement thrust was halted in the West after the defeat of the Louis Riel struggles in 1870 in Manitoba and 1885 in Saskatchewan. The French presence, though, is still evident.

The region we call the Bilingual Belt straddles the boundaries of Quebec with New Brunswick and Ontario. In every region that we have defined for this study, there are important internal variations which we cannot explore because of the limitations of space. Internal variation is nowhere greater and more important than in the Bilingual Belt. For instance, the Montreal metropolitan area, with 3,000,000 inhabitants, is usually analyzed as a distinctive language zone (Lachapelle, 1979). Obviously, there are very important differences between the Quebec, New Brunswick, and Ontario parts of this zone. These and other variations are not examined here. Rather, we focus on the similarities in pattern shared by all parts of this region.

One is impressed with the sheer magnitude of the language populations in the Bilingual Belt. Sharing this geographical space are 1,223,485 unilingual English; 1,891,095 unilingual French; and 1,633,580 officially bilingual speakers. Because of the salience of English-French language issues in this region, it is often overlooked that in it there are a half-million persons with mother tongues other than English or French, the largest portion of whom are what we have termed unofficially bilingual or English.

Two striking and related sociological features of this region should be noted. One is the high degree of segregation between language categories. The other is the large number of parallel institutions providing strong support for the English and French. There are English and French school systems, universities, hospitals, undertakers, radio and television networks, and the like (Vallee and Dufour, 1974).

The limited information available shows that some languages other than English and French fare as well as, or even better than, those in some other multicultural areas in terms of schools, press, radio, organizations, and so on (Secretary of State, 1972). It should be noted that the degree of maintenance or retention for languages other than English and French is higher in the Quebec portion of the Bilingual Belt than it is for Canada as a whole. That is, there is a stronger tendency in this region than in all others for people with mother tongues other than English or French to speak that mother tongue most often at home (deVries and Vallee, 1980).

In Figure 4-5, we see that the Soo-Moncton Bilingual Belt has raised the bilingual populations in each of the three provinces it affects. Approximately one-third of the population in Quebec (35%) was officially bilingual (English and French); almost one-third of New Brunswick's population (30%) in 1991 was bilingual; and one-tenth of the population in Ontario (11.4%) was officially bilingual in 1991. Between 1981 and 1991, bilingualism rose in every province, but the heart of official bilingualism is in this Soo-Moncton bilingual-belt region. The number of offically bilingual people increased from 7.6% in 1981 to 8.5% in 1991 among anglophones and it increased from 36.2 to 38.9% among francophones during the 1981–91 decade. This increase occurred most noticeably in the bilingual belt region, where opportunities for the use of both official tongues are best (Harrison and Marmen, 1994: 39). In 1991, 4 million Canadians could speak both official languages. More than one-third of Quebec's population can speak both official languages. Bilin-

FIGURE 4-5 PERCENTAGE OF THE CANADIAN POPULATION WHO ARE
OFFICIALLY BILINGUAL, BY PROVINCES AND TERRITORIES, 1991

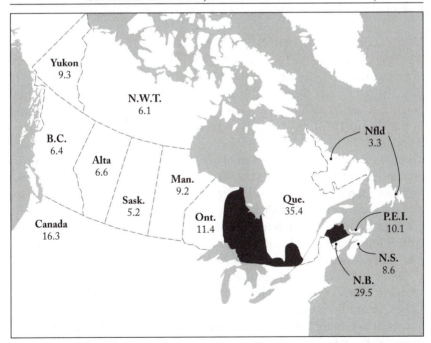

SOURCE: Brian Harrison and Louise Marmen, *Languages in Canada*, Catalogue No. 96–313E. Scarborough, ON: Prentice-Hall and Statistics Canada, 1994, p. 36.

gualism is related to proximity to the Quebec French Heartland, and rates of official bilingualism drop as distance from Quebec increases. More than half the English mother tongue group is bilingual in Quebec (Harrison and Marmen, 1994: 38). Citizens in the rest of Canada outside the Bilingual Belt have not seen bilingualism as one of their priorities and are not as willing to put forth the effort to accomplish bilingualism.

Language conflict in this region draws worldwide attention for the obvious reason that Quebec is probably one of the very few regions in the world where English speakers feel threatened by language legislation. In New Brunswick and Ontario, French speakers have to fight to acquire or retain language rights, particularly in the educational system. There is a substantial body of literature on these language conflicts (Jackson, 1975; Juteau-Lee and Lapointe, 1977). The only points we want to make here are: 1) that this is the only part of Canada where the Official Languages Act designating English and French as the official languages of the country is likely to produce the results desired by legislators; and 2) despite the general acceptance of the ideology of bilingualism and multiculturalism *de facto*, multiculturalism probably has a bright prospect for realization insofar as cultural maintenance and development depends on language, for in this region continental European and Third World languages show a fair degree of staying power.

UPPER CANADA: ANGLOPHONE AND MULTICULTURAL
The first United Empire Loyalists settled in Upper Canada, the southern part of Ontario in 1784, shortly after the American Revolution (Armstrong, 1981: 274). In those early days the British in Upper Canada were surrounded by potential enemies with the Americans to the south (whom they had to battle in the War of 1812), the larger French settlement to the east, and the many Aboriginals to the northwest. At that time it was not clear that York (now Toronto) and southern Ontario would become the stronghold of the British establishment (Armstrong, 1981: 274).

The region we have labelled Upper Canada comprises all of Ontario outside the parts we have included in the Bilingual Belt and the Northlands. At one time Upper Canada referred to a political entity settled and controlled by British immigrants and United Empire Loyalists, and separate from what is now the province of Quebec, then called Lower Canada.

One outstanding sociological feature of the region is the dominance of southern Ontario, in particular that portion stretching along the shore of Lake Ontario from Oshawa through Toronto to Niagara Falls. This portion has about one-fourth of the entire Canadian population and within it is concentrated the financial and manufacturing core of the country. Its economic dominance continues to make it a magnet for most of the immigrants who have come to Canada since the Second World War.

In many ways the ethnolinguistic profile of Upper Canada is similar to that of the West. As Figures 4-1 and 4-2 show, in both regions there are substantial numbers whose origins are other than English or French. However, Upper Canada did have a higher proportion of people of British origin than the West. Many of its smaller cities, towns, and rural areas still retain some British-Canadian flavour.

Although English unilingualism in this region is as high as in the West (73–83%), Ontario has a longer anglophone British history. Very strong objections have been raised to the establishment of French-language educational and media institutions at local levels. This has been the case even where the French presence goes back several generations (e.g., Penetang, Welland, and Windsor). It appears that the idea of an officially bilingual country is acceptable to many people in this region provided that French language rights are given concrete recognition in Canada as a nation.

Institutional supports for non-English languages and cultures are many and varied, especially in cities like Toronto. Even more than in the West, the stronghold of multiculturalism, one is impressed with the array of ethnic and foreign-language radio and TV programming, newspapers, shops, and the like. The trend is toward multiculturalism as an ideal, particularly in the larger cities where those of British origin are a declining proportion of the population.

Because Ontario is the industrial hub of Canada, it tends to set the economic pace for the country. With a concentration of the British economic élite (Porter, 1965) and with more than one-third of the entire Canadian population, this region has enormous political influence in Canada. The attractiveness of urban industrial activity draws immigrants and migrants from all directions. Thus, the use of English in the economic process will likely gain strength. More study is needed to see to what extent economic and political élites are moving increasingly into Toronto, and the extent to which persons of non-British stock are able to enter the economic and political arena. Have the French, the Germans, the Ukrainians, the Italians, and the Jews broken into this power élite? Is learning French a factor in gaining a place within the economic élite?

Recently this urban industrial area has attracted many immigrants into its labour market so that over half of the population is foreign-born. These immigrants represent many cultures from northern and southern Europe and the Third World. Thus, the urban areas of Ontario are changing from highly British cultural areas to multicultural and multiracial areas where many languages are used. These new immigrants, however, are competing for jobs and are learning English. Although the British culture is not threatened in Upper Canada, multiculturalism is certainly on the rise.

In Ontario approximately 85% of the people use English at home (Harrison and Marmen, 1994:10). Only about three per cent speak French at home.

Although the population of Ontario has made some efforts to become bilingual in French and English, the English language is dominant and other languages constitute a small minority. This region could best be described as Anglophone with strong multicultural trends.

Although the linguistic and cultural conditions of the West and Upper Canada seem to be similar, they are very different historically. The West has been strongly multicultural and multilingual throughout its comparatively short history. Because it is less industrialized, however, it does not attract great numbers of immigrants. Consequently, its cultural diversity is not increasing. In Ontario, however, with a very strong influx of new Third World immigrants, multiculturalism and multiracialism are growing.

THE WEST: MULTICULTURAL AND ANGLOPHONE
The many wars and animosities between the British and French during the colonization of early North America spilled into the settlement of the West. The French settlers who expanded westward from the Quebec heartland extended their bilingual belt well beyond Sault Ste Marie to St Boniface, now part of Winnipeg. Louis Riel, a Métis, was a leading force in convincing the East to recognize Manitoba as the fifth province in Confederation, as it did in 1870. Both the British Hudson's Bay Company and the French Northwest Company extended their fur trade to the forks of the Red and Assiniboine rivers, where they established their forts. The first of eleven treaties was signed with the Indians of the West in 1871 in Fort Garry, when Manitoba was a new province. Because the population was half French and half English, Manitoba was declared a bilingual province. After the defeat of Riel in St Boniface in 1870, however, the French ceased to expand westward. Soon other European immigrants converged on the West so that the French proportion of the population declined.

The West, which includes the southern portions of the four most westerly provinces (British Columbia, Alberta, Saskatchewan, and Manitoba), was the domain of food-gathering Aboriginal peoples and it was settled in the last century by immigrants of many European origins. This is the only region where no group is in the majority, although the British form the largest group. The region is highly rural, involving agriculture and fishing; it includes a multitude of substantial enclaves of British, German, Ukrainian, French, and smaller ethnic groups. Although the Hudson's Bay Company, administered from Britain, traded in the area for 200 years previous to Manitoba's entry into Confederation (1670–1870), a diversity of European ethnic groups settled the region and began social institutions.

Although many ethnic groups seek to maintain their ethnic languages, the language used at home by the majority (86–93%) is English (Harrison and Marmen, 1994: 10). Many of these groups promote British, Ukrainian,

German, French, and other cultures because no one group dominates the region culturally. Many of the people in the region desire a form of bilingualism that includes English and their own ethnic tongue (O'Bryan et al., 1976). Few Westerners aspire to learn French, and Gagnon (1974) found that positive attitudes to a language were important in attempts to learn it. Most Westerners consider official bilingualism (French and English) an impractical imposition because the French are only the fourth-largest population on the prairies. The need for French is limited, so there is little motivation for those who do not speak it to learn it (Gardner and Smythe, 1975).

One hundred years ago, when the European population in Manitoba was half French and half British, the potential for a bilingual province looked bright (Flanagan, 1991). However, because the British refused to support Riel, and the French did not immigrate in numbers sufficient to reinforce their proportion of the population, the demographic mass swung in favour of the British. Since then the mass migrations of other ethnic groups into the West have turned the region into a multicultural region. With the rise of other ethnic groups, the demographic change is being reinforced by increasing political and economic activity by all groups in all provinces. The ethnic diversity of provincial cabinets is evidence of this multicultural approach to life. The official working language is English; other languages such as French, German, and Ukrainian are kept up by many groups as part of their ingroup cultural heritage. History bears out that French and languages other than English have not been encouraged and have often been systematically legislated against by provincial governments, especially in Manitoba and Saskatchewan.

Three-fourths or more (73–83%) of the population in the four most westerly provinces reported their mother tongue as English; less than one in twenty (2–5%) claimed the French mother tongue (Harrison and Marmen, 1994: 24). Up to one-fourth in Manitoba reported a non-official mother tongue (15–22%) (Driedger and Hengstenberg, 1986). English is clearly the language of a large majority, and non-official languages run a strong second. In fact, the German mother tongue ranks after English, followed by Ukrainian and French. The West is clearly an English-language region.

Culturally the West is strongly diversified with strong multiple responses (MR). As seen in Figure 4-2, well over half of the population in the West reported non-charter ethnic origins. Less than 5% reported French as their ethnic origin, and less than half (23–35%) reported British origins in 1991 (Harrison and Marmen, 1994). The charter groups do not dominate in the West as they do in the East. Except for multiple responses, the British are the largest group; the French rank fourth in size after the British, Germans, and Ukrainians. The West is made up of many ethnic groups, largely from northern and eastern Europe, who were part of the great migrations before and between the great wars. The West is the most multicultural region of Canada with high European other (EO) and multiple responses (MR). Official bilingualism and biculturalism (meaning English and French language usage and culture) seems unrealistic for the West. A more appropriate formula would be multiculturalism and anglophone. English is spoken and accepted by most Westerners. Because no group dominates the region culturally, nor has the right to such a claim historically, demographically, economically, or politically, it is realistic to promote a variety of cultures and languages.

The concept of Canada as an officially bilingual country does not have much of an appeal to the majority of people in this region (Driedger, 1989). According to one study, the goal of 'unofficial' bilingualism—the combination of English with any other language—is more acceptable than that of English-French bilingualism (O'Bryan et al., 1976). In other words, the French and their language are regarded as another minority in the region with no stronger claim to official recognition than other groups such as Germans, Poles, or Ukrainians (Vallee and deVries, 1978: 162f).

It would appear that language, as such, is not a major issue in this region and that the vast majority assume that English is and ought to be the only official language for the West. On the other hand, there is a strong resistance to the idea that any one culture should be regarded as the official one. The ideal is that of multiculturalism, brought to the West by thousands of immigrants who form an ethnic mosaic. The bulk of new immigration which might replenish the older ethnic enclaves is, however, flowing into Upper Canada (Driedger, 1989).

Dawson's *Group Settlement: Ethnic Communities in Western Canada* (1936) is a good example of research about the West, using the Chicago School's approach. He examines the prairies as an ecological area into which a multitude of ethnic groups entered, establishing their many communities. He then selects five groups (the Doukhobors, Mennonites, Mormons, German Catholics, and French Canadians) and devotes the entire volume to various topics: their settlement, invasion, and succession; their means and modes of living; their resistance to secularization; their community building; their establishment of organizations; and their social adjustment and persistence. Dawson's emphasis on ethnicity and religion is similar to many other studies made by sociologists of the Chicago School, who sought to research the patterns of settlement, the forms of community organization, and the extent to which these new immigrants persisted or assimilated (Driedger, 1984: 168–71). The focus was on a variety of distinctive groups living first in rural segregated bloc settlements, and later converging upon emerging urban areas.

To understand the Canadian West, we must first discuss the unique diverse regional context and assumptions of other regions. From the Western view, we must ask such questions as why the East sent two armies to suppress Riel;

why land claims with Aboriginals are not being dealt with; why the West produced so many new political parties (such as the Progressive, Social Credit, CCF, and Reform); and why there was so much western opposition to a new constitution. While economic and political modernity factors are certainly relevant, we propose that traditional factors of counter-modernity (such as ethnicity and religion) are important.

Reginald Bibby (1987a: 161–4) found in his three national surveys of Canada in 1975, 1980, and 1985 that more than half (57%) of all Canadians endorsed official bilingualism in 1985, a rise from 49% in 1975. He found that official bilingualism was accepted by most of the population in Quebec (91% in 1985), and that it was least accepted on the prairies (36% in 1985). Almost half of the people outside Quebec (46% in 1985) endorsed official bilingualism. In each of the regions, however, acceptance of bilingualism increased between 1975 and 1985.

Bibby (1987a: 161) also found that a majority in Canada (56%) preferred an ethnic mosaic (multiculturalism), while only half as many (27%) preferred to see a Canadian melting pot (amalgamation or assimilation). This did not vary as much by regions, with 58% of the Canadians in Quebec, Ontario, and the Prairies favouring the mosaic, and 49% in the Atlantic region doing so. Multiculturalism is accepted by half or more of the population in all regions, and it is in fact a reality in all of Canada except, perhaps, in the Quebec and Atlantic regions. Berry et al. (1976) found similar tendencies in their 1974 Canadian national sample. Canadians have adopted a policy of diversity in religion and politics for years, and the same choice is also increasing with respect to language use and cultural pluralism. However, Canadians in the various regions seem to see the ethnic future of Canada differently. Some want more pluralism, others more assimilation, and still others prefer modifications or variations in between.

SUMMARY

As Prime Minister Trudeau announced in 1971, Canada is officially bilingual, with French the dominant language in Quebec and English dominant in the rest of Canada. Although official bilingualism is increasing in all of Canada, the region surrounding the federal government in the Ottawa–Hull centre is actually practising official bilingualism best. Unofficial bilingualism (English and another language) is practised most in the northwest.

Aboriginals still dominate in the vast Northlands of Canada where multilingualism and multiculturalism reign. Remnants of Aboriginals still remain in the northern parts of the prairies. Unilingualism and uniculturalism are dominant in French Quebec, part of the first European settlement along the St Lawrence River. Such single linguistic and cultural British dominance is also evident in Atlantic Canada, especially in Newfoundland. Joy's bilingual belt represents the remnants of old Acadia especially in New Brunswick, and stretches east and west from bilingual Ottawa. In anglophone Ontario and the West multiple ethnic responses are now the largest category. Visible minorities are on the rise in urban Ontario, as are remaining Aboriginals in the western half of Canada.

Indeed, we found that Canada is predominantly bilingual and multi-cultural. Canada is multicultural both in governmental policy and in fact, although not all residents recognize this reality equally. Likewise, many people recognize that Canada is officially bilingual, but that there are great variations in the numbers who actually know and use two official languages. A sense of place has been developed historically, linguistically, and culturally in the many distinct regions of Canada.

PART III

Dimensions of Identity and Solidarity

Language and the Québécois 'Nation'

Canada is unique on this continent because it contains within its borders six million francophone citizens, most of them located in the province of Quebec. These French Québécois represent a large bloc (23%) within Canada, but are a small francophone island in the continental sea of 270 million anglophones (McRoberts, 1990: 98; Taylor and Sigal, 1982: 59–70). French Quebeckers are distinctive in that all five of Weber's markers of identification apply to them. They are of Caucasian European origin, their French culture provides a consciousness of kind, they are largely Roman Catholic, they have emerged as a distinctive 'people', and they still think of themselves as a 'Volk' or 'nation'.

The French Québécois are an ethnic 'nation' that has maintained its identity for 385 years. They are the reason that Canada is now constitutionally bilingual. They have made more plural options increasingly possible, and multiculturalism a national option (Breton and Savard, 1982; Guindon, 1988). Let us examine their origins, region, ideologies, language, and culture to see why they are the major voluntary pluralist force in cell E of the Conformity-Pluralist model, resisting assimilation and amalgamation.

THE QUÉBÉCOIS SETTING

New France was one of the first European settlements in North America. In its demographic and regional setting a francophone symbol system emerged, which has become Canada's second official language (Burnet, 1988: 13–16).

THE ORIGIN OF NEW FRANCE

Almost four centuries ago, Samuel de Champlain founded what is now Quebec, only a year after the first permanent European settlement was founded in Williamsburg, Virginia, in 1607. New France was a French colony, the first European settlement in what is now Canada. No more than 10,000 French immigrants came to settle along the St Lawrence River (Rioux, 1971: 12).

These French settlers, who came to be called 'habitants', had to defend themselves against the Iroquois Indians in a harsh environment. As rural, unlettered settlers they began to develop a 'little' tradition, which became very important after the 1760 conquest by Britain. They adapted to the new environment and were left to their own devices after the conquest. The 'great' tradition cultivated in schools and by the élite was represented by French military, clergy, and businessmen who were mostly interested in the fur trade and profit. After the conquest most of them left the St Lawrence region and returned to France, and it took several generations for new leaders to emerge from within the habitant nation (Guindon, 1988: 3–17).

According to Jacques Henripin (1993), the largest waves of immigration had come in 1663 and 1671, so that by 1700 the French settler population was about 15,000. They were divided into 82 parishes: 48 on the left and 34 on the right banks of the St Lawrence River. By 1771 the agglomerations of Quebec City, Montreal, and Trois-Rivières were beginning to emerge as urbanized areas. Two classes developed—the élite and the habitants. The élite consisted of the administrators and higher clergy who had arrived recently and lived in the urban areas, while the habitants had lived in small, rural, strip villages for generations. The élite used France as their reference point, while the rural habitants soon developed their own French-Québécois characteristics and formed their own indigenous lifestyle. Even some of the village French priests began to have their differences with the élite clergy linked to France. It was the habitants who continued the Quebec nation after the conquest (Juteau, 1992: 323–41).

THE DEMOGRAPHIC AND REGIONAL SETTING
The French settled on both shores of the St Lawrence, which today is part of the province of Quebec. While the British first settled in Virginia in 1607, in Canada they were fur traders for the Hudson's Bay Company which began in 1670 in the Canadian northwest. The British did not settle permanently in Canada until the mid-1700s. Thus, the French settlers on the St Lawrence were for about 150 years the first and only European settlers in what is now Canada. They were starting to develop a French colony that was really the beginning of a new nation called New France. The original 10,000 French settlers grew so that before the conquest, and even after 1760, the French settlers were a large European majority in Canada (McRoberts, 1990). The British conquerors after 1760 were faced with integrating a very large bloc of French habitants who had lived here for many generations in segregated, contiguous, solidly French communities, unbroken by non-French settlers. The French habitants were basically a sociocultural society that could most naturally rule itself as a Quebec nation. However, the conquest interrupted this natural development of a uni-ethnic people. About 1000 of the élite leaders—

including administrators, businessmen, and the educated élite—returned to France, leaving the less educated rural habitants to their oral traditions (Rioux, 1971: 30). Many habitants were not entirely displeased with the departure of these French élite colonists, although future prospects without experienced leaders would not be easy.

The French settlements along the St Lawrence were fashioned after the Old French feudal system with some modifications (Guindon, 1988: 3–24). A feudal estate was granted to a seigneur, who then was obligated to get settlers and to develop the land. A rang system was developed in which settlers received a strip of land, called a rang, on the waterfront. It was 200 to 250 metres wide and extended away from the water in a long narrow strip into the treeline. New France literally was the opening up of a river civilization, first along the south shore and later along the north shore. Later, tributary rivers were settled so that:

> Toward the end of the French regime, one had only to take a canoe trip along the St Lawrence and the Richelieu rivers for an almost complete enumeration of Canadian homes; the waterfront or shoreline was synonymous with settled country. (Deffontaines, 1965: 4)

This rang system had several advantages in the pioneer setting. It allowed settlers to have large narrow land tracts extending away from the river. The layout of the lots afforded protection because the farmyards were lined along the river not far from each other. This fairly close proximity provided more protection and social contact, as well as access to the river for transportation and fishing. Indians, home and forest fires, famine, sickness, and the long cold winters were all a threat (Guindon, 1988: 3–17). Mutual aid and protection were more readily available because of the ecological layout. Later, roads which each habitant had to keep passable followed the river; eventually, modern highways, electricity, telephone lines, and bus services followed the same river shore.

Soon Catholic parishes were established, their churches lining the river shore at intervals. These churches were named after saints such as St Denis and St Pascal. Soon stores, commerce, social halls, and agencies surrounded these churches and the elderly moved closer to church, leading to the establishment of these parish centres as villages and towns. Professionals such as doctors, lawyers, and notaries joined some of the centralized settlements (Guindon, 1988). With this rural social order, residents of the seigneurial system were slow to consider going to the city and urbanization did not develop quickly. After the conquest, the Quebec population became even more rural (Rioux, 1965: 34). By 1871, only one person in five lived in the city. Today if you take a car going northeast from Montreal along the north shore toward Quebec City, you will find that the population becomes increasingly francophone. Beyond Quebec City, toward Sept Iles and Labrador, only French radio can be heard. French Canadians are still segregated in rural eastern Quebec.

After the conquest Quebec became more isolated and more homogeneous than before. In 1760, one-fourth of the Quebec population was not engaged in agriculture; by 1825, 88% of the population was rural. In 1871 four-fifths of the population was still rural. High birthrates doubled the rural habitant population every twenty-five years, and it was largely illiterate: 'barely ten per cent had learned, imperfectly, to read and write' (Rioux, 1965: 36). The French revolution occurred shortly after the conquest, which isolated Quebec even more, and it influenced the Quebec habitants very little (Guindon, 1988: 4–11).

'By 1840 Lower Canada contained 500,000 French-speaking people and 75,000 English-speaking people' (Rioux, 1965: 45). A rebellion had taken place in 1837 and 1838, after which Lord Durham was sent from Britain to assess the problems. When he came, he found 'two nations warring in the bosom of a single state: [he] found a struggle, not of principles, but of race . . . every contest is one of French and English in the outset, or becomes so ere it has run its course' (Wade, 1968: 197). Durham's remedy was simple, namely to assimilate the French of Lower Canada into English-speaking Upper Canada. He wrote:

> We entertain no doubt of the national character that must be given to Lower Canada; it must be that of the British Empire; that of the majority of British America; that of the great race which must, in the lapse of no long period of time, be predominant over the whole of the North American continent. . . . Much as they struggle against it, it is obvious that the process of assimilation to English habits is already commencing. (Wade, 1968: 212)

Durham unabashedly proposed assimilation after the rebellion; in particular, he proposed Anglo-conformity, an amalgamation into the dominant group. The Act of Union in 1840 was supposed to bring about the Anglicization of French-speaking Lower Canada. Three decades later, the 1870–85 Louis Riel affairs opened up the same French-English conflict in the West; it was dealt with by sending armies from the East to ensure Anglo-conformity.

THE DEVELOPMENT OF IDEOLOGIES IN QUEBEC

Marcel Rioux (1973), analyzing the development of the various ideologies of francophones in Quebec, suggests that three ideologies have appeared in Quebec since 1840: 1) the conservative ideology, 2) an ideology of confrontation, and 3) the affirmation of Quebec by development and participation. Let us look at each briefly.

After the rebellion of 1837–38, the Québécois sensed that they were to become a minority. They no longer sought to become an independent society, but turned their attention to the preservation of their language and culture.

Rioux (1973: 263) calls this practice the conservative ideology. It marked a time of tragic contraction when the Québécois gave up their sense of nation, but became an ethnic group which wanted to maintain its heritage. The English sought to divide the French along the St Lawrence from those in Acadia to dissipate their demographic strength. The clergy and the Catholic parish turned inward, seeking to promote their religious ideology with less emphasis on larger political aims. The church helped to build an ideology of conservation of tradition. Demographically, politically, and religiously, the Québécois reserved control. The English, however, dominated Quebec's commerce, industry, and finance from Montreal (McRoberts, 1990: 98–107).

During the fifteen-year tenure of the French prime minister Wilfrid Laurier (1896–1911), Quebec had begun to change extensively. In 1871 Quebec was 77% rural; by 1911, it was half urban (Henripin, 1993: 304–18). As Montreal's English commerce and industry developed, many rural Québécois had moved to the city to find work as labourers. The French habitants were poorly educated in their Catholic schools, and they were not encouraged to enter higher learning. Therefore, they were destined for only lower status jobs with little opportunity for promotion and upward mobility. The conservative ideology lasted until the end of the Second World War, but between the wars changes had taken place which provided opportunities for a new ideology (Guindon, 1988: 18–24).

Rioux (1965: 73–84) called the period after the Second World War 'the springtime of Quebec'. The war effort had escalated the industrialization and urbanization process in Quebec as well as elsewhere in Canada. With the death of the Conservative premier Duplessis in 1959, the Liberals and Jean Lesage came into power in 1960, starting the 'quiet revolution' in Quebec. Quebeckers began to shrug off the fatalism of their conservative ideology and began what Rioux (1973: 269–73) calls the ideology of contestation and recoupment. The population involved in agriculture dropped by 64,000 and numbers in non-agricultural occupations increased from 79,000 to 237,000 between 1911 and 1951 (Keyfitz, 1965: 227). In 1960 the Liberals began to modernize the state, and instilled the hope of change. Québécois turned from seeing themselves as only an ethnic group that wanted to preserve its culture and language to a French society that wanted to compete in the larger marketplace. This ideology of recoupment tended to discredit the traditional power élites and the ideology of conservatism and turned Quebec's attention to the future.

While the first ideology was directed toward the past, the second was turned toward the present and called for an update. Rioux (1973: 274) believes the third ideology of René Levèsque and the Separatist movement combines the old and the new in what he calls the ideology of development and participation. This ideology recognizes Quebec as a culture different from others in North America, and reaches back to the earlier visions of a Quebec that hoped for independence and a separate nation before the union and confederation. It calls for a Quebec with a unique culture, language, religion, and traditions, but also for an independent economic and political society that can control its own destiny. The third ideology is most radical because it no longer wishes to be dominated by the rest of Canada. Thus, separatism calls for drastic structural and political changes to liberate Quebec (McRoberts, 1990: 110–17).

The referendum over which René Levèsque presided called for sovereignty-association with Canada and was defeated by Quebeckers by a 60–40 margin in 1980 (Guindon, 1988: 112–24). In a second referendum (30 October 1995) the sovereigntists lost only by a margin of one per cent. There are already talks about another referendum. What new ideology will now follow is hard to predict. The latest separatist ideology and new guarantees for bilingualism and the preservation of the French language and culture show that the French have at least forced Canada to take a second language and culture seriously. This is an important step toward pluralism. In the case of the French in Canada, assimilation was tried but failed; amalgamation into Anglo-conformity has not worked, either. Neither the cultural nor the structural parts of the Quebec society have followed Gordon's modified assimilation model. The French in Quebec are a clear example of ethnic or national pluralism.

Crean and Rioux (1983: 1) stated that many people predicted that the referendum on sovereignty-association would not resolve the fundamental questions raised by the separatists in Quebec, and that Canadians and Quebeckers will need to sit down together to work out a new type of association. Their book, *Two Nations*, assumes that both the British and the French in Canada will not rest until they have sovereignty over their respective languages, cultures, and destinies because in essence they live in two countries. The problem is that even if Quebeckers gain political independence, what will happen to other francophones in Canada and what will happen to the multicultural pluralist model remains unclear. Separatists assume that a uni-ethnic state is the ideal. McNeill says this state is hardly possible for all groups in our industrial society. A Quebec which stays within Canada can help the pluralist vision. A sovereign Quebec nation will likely perpetuate Franco-conformity and will seek to amalgamate and dominate others as Anglo-conformists have sought to do in the past.

LANGUAGE: A FRANCOPHONE SYMBOL SYSTEM

In Chapter Four we discussed linguistic and cultural factors as a means of differentiating the various regions of Canada. The southern part of Quebec, which we called the Québécois heartland, is one of these distinct regions, and

is francophone and francocultural. It includes the largest majority of francophones in Canada: 82% of the population report French as their mother
tongue, and 83% speak French in their homes. We also discussed the importance of language as a symbol system into which humans are introduced when
they first learn their mother tongue; in turn, how cultural learning is transmit-
ted through the symbolic language code shapes their social world view. Those
who learn French and do not learn another language, for example, are locked
into communicating in French and are separated from easy communication
with others who do not speak French. Thus, language is a boundaried
'Québécois heritage' system which includes or excludes those who do or do
not learn the symbol system (Taylor and Sigal, 1985).

Region may be a form of restriction for people, and regions can become
boundaried spaces within which people create their cultures and social interaction. A second important system which humans learn and identify with, is
language (Lieberson, 1970) More than 80% of Quebec's population is of
French origin, and as many also use French as their language of communication as they have now done for 385 years.

THE BILINGUALISM AND BICULTURALISM COMMISSION
For a hundred years after the 1837–38 rebellion the Québécois retreated into
a conservative ideology. However, after the Second World War and the leadership of Duplessis, there was what Rioux (1965) called springtime in Quebec, which began as a quiet revolution in search of greater freedom again. By
1963 the crescendo of discontent had developed to the point that a special
ten-person federal Royal Commission on Bilingualism and Biculturalism was
established to hear these voices of change, and to assess to what extent other
Canadians were willing to allow greater change (Burnet, 1988: 175–80). Let
us hear how the commission saw the problem:

> . . . There have been strains throughout the history of confederation . . .
> They have been driven to the conclusion that Canada, without being fully
> conscious of the fact, is passing through the greatest crisis in its history. . . .
> The source of the crisis lies in the province of Quebec. . . . Although a
> provincial crisis at the outset, it has become a Canadian crisis, because of
> the size and importance of Quebec, and because it has inevitably set off a
> series of chain reactions elsewhere. . . . The state of affairs established in
> 1867, and never since seriously challenged, is now for the first time being
> rejected by the French Canadians in Quebec. (Royal Commission on Bilin-
> gualism and Biculturalism [RCBB], 1965:13)

In the opinion of the commission, the dominating idea in its terms of reference was 'equal partnership' between the two founding peoples. The commission was appointed, at least to some extent, for the purpose of studying the

grievances which French Canadians, and particularly Quebeckers, were voicing more vigorously (Burnet, 1979). As the name of the commission implied, French Québécois thought of equality between the founding peoples as a dual postulate, even though no mention was made in the constitution of such a partnership.

The first preliminary report of the commission said that 'these notions and expressions—"equal partnership", "two founding groups", "a compact"—are traditional in French Canada. "Two Nations" is a more recent and vivid way of expressing this desire for a recognition of the dual character of the country' (RCBB, 1965: 47). To many people, these expressions of dualism seemed a continuation of the age-old battle of the European British and French nation states, which could think in terms only of unitary sovereignties and who had faced each other across the Ottawa River for centuries. Did the multi-ethnicity of Canada not matter? Why should the rights of the charter groups be corrected without hearings given to the rights of others as well? Indeed, one of the commissioners, Ukrainian Jaraslov Rudnyckyj, felt so strongly about the rights of 'new Canadians', which supported not duality but a mosaic, that he made a separate statement published in Volume One of the Official Languages book (RCBB, 1965: 155–69). Others, however, thought that more than two official languages would lead to Balkanization.

Volume One of the Bilingualism and Biculturalism Commission report was devoted entirely to the official languages, English and French. It portrays Canada as a unique state with English and French as two languages of international status:

> English is today the mother tongue of more than 250,000,000 people. To this figure should be added some 200,000,000 who speak English as their second language or who have a good working knowledge of it. French, for its part, is the mother tongue of around 65,000,000 people and is constantly used by another 150,000,000 throughout the world. These two languages thus have worldwide prestige. (RCBB, Volume 1, 1967: 15)

The seven-volume report involved an enormous amount of research that became a basis of demographic, ecological, economic, political, and social facts sparking a flurry of research on language, culture, ethnicity, and race (Burnet, 1988: 175–80; Pendakur, 1990). Volume One clearly showed that, while the mother tongue of over half of all Canadians was English, almost one-third spoke French and a sizeable number had non-charter mother tongues. However, most of these francophones resided in Quebec, where the French dominated, while the rest of Canada was anglophone. The two languages represented two 'national' solitudes that were separated regionally, politically, and socially. These conclusions led Prime Minister Trudeau in 1971 to declare Canada a bilingual nation (Crean and Rioux, 1983).

The pressures of Commissioner Rudnyckyj, who made a separate report on languages in Volume One based on the outcry of more than one-fourth of the population who then were not charter Canadians, led the commission to publish a fourth volume titled *The Cultural Contribution of the Other Ethnic Groups* (1970), a study which at first they had not envisioned. This no doubt partially contributed to the second part of Trudeau's declaration in 1971 of a bilingual and multicultural Canada, and modified what had originally been a commission on bilingualism and biculturalism. Thus, the commission, which had been asked to explore more than one unitary linguistic and cultural state, actually opened up the arena to the possibility of a broader pluralism beyond charter group dominance (Burnet, 1979: 43–58).

JOY'S BILINGUAL BELT

In the French Québécois heartland, 82% of the population report French as their mother tongue. French Canadians have lived there for many generations and have become quite distinct from the culture of France, their original mother country. Of the 82% who in 1991 reported French as their mother tongue, 83% speak French at home. English home-language use has declined from 13% in 1971 to 11% in 1991. The French nation has survived in Quebec for almost four centuries. They are a people who have not assimilated, and who clearly represent the pluralism end of our continuum (p. 39) discussed as cell E.

Richard Joy (1972; 1992) proposed that there is a Bilingual Belt in the south of Quebec. It hugs the southern underbelly of the heartland, where large numbers of French-speakers reside adjacent to, and in continuity with, the 'mother' core of French Quebec. In our discussion of regions (p. 89) we plotted this Bilingual Belt and discussed it briefly. Here let us demonstrate how it fits into the total pattern of the French presence in Canada.

Joy's thesis is that the French language and culture have survived and will continue to do so in the Québécois heartland because there is a sufficient demographic mass of six million French Canadians who have maintained their French language and who are dominant politically in that provincial region. He predicted that French-speaking Canadians in the Bilingual Belt— especially in northern New Brunswick, northwestern Ontario, and the Ottawa area—will also have a very good chance of maintaining their French language because they are adjacent to the heartland, can remain in contact with this core, and meet other francophones where their language is of use and can be practised among those who value it. While there may be somewhat less opportunity to use French than in the French Québécois heartland, those people in the Bilingual Belt should be able to retain their French.

Joy (1972; 1992) also predicted that as we move farther away from the Quebec core and beyond the Bilingual Belt, it will be increasingly harder to maintain the French language where French communities are smaller, and where support from the Québécois heartland is less because of distance. Thus, it would be even more difficult to sustain the French language in communities such as Yarmouth, Nova Scotia, an area which used to be a part of French Acadia; Tecumseh, Ontario, near Windsor; Penetanguishene, Ontario, one of the earliest French missions to the Hurons on Lake Huron; and St Boniface, Manitoba, even farther away and now part of Winnipeg, where the French Northwest fur trading company and the Hudson's Bay Company had often clashed. Using the 1961 census data, Joy tried to show that the French language was best maintained and even advanced in core parts of the Québécois heartland, that it was well maintained in the Soo-Moncton Bilingual Belt, and that it declined at points farther away, especially in Atlantic Canada where the population is almost entirely British and anglophone.

Joy summarized seven regions based on the order in which the respective populations speak French: 1) Interior Quebec, where 95% of the population reported French as their mother tongue and only 2% speak English exclusively; 2) southern Quebec and the Ottawa Valley, where 70% of the population report French as their mother tongue, and where French is dominant in government, but English is dominant in industry; 3) northern New Brunswick, where 59% of the population report French as their mother tongue, but where fewer spoke it; 4) eastern and northern Ontario close to the Quebec border, where French is the mother tongue of 30% of the population; 5) the Atlantic region, where French is spoken by only 5% of the population; 6) the western provinces, where French is the mother tongue of only about 5% of the population and is spoken at home by fewer still; and 7) southern Ontario, the industrial heartland where less than one person in forty gave French as his or her mother tongue. Joy claimed that, while in the first region the French language was not declining, language assimilation progressed increasingly in regions five through seven. Assimilation was proceeding quickly, especially since there are few reinforcements from Quebec. More recently Joy (1992) has updated his original thesis using language use at home, rather than only mother tongue, as his measure of the state of French in Quebec and Canada. He has worked on more qualitative assessments saying, 'They're not going to get jobs at age 20 with a 14-year-old's vocabulary' (Joy, 1992: 11).

LANGUAGE CONTINUITY AND SHIFT

To what extent has the language continuity of the French core in the Quebec heartland extended into the nineties? Do Joy's predictions follow for the regions more distantly removed from this core? How does this affect other language groups, and how does the French language compare with others in Canada?

Of the two million people who experienced a language shift between 1981 and 1991, 70% have mother tongues other than English or French. Twenty

TABLE 5-1   LANGUAGE CONTINUITY INDEX FOR ENGLISH, FRENCH AND OTHER (NON-OFFICIAL) LANGUAGES, CANADA, 1991

Regions	English %	French %	Other %
Canada	113.1	95.8	54.9
Newfoundland	100.7	44.8	60.8
Prince Edward Island	103.3	52.6	25.0
Nova Scotia	103.1	59.5	48.6
New Brunswick	105.6	91.6	47.5
Quebec	121.7	101.2	66.3
Ontario	114.7	63.3	57.1
Manitoba	112.3	49.2	45.6
Saskatchewan	113.3	33.0	33.8
Alberta	112.7	35.6	46.5
British Columbia	113.6	28.3	51.0
Yukon	108.5	44.4	22.7
Northwest Territories	121.1	46.7	75.7

SOURCE: *Home Language and Mother Tongue: The Nation*, Catalogue 93-317, 1991 Census. Ottawa: Statistics Canada, 1993, pp. 16-45, 142-219.

per cent switched from French, and only ten per cent from English (Statistics Canada, 1991). Language mobility (that is, the tendency of persons to speak a language at home that is different than their mother tongue) can be compared. We have developed a language continuity index by calculating the ratio of persons speaking a particular language at home to the number of individuals who have the same language as their mother tongue (deVries, 1990: 163–77).

In Table 5-1 we see that language mobility favours English (113.1%) for all of Canada, followed by French (95.9%) and the other languages (54.9%). The value larger than 100% means that the English recruited more English-speakers during the decade than they lost, which was the case in each of the regions. The French, over all, lost more speakers than they recruited. Of the other groups, only half (54.9%) continued to use their mother tongues at home. We have the data to examine where these losses for the French and others occur.

In Quebec, which has a language continuity of 101.2%, the French are able to maintain their language continuity and gain some because of their solid French heartland and their political control over their institutions. There is some loss by the French in New Brunswick (at 91.6% continuity), where they are solidly concentrated in the north but not as much in control as they are in Quebec. In Ontario, French language continuity dropped (to 63.3%); in the

TABLE 5-2   LANGUAGE CONTINUITY FOR OTHER NON-OFFICIAL LANGUAGES BY ETHNIC GROUP, CANADA AND PROVINCES, 1991

Regions	Canada Non-Official	Dutch	German	Ukrainian	Italian	Polish	Portuguese	Greek	Aboriginal	Chinese
	(Percentages)									
Canada	54.9	14.4	25.9	26.7	56.4	61.9	71.7	73.8	78.0	86.2
Newfoundland	60.8	29.2	13.4	33.3	37.5	42.1	44.0	77.8	58.5	74.1
Prince Edward Island	25.0	22.8	12.5	50.0	60.0	50.0	55.6	—	—	76.9
Nova Scotia	48.6	14.9	27.3	8.1	39.4	56.2	61.6	74.7	90.5	72.9
New Brunswick	47.5	21.1	25.1	.8	30.6	62.5	77.2	68.1	85.0	77.1
Quebec	66.3	24.2	34.3	49.2	63.2	66.0	74.5	82.6	88.0	91.5
Ontario	57.1	11.0	30.1	40.4	55.6	64.7	74.0	70.5	76.0	87.6
Manitoba	45.6	20.7	36.8	24.7	44.0	48.9	65.1	59.7	78.8	85.9
Saskatchewan	33.8	12.4	21.0	33.0	34.7	31.4	51.3	59.2	76.6	76.8
Alberta	46.5	15.3	32.2	17.6	44.0	58.4	62.2	55.7	70.5	85.2
British Columbia	51.0	12.6	20.2	10.5	42.8	53.6	51.4	55.4	47.0	84.3
Yukon	22.7	12.5	23.1	7.0	—	—	—	75.0	27.3	87.5
Northwest Territories	75.7	9.5	10.6	7.1	40.9	46.2	60.0	40.0	85.6	78.0

SOURCE: *Home Language and Mother Tongue: The Nation*, Catalogue 93-317, 1991 Census. Ottawa: Statistics Canada, 1993, pp. 16-45, 142-219.

other Atlantic provinces, formerly Acadia, it drops into the fifties; and in Manitoba (including St Boniface) it drops even more, to 49.2%. Joy's theory continues as predicted into the 1990s. It is the non-Quebec French Canadians, not those who live in Quebec, who bring the total French-Canadian continuity index down to 95.9% (Henripin, 1993: 316–17).

Even within the province of Quebec, however, there are interesting shifts which deVries and Lewycky (1985), Kalbach and Richard (1990), and Henripin (1993: 304–20) have researched. Quebeckers whose mother tongue was English were able to maintain their continuity until the 1970s. However, by the 1980s the English language continuity percentages began to decline, a considerable difference from the fifties and sixties when they were gaining. The separatist independence drive and Quebec's laws that were favourable to the French language certainly had their impact. The departure of many anglophone Quebeckers for Ontario has also increased francophone ratios in Quebec (Henripin, 1993: 310–15).

For other non-official language users, continuity has dropped to 54.9% in Canada. The aboriginals most often speak their mother tongues at home (75.7%), but language continuity ratios drop to less than fifty per cent in over half of the regions (Statistics Canada, 1993).

The continuity and language shifts vary considerably for non-charter Canadians (as we would expect) since they each represent smaller demographic masses and they do not have political control over territory as charter groups do (Driedger and Hengstenberg, 1986; Herberg, 1989: 115–19). In Table 5-2 we see some interesting variations. Over half (54.9%) of these non-charter peoples still speak their mother tongues at home; two-thirds do so in Quebec, and only one-fourth in the Yukon. Interestingly, most of the nine ethnic groups listed have highest language continuity in Quebec. The French Québécois concern for maintaining their own French language seems to also spill over to other groups.

Language continuity varies greatly by ethnic group. North Europeans like the Dutch and Germans have the lowest continuity; south and east Europeans, such as the Ukrainians, Poles, and Italians, who have been here longer, rank in between, and the recent south Europeans such as the Portuguese and Greeks (many first-generation) rank highest (Herberg, 1989: 115–19). Roughly three out of four Aboriginals who are segregated in the Northlands speak their mother tongues at home, and the Chinese (86.2% continuity) rank highest with almost all speaking their mother tongues at home. Time of immigration, degree of segregation, demographic mass, and regional residence all influence language continuity rates (Driedger, 1989).

Scholars have devoted considerable attention to the relationship between language and ethnic identity of immigrant groups in multilingual settings and have frequently claimed that preservation and continued use of the traditional mother tongue is one important—if not the most important—component of ethnic identity.

In the 1960s and early 1970s it was mainly social psychologists and psycholinguists who began to study the context and the dynamics of language groups. They concentrated mostly on English and French as official languages, dealing with questions of bilingualism, second language learning, and the like (see, for example, Taylor and Gardner, 1970; Berry and Wilde, 1972). Similarly, demographic studies based on census data concentrated on the official languages with only passing reference to the non-official language groups that were frequently lumped into a category called 'Others'.

The 1975 study conference 'The Individual, Language and Society in Canada' (Coons et al., 1977) was an early interdisciplinary effort by psychologists, sociologists, and sociolinguists to deal with different aspects of the languages-in-contrast situation and to include non-official languages. While psychologists brought their research on official languages to the meeting (Berry, 1977; Taylor and Gardner, 1977), sociologists stressed the broader multilingual and regional dimensions of linguistic research in Canada (cf. Driedger, 1977; Jackson, 1977). These sociologists saw competence in the traditional mother tongue and its continued use as one of a number of ethnic identity factors along with religion, endogamy, parochial education, participation in voluntary associations, etc. (Driedger, 1978; Isajiw, 1981; Reitz, 1980). Later sociological studies have increasingly focused on language as an important variable related to ethnic identity (deVries and Vallee, 1980; deVries and Lewycky, 1985; Bourhis, 1983, 1994; Bourhis and Lepicq, 1993).

Several Canadian studies have demonstrated the importance of controlling for immigrant generation and community size in the analysis of language maintenance. For the urban context, O'Bryan et al. (1976) sampled ten groups of adult speakers of non-official languages in five Canadian metropolitan centres and found a fairly rapid decline in traditional mother tongue competence from first- to third-generation Canadians. Fluency in the respective languages was fairly high for the first generation (between 56.0 and 80.7%), but had virtually disappeared by the third. These ethnic groups were able to maintain 'some knowledge' of their ethnic language only into the third generation (38.7%; cf. O'Bryan et al., 1976: 45–6). DeVries and Vallee (1980) amply describe this phenomenon as 'the levelling effect of the third generation' (132), also discussed by deVries and Lewycky (1985), Breton et al. (1990), and Henripin (1993: 316–17).

Comparable studies for rural environments have shown that ethno-linguistic or ethnoreligious groups in more segregated rural enclaves have been somewhat more successful in maintaining ethnic language (Anderson, 1980; Anderson and Driedger, 1980). While an extremely high proportion of all respondents was still competent in an ethnic mother tongue (though most of them were bilingual), actual use and the desire to speak it was consistently lower and varied significantly among the different groups, most markedly among the three German groups (Hutterites, 100%; Mennonites, 68.9%; Catholic, 29.0%). Li and Denis (1983: 18–32) who studied Gravelbourg, a French community in Saskatchewan, found that 9% of the French residents spoke French only, and 91% were officially bilingual. While most in their sixties spoke French at home, less than half under 30 did so.

All these studies support previous observations that ethnolinguistic minorities tend to lose their traditional mother tongue over time, though their capability to resist linguistic assimilation may vary considerably. Language shifts towards the official language(s) do not necessarily imply a complete loss of the heritage language, nor do they mean that a group ceases to exist as an identifiable entity. Therefore, it seems to be more appropriate to describe these processes in terms of linguistic accommodation and to keep in mind that the linguistic factor 'is not always an important, much less the only component of ethnic identity. The varied significance of language, religion and diverse customs as components of ethnic identity can be very complex' (Anderson, 1980: 67).

STUDIES IN QUÉBÉCOIS SOLIDARITY AND CHANGE

Having provided the French Québécois setting and the importance of the francophone symbol system, let us turn to early studies that illustrate some of the research done on the traditional habitant village, the industrialization of a small urban community, and French-English power relations. Each will illustrate different features of French-Canadian solidarity and change.

MINER'S FRENCH HABITANTS IN ST DENIS

One of the earliest community studies in Canada was that by Horace Miner (1939), which has become a classic (Guindon, 1988; Juteau, 1992: 322–5). Miner was a student of Robert Redfield at Chicago and casts his study in Redfield's peasant or folk society mode. Miner (1939: ix) states that his objectives are to provide an ethnographic description of the old rural French-Canadian folk culture, to analyze the social structure, and to find factors of social change in the direction of urbanization and anglicization. The first two aims are that of an anthropologist; the third is a major focus of the Chicago School. Miner did participant observation for a year (1936–37) and spent some time at McGill. Two chapters were published in *The American Sociological Review* in 1938. In 1949 Miner revisited St Denis and published his findings of change in the *American Journal of Sociology* (1950).

St Denis is a rural French-Canadian parish located on the lower south side of the St Lawrence River between Montreal and Quebec City. When Miner

studied St Denis in the 1930s, life there was typical of the French conservative ideology. It was one of many 'sacred' communities symbolized by the
steeple of the Roman Catholic church, located in the centre of each parish
like a hen with her brood of chicks. Miner briefly describes some of the historical context which has since been elaborated more fully by French scholars
such as Rioux and Martin (1964), Rioux (1969, 1973), and Guindon (1988).
St Denis was located in the centre of the agricultural rang system, in which
narrow strips of land began at the river and extended inland with the farm
buildings bordering the river, forming a long snake-like village.

Miner (1939) describes kinship and the family cycle, the role of religion, the
agricultural means of making a living, and patterns of community organization
in typical anthropological fashion. The autobiography of a habitant gives
insight into experiences such as childhood, schooling, first communion, family
reunions, marriage, a death in the family, land improvement, and travel. These
ethnographic insights provide a sense of the peasant atmosphere.

Miner compares the changes which had taken place between life in the
1800s and in 1936, when he studied St Denis. Flail threshing was replaced by
mechanical tools and hand bucksaws were replaced by circular saws. Local
bean-and-barley coffee had been replaced by store-bought tea and coffee.
Kerosene lamps replaced candles. Homemade clothes were replaced by store-
bought shoes and clothes, and bobsleighs and buggies replaced traineaus and
carrioles. Although changes through the 1800s were evident, they escalated in
the early 1900s.

Miner returned to St Denis in 1949 to compare the changes since 1936.
He found that 'life is now less "like a turning wheel", as an old habitant
described it, for the repetitive cycle of life no longer returns to the same point
with each succeeding generation' (Miner, 1939: 255). In 1949 television had
spread to many households; roads once gravelled were now surfaced, and
many more automobiles had appeared; easier communication through buses,
trucks, telephones was possible; on farms tractors replaced horses, electricity
made electric washers, milkers, refrigerators, electric pumps, and running
water possible; store-bought furniture, packaged foods, and clothes no longer
required as much home woodwork, cooking, and sewing. We are fortunate
that sixty years later, we have such a classic ethnographic study of one French-
Canadian parish as an important point of traditional reference.

While Miner's community study of traditional and conservative St Denis
was one of the first such projects, we have several more to add to our rich
understanding of French communities. In 1975, anthropologist Gerald Gold
at Laval studied St Pascal, a parish adjacent to St Denis. St Pascal is just
southeast of St Denis, located not on the river, but in the second tier of inland
rangs. The small map (Figure 5-1) also shows a dozen Catholic parishes
named after saints, which clearly emphasizes 'the sacred' milieu that we are

FIGURE 5-1   ST DENIS AND ST PASCAL PARISHES ON THE SOUTH SHORE OF THE
ST LAWRENCE RIVER IN QUEBEC

SOURCE: G. Gold, *St Pascal: Changing Leadership and Social Organization in a Quebec Town.* Toronto: Holt, Rinehart and Winston, 1975, p. 23.

dealing with. Paul Charest (1975: iv) writes in his foreword, 'The non-Québécois reader, familiar with the now classic works of Hughes and Miner, will here find an image of Quebec that is not only different but also much more contemporary and realistic.' Gold (1975) focuses on the changing leadership and social organization of St Pascal. He is concerned with showing the social structure of the town and the influences of industry, combining the interests of both Miner and Hughes. Much more local French control of the economic welfare of the community has developed, and more important linkages have been made with the larger networks outside. Small-town St Pascal has prospered and joined the larger scene in the nineties. The French are no longer as economically isolated as they were.

HUGHES'S INDUSTRIALIZED CANTONVILLE
Like Dawson, Everett Hughes was one of the few sociologists in Canada located at McGill. He too was trained at Chicago, and in their respective 1936 and 1943 publications they acknowledge each other for support. As we might expect of a Chicago School sociologist, Hughes is interested in the industrialization process in Quebec, an interest illustrated in *French Canada in Transition* (1943). Hughes's study explores charter French-English relations and British-French relations in the Quebec industrial town of Cantonville.

In his preface, Hughes (1943: x) says he chose Cantonville (actually Drummondville) for study because 'it stands in between the two extremes' of Horace Miner's community study of the traditional rural French St Denis parish prototype and Montreal, the largest metropolis in Quebec. Industries, all started and managed by English-speaking people, had both 'enlivened and disturbed' Cantonville. In 1941 Cantonville (near Montreal in southwest Quebec) had a population of 20,000 which was 95% Catholic and French. It was the first of a series of French towns that Hughes planned to study (Hughes, 1943: xv). The industrial invasion of English-speakers was in many ways alien to French Quebec, and the fact that the English held the top industry positions while the French in their own territory filled in as lower-class workers created potential conflict in French-English relations. These ethnic relations resulted in Hughes's exploring minority-majority relations more particularly than many sociologists of the day (Juteau, 1992).

Hughes (1943: 21) begins his book by sketching the rural Quebec context, the French-Canadian family farm, the centrality of the Catholic parish, the first institution of local self-government, the rural village and parish populations, and the homogeneity for more conspicuous living, clearly showing where the money is. Thus, two ethnic solitudes live side by side, each in its own place encouraged by the differentiation of industrialization.

While the St Denis and St Pascal studies focus on French communities in the Québécois heartland, Hughes's study of Cantonville shows the impact of industry parachuted into a French community and the need for adjustment and cooperation with those of other ethnic traditions. French communities outside the Quebec heartland have additional problems with maintaining their identities, because outside Quebec they no longer are a majority who can influence and shape their French destiny. Let us examine several French communities in Ontario and Alberta, to illustrate their struggles.

John Jackson (1975) made a community study of French-English relations in Tecumseh, near Windsor in English-speaking Ontario. The research focused on conflict between the Franco-Ontarians and Anglo-Ontarians over language. In 1921, 86% of the population of Tecumseh was French; by 1971, the French had declined to 48%, still the largest ethnic group (Jackson, 1975: 9). Religion also added to the complexity; in 1921, 94% of the population were Roman Catholic; by 1971 they had declined to 75%, with the French-Ontarians mostly Catholic, and the British and others both Catholic and Protestant. Ethnic origin, language, religion, and social class were all factors that influenced the amount of conflict over social issues such as French-language education and Catholic schools. Jackson (1975: 1–15) suggests that 'using language as an index ... Tecumseh Francophones, though not as strong as their confreres in the Ottawa Valley and northwestern Ontario, have maintained an amazing viability against the extreme pressure of anglicization in the Detroit-Windsor metropolitan complex.'

Farther west, Robert Stebbins (1994) made the first metropolitan study of the French outside Quebec in Calgary where some 15,000 represent only two per cent of the metropolitan population. Stebbins (1994: 113–14) lists four core activities as crucial to their survival: 1) activities with children, 2) French schools, 3) routine passive leisure, and 4) interactive leisure. Most are bilingual, 75% speaking French at home, although intermarriage is a problem. These are not highly segregated French communities in Calgary, but many are retaining a modified French identity.

Stebbins (1994: 113–21) discusses the future of Franco-Calgarians, saying that they face levels of importance of activities which he classified into core and semi-peripheral activities. He sees their core as centred around the school-community centre which they were planning to construct with governmental authorization. This centre will contain space for offices, educational facilities, and room for the performing arts. This they hope will raise the profile of francophones in the surrounding anglophone milieu, which should act as a magnet to draw increased involvement of the 14,490 francophones in the city. Here francophones would have increased opportunities to use their language, and build networks and community where francophones can interact and find each other. Hopefully more of their own kind would marry each other and stem the trends of exogamy. The sizeable flow of francophone immigrants into the city adds to the hopes of a revitalized francophone community (Stebbins, 1994: 120). Clearly, the identity maintenance of such a francophone community is more similar to that of other non-charter ethnic communities than to French communities supported by a massive regional, demographic, institutional, and political French core in Quebec.

FEDERALIST VERSUS SEPARATIST DIALECTICS

Lord Durham's observation that he found two peoples warring in the bosom of one nation is not surprising in light of our findings in this chapter (Axworthy and Trudeau, 1992: 7–50; Denis, 1995: 162). New France, created almost 400 years ago, was designed to be a French Québécois nation, and the original demographic European origin in a distinct region along the St Lawrence was headed that way until the conquest. The various ideologies in Quebec have worked to preserve this French nation whose French-language symbol system is in continuity with its long historical past. The studies by Miner and Hughes just reviewed show both the earlier French parish system, which sustained them through their years of conservatism, and the distinct French-English polarities during the time of more recent industrialization. A great deal of research has gone into this English-French power dialectic (Breton et al., 1980; Bell and Tepperman, 1979).

In Chapter Two our model of conformity and pluralism (p. 39) placed the British and French in opposite corners B and E, with the industrial melting pot and many arrows of conflict between them. The British and French have remained two economic, political, and social solitudes. According to Breton (1980: 139), 'to a significant degree, Anglophones and Francophones live separately in their own social circles and institutions. . . . Many Canadians perceive problems of national unity as problems pertaining to English-French relations.' The two are segmented, encircled by institutional boundaries and enclosures, and Breton et al. (1980: 142–304) describe these in three basic economic, political, and social dimensions. The conflict and dynamics of these dialectics are still unresolved in the nineties.

TRUDEAU'S FEDERALIST ALTERNATIVE

Two federalist and separatist French-Canadian alternatives for survival were clearly spelled out by Quebeckers Pierre Trudeau and René Levèsque in the 1960s. Trudeau's (1962; 1968) *Federalist alternative* proposed that Quebec's future lies within confederation; Levèsque's (1963) *Separatist alternative* (attempted again in the nineties by Jacques Parizeau) was to lead Quebec out of confederation to form a separate sovereign Quebec nation-state. Both called for the survival of the Québécois as a distinct people, but their models for survival are quite different. Both men are examples of very able modern leaders spawned by Quebec, evidence of changes which have taken place there. Let us look at the federalist and the separatist alternatives briefly.

Pierre Trudeau, the prime minister of Canada for fourteen years (1968–1983), was born in Montreal in 1921 and brought up in a bilingual and bicultural home. He was educated at the universities of Montreal, Harvard, Paris, and the London School of Economics, doing postgraduate studies in economics, political studies, and law (Saywell, 1968: viii). During the conservative Duplessis years, to combat Duplessis, Trudeau, Gerard Pelletier, and others founded a new journal, *Cité Libre*, in which they began to expound their visions for change. Later Trudeau, Pelletier, and Jean Marchand—all from Quebec—entered federal politics and became known as the 'three wise men'.

As professor of law at the University of Montreal, Trudeau continued to write. An important article in *Cité Libre* (1962) outlined his position on French nationalism and the need for a multinational state. He rejected any movement toward Quebec's independence, which in the past had failed and which he thought would not succeed but would lead only to further misery. Instead, he proposed a multinational state, rejecting the idea of a nation-state but opting for what he called 'more civilized goal of polyethnic pluralism . . . dreamed about by Lafontaine, realized under Cartier, perfected by Laurier, and humanized with Bourassa' (Trudeau, 1962: 58). Trudeau believed that the British North America (BNA) Act and the Constitutionalists had indeed made a first step away from a nation-state toward a multinational option, and that this needed to be refined.

Trudeau had harsh words for 'Separatists and Nationalists of all shapes and sizes baying after independence, who devote all their courage and capabilities to stirring up French-Canadian nationalism in defiance of the Anglo-Canadian variety . . . incessantly promoting the "state-of-siege mentality"' (Trudeau, 1962: 59). He felt that French Canadians had failed to make themselves indispensable to Canada's future because of weak leadership and their failure to enter the ranks of senior civil servants. He claimed Anglo-Canadians had been strong because of French weakness, and that the French language had lost its status because Quebeckers had let their language and education be reduced to mediocrity. Trudeau thought that Canada must look for an alternative to a unitary nationalist state because:

> A nationalist government is by nature intolerant, discriminatory, and, when all is said and done, totalitarian. A truly democratic government cannot be nationalist, because it must pursue the good of all its citizens, without prejudice to ethnic origin. (Trudeau, 1962: 63)

These words of Trudeau sound like McNeill's call for polyethnicity which we quoted in Chapter One. Trudeau's call for modification by all sounds much like modified pluralism. He continues:

> The die is cast in Canada: there are two main ethnic and linguistic groups; each is too strong and too deeply rooted in the past, too firmly bound to a mother culture, to be able to engulf the other. But if the two will collaborate at the hub of a truly pluralistic State, Canada could become the envied seat of a form of federation that belongs to tomorrow's world. Better than the American melting-pot, Canada could offer an example to all . . . who must discover how to govern their polyethnic populations with proper regard for justice and liberty. (Trudeau, 1962: 67)

Later, in his volumes *Federalism and the French Canadians* (1968), and *Toward a Just Society* (1992), Trudeau more systematically argues the Federalism case. He argues that the provinces in Canada now have jurisdiction over education and land resources. This jurisdiction provides Quebec and others the opportunity to train their people and develop their regions. He outlines some necessary constitutional changes, including a Bill of Rights, and the deletion of some of the imperial phraseology, which was done later in the passing of the new Canadian constitution. (We will examine the content of the Charter of Rights and Freedoms in more detail in Chapter Twelve.) Trudeau was always very critical of the Separatist movement, which he called 'the Wigwam Complex', as a powerless petit-bourgeois minority left behind by the twentieth century.

In 1963, Lester Pearson had appointed the Royal Commission on Bilingualism and Biculturalism to study English-French relations in Canada. In 1965 the three wise men from Quebec—Trudeau, Pelletier, and Marchand—

were added to Pearson's cabinet to bolster French representation. By 1968, when the commission's recommendations began to appear, Trudeau had replaced Pearson as leader and prime minister. Trudeau personally piloted through Parliament new legislation designed to establish English and French as Canada's official languages. The Official Languages Act was supported by all political parties and passed in 1969 with few dissenting votes (Bell and Tepperman, 1979: 135). At the same time, Separatism was also growing in Quebec, led by René Levèsque, and more recently by Jacques Parizeau.

LEVÈSQUE'S SEPARATIST SOLUTION
While Trudeau stayed in power federally as prime minister of Canada for fourteen years to promote his Federalism experiment, René Levèsque promoted the Separatist option during the seventies through the Parti Québécois, as First Minister of the province of Quebec. Levèsque was part of the Liberal Party with Trudeau, but in 1967 he wanted the Liberal Party to favour sovereignty for Quebec within a common market association with Canada. The party did not accept this option (Milner, 1978: 153). In 1968, various Separatist political groups joined to form the Parti Québécois with René Levèsque as president. It took just eight years (until 1976) for the party to take power in Quebec, with Separatism as one of its main goals (Milner, 1978: 151–8). The party was considerably to the left of centre, but continually tried to keep the radicals farther to the left in check in order to get elected and to stay in power. Their goal was to rationalize and modernize Quebec and eventually to separate from Confederation with Canada.

'Over 80 per cent of Québécois surveyed in June 1978 wanted either a change in Confederation or outright independence' (Bell and Tepperman, 1979: 137). Large numbers, however, considered themselves to be in the middle ground, neither extreme Separatists nor extreme Federalists. Slowly many Québécois began to see that some third option was needed. Trudeau stopped insisting that Confederation did not need to be altered, and Levèsque increasingly tried to persuade his radical Separatists that a more modified sovereignty association was needed. After the Parti Québécois had been in power for four years, a referendum was held in 1980, in which Quebeckers had to choose for or against sovereignty association. Did they want to separate to become an independent sovereign nation linked and associated with Canada, especially economically, or did they wish to remain in Confederation? Sixty per cent voted in favour of staying in Confederation. Even a modified form of Separatism with sovereignty association was not acceptable to a majority, even though the Parti Québécois had extensively promoted modified independence (Denis, 1995: 166–8).

The defeat of the referendum in Quebec in 1980 put the Quebec drive for Separatism on hold; 60% voted against separation. Once again, Quebec had not become an independent sovereign nation as many wished, but this time the Québécois had decided the question internally and without violence. Quebec had passed Bill 101, which strengthened the French language within the province, and the federal bilingual act strengthened French as an official national language in Canada. The nationalist Parti Québécois came to power in 1976 and legislated Bill 101, in 1977 which declared French to be the official language of Quebec for the courts and the legislature (Denis, 1995: 167). It made French compulsory in the public service, and restricted access to English schools to children who have one parent educated in English in Quebec, which boosted continuity of the French language in Quebec (Axworthy and Trudeau, 1992).

To many Canadians it seemed unfair that after great efforts, during the Trudeau years, to bring about an officially bilingual English and French Canada, Quebec would now legislate French as the only official language in Quebec in Bill 101. From the French Québécois perspective, however, Bill 101 was essential. The Quebec population in Canada had dropped from one-third to one-fourth because of the severe drop in birthrates and less than average immigration into the province. Four major factors account for the language-planning efforts in Quebec during the fifties and 1960s and 1970s. First, the demographic decline of francophones in Canada meant that Quebec was the last enclave of a French-speaking society. Second, the demographic birthrates in Quebec itself were declining from the highest to the lowest in Canada (Henripin, 1993: 304–10; Bourhis, 1994: 329). Third, freedom of language choice in Quebec schools meant that immigrants chose English rather than French schools. Fourth, the anglophone dominance of business and economic activity in the province required a more prominent place for the French language. Bill 101 was designed to enhance the status of French generally and it had its intended impact (Bourhis, 1994: 330–1). Both anglophones and allophones learned and used more French, and francophone status was enhanced.

MEECH LAKE AND THE 1995 REFERENDUM
With the rise of the Parti Québécois and its work like Bill 101, the French Québécois cause was enhanced. However, when the Canadian Constitution was repatriated and signed in 1982, René Levèsque, then First Minister of Quebec, did not sign, while the other nine premiers did. Levèsque's refusal to sign was a clear indication that the question of Quebec's integration into Canada had failed (Denis, 1995; Parel, 1988: 129–37). The question of a 'Quebec Nation' had not been resolved.

In the 1980s Brian Mulroney, prime minister of Canada, opened up discussions again, trying to get the first ministers to sign an agreement which would include Quebec. The new Liberal Party now in power in Quebec outlined five conditions that had to be met for Quebec to agree: 1) recognition of Quebec as a distinct society, 2) a veto or compensation over constitutional amendments, 3) participation in appointment of three Supreme Court justices from Quebec, 4) Quebec rights to help select immigrants for Quebec, and 5) limitation of Parliament's spending power (Denis, 1995: 178–9). The first was a version of the concept of 'nation'. The other four would make Quebec a more active player in Canadian decision-making. These were moves toward sovereignty association. Quebec was the first to sign the Meech Lake Accord in 1987, and so did seven other provinces. The Canadian Parliament passed the Accord in 1988, but Manitoba and Newfoundland did not, and 'Meech' expired in 1990 (Fournier, 1991).

Another Charlottetown Agreement occurred in 1992, but the Canada-wide referendum on October 26, 1992 was defeated by a vote of 54.5% (Denis, 1995: 182). The Charlottetown referendum failed because outside Quebec it appeared that it gave Quebec too much, while inside Quebec, Quebeckers thought it did not give Quebec enough (Russell, 1993: 226). In 1994 the separatist Parti Québécois again came into power, with Jacques Parizeau promising to hold another referendum in Quebec in 1995. In early 1995 the public opinion polls in 1995 predicted that a simple question on 'Should Quebec separate from Canada' would be defeated 55–60 to 40–45, similar to the results of the first 1980 referendum to separate. This tended to lull the Federalist forces to inactivity. In the meantime politicans argued as to whether some form of sovereignty association should again be proposed (Drache and Perin, 1992).

Figure 5-2 illustrates well the extent to which Quebeckers were split by the October 30, 1995 referendum. Basically, metropolitan multi-ethnic Montreal, where 3.1 million or half of all Quebeckers live, voted 'No' and the rest of Quebec, which is much more rural and less metropolitan, voted 'Yes'. Quebeckers farthest to the west, near Ottawa and Ontario, had voted 'No', in some regions as strongly as three to one. Those farther east, more deeply into the core rural French Catholic heartland voted 'Yes', as strongly as two to one farthest east. In his agonized concession of defeat, Parti Québécois leader and premier Jacques Parizeau lamented that it was 'money and the ethnic vote' which had brought the separatists down to defeat. What many thought, but dared not utter, had been said by their leader. It was true that non-francophones had voted 'No' overwhelmingly, but Parizeau's racist remark raised a storm of protest even among his own followers. The next day, on Hallowe'en, Parizeau resigned.

The question that the Parti Québécois posed for the referendum of October, 1995 was not clear-cut: 'Do you agree that Quebec should become sovereign, after having made a formal offer to Canada for a new Economic and Political partnership, within the scope of the Bill respecting the future of

FIGURE 5-2   REFERENDUM POLLS AND RESULTS, 1980 AND 1995.

1980

			YES	NO
Dec. 24	1979	IQOP	38.5	47.2
March 7	1980	CROP	41.0	52.0
March 16	1980	IQOP	47.4	43.8
April 20	1980	IQOP	41.2	40.9
April 25	1980	CROP	44.4	43.9
May 9	1980	CROP	39.6	45.5
May 11	1980	IQOP	37.0	40.0
May 16	1980	Pinard-Hamilton	37.0	40.0
May 18	1980	IQOP	40.4	36.5

May 20, 1980 results

Yes 40.5%   No 59.5%

Official question

The Government of Quebec has made public its proposal to negotiate a new agreement with the rest of Canada, based on the equality of nations; this agreement would enable Quebec to acquire the exclusive power to make its laws, administer its taxes and establish relations abroad—in other words, sovereignty—and at the same time, to maintain with Canada an economic association including a common currency; any change in political status resulting from these negotiations will be submitted to the people through a referendum; on these terms do you agree to give the Government of Quebec the mandate to negotiate the proposed agreement between Quebec and Canada?

1995

			YES	NO
Sept. 7-8	1995	Leger & Leger	43.8	42.9
Sept. 8-12	1995	SOM Inc.	37.0	45.0
Sept. 19-25	1995	SOM Inc.	39.0	48.0
Sept. 20-25	1995	CROP	39.0	47.0
Sept. 25-28	1995	Leger & Leger	43.8	45.1
Oct. 1-5	1995	Leger & Leger	42.9	43.7
Oct. 8-12	1995	Leger & Leger	45.0	42.4
Oct. 10-12	1995	Gallup	39.0	43.0
Oct. 13-16	1995	SOM Inc.	42.9	43.4
Oct. 13-16	1995	CROP	43.6	42.6
Oct. 16-18	1995	Angus Reid	45.4	43.6
Oct. 16-20	1995	Leger & Leger	45.8	42.2
Oct. 19-23	1995	CROP	44.5	42.2
Oct. 23-25	1995	SOM Inc.	46.0	40.0
Oct. 23-25	1995	Angus Reid	44.0	40.0

October 30, 1995 results

49.4%   50.6%
Yes   No

Official question

Do you agree that Quebec should become sovereign, after having made a formal offer to Canada for a new Economic and Political Partnership, within the scope of the Bill respecting the future of Quebec and of the agreement signed on June 12, 1995?

SOURCE: Nancy Gill, Canadian Press. 'Referendum Polls and Results, 1980 and 1995'. Winnipeg: *Winnipeg Free Press*, 28 October 1995, p. A3.

FIGURE 5 - 3   QUEBEC REFERENDUM RESULTS BY REGION, 1995

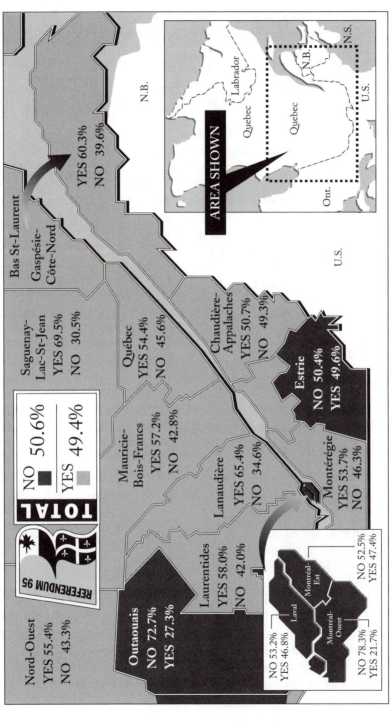

SOURCE: Canadian Press, '1995 Referendum Results by Region'. Winnipeg: *Winnipeg Free Press*, 31 October 1995: p. B2.

Quebec and of the agreement signed on June 12, 1995?' The debate centred around the new division of power (Drache and Perin, 1992: 13–19), Quebec-Canadian association (Smith, 1992: 61–70), sovereignty and the aboriginals (Turpel, 1992: 93–106), a common currency (Donner and Lazar, 1992: 127–38), and dividing the debt (Chorney, 1992: 156–70). Indeed, just days before the referendum, the Cree of northern Quebec held their own referendum with 97% voting to stay in Canada. With the failure of Meech Lake, Federalists had little to offer Quebeckers who wanted to stay. Federalists mostly warned of dire economic consequences for Quebec.

As we can see in Table 5-3, six of the 1995 polls in the last half of October, two weeks before the vote, the 'Yes' vote for Quebec sovereignty ahead. The 'Yes' vote gained an enormous boost when charismatic Lucien Bouchard, the leader of the Bloc Québécois, and federal leaders of the official opposition vigorously entered the referendum debate. Whereas polls a month earlier had the 'No' vote leading by as much as ten points, the race became neck and neck toward the end. The 'No' side won by a narrow 1.2% margin only because the 12–15% undecideds voted four-to-one 'No' as they had in 1980, and large 'No' crowds rallied in Montreal and cities across Canada. Whereas the 'No' side won by a 20% margin of 59.5 to 40.5% in 1980, by 1995 the margin had been cut to a 49.4 to 50.6% margin of victory. Basically, Quebec voters' opinions split down the middle, where very little had been decided. The survival of Canada had been on the brink, with both sides shaken and dissatisfied!

SUMMARY

In Part Three we focus on ethnic solidarity and identity. In this chapter we have examined the French in Quebec as the most important evidence of pluralism. In Max Weber's terms, French Québécois are European racially; they have maintained a distinct language, culture, and consciousness of kind for 385 years; their religious ideology is solidly Roman Catholic; they have definitely remained a distinctive 'people' with the will to fight for their identity; and they think of themselves as a nation. Their macro sociocultural structures are clearly French-Québécois, and they interact extensively with other French Canadians in symbolic interactionist terms.

The regional setting in the province of Quebec has made French solidarity possible. They were the first Europeans to settle in Canada, founding what was to become the nation of New France. Demographically, more than 80% are French, and they speak French in the region of Quebec. During their 385 years, these Québécois have resorted to a series of colonial, conservative, quiet revolutionary, and Separatist ideologies to survive, especially since the conquest by the British.

A francophone symbol system has remained the dominant language of Quebeckers. Recently the recommendations of the Royal Commission on Bilingualism and Biculturalism to make French an official national language along with English has been enacted and promoted nationally. Francophones outside of the province of Quebec are struggling to retain their French identity, but those within the Bilingual Belt adjacent to the French core are maintaining their French-Canadian identity extensively. While fewer others are shifting to speaking French than shifting away, francophones are clearly maintaining themselves in the Quebec core.

Miner's study of the St Denis parish illustrated the rural life of the habitants during the conservative ideological period. Hughes's and Gold's studies illustrate the impact of industrialization and the resulting changes. Quebec is fast becoming more urban and more industrial, but the desire to remain French continues unabated. The recent quiet revolution, the Separatist movement, the two Quebec referenda, and Bill 101 have all served to strengthen francophones and French Québécois, while more and more people are learning French across Canada and accepting Canada as a bilingual nation. French Canadians are the best example of a macro sociocultural 'nation' which has not assimilated, but which has instead fought for an alternative to unitary Canadian nationalism. Plural French identity and solidarity is an empirical fact in Canada. We turn next to ethnic cultural identity, and the extent to which smaller ethnoreligious groups have been able to establish plural ethnic identity and solidarity.

CHAPTER 6

Ethnic Identity and Identification

In Chapter Five we presented language as an important symbol system, anchored in the distinctive French Québécois territorial 'nation'. The French fact, as one of the two founding charter peoples, has been a solid example of voluntary pluralism centring cell E in our theoretical model. To what extent can other ethnic groups also voluntarily perpetuate their heritages, even though they may not be as large or as powerful as the French in Quebec? What is the salience of their ethnic identity? What are some of the cultural indicators of their distinctive identification? How do some minority groups compare to others?

Gordon (1964: 24) defines an ethnic group as a group of individuals with a shared sense of peoplehood based on presumed shared sociocultural experience and/or similar physical characteristics. Dashefsky defines group identification 'as a generalized attitude involving a personal attachment to a group and a positive orientation toward being a member of a group. Therefore, ethnic identification takes place when the group in question is one with whom the individual believes he has a common ancestry based on shared individual characteristics and/or shared sociocultural experiences' (1975: 8). Erickson suggests that 'identity is not only the sum of childhood identifications, but rather a new combination of old and new identification fragments' (1968: 90).

'Identity may best be understood if it is viewed first as a higher order concept, i.e., a general organizing referent which includes a number of subsidiary facets' (Dashefsky, 1972: 240). Dashefsky has reviewed some of the literature on identity and identification which illustrates the many dimensions of identification:

> Foote (1951) and Lindesmith and Strauss (1968) have suggested that identification involves linking oneself to others in an organizational sense (as becoming a formal member of an organization) or in a symbolic sense (as thinking of oneself as a part of a particular group). Stone (1962) argues further that identification subsumes two processes: 'identification of' and 'identification with'. The former involves placing the individual in socially defined categories. This facilitates occurrence of the latter. In Stone's terms it is 'identification with' that gives rise to identity.

Rosen has gone further in arguing that an individual may identify himself (herself) with others on three levels: First, one may identify oneself with some important person in one's life, e.g. a parent or a friend (i.e., a significant other). Second, one may identify with a group from which one draws one's values, e.g. family or coworkers (i.e., reference group). Last, one may identify oneself with a broad category of persons, e.g. an ethnic group or occupational group (i.e., a society category). . . . (1972: 242)

THEORIES OF ETHNIC IDENTITY

Because sociologists and psychologists have studied ethnic identity at macro and micro levels there is a great deal of confusion about the nature of ethnic identity. Some of this is due to the different theoretical biases which researchers bring to their studies. Dashefsky (1975) has tried to systematize some of these macro and micro emphases. He suggests that four frameworks (sociocultural, interactionist, group dynamicist, and psychoanalytic) have generally been used: the first two by sociologists, the second two by psychologists.

Dashefsky (1975: 11) classifies these four theoretical orientations along two axes (Figure 6-1), using ontology (theory of reality) and methodology axes which intersect to form four cells. The first two cells deal with macro and micro sociological orientations, and the second two with macro and micro psychological orientations. Sociological methods of research rely on field study, survey research, and sociohistorical analysis, while psychological methods deal primarily with experimental and clinical studies.

The top left sociocultural cell represents a macro sociological approach in which social structure and culture are the dominant foci of ethnic identity research. In the lower left cell, the interactionist approach is micro sociological and deals with the social-psychological concern with symbols and their importance for social relationships. In the upper right cell, the group dynamicist approach is a macro psychological method in which the group context is

FIGURE 6-1   THEORETICAL ORIENTATION IN THE SOCIAL PSYCHOLOGY OF ETHNICITY

		METHODOLOGY	
		Sociology	Psychology
ONTOLOGY	Macro	SOCIOCULTURAL	GROUP DYNAMICIST
	Micro	INTERACTIONIST	PSYCHOANALYTIC BEHAVIOURIST

SOURCE: Arnold Dashefsky, 'Theoretical Frameworks in the Study of Ethnic Identity', *Ethnicity* 2, 1: 1975.

important in examinations of ethnic identity. The sociocultural and the group dynamicist traditions are both macro approaches. Both look at the social system, but socioculturalists stress the importance of historical experiences, while group dynamicists focus more on immediate individual and group structures. The lower right cell represents the micro psychological approach often called behaviourist, in which identity is explained in terms of reinformed responses to stimuli (Dashefsky, 1975: 11). Very little research has been done in this behaviourist area of ethnic identity. In this chapter we shall confine our theoretical review to the first two sociological macro and micro approaches (sociocultural and interactionist). The interactionist approach is largely an attempt at rebutting the mechanistic image of humans portrayed by behaviourists. Interactionists also want to stress the symbolic dimensions of human behaviour, which structural functionalists tend not to emphasize. The ethnocultural approach can focus so intensely on structures that the dynamic features of change tend to be overly restrictive and deterministic.

THE MACRO SOCIOCULTURAL APPROACH

Dashefsky (1975: 12) summarized the socioculturalists' assumptions very well. The macro sociocultural framework assumes that individual behaviour is shaped by, and occurs within, social and cultural systems. The social system tends to define the relationships among individuals within the structure, and the cultural system defines the mutual expectations that individuals share and the norms that they hold. The cultural and social system is the result of cumulated historical experiences; individual behaviour is shaped within this context. The study of human behaviour is more important to these socioculturalists than is the study of attitudes, perceptions, and self-conception.

A review of the literature shows that the multidimensional approach to identity has been expounded first by a host of researchers interested mostly in Jewish identity (Segalman, 1967: 92–111; Levinson, 1962: 375–99; Fathi and Kinsley, 1968). Many of the factors used by Lazerwitz (1970) include some distinctly Jewish cultural items such as Zionism, although other of his factors such as education, religion, friendships, and dating patterns could be extended to apply to any minority.

Studies show that ethnocultural identity tends to be multidimensional, clustering around a multiplicity of factors, among them language use, religious practice, endogamy, parochial education, choice of ingroup friends, use of ethnic media, and participation in ethnic voluntary organizations (Ishwaren, 1980; Weinfeld et al., 1981; deVries, 1988; Driedger, 1989; Breton et al., 1990; Burch, 1990; Friesen, 1993). Because individuals and ethnic groups vary in the extent to which they emphasize different identity factors, researchers need to sort out the different factors and the patterns or profiles of ethnocultural identity.

Historical, national, and regional experiences also add to Canada's ethnic diversity. Because of the Canadian policy of pluralism, ethnic identity often persists. For some groups, however, shifts of interest reinforce identification and account for greater ethnic identity. This trend may be seen in the French, with the present emphasis on bilingualism, and the Jews, who are concerned with events related to the state of Israel. Glazer and Moynihan (1975), for example, suggest that such events as the Nazi holocaust, Zionism, and the Catholic school controversy have provided foci for ethnic identification. Charter group status, entrance status, and ethnic institutional completeness are influential also. Thus, it is reasonable to expect that modes of identification will vary with historically important causes and events. The measures of these modes will therefore exhibit a multifactor structure, to distinguish the components that different individuals and groups stress. This raises the problem of selecting crucial elements to measure ethnic identity (Driedger, 1989; Breton et al., 1990; Weinfeld, 1994: 238–66).

THE MICRO SOCIOLOGICAL INTERACTIONIST APPROACH
Max Weber assumed that humans live in a symbolic world, are stimulated by symbols, and stimulate others through symbols. Indeed, it is the ability to use symbols in a complex way that makes humans distinctive. Humans learn through symbolic communication—especially language—and become reflective beings who can think abstractly, take roles, and create feelings and values. As a result they learn to predict each other's behaviour and to adjust their behaviour based on these predictions. In this way they define themselves in relationship to other persons and situations (Dashefsky, 1975: 13). It is therefore important to ethnic identity that groups of individuals share symbols and their meanings and values in what we call group identification. Religious institutions, newspapers, and schools can all symbolically reinforce ethnic identification.

Further investigation is needed to determine the relationship between attitudes toward ethnic identification and actual activity based on those attitudes (Edwards and Doucette, 1987). Lazerwitz (1953: 3–24) developed three categories—behavioural, attitudinal, and conceptual—for Jewish identification. He gave the most weight to behavioural items, middle weight to attitudinal items, and the least weight to conceptual items. According to Segalman, 'the decision to give more weight to the behavioural than to attitudinal data is a matter for continued examination and study' (1967: 98).

Kurt Lewin (1948) proposed that individuals need a firm, clear sense of identification with the heritage and culture of their ingroup to find a secure basis for a sense of well-being, and that insufficient ingroup security results in self-hatred and ingroup denial. Rothman's (1960: 82) summary of Lewin's theory suggests that such factors as ethnic self-affirmation, ethnic self-denial, and marginality need to be examined as independent but related variables which form a sense of ethnic self-identity for members of a particular ethnic group.

Many social psychologists hold that the preservation and enhancement of the self is a basic human need. To determine the extent to which members of an ethnic group consider their ingroup an essential part of their self-identification, it is necessary to review studies related specifically to ethnic self-identity. Segalman's early extensive review of Jewish identity indicates that few scales include social-psychological items. Since then some studies have been done (Mackie and Brinkerhof, 1984; Weinfeld, 1985; Edwards, 1987; Berry, 1990), a number of which have centred around salience of ethnic identity and means of measuring salience. Driedger (1976) examined ethnic self-identity in Canada and found considerable differences among Winnipeg groups in their real and ideal ethnic affirmation, and their levels of denial and marginality. Isajiw (1981: 90) studied symbolic ethnic identity in Toronto, and later Isajiw and Driedger (1987) developed a Symbolic Ethnic Identity (SEI) Index.

Lewin's theory deals with ethnic self-hatred. The first proposition, *ethnic affirmation*, describes the extent to which members identify with the ethnic support provided by their ingroup. It examines whether they are proud of their ingroup, whether it provides them with a rich heritage, and whether they wish to remember it or participate in it if they are given a choice. Ethnic affirmation refers not only to behavioural indicators of identity such as language use, attendance in parochial schools, and choice of ingroup friends, but also to a desire to be affiliated with one's ethnic group. Driedger (1976) found much Jewish and French ethnic affirmation in Winnipeg.

On the other hand, *ethnic denial* might include feelings of inferiority, of being restricted by or annoyed with the ingroup, or of a desire to hide cultural identity. These feelings of insecurity, inferiority, and discomfort caused by association with the reference group may be due to the negative stereotypes of the ingroup created by members of the majority culture.

Marginality is another important concept derived from Lewin's theory. Sociologically, this term has generally referred to the uncertain position of persons experiencing two cultures but identified with neither; it can also include the idea, at the psychological level, of a *discrepancy* between ingroup members' real and ideal identifications. The format of Worchel's Self Activity Inventory (SAI) (which involves a description of who a person is as well as an assessment of who he *would like to be*) is useful in this connection. The discrepancy between the two is important to a study of student aspirations (Wylie, 1961). A low degree of discrepancy suggests that persons see themselves as consistently successful in meeting their expected needs, while a high degree of discrepancy reveals a sense of being unable to meet expectancy levels. Driedger (1976) used real and ideal discrepancies as indicators of marginality because ethnic solidarity is perceived as an inferior goal which is not in harmony with the aspirations of the individual showing these discrepancies.

Having reviewed the two major sociological macro and micro perspectives on ethnic identity, let us identify some of the ethnic identification factors evident in the empirical literature. We begin with three structural sociocultural forms of identification (territory, institutions, and culture), and end with three symbolic forms of identification (history, ideology, and leadership). These two theoretical perspectives tend to summarize the many forms of ethnic identification on a structural-symbolic continuum. In the middle of this continuum, the two approaches overlap considerably; the respective poles, in contrast, are clearly distinctive ontologically and methodologically.

ETHNIC IDENTIFICATION FACTORS

In our discussion of ethnic identification, we shall touch on six factors: ecological territory, ethnic culture, ethnic institutions, historical symbols, ideology, and charismatic leadership (Driedger, 1989). We suggest that these factors are some of the basic components which constitute an ethnic community, which Weber referred to as a group of individuals having a shared sense of peoplehood including both structural and symbolic dimensions (Breton, 1991; Weinfeld, 1994).

IDENTIFICATION WITH A TERRITORY

Both Joy (1972) and Lieberson (1970) argue that maintenance of an ethnic language and culture is not possible unless there is a sufficiently large number of the same ethnic group concentrated in a territory. Joy demonstrates how Quebec's French were in control of the provincial territory, thus perpetuating their language and culture through religious, educational, and political institutions. Indian reservations also demonstrate ethnic territorial segregation. Most minorities cannot maintain such exclusive control over a territory; however, it is a model to which many minority groups seem to aspire. Ethnic bloc settlements are common, especially in the West. Examples include the French in Quebec, the Germans in the Kitchener-Waterloo area in Ontario, and the Ukrainians in the Aspen Belt stretching from the Manitoba Inter-Lake region to Edmonton. Rural hinterlands often contribute immigrants to the city. These migrants often perpetuate the urban villager way of life, as best illustrated by the North End of Winnipeg—the stronghold of Ukrainians, Poles, and Jews until recently (Driedger and Church, 1974). Balakrishnan and Kralt (1987; Balakrishnan and Selvanathan, 1990; Kalbach, 1990) also found extensive residential segregation in Toronto. Territory is an essential ingredient of any definition of a community. Individuals can identify with a territory, and it is the place within which ethnic activity can take place.

ETHNIC INSTITUTIONAL IDENTIFICATION

Breton (1964: 193, 194; 1991: 125–61) argues that the direction of the immigrant's integration will to a large extent result from the forces of attraction (positive and negative) stemming from three communities: the community of the respondents' ethnicity, the native (receiving) community, and the other ethnic communities. These forces are generated by the social organization of ethnic communities and their capacity to attract and hold members within their social boundaries. Integration into their own ethnic community, supported by institutional completeness of their group, will reinforce solidarity.

The rationale for institutional completeness is that a minority can develop a social system of its own with control over its institutions, and then the social action patterns of the group will take place largely within the system. Breton (1964) suggests that religious, educational, and welfare institutions are crucial, while Joy (1972) adds the importance of political and economic institutions. Vallee (1969) confirmed Breton's claims by summarizing the need for organization of group structures and institutions that influence socialization and ethnic community decision-making. Driedger and Church (1974) found that, in Winnipeg, the French and Jews maintained a more complete set of religious, educational, and welfare institutions than other ethnic groups in the city. These two groups were also the most segregated in St Boniface and the North End respectively, where they established their institutions. Residential segregation and ethnic institutional completeness tend to reinforce each other. The French and the Jews identified with both territory and ethnic institutions.

IDENTIFICATION WITH ETHNIC CULTURE

Kurt Lewin (1948) proposed that the individual needs to achieve a firm sense of identification with the heritage and culture of the ingroup to find a secure 'ground' for a sense of well-being. We assume that a minority culture can be better groomed within the territorial enclave where an ethnic group can build a concentration of its own institutions. The territory becomes an enclave within which ethnic institutions can be built, and the ethnic culture should flourish within these boundaries which support it.

Ethnic cultural identity factors have been studied by numerous scholars (Berry et al., 1987; Isajiw, 1990; Richard, 1991; Isajiw, Sev'er, Driedger, 1993; Friesen, 1993; Weinfeld, 1994). Driedger found at least six cultural factors which tended to differentiate group adherence to culture (language use, endogamy, choice of friends, and participation in religion, parochial schools, and voluntary organizations). French and Jewish adherents in Winnipeg, who were residentially segregated and maintained their ethnic institutions to a great degree, also ranked high on attendance at parochial schools (79 and 74%); endogamy (65 and 91%); and choice of ingroup friends (49 and 63%). This would seem to support use of French language at home (61%) and attendance in church (54%) for the French; that was not the case for the Jews. Other ethnic groups such as the Germans, Ukrainians, Poles, Scandinavians, and British supported their ingroup cultures less actively.

Examination of territorial, institutional, and cultural identity factors suggest that these three tend to reinforce each other. When individuals of a given ethnic group identify with their ingroup along these dimensions, they tend to remain more distinctive which blocks tendencies toward assimilation. Such maintenance of distinctive ethnic features is necessary if the Canadian ethnic mosaic is to remain a distinct reality.

IDENTIFICATION WITH HISTORICAL SYMBOLS
Minority rural villagers may perpetuate their social structures and community as ends in themselves, without much reference to where they came from and their future purpose. Among ethnic urbanites knowledge of their origins and pride in their heritage would seem to be essential for a sense of purpose and direction. Without such knowledge and pride, the desire to perpetuate tradition rapidly diminishes. The Jews have ritualized their history by placing it before their youth in the form of special days, fasts, candles, and food habits— symbols of their past history. Such historical symbols can create a sense of belonging, a sense of purpose, and a sense of continuing tradition that is important and worth perpetuating. Although tragic for the Jews, the Nazi holocaust in the 1940s and the present struggles in the Near East may be a reminder of the conflict that is a part of their historical past (Davis, 1992; Levitt and Shaffir, 1993; Brym and Lenton, 1993).

The ethnic heritage of the past can be a positive or negative influence on identity. A comparison of the sense of identity of seven ethnic groups in Winnipeg using a Worchel-type scale indicated strong French and Jewish ingroup affirmation and low ingroup denial, while Scandinavians scored low on both (Driedger, 1976b). Jewish and French students were proud of their ingroups, felt strongly bound to them, wished to remember them, and contributed to them. Their ingroups were positive symbols. The French indicated a very low ingroup denial. They did not try to hide their ethnicity, nor did they feel inferior about it. They seldom felt annoyed or restricted by their identity. The Ukrainians, Poles, and Germans felt less positively about their ethnic identity and, at the same time, were more inclined to deny their ethnicity.

IDENTIFICATION WITH AN IDEOLOGY
A religious or political ideology can rally followers to a goal beyond cultural and institutional values (Glazer and Moynihan, 1975). For many of the younger generation, territory, culture, and ethnic institutions seem to be means to an end rather than an end to be perpetuated indefinitely. As urban ethnic groups become more sophisticated, it is doubtful that enclavic means will hold them within an ethnic ingroup orbit. A political or religious ideology, however, provides a purpose and impetus for values which are considered more important than cultural and institutional means (Bibby, 1987; Kauffman and Driedger, 1991; Brym, Shaffir, and Weinfeld, 1993).

In our study of Winnipeg clergymen, we found doctrinal belief, for example, to be an important factor in differentiating attitudes toward a variety of social issues (Driedger et al., 1983). Beliefs had an independent effect on positions taken on issues related to social control, personal morality, use of power by the élite, civil liberties, minority rights, and welfare support. Absolutist clergy, those with a conservative other-worldly focus, were reluctant to change society; clergymen who were more doctrinally liberal were open to change. There is often a very strong correlation between religion and ethnicity in French and Polish Roman Catholics, Orthodox and Catholic Ukrainians, Scandinavian Lutherans, German Lutherans and Baptists, the Jews, and British Anglicans and United Church adherents.

Identification with religious beliefs or a political philosophy provides a more social-psychological dimension, which again emphasizes the importance of decisions to perpetuate or change territory, institutions, and ethnic culture (Driedger and Kraybill, 1994; Friesen, 1993).

CHARISMATIC LEADERSHIP AND IDENTIFICATION

The importance of charisma is demonstrated in a variety of new minority movements as shown by the leadership of Martin Luther King and Malcolm X among the Blacks in the United States, and René Levèsque among the Québécois. Individuals with a sense of mission often adapt an ideology to a current situation, linking it symbolically with the past and using the media to effectively transform the present into a vision of the future.

Most religious movements began with charismatic leaders as demonstrated by the founders of the great religions: Abraham, Buddha, Confucius, Jesus, and Mohammed. The importance of Martin Luther to the Lutherans, John Calvin to the Presbyterians, Joseph Smith to the Mormons, and Menno Simons to the Mennonites illustrates this also. The same is true of political movements led by Ho Chi Minh of Vietnam, Mao of China, Lenin of Russia, Hitler, Churchill, Castro, Tito, Mahatma Gandhi, Lincoln, and Levèsque.

Such charismatic leaders use social-psychological means designed to create trust with which they mould a cohesive loyalty to both leader and ingroup. They are true believers in a cause that is passed on to their followers, resulting in new potential for change. In the beginning they may be less oriented to territory, institutions, culture, and heritage; as the movement ages, however, such structural features slowly become more important.

Although there may be many more ethnic dimensions of minority identification, we have suggested that territory, institutions, culture, heritage, ideology, and leaders are important. Studies show that some ethnic groups identify more with some of these dimensions than do others, and that some groups are more successful at maintaining a distinct community. The Hutterites are perhaps one of the most obvious groups that have survived in the rural setting, and the Jews have done so effectively in the cities for centuries. The task in this volume is to explore the various dimensions and foci of ethnic identification for various ethnic groups. It will not be possible to explore all of these dimensions with each group; all we can do is provide a small sample of studies to illustrate the multidimensional and multilinear complexity of the ethnic mosaic.

ETHNO-CULTURAL IDENTITY DIMENSIONS

It is not easy to measure ethnic identity because we are dealing with a phenomenon that involves many levels, both macro and micro, each of which is multidimensional. A number of studies in search of the macro sociological-sociocultural dimensions have compared the numerous ethnic groups that we wish to examine here. Max Weber often did comparative studies. Anderson first compared rural ethnoreligious identity on the prairies. Driedger began the urban search by selecting students representing many groups in one university. O'Bryan et al. sampled adults representing ten groups of non-charter adults in five cities, and recently Breton et al. (1990) took a sample of adults in Toronto. All probed the sociocultural dimensions of ethnic identity, and the findings are fairly consistent and cumulative. Let us begin with rural studies that focus on structure and culture, and end with urban studies that show symbolic identity more.

RURAL ETHNORELIGIOUS IDENTITY

Anderson (1972) collected 1,000 interviews with adults from eighteen rural ethnoreligious bloc settlements (seven French Catholic, two Hutterite, two Scandinavian Lutheran, two Mennonite, and one each of German Catholic, Russian Doukhobor, Ukrainian Orthodox, Ukrainian Catholic, and Polish Catholic) located between Saskatoon, North Battleford, and Prince Albert (census divisions 15 and 16) in Saskatchewan. He collected data on church attendance, endogamy, ethnic language ability and use, ethnic food habits, and involvement in ethnic crafts. The French and German Catholics, the Mennonites, and the Doukhobors in Anderson's sample comprise four of the five prairie groups Dawson studied in 1936.

In Table 6-1 we see that sociocultural identity is high for most of the nine ethnic groups, although there are considerable variations. More than nine out of ten could speak their mother tongue, and two-thirds or more attended church regularly and married their own kind (endogamy). Except for the Germans and Scandinavians, two-thirds or more used their mother tongue at home frequently. Except for the French and German Catholics, a majority cooked and ate traditional ethnic foods. Over half of the groups reported extensive involvement in making traditional ethnic crafts. Generally, ethno-cultural identity was very high in rural northern Saskatchewan.

The Hutterites, segregated on colonies, had a perfect score of 100 on all five ethnocultural identity indicators, while the German Catholics had the lowest average identity score of 64. Interestingly, two of the Catholic groups (Ukrainian and Polish) scored very high, and two (French and German)

TABLE 6-1   COMPARISON OF NINE RURAL ETHNO-RELIGIOUS GROUPS AND
ETHNIC IDENTITY FACTORS

ETHNIC IDENTITY FACTORS (percentages):

Groups	N	Average Identity Scores	Ability to Speak Mother Tongue
Hutterites	(6)	100	100
Ukrainian Catholic	(154)	86	99
Polish Catholic	(15)	82	100
Ukrainian Orthodox	(83)	82	100
Mennonite	(244)	81	97
Doukhobor	(20)	76	95
Scandinavian Lutheran	(86)	76	90
French Catholic	(15)	73	99
German Catholic	(190)	64	93
Total Sample	(813)	80	97

SOURCE: Alan B. Anderson and Leo Driedger, 'The Mennonite Family' in K. Ishwaren (ed.), *Canadian Families: Ethnic Variations*. Toronto: McGraw-Hill Ryerson, 1980, pp. 161–80.

scored the lowest. This seems to indicate that ethnicity is more important to them than is religion. Religion does, however, seem to be an important factor in maintaining such a generally high rural ethnic identity. Church attendance is generally high. It is somewhat surprising to see that the Mennonites and Doukhobors are in the middle of the church attendance rankings, between the high and low Catholics, when we expected to see them among the highest rankings with the Hutterites.

All of these groups were segregated in rural ethnic enclaves where they could develop some demographic and institutional mass to build their ethnic institutions, although this varied by ethnic group. The Anderson findings confirm the findings of Dawson: the Mennonites and Doukhobors were more sect-like and retained their identity more, while the French and German Catholics, who are more church-like and somewhat more secularized, did not score as highly on the ethnic identity scale. In general, Anderson's findings show that ethnocultural identity in rural Saskatchewan is high, and that, although it declined somewhat by the third generation for which Anderson and Driedger (1980: 166–7) controlled, identity remained high.

A later study of the French Saskatchewan town of Gravelbourg, by Li and Denis (1983: 18–32), does show that there is a language shift to English. Although the majority in Gravelbourg are French, English is used widely in the school board and Board of Trade meetings. Younger, more educated third generation Gravelbourgians are shifting to English the most. Exogamy is the

TABLE 6-1 (CONTINUED)

ETHNIC IDENTITY FACTORS (percentages):

Groups	Extent of Endogamy	Regular Church Attendance	Frequent Use of Mother Tongue	Eating Ethnic Foods
Hutterites	100	100	100	100
Ukrainian Catholic	88	82	69	92
Polish Catholic	69	53	87	100
Ukrainian Orthodox	89	70	63	87
Mennonite	98	86	69	51
Doukhobor	60	55	70	100
Scandinavian Lutheran	96	87	37	69
French Catholic	91	91	78	4
German Catholic	90	94	29	2
Total Sample	91	86	60	47

greatest factor in shifting away from using French in the home (Li and Denis, 1983: 26, 27).

SOCIOCULTURAL FACTORS IN WINNIPEG

Numerous samples of ethnocultural identity in urban areas have been made, so we turn now to metropolitan ethnic studies which we expect will be harder to maintain. A random sample of 1560 questionnaires was collected by Driedger from seventy-six classes representing 15% of the undergraduate enrolment on the campus at the University of Manitoba. The following seven groups were represented in sufficient number (fifty or more) for the purpose of group comparisons: British (157), French (86), Germans (160), Jews (112), Poles (56), Scandinavians (61), and Ukrainians (188).

Driedger (1974, 1987) was the first to develop an Ethnic Cultural Identity (ECI) index in Canada involving both behavioural and attitudinal items in comparing seven groups of ethnic university students (French, Jewish, German, Ukrainian, Polish, British, and Scandinavian). A series of behavioural items were designed and analyzed. Six cultural identity factors emerged: religious practice, endogamy, ethnic language use, ethnic organizational participation, attendance in parochial schools, and extent of ethnic best friendships. Religion, endogamy, and language clearly were the most salient factors in that order, but this varied by ethnic group.

In Table 6-2 we see that one-half to three-fourths of the French students scored well on five of the six identity factors. They attended church at least twice a month; all their immediate family members had married French

TABLE 6-2 COMPARISON OF ETHNIC GROUPS BY SIX ETHNOCULTURAL FACTORS

BEHAVIOURAL IDENTITY FACTORS (percentages):

Ethnic Groups	Average Identity Scores	Religious Practice	Endogamy
French	55.0	54	65
Jewish	44.2	7	91
German	40.8	56	636
Ukrainian	36.8	44	76
Polish	31.5	46	53
British	29.3	3	72
Scandinavian	16.4	15	67

SOURCE: Leo Driedger, 'Ethnic Boundaries' in G.A. Theodorson (ed.), *Urban Patterns*. University Park, PA: Penn State University Press, 1982.

spouses; they spoke French to their parents at home; they participated in French voluntary organizations and attended a French school for at least a year; and a majority of their best friends were French. Their total composite identity score of 55.0 (the sum of the six factor scores divided by six) was the highest of the seven ethnic groups. Scandinavian students ranked lowest (16.4) with one-fourth or less who scored on any of the five factors excluding endogamy.

The profiles of the seven ethnic groups vary greatly. The French regularly scored high and the Scandinavians scored low most consistently. Jewish students scored very high on endogamy and attendance at Jewish schools, but very low on religious attendance and ethnic language use. The Germans and Ukrainians scored moderately on most factors. Driedger (1976) concluded that the ethnic cultural identity of the French and Jews was high, and that the sense of identity of the Scandinavians was low. In terms of the theories discussed in Chapter Two, the French and Jews followed the pluralist pattern, retaining their identity; the Scandinavians followed the assimilationist patterns with loss of identity; and the Germans, Ukrainians, and Poles demonstrated varied states of modified pluralism and assimilation. Driedger (1975) found that measures of both behavioural (ECBI scale) and attitudinal (ECAI scale) identity correlated very highly, and these in turn correlated highly with the degree of institutional completeness that ethnic groups had developed (Breton, 1964).

NON-CHARTER IDENTITY IN FIVE CITIES

The Anderson and Driedger studies involved rural adults and urban students in two provinces of the prairie region. O'Bryan, Reitz, and Kuplowska (1976),

TABLE 6-2 (CONTINUED)

BEHAVIOURAL IDENTITY FACTORS (percentages):

Ethnic Groups	Ethnic Languages Use	Ethnic Organizations Participation	Parochial Education Attendance	Best Friends Ethnic
French	61	23	79	49
Jewish	2	29	74	63
German	29	16	44	36
Ukrainian	22	23	41	16
Polish	14	13	57	5
British	—	10	27	45
Scandinavian	0	2	25	0

in contrast, collected data on ethnocultural identity of adults in five cities (Montreal, Toronto, Winnipeg, Edmonton, and Vancouver) which provide us with information from at least three of the Canadian regions discussed in Chapter Four. They also used six ethnocultural identity indicators but confined their study to adults of ten non-charter groups: Chinese, Dutch, German, Greek, Hungarian, Italian, Polish, Portuguese, Scandinavian, and Ukrainian, randomly selected to represent the urban populations of the ten ethnic groups in these five cities. The charter groups (British and French), who represent over half of the Canadian population, were not included.

In Table 6-3 we present comparative data on five ethnocultural indicators: church attendance, language use, ethnic language fluency, listening to ethnic radio, and reading ethnic ingroup newspapers. Except for the Chinese, weekly attendance at church was extensive in all ethnic groups (55–86%) as a strong indicator of identity. Ethnic radio and newspapers were the least important; language use and ability were important for respondents of half of the groups (Hungarian, Greek, Chinese, Italian, and Portuguese).

We have ranked the ten ethnic groups using average ethnic identity scores (the sum of the five indicators divided by 5), with the Hungarians on top and the Scandinavians at the bottom. We note that the Chinese and those immigrants who came after the Second World War rank in the top half, indicating the highest identity, while North Europeans who have been in Canada for one hundred years or more rank the lowest. Except for church attendance, the Scandinavians indicate low ethnic identity; this is similar to Driedger's findings in Winnipeg. Interestingly, groups such as the Greeks, Portuguese, Italians, and Chinese (who Balakrishnan and Kralt found highly segregated in Montreal, Toronto, and Vancouver) also show higher ethnic identity. Indeed, Reitz (1980:118) used the same data and found high correlations (Pearson's r)

Tꓮꓐᒪꓰ 6-3   Comparison of Ten Non-Charter Urban Ethnic Groups by Five Ethnocultural Factors

Ethnic Group	Average Identity Score	Weekly Ingroup Church Attendance	Frequent Ingroup Language Use
Hungarian	57	75	64
Greek	56	75	92
Portuguese	54	86	95
Italian	51	75	84
Chinese	45	36	88
Polish	42	74	46
German	39	69	46
Ukrainian	39	63	49
Dutch	38	80	40
Scandinavian	29	55	14
Totals		72	63

SOURCE: K.G. O'Bryan, J.G. Reitz and O.M. Kuplowska, *Non-Official Languages: A Study in Canadian Multiculturalism*. Ottawa: Minister of Supply and Services, 1976, pp. 214–45.

among these ethnic identity indicators ranging from .50 to .56. The Pearson r method correlates high or low statistical correlations between two variables on a scale of zero to unity. The correlation between residential segregation and identity factors was somewhat lower, but still significant.

Comparisons of the five cities from which data were collected show some interesting variations as well. Mother-tongue fluency tended to be highest in Toronto, the most multicultural urban setting. Ethnic language use was most common in Montreal and Toronto. O'Bryan et al. (1976) and Breton et al. (1990) also controlled for generation, and they found that there was a great decline in language knowledge and use by the third generation, but that church attendance declined only marginally in the same period. This suggests that more indicators of ethnic identity are needed to trace the total ethnic identity profile. These indicators should include controls for generation, size of community, types of indicators, and ethnic groups.

ETHNIC IDENTITY IN TORONTO

Raymond Breton et al. (1990) did a random survey of 2,338 adult respondents in Toronto. The survey included a series of sub-projects, one of which was designed to measure ethnic identity, This is an in-depth study of ethnic identity in Toronto, the largest and most multicultural city in Canada.

Isajiw and Driedger (1987) developed two ethnic identity indexes using

TABLE 6-3 (CONTINUED)

Ethnic Group	Fluent in Ingroup Language	Regular Ingroup Radio Listening	Regular Ingroup Newspaper Reading
Hungarian	64	58	24
Greek	79	10	26
Portuguese	56	15	18
Italian	60	10	24
Chinese	53	17	34
Polish	36	32	21
German	50	19	19
Ukrainian	31	32	20
Dutch	49	6	13
Scandinavian	23	42	10
Totals	50	24	21

the Toronto data: one a six-item Ethnic Cultural Identity (ECI) index, and the other a Symbolic Ethnic Identity (SEI) index. In Table 6-4 we show the Ethnic Cultural Identity Index and how eight ethnic groups (West Indian, Jewish, Chinese, Italian, Ukrainian, Portuguese, British, and German) scored on ethnic cultural items. This ECI index is similar to Driedger's ECI index used to measure ethnocultural identity in Winnipeg.

The average ECI ranking shows that the West Indians, Chinese, and Jews ranked the highest; the Germans and British ranked lowest; and the Italians, Ukrainians, and Portuguese ranked in between. West Indians chose a majority of their friends (79%) from their ingroup and used their media (66%) more than any of the others. The Chinese cooked Chinese foods on holidays (98%) and read Chinese newspapers (69%) more than any of the others, and Jews felt obligated to marry within the group (75%) more than others. The extent of Jewish identity behaviour should be noted, since a majority were second- and third-generation Canadians (Isajiw and Driedger, 1987).

The Germans and British ranked lowest, indicating the least activity in ingroup ethnic cultural behaviour. The Germans ranked last or second-last on all but one of the six indicators; except for cooking German food on holidays (50%), fewer than half were engaged in any ingroup activities. Activities of Britsh respondents were also low, except that 70% indicated that a majority of their best friends were British. Italian, Ukrainian, and Portuguese respondents ranked intermediately. It should be noted that, while the Italian and Ukrainian groups included three generations, the Portuguese were all first-generation.

TABLE 6-4   ETHNIC CULTURAL IDENTITY (ECI) IN TORONTO USING SIX
INDICATORS

ETHNIC CULTURAL IDENTITY (ECI) INDEX (percentages):

Ethnic Origin	ECI Average Scores & Rank	Use Ingroup Language	Consider Endogamy Obligatory
West Indian	68.4	—	39
Chinese	65.9	83	42
Jewish	58.6	0	75
Italian	51.6	65	25
Ukrainian	44.1	50	33
Portuguese	43.5	99	24
British	39.3	—	10
German	26.5	35	1

SOURCE: Breton et al., *Ethnic Identity and Equality.* Toronto: University of Toronto Press, 1990, pp. 51–83.

We expect that their extensive language use will drop considerably as they proceed through the second and third generations (as it does for most others).

As Driedger found in his sample, different ethnic groups score differently on the six factors. For example, use of ethnic food ranked first for all groups except the Portuguese and British, for whom it ranked second. This holds true even for the Jews, Italians, Ukrainians, and Germans, who were represented by many second- and third-generation members. It seems to be one of the most stable indicators over time. On the other hand, groups which included only first-generation members (such as the Portuguese and Chinese) scored high on language use, which usually declines greatly in succeeding generations. This shows that it is difficult to control for all the variations, and it is most important that a number of indicators of ethnic cultural identity be used in an index so that the different groups have some opportunity to score well.

By using ethnic cultural identity (ECI), we find that West Indians, Chinese, and Jews scored high on ethnic identity, and that Germans and the British scored low. Isajiw and Driedger (1987) turned to symbolic measures of identity to see whether different items measuring another dimension of ethnic identity correlated with the index just designed, and to see how eight ethnic groups in the sample fare with respect to a second index using symbolic items.

SYMBOLIC INTERACTIONALIST ETHNIC IDENTIFICATION

Max Weber was one of the first to focus on the symbolic features of society. Recently, Raymond Breton (1984: 124) followed Weber's lead:

TABLE 6-4 (CONTINUED)

ETHNIC CULTURAL IDENTITY (ECI) INDEX (percentages):

Ethnic Origin	Majority of Friends Ingroup	Use Ingroup Media	Read Ingroup Newspapers	Use Ethnic Foods
West Indian	79	66	69	88
Chinese	54	49	69	98
Jewish	78	29	59	91
Italian	68	26	38	86
Ukrainian	48	34	39	80
Portuguese	17	36	23	63
British	70	49	25	42
German	49	5	20	50

I would like to argue that much of society's activities cannot be adequately understood if we over-emphasize the material dimension to the detriment of the symbolic dimension of social organization. This analysis will apply notions and propositions from Weber, analysts of symbolic behaviour, including symbolic inter-actionists. . . . Attention will be given to the processes involved in attempting to regenerate the cultural-symbolic capital of the society—to restructure the collective identity and the associated symbolic contents.

Breton (1984: 127) suggests that, historically, nation-building was symbolically oriented toward the construction of a British type of society in Canada. Being Canadian was defined as speaking English within a British legal, educational, and economic institutional system. However, since the work of the Bilingual and Bicultural Commission in the 1960s, efforts have been made to change the symbolic system to include the French:

Numerous changes in the symbols themselves were introduced: for instance a Canadian flag was adopted in 1965; Trans-Canada Airlines became Air Canada; the Dominion Bureau of Statistics became Statistics Canada; 'O Canada' was proclaimed as the national anthem; stamps were changed; money was redesigned with more Canadian symbols; and the Constitution was patriated (formerly called the British North America Act). (Breton, 1984: 127)

In 1971, when Prime Minister Trudeau proclaimed Canada a multicultural society within a bilingual framework, he was symbolically including all

Canadians, especially non-charter groups, when he said, 'Such a policy should help to break down discriminatory attitudes and cultural jealousies. National unity, if it is to mean anything in the deeply personal sense, must be founded on one's own individual identity. Out of this can grow respect for that of others . . . based on fair play for all' (House of Commons Debates, 1971: 8545).

In this section we shall examine the extent to which Canadians indeed identify with various 'ethnic', 'hyphenated', or 'Canadian' symbols. So far, relatively few scholars (O'Bryan et al., 1976; Berry et al., 1977; Frideres and Goldenberg, 1977; Mackie, 1978; and Driedger, 1980) have addressed the problems of ethnic, regional, and national identification. Among the studies that have sought to clarify and solve problems of Canadian ethnic identification, and that illustrate ethnic identification variations within regions of Canada, are those made by Boyd et al. (1981), Berry et al. (1977), O'Bryan et al. (1976), Mackie (1978), Frideres and Goldenberg (1977), (Reitz and Breton, 1994), probing Canadian ethnic, regional, and national identification.

NATIONAL ETHNIC IDENTIFICATION

Berry et al. (1977) collected a national sample of 1,849 respondents. The survey provided individuals wider opportunity to identify both their national and their ethnic identity. Berry et al. analyzed their data by regional representation and showed the preferences expressed by various ethnic groups. Their study illustrates a richly varied combination of national and/or ethnic preferences.

The sample gave Canadian adults the opportunity to place themselves in one of eight categories (father's ethnic origin, mother's ethnic origin, father's ethnic-Canadian identity, mother's ethnic-Canadian identity, or respondent's choice of English-Canadian, French-Canadian, Québécois, or Canadian identity). The results are shown in Table 6-5.

Approximately one-fourth (23%) preferred a specific ethnic category, almost one-fifth (18%) preferred a hyphenated identity, and over one-half (59%) preferred the 'Canadian' identification.

More detailed analysis shows that most respondents of British origin (81%) preferred the 'Canadian' category, respondents of French origin (66%) favoured the 'hyphenated' option, and 'other' adults (33%) chose the 'ethnic' category (Berry et al., 1977: 36–8). Because ethnic groups are not proportionately represented in all regions of Canada, Berry et al. found that 'Canadian' was most popular in the Atlantic provinces where the population is mainly of British origin; the 'hyphenated' version (French-Canadian) was most popular in Quebec since 80% of the province's population is of French origin and whose ancestors have been in Canada for centuries; the straight 'ethnic' choice was made more often on the prairies where no group comprises a majority, forming a multicultural pattern.

The data of Berry and associates (1977) show how important it is to get a national sample if we wish to get some sense of preferred ethnic and regional

TABLE 6-5   A COMPARISON OF FOUR ADULT STUDIES ON ETHNIC AND
NATIONAL IDENTIFICATION

Ethnic Categories of Identification	Berry, et al. National Sample 1974		O'Bryan, et al. 5 cities Sample 1973		Kennedy, et al. Edmonton Sample 1980	Driedger, et al. Winnipeg Sample 1980
Ethnic	23		18		37	50
Ethnic		16				
Québécois		7				
Hyphenated	18		46		8	10
French-Canadian		14				
English-Canadian		4				
Ethnic-Canadian				33		
Canadian-Ethnic				13		
Canadian	59		36		48	30
Other					7	10
	N= 1849		N= 2433		N= 398	N= 332

SOURCE: Leo Driedger et al., 'Ethnic Identification: Variations in Regional and National Preference', *Canadian Ethnic Studies* 14 (1982): 57–68.

identification in Canada that considers regional differences. A sampling in any one region cannot be presumed to represent the whole of Canada. The Québécois preference show how intense such ethnic identification can become. On the other hand, it also shows how respondents of British origin chose to relabel their loyalties by adopting the 'Canadian' label. As the largest and most powerful group, the British can afford to abandon the 'ethnic' symbol, hoping that others will join them under a new national symbol strongly influenced by British history, culture, and language.

ETHNIC IDENTIFICATION IN CITIES
O'Bryan, Reitz, and Kuplowska (1976) collected a sample of ten non-official language groups in five cities (Montreal, Toronto, Winnipeg, Edmonton, and Vancouver). The charter groups (British and French), adults in rural areas, and the Atlantic region were not represented. If the Berry (1977) national study is representative of ethnic and national preferences, then we would expect respondents in the O'Bryan (1976) sample to prefer the straight 'ethnic' symbol more than the 'Canadian' and 'hyphenated' ones that are most popular with the British and French respectively, who are not represented in this sample.

In Table 6-5 we see that, as expected, only 36% chose the 'Canadian' category, and that the 'hyphenated' identification was most popular (45%). This suggests that modifications are taking place, as suggested by modified assimilation and pluralism theories in Chapter Two. Respondents were given four

TABLE 6-6   ETHNIC PREFERENCE OF WINNIPEG AND EDMONTON ADULTS, 1980

| | | WINNIPEG | | |
| | | Respondent's Classification of: | | |
Ethnic Categories	Self	Spouse	Mother	Father
Ethnic	50	55	70	70
Hyphenated	10	10	8	7
Canadian	30	28	15	16
Other	10	7	7	7
	N 332	198	333	332

SOURCE: Leo Driedger, Charlene Thacker, and Raymond Currie, 'Ethnic Identification: Variations in Regional and National Preferences'. *Canadian Ethnic Studies* 14 (1982): 57–68.

options (ethnic, ethnic-Canadian, Canadian-ethnic, and Canadian). In the Berry sample, the Québécois and rural respondents inflated the 'ethnic' and 'ethnic Canadian' first, indicating the salience of a somewhat modified ethnicity that leans toward pluralism rather than assimilation. The high number in the hyphenated category seems to suggest that urban 'ethnics' have accommodated themselves somewhat as a result of urbanization, although 'ethnic' still precedes 'Canadian'. This clearly shows the need for modified theories of ethnic change.

Jeffrey Reitz (1980: 113) based his entire book on the O'Bryan et al. (1976) data and found a direct correlation between ethnic identification and ingroup friends. Nearly two-thirds (64%) of those who reported no ethnic ingroup friends also designated themselves as 'Canadian', while only 7% of those who designated themselves as 'ethnic' reported no ingroup friends. The first group shows assimilation, and the second shows pluralism. The correlations between ethnic identification and language retention (Pearson's r of .53), ingroup interaction (.46), ethnic church affilation (.40), ethnic neighbourhood residence (.32), and endogamy (.31) were all quite significant (Reitz, 1980: 116, 118). Identification under such categories (ethnic, ethnic-Canadian, Canadian-ethnic, and Canadian) may well be more a measure of ethnic salience (identity or assimilation) than an objective measure of ethnic heritage. Reitz (1980: 20) clearly shows that correlations of ethnic origin and ethnic identification also vary considerably by ethnic categories (Chinese, 82%; South Europeans, 71%; East Europeans, 39%; and North Europeans, 30%).

IDENTIFICATION IN THE PRAIRIES

Edmonton and Winnipeg area studies were coordinated by Driedger et al. (1980) using the same sampling design, interview schedule, and data collection method. Respondents were given the opportunity to choose their own category of identification without pre-classification. In Table 6-6 we see that

TABLE 6-6 (CONTINUED)

| | EDMONTON | | | |
| | | Respondent's Classification of: | | |
Ethnic Categories	Self	Spouse	Mother	Father
Ethnic	37	40	57	62
Hyphenated	8	9	8	7
Canadian	48	45	28	27
Other	7	7	7	4
	398	261	390	394

most of the respondents in Winnipeg and Edmonton answered the question 'How would you define your ethnicity?' in three categories (ethnic, Canadian, and hyphenated). Most of them also used the same categories to define the ethnicity of their spouse, mother, and father. Overall the 'ethnic' category was the most popular, with 'Canadian' a strong second. The 'hyphenated' category (e.g., Greek-Canadian) was chosen by 10% or less, making it a fairly insignificant category compared to the other two. As expected, these three categories were most popular.

Comparing Winnipeg and Edmonton, we note that one-half (50%) of the respondents in Winnipeg preferred the 'ethnic' category, and about one-third (30%) the 'Canadian' category, while in Edmonton the preferences were reversed (49% 'Canadian' and 37% 'ethnic'). As expected, respondents in the slower growth centre of Winnipeg preferred 'ethnic', while more respondents of the faster-growing Edmonton preferred 'Canadian'.

Third, the respondents' classification of their spouse and parents tended to be more 'ethnic' than the respondents' self-identification in both Winnipeg and Edmonton. This suggests that respondents have the tendency to apply the 'ethnic' criterion more to others than to themselves or that their own ethnic identity is no longer as salient as that of their parents. It is clear that respondents in both Winnipeg and Edmonton classified their parents as highly 'ethnic' (70 and 60% respectively). In Winnipeg, only one-seventh classified their parents as 'Canadian', and in Edmonton only one-fourth did so. Over all, the 'ethnic' category is still very popular (Driedger et al., 1982).

We conclude that regionalism must be controlled. As the Berry study shows, the British in the Atlantic region prefer to be known as 'Canadian', the French in Quebec prefer hyphenated or ethno-local (Québécois) categories, and straight 'ethnic' labels are popular in the multicultural West. We cannot assume that preferences in any one region will be uniform. Increasing preferences for 'Canadian' identification in Edmonton and Calgary as compared to

Winnipeg suggest that rapid change does wean some people from 'ethnic' identification into assimilation or Anglo-conformity.

The use of adult samples collected randomly is of crucial importance if we wish to get some sense of proportion and the importance of ethnic, regional, and national identification. The national data collected by Berry and associates is clearly preferable.

Free ethnic classification of oneself (as used by Driedger et al., 1982) seems to be a more subjective approach and it is difficult to know which criteria guide the respondent's choice. Moreover, free ethnic classification seems to be a measure of identity and assimilation, showing whether the original ethnic milieu or the Canadian context is the more influential cultural pole.

This seems to suggest that the most objective data we can collect is 'ethnic origin' as the census has done for over a century. Other studies suggest the value of additional smaller studies designed to measure the degree to which ethnicity is still salient. If we should abandom the 'ethnic origin' questions, then we would be left only with more subjective data which is less longitudinal, and less consistently and systematically collected.

We recommend that in the future both objective and subjective dimensions of ethnic research are needed. The objective ethnic origin data are useful as a measure of the cultural and social milieu in which respondents were raised; the subjective choice may be more valuable as an assessment of the individual's self-identity and as a measure of assimilation.

SUMMARY

Ethnic identification may be defined as a positive personal attitude and attachment to a group with whom the individual believes he has a common ancestry based on shared characteristics and shared sociocultural experiences. Such identification can take place at various levels, ranging from persons to groups and categories such as ethnicity. Similarly there may be identification with a territory, ethnic institutions, culture, historical symbols, ideology, or leaders.

The sociocultural theory of identity deals with a macro ontology and sociological methodology using survey field study, survey research, and sociohistorical analysis focusing on social and cultural items of ethnicity. The interactionist orientation is more micro-sociological, dealing with symbols and their importance for social relationships. A review of the literature shows that more work has been done on sociocultural macro orientation, out of which a multiplicity of factors has developed, demonstrating that sociocultural ethnic identity is multidimensional and complex.

Anderson's ethnoreligious probing of identity of nine groups in rural Saskatchewan showed that some identity factors are more important than others, and that the various ethnic groups also vary in the importance they attach to each of these identity factors. Driedger's study of sociocultural factors in Winnipeg found that of the seven ethnic groups compared, the French and Jews indicated high identity and the Scandinavians low identity, but that all groups scored differently on the six factors used. O'Bryan et al., comparing the ten non-charter groups in five Canadian cities, found them similarly diverse of identification; they also found a decline in the use of language by the third generation, but little decline in ethnic food-eating habits. Isajiw's findings on ethnic identity in Toronto using six factors and eight groups found similar diversity in the importance of the various identity factors and the weight the ethnic groups gave to each.

Studies on symbolic ethnic identification revealed that here, too, there were ethnic group, regional, and other factors which resulted in varied forms of symbolic identification. Berry et al., in their national sample, found that the 'Canadian' designation was most popular, followed by 'ethnic' and 'hyphenated' identification, followed by 'Canadian' and 'ethnic' symbols. Driedger et al. found that the 'ethnic' designation was most popular in Winnipeg, but in Edmonton, also a prairie city, scholars found that the 'Canadian' designation was more popular. These findings show that symbolic identification varies by ethnic group, region, city, and generation.

Generally, for some ethnic groups in Canada both ethnocultural and symbolic ethnic identity are clearly present. The diversity of the population makes for a variety of expressions of identity, so that other ethnic groups no longer expressed high ethnic identity; presumably they had amalgamated or assimilated. Some groups contribute to a multicultural plural society, while others follow the assimilation or modified assimilation models discussed in Chapter Two. Anglo-conformity is also evident for some.

Ethnic identity is always in the process of change, and the modified forms of pluralism and assimilation as discussed in Chapter Two make for a variety of changes among groups. Sorting and controlling for these many factors makes for interesting but very complex research challenges. The theories and methodologies required to document these changes are too often inadequate.

CHAPTER 7

Construction of a Sacred Reality

Chapter Six outlined Arnold Dashefsky's (1975) fourfold theoretical classification of ethnic identity, and discussed the two sociocultural and interactionist, macro and micro, forms of sociological ethnic identity.

This chapter will focus on Dashefsky's micro interactionist cell of ethnic
identity by considering smaller, less influential ethnic groups such as the
Aboriginals, the Hutterites, and the Jews. While sociocultural characteristics
will again be considered, this time we want to look increasingly at symbolic
interactionist characteristics, with a focus on the concept of 'The Sacred'.
While religion will be one aspect of 'The Sacred', we need to look at this phenomenon much more broadly to include sociocultural elements as the
Aboriginals, Hutterites, and Jews all do. We shall propose that these three
religio-ethnic groups represent three types of development along a tradi-
tional-urban continuum into which most other ethnic groups in Canada can
be fitted. It is the identity of groups such as these that has led Canadians to
consider multiculturalism as an option.

IN SEARCH OF SACRED SOCIALIZATION

Durkheim was interested in social cohesion and the forms of solidarity that
humans developed to stave off anomie and alienation. In his early writings,
Durkheim concluded that features such as contract, beliefs, and ritual were
important elements of a sense of 'The Sacred'. To study this subtle and pro-
found phenomenon, he changed his methodology from using empirical data
collection as he had in *Suicide*, to using the more qualitative methods of
inquiry often used by anthropologists: studying whole communities to better
gather the quality of relationships found in more primitive religions. He used
the latter approach in *Elementary Forms of Religious Life*.

Durkheim went back to a study of pre-modern societies because he wanted
to see what the sense of wholeness of life entailed; he concluded that human
contact with forces sometimes labelled mana, orenda, or a totemic principle

was always present (Durkheim, 1912: 363). Thus, he concluded that a focus of beliefs on a Sacred force or forces that guides humans is central. Humans then are faced with linking to these forces of belief and developing rituals that direct human action in line with them. Durkheim concluded that this focus on the Sacred was socially created, thus emphasizing the importance of ritual to reinforce beliefs in the Sacred. He found that in the pre-industrial societies he studied, all of life became a part of religious ritual and the whole community was seen as a sacred endeavour or enterprise. This, he concluded, brought wholeness and a sense of the sacredness of everything that was done as 'a people'. He thought that this sensibility was partly or largely lost in the process of industrialization, his major concern for modern France. This integration of the all into the Sacred is the means to fight anomie, or normlessness, which often leads to the hopelessness and suicide prevalent in modern industrial society.

Bronislaw Malinowski (1945) was also concerned with similar questions of cohesion and ritual; he found that the most elaborate rituals among the Pacific Trobriand Islanders occurred when they prepared for dangerous deep-sea fishing. Religious practitioners engaged in prolonged and elaborate regularized rituals to protect fishermen who were going offshore, but not those who engaged in safer fishing on the shores. He too concluded that the Sacred was an important part in a sense of community and human well-being.

Many anthropologists conclude from their studies that 1) religion or magic is a vital mechanism in unifying life-giving symbols and integrating humans socially; 2) creeds, beliefs, ritual, and ceremony are enduring elements of community solidarity; and 3) religion is an integral part of social integration as well as a seedbed for social change (Nisbet, 1974: 165).

Recent modern sociologists have suggested that becoming Sacred is very much a process which they have called sacralization of identity (Mol, 1976: 1). Andrew Greeley (1989: 11) said the 'Sacralizing tendency' involves a process in which 'the symbols even of a secular faith are so set apart from the profane, and eventually so cloaked with ritual and tradition, that they become in fact "functionally sacred".' It is in this sense that we shall consider the Sacred as more than religion, but as the whole process of setting apart and preserving as special some aspects of life (such as ethnicity) which are considered very important and which should endure. In line with this trend of thinking, Hans Mol (1976: 5, 15) defines sacralization as:

> the process by means of which man has preeminently safeguarded and reinforced this complex of orderly interpretations of reality, rules and legitimations. . . . It is a sort of brake applied to unchecked infinite adaptations in symbolic systems . . . for the emotional security of personality and the integration of tribe or community. . . . It safeguards identity, a system of meaning, or a definition of reality; and it modifies, obstructs, or legitimates change.

Thus, it is a process rather than a state.

Max Weber's (1978) concept of charisma has many sacred elements such as being set apart or qualities that seem to be supernatural or not accessible to the ordinary person (Hamm, 1987: 14–18). Weber's symbolic emphases have been taken farther by Peter Berger, who suggests that rather than looking at the structural functional outward dimensions of religion, we need to also look within from the standpoint of Weber's *Verstehen* or deep understanding (Berger, 1967). Thus, we need to look at Berger's 'sacred canopy' and the whole idea of nomos-building which has to do with symbolic forms of the Sacred and human experience as part of ethnic identification.

NOMOS-BUILDING OF SACRED CANOPIES

Peter Berger (1967: 19) writes about the socially constructed world as 'an ordering of experience, into a meaningful order, or nomos, which is imposed upon the discrete experiences and meanings of individuals. . . . To participate in the society is to share its "knowledge", that is, co-inhabit its nomos.' He continues:

> The socially established nomos may thus be understood, perhaps in its most important aspect, as a shield against terror. Put differently, the most important function of society is nominization. The anthropological presupposition for this is a human craving for meaning that appears to have the force of instinct. Men are congenitally compelled to impose meaningful order upon reality. This order, however, presupposes the social enterprise of ordering world construction. To be separated from society exposes the individual to a multiplicity of dangers which he is unable to cope with himself. . . . The ultimate danger of the individual separation from society is meaninglessness. (Berger, 1967: 22)

Thus, anomie is normlessness or life without a meaningful construct of reality (Durkheim, 1965; Berger, 1967).

A key element of the Sacred is the 'sharing of society's knowledge and the co-habitation of its nomos' (Driedger, 1980b: 342). This suggests the need of humans to belong to a fairly stable community or network where indepth sharing and participating can take place. 'Co-habitation' implies the considerable commitment to a group of people that usually takes place in families, but Berger thinks this must be extended to a larger community, because the nuclear family is no longer a sufficiently large network. Co-habitation also suggests that considerable quality time be spent within the context of a cohesive *gemeinschaft*, a meaningful support which satisfies real social needs (Driedger, 1980b: 342). 'Sharing of knowledge' implies identification with some ideals and being able to contribute to a sense of richness of belonging which uplifts and challenges. Industrialization usually has a way of detracting from this sense of wholeness and meaning, substituting the drive for materialism. It is at this point, Berger says, that religion enters significantly into the argument.

> Religion is the human enterprise by which a sacred cosmos is established. Put differently, religion is cosmization in a sacred mode. By sacred is meant here a quality of mysterious and awesome power, other than man and yet related to him, which is believed to reside in certain objects of experience. (Berger, 1967: 25)

The sacred cosmos is confronted by humans as an immensely powerful reality other than humanity. Some post-moderns are willing to call this 'spiritual' reality.

To bridge the macro and micro realities, we propose to use the concept of a sacred canopy, also introduced by Peter Berger (1967). While Berger speaks of the socially constructed world as an ordering of experience into a meaningful order, or nomos, which acts as a shield against terror, he also speaks of a 'sacred canopy'—a tent-like roof used by the Jews as a symbol of protection. It was a large blanket with long stakes attached to each of the four corners to hold it up. This symbolism is useful for our discussion because the blanket can be seen as a roof that protects those who are inside from the onslaughts outside. The stakes are also important because without stakes there would be nothing to hold up the roof. One or two stakes are hardly adequate: four or more provide a better cover. Furthermore, stakes in the canopy can be replaced or substituted by new ones, or better ones, and the various components of the canopy are adjustable. And finally, the canopy is mobile. It can be folded, transported, and pitched again in new places. Nomos-building can be seen as pitching a sacred tent which shields the individual or group from terror or meaninglessness. It houses a 'reality'—a meaningful order or nomos.

Four stakes which hold up the canopy will be considered: 1) an ideology or religion, 2) a community, 3) an ethnic culture, and 4) land or territory in which the group resides (Driedger, 1989). All four components are in a symbiotic relationship. That is, the land will act as a crucible in which the community and culture are formed, and the religious ideology is moulded by these outer circumstances and is a driving force that in turn shapes the community and culture. The task will be to delineate the state of the sacred reality in its original time and place, and to examine how the ideology, community, culture, and territory were either reconstructed, transferred, or transformed as the sacred canopy.

Since there are many ethnoreligious groups in Canada, we need to select several so that we can examine changes in their sacred canopies. Aboriginals (especially the Blackfoot), the Hutterites, and the Jews have been chosen for specific reasons. As food-gathering people, the prairie Indians were faced with a complete reconstruction of their sacred canopy when they were forced from the open plains onto reserves. The Hutterites, as food-gathering agriculturists, literally transferred their communal society from Europe to the North American prairies with its ideology and structure intact. The Jews represent yet another form of change because they transformed their east European *shtetl* ghettos into segregated urban communities. We plan to discuss the changes in these three sacred canopies as three different types into which the many other religious and ethnic groups can be fitted. We propose that some canopies provided a better shelter from terror and meaninglessness than others. First, we shall examine the original structures of these sacred canopy types, the changes and adaptations made to them, and the social processes involved in these changes.

CONSTRUCTION OF SACRED CANOPIES

Berger's (1967) concept of constructing a nomos to create meaning is directly applicable to the Canadian ethnic scene. Numerous historical events could illustrate the formation of sacred canopies, but we shall briefly sketch early Aboriginal food-gathering, the coming of the agrarian European immigrants typified by the Hutterites, and the more recent migration to the cities represented best by the Jews, but also the Chinese. Each of these three types was threatened by anomie; however, reconstruction, transferral, and transformation of their social and sacred realities occurred with new identification in various changing situations.

RECONSTRUCTION OF THE CANOPY: ABORIGINAL FOOD-GATHERERS

'An area as large as Europe, bounded on the north by the "Barren lands", on the west by the snow-capped Rockies, and on the south by the arid plains, was transferred by Charles II's sweeping gesture in the overlordship of the Hudson's Bay Company' (Stanley, 1960: 3). This happened in 1670, when scattered throughout the area were thousands of aboriginals, who made up three great linguistic groups: the Algonkin, the Athapascan, and the Siouian. Several expeditions were dispatched inland to draw the remote tribes to the trading posts of the Hudson's Bay Company. As early as 1690, Henry Kelsey was sent to visit some of the tribes in the interior, and it appears he reached what is now Saskatchewan. While the English were penetrating Rupert's Land from Hudson Bay, the French also pressed westward. La Vérendrye and his sons opened the door to the Northwest during 1732 to 1743, when they discovered the Red River, built Fort Rouge on the site of what is now Winnipeg, and pressed onwards to the Saskatchewan River.

The Indians that the Whites described between 1830 and 1880 had the most highly developed hunting culture in the world. It was a materially rich situation for hunters. A Native population of only 150,000 people was harvesting the herds of millions of buffalo. They were extremely diverse in languages, speaking some 25 languages related to each other in six families, and four phyls. Still, it was a generally uniform culture, as though a few patterns for the region had developed over thousands of years. (Price, 1979: 165)

Price (1979: 167) suggests that the Blackfoot stayed in place in Alberta on the northern plains for approximately 10,000 years, so we shall use ethnographic sources by Price (1979), Ponting (1986), Dickason (1992), Frideres (1993), and McMillan (1995) as background.

Perhaps the most important stake in the sacred canopy of the Aboriginals were the plains, a land area which was sometimes referred to by the Europeans as 'The Great American Desert', a myth that persisted because Europeans who populated the Canadian east were used to woodlands territory. In 1700 there were an estimated sixty million buffalo on the plains; they were the major source of food for the plains Indians (Price, 1979). By 1885, because of the earlier introduction of the horse and the excessive hunting that followed, the buffalo had become virtually extinct. The economic base of the prairie Indians was destroyed, causing severe starvation. The eleven treaties made with the prairie Indians beginning in 1871 herded them onto segregated Indian reserves and restricted their lifestyle. They were to become relatively immobile, like the agriculturists, without the will or the skills to eke out a new life. A major stake in the sacred canopy had been severed (Cardinal, 1977; Asch, 1984; Ponting, 1986).

When the economic base of the plains Indians in the West had been demolished with the demise of the buffalo, the great plains lay open for a final onslaught by European agricultural immigrants. A series of treaties numbered 1 to 11 was signed, beginning with Treaty One at Fort Garry, near Winnipeg. In Figure 7-1 we see that a few treaties (A-E) had been made in southern Ontario or Upper Canada and the west coast, but none were made in the five most easterly provinces and most of British Columbia (Ponting, 1986; McMillan, 1995). The signing of the eleven treaties began in 1871, a year after Manitoba became a part of the Canadian Confederation. Manitoba became the European foothold in the West once the Selkirk settlement was established. The treaties fanned out in horseshoe fashion westward and then in a northerly and easterly direction as the European immigrants continued to invade the territory. By 1921 these treaties had reached up the Mackenzie Valley into the Yukon and the western Northwest Territories with the signing of Treaty Eleven. The land stake in the sacred canopy of the aboriginals was greatly eroded by herding the Aboriginals onto Indian reserves in much of this new treaty territory. Much of the eastern Northwest Territories, eastern Canada, and the west coast still remain untreatied (Frideres, 1993; McMillan, 1995).

FIGURE 7-1   TREATY AREAS IN CANADA

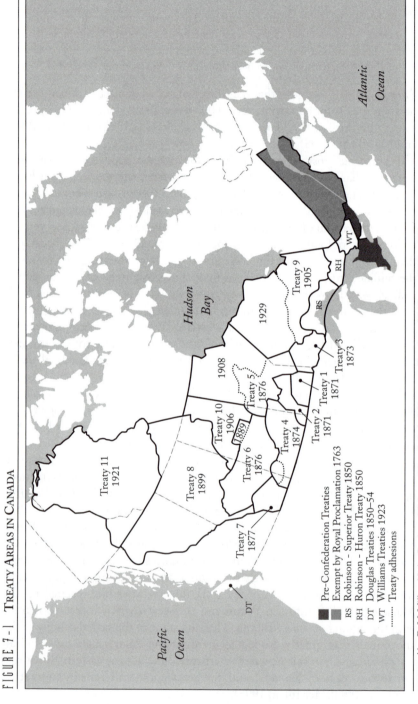

SOURCE: Alan D. McMillan, *Native Peoples and Cultures of Canada*, 2nd ed. Vancouver: Douglas and McIntyre, 1995, p. 317.

Price (1979: 164) says the culture of the prairie and plains Indians had many features in common: 'All the societies had the hide tipi; bows and arrows; leather containers, breechcloths, leggings, shirts and moccasins, and buffalo robes. Things were light and portable, adapted to a nomadic hunting way of life.' At first they hunted on foot, but later the horse was introduced and greatly increased their effectiveness in buffalo hunting. The Blackfoot farther to the west generally did not make canoes or eat fish, traits that were common almost everywhere else in the Plains. The men were the hunters and warriors and did heavy butchering of meat. They made weapons, shields, drums, pipes, and often their own leggings and coats (McMillan, 1995). This exciting nomadic life and culture was destroyed when the buffalo disappeared and when the Indians were forced onto reserves. Most of the activities centred on the buffalo, and these buffalo-centred activities disappeared in a very short time, so that cultural substitutes were not developed.

In 1700 there were an estimated 60 million buffalo in North America. When the whites arrived in numbers in 1850 the buffalo had already been reduced to about 20 million animals. By 1885 the buffalo was close to extinction. (Price, 1979: 165)

Price suggests that the extinction of the buffalo was due to two factors. One of these factors was the introduction of the horse by the Spaniards in the South, which enabled the Indians on horseback to exploit and overkill the buffalo. Previously their hunting was confined largely to buffalo pounds, into which the animals were herded, forced over cliffs, and then butchered. The second factor was the coming of Europeans who slaughtered buffalo for their hides and for pemmican to trade, so that by 1885 the herds were almost extinct. This had radical implications for all plains Indians because their sacred canopy and culture were built around the buffalo. Their whole way of life involved this major means of economic survival. A second major stake in the sacred canopy vanished.

Many horse-related traits died out soon after the extermination of the buffalo. The camps were now permanent, so horses were less useful. The Blackfoot were faced with building a new *community* centred on ranching or farming. Price (1979: 185) says that many Blackfoot are successful entrepreneurs in ranching, petroleum, mining, and a few in manufacturing. On some reserves, however, especially among the plains Cree and Cheyenne there is a great deal of inertia and despair (McMillan, 1995). While the Indians are still together on reserves as they were in their hunting camps, the buffalo culture is gone, leaving a sense of purposelessness. The foci for nomos-building seem to be gone.

Many Indian chiefs, such as Big Bear in Saskatchewan, did not want to give up their hunting freedoms and resisted confinement on reserves.

Although in the United States there were extensive wars between the national government forces and the Indians, this was not usually the case in Canada. However, during the Louis Riel conflict in 1870 in Manitoba and 1885 in Saskatchewan, there was considerable resistance from both the Métis and the Indians (Flanagan, 1991). With the destruction of the buffalo by 1885, the Métis—who were middlemen in the buffalo hunt and trade—were faced with a complete change of lifestyle and culture. The food-gathering Indians, however, were faced with a much greater cultural change: a change to either an agricultural way of life, or to attempts at food-gathering where their territory was almost gone. Reserves were too small for effective hunting and fishing, and much of the land was not very good for farming. The community stake was completely disrupted and had to be reorganized spatially, economically, politically, religiously, and symbolically. Such a drastic community change in so short a time was almost impossible.

Religion, the fourth stake in the sacred canopy, is in many ways a symbolic expression of the total way of life of a people. For food-gathering people especially, religion is fully integrated into the cultural, economic, organizational, and spatial way of life. When the land, culture, and community base had been stripped, the integrating religious expression had no foundation. The prairie Indians were faced with a vacuum, which in Durkheim's terms was tailored for anomie. Thus, their religious expression no longer symbolized the reality around them.

Many of the religious traits were institutionalized in medicine bundles. These might include feathers, beaks, claws, teeth, or stones that acted as the focus of religious ritual. Rituals and dances were performed and individuals developed relationships with supernatural powers and spirits. After the Blackfoot signed a treaty with the Whites in 1877,

> the White Indian agent and the Anglican missionaries forced the Blackfoot to stop the Sun Dance. They pressured them to substitute tree platform burial with underground burial, though the people were afraid that the spirits would be eternally trapped below the ground. Plural marriages were dissolved and the extra wives sent away. Sacred bundles and regalia or traditional societies were destroyed. (Price, 1979: 183)

The religious ideological drive for nomos-building was also stripped from them, while the surrounding cultural, community, and territorial context had been destroyed.

Essentially the four stakes (land, culture, community, and ideology) that held up the sacred aboriginal canopy to protect them from normlessness and terror had been destroyed. They were left with the task of a complete reconstruction of a new canopy amidst the ashes of their old sacred reality. As a food-gathering people, many prairie Indians were soon faced with the oncoming agricultural European immigrants who had made the transfer from food-gathering to producing over thousands of years (Dickason, 1992). As if the transition from food-gathering to food producing was not enough, in less than a hundred years many prairie Indians were also faced with entering the industrial urban society (Frideres, 1993). By 1991, 44,000 had moved into Winnipeg, 33,000 into Edmonton, and 22,000 into Calgary (1991 census). Very few societies manage to reconstruct canopies that quickly or have the ability to sacralize them into a meaningful nomos.

TRANSFERRAL OF THE CANOPY: HUTTERITE AGRICULTURALISTS
In contrast to the native Indians' shattered canopy, the Hutterites transferred their sacred canopy intact from Europe to the North American prairies in Alberta, Saskatchewan, Manitoba, Montana, and North and South Dakota (Driedger, 1996). They were experienced agriculturalists familiar with farm- ing the *land*; they perpetuated a distinctive Germanic *culture* and customs; they were a *communal* society living in colonies; all of this was firmly anchored in a *religious* ideology formed during the Reformation in the sixteenth cen- tury. The Hutterites represent one of the most stable types of canopies, anchored firmly in an ideology, community, culture, and land base.

The Hutterite canopy emerged in Moravia in 1528, and shortly thereafter Jacob Hutter, after whom they are named, joined the community (Hostetler, 1974; Gross, 1980). They began as a distinctive *religious* group when a group of refugees pooled their possessions and introduced the practice of the 'com- munity of goods'. Since their community of goods was a unique interpretation that most other Christians did not share, and since they also believed in non- resistance and adult baptism, they became the target for persecution, espe- cially in a Europe that was not tolerant of pluralism (Gross, 1980: 26–31). Jacob Hutter, by then their leader, was burned at the stake in 1536, as were many others. Their frequent migrations to escape persecution finally brought them to North America in 1874 (Hostetler, 1974; Hofer, 1988).

Hutterite *communities* are perpetuated in colonies of one hundred or more members, a second stake in the canopy firmly tied to their religious beliefs. Whereas in the past they were engaged in trades in addition to agriculture, they now are mainly agriculturalists (Ryan, 1977; Driedger, 1996). The preacher is the primary leader of the colony, with the farm boss second in authority. The social structure has been developed over many years and has been sanctioned by religion and tradition. Although some colonies are more economically and politically stable than others, on the whole they compete very well in society and have become an economic threat to neighbours on occasion. While much of their community structure does not change rapidly, they adopt the most modern farming methods, which—together with their simple lifestyle and cooperative work—makes them very competitive economically (Peter, 1987). The community stake is both sacred and functional in Hutterite society, and boundaries are securely maintained (Driedger, 1982: 207–17).

'The Hutterite world view leads to the creation of an earthly environment that is ordered spatially, temporally, socially and symbolically; within this created environment the individual matures and ages' (Hostetler, 1974: 155). The Hutterites' colony is the centre of their universe and they sometimes compare the colony to the ark of Noah in the biblical account of the flood, claiming that those within the ark or colony will be rescued from the technological secular flood (Hostetler, 1974: 155). Because they spend much time socializing their children to internalize their orderly community, very few of them leave. The whole community is tightly ordered with the preacher at the head, followed by the farm boss, and the sub-heads of the various chicken, hog, grain, household, and gardening sub-divisions. The men work and eat together, the women eat and work separately, and the children eat, study, and play under the supervision of the teacher. Although some colonies now have a separate church building, many still meet in the schoolhouse for worship because the whole colony is their sanctuary, an integral part of their religious life.

While religion and community were the major components of the Hutterite canopy in the beginning, Germanic *culture* was slowly sacralized. In the sixteenth century, their German culture was part of the larger society. Over time, however, traditional forms of female attire such as long dresses, polka-dot kerchiefs, shawls, and parting of the hair in the middle and braiding became sacralized so that now they are required. The men do not wear ties; they wear distinctive hats, suspenders, and hairstyles (including beards) as an essential part of the sacred canopy. A distinctive traditional culture has emerged as a third stake in the sacred canopy (Stephenson, 1991).

The Hutterites speak a German dialect that they adopted in central Europe and transported and used in many parts of Europe before it was transplanted to North America. This dialect also is considered a part of a sacred form of familiar communication and distinguishes them from 'the English' who reside outside in the secular world. These concepts unique to their culture are laden with religious meaning. They live in a *Bruderhof,* or a brotherly yard; they see themselves as a *Gemein,* or a community of believers; they refer to their sub-divisions as *leut,* or people, a practice common among others like the Inuit; their written rules are *ordnungen,* or rules to be followed, all of which symbolize the sacred canopy in which God's people are sheltered (Hofer, 1988).

Interestingly, their community is so tightly knit that they can afford to adopt the most modern machinery to compete exceedingly well with farmers around them. They can pool and develop their captial, buy in bulk, make the most efficient use of machinery and labour, and, as a larger working unit, act as their own insurance body. They can diversify into all branches of mixed farming on a large scale, which acts as another flexible means of survival in the competitive market.

Agricultural *land* was not an essential part of the Hutterite sacred canopy in the beginning. In addition to agriculture, their early activities included ceramics, cutlery, milling, wine-making, spinning, weaving, tailoring, clock-making, and carriage-making. Hutterite nurses, midwives, and physicians were in great demand (Hostetler, 1974). By the time they came to the North American prairies, however, farming agricultural land and raising livestock had become a sacred part of their nomos-building. The norm is to work on the land. Other economic activities are frowned upon and are usually forbidden (Hofer, 1988).

To illustrate the extent of the transferral of the Hutterites from Europe to North America, we see in Figure 7-2 that all of the Hutterites that exist today now reside on the North American prairies in three provinces of Canada (Alberta, Saskatchewan, and Manitoba) and five of the United States (Washington, Montana, North and South Dakota, and Minnesota) (Driedger, 1997). None of them exist in Europe any longer. In 1993 there were 262 colonies in Canada and 106 colonies in the United States; of these over half were in Alberta (130) and Manitoba (85) (Driedger, 1997).

In Table 7-1 we see that the Hutterites are divided into three major *Leut* (people): the *Schmiedeleut* (15,855), the *Dariusleut* (10,922), and the *Lehrerleut* (8,544), with a total population of 35,321. The Hutterites of the world are located in a total of 368 prairie colonies, with an average of 96 people in each colony. The Hutterites began in 1528, grew very quickly to about 20,000 just before 1600, then declined; however, today there are more than there ever have been. Since 1874, when they arrived on the prairies, their numbers have grown due to high birthrates and favourable means of agricultural expansion (Peter, 1987).

In contrast to the Aboriginal experience of nomos-building on the prairies, the Hutterites have built a very stable sacred canopy, firmly staked by religious, communal, cultural, and territorial norms. Tested over time in Europe and transferred intact to the Canadian prairies as a rural ideal type, it appears to be quite functional and protective. The Hutterites illustrate that small groups can survive if they have a clear, ideological symbolic focus to which they are committed, and if they develop tightly knit structures which open and close selectively (Driedger, 1995). They illustrate a micro version of Dashefsky's sociocultural identity and demonstrate the importance of symbolic relations, a major emphasis of Max Weber. They are definitely a tile in the pluralist mosaic.

FIGURE 7-2   LOCATION OF HUTTERITE COLONIES IN NORTH AMERICA, 1990

SOURCES: Taken from maps prepared by Lawrence C. Anderson, 1991, and Enco Supply, *Hutterite Colonies of Manitoba*, 1993. Leo Driedger, 'The Hutterites', in P.R. Magocsi (ed.), *The People of Canada: An Encyclopedia for the Country*. Toronto: University of Toronto Press, 1997.

TABLE 7-1   HUTTERITE POPULATION IN NORTH AMERICA BY LEUT AFFILIATION
AND LOCATION, 1988

Category	Schmiedeleut	Dariusleut	Lehrerleut	Total
Population	15,855	10,922	8,544	35,321
Number of colonies	146	126	96	368
Mean colony size	105	86	89	93
Location and number of colonies in U.S.				
South Dakota[a]	51	0	0	51
Montana[a]	0	13	27	40
North Dakota[a]	6	0	0	6
Washington	0	5	0	5
Minnesota[a]	4	0	0	4
Total in U.S.	61	18	27	106
Location and number of colonies in Canada				
Alberta[b]	0	84	46	130
Manitoba[c]	85	0	0	85
Saskatchewan	0	23	23	46
British Columbia	0	1	0	1
Total in Canada	85	108	69	262

SOURCES: John Hofer, David Wiebe, and Gerhard Ens, *The History of the Hutterites*, rev. ed. Altona, MB: D.W. Friesen, 1988, p. 68, plus checks of maps:
[a] Lawrence C. Anderson, 1991
[b] *Hutterite Colonies in Alberta*, June, 1988; and
[c] Enco Supply, *Hutterite Colonies of Manitoba*, 1993
Leo Driedger, 'The Hutterites', in P.R. Magocsi (ed.), *The Peoples of Canada: An Encyclopedia for the Country*. Toronto: University of Toronto Press, 1997.

TRANSFORMATION OF THE CANOPY: JEWISH URBANISM
While the sacred canopy of many prairie Aboriginals was shattered awaiting reconstruction, and the Hutterite canopy was transferred intact and transplanted, the Jewish experience illustrates some of both processes. Like those of the Hutterites, their ideology and community components were transplanted fairly intact, but the cultural and land components, like those of the Aboriginals, were extensively changed. Like Glazer and Moynihan's (1970) theory that a shift may take place from traditional identities to new interest foci without losing a sense of a distinctive identity and reality, the Jewish sacred canopy was transformed from a traditional east European shtetl community into a segregated urban community located typically in Toronto, Montreal, Vancouver, or Winnipeg (Brym, Shaffir, and Weinfeld, 1993).

While the Jewish community formed one of the most important stakes in the canopy, their *religious* ideology was really the driving force. For nearly

3000 years they found themselves in religiously hostile environments. Within the minority Jewish community, religious (Judaic) law provided the Jewish rules—the world view and the codes of behaviour—which clearly defined the boundary between insider and outsider (Kallen, 1977: 20). Numerous prescriptive and proscriptive commandments regulated religious learning, establishment of the family, and the observation of religious laws. These involved such observances as circumcision, eating Kosher foods, and holding the sabbath which were transferred to urban settings mostly intact.

Religiously, Jews in Canada can best be discussed under the three categories: Orthodox, Conservative, and Reformed. The Orthodox focus on Jewish religion and customs as their primary reference groups and feel obligated to support their own kind. The Jewish family is of primary importance. Most Orthodox Jews also reside within an Orthodox neighbourhood where they have access to a synagogue, which accounts for the high Jewish residential segregation.

Kallen (1977: 72–4) says that Conservative Jews tend to be oriented to the broad ethnic category of Jews as a primary ethnic group, but that they are decidedly more secular and more pragmatic in outlook. Many rituals are still maintained within the home, and they tend to identify strongly with the state of Israel. Like the Conservative Jews, the Reformed Jews have become secular in outlook, but they have become far more critical and questioning about their tradition. Both the Jewish community and the larger society become their dual reference groups, although most Reformed Jews still continue to have their closest friendships with other Jews. Basically, Orthodox Jews attend to boundary-maintaining most, while the Reformed Jews do so least (Shaffir, 1993).

Kallen describes the Jewish settlements in Europe as a change from nomadism: 'For almost two hundred years the Jewish people were dispersed throughout the nations of the world where they earned the epithet "wandering Jew"—a migratory people without a national homeland. . . . By the nineteenth century most of the European Jewish population was concentrated in the countries of eastern Europe' (1977: 17). Jews have frequently faced pogroms and near-extermination (Levitt and Shaffir, 1993; Brym and Lenton, 1993). A majority lived in small towns and *shtetls* before they came to Canada.

The 318,000 Jews reported by the 1991 census in Canada represent only .9% of the Canadian population, and 98.5% of these are located in cities. Three-fourths of all Canadian Jews live in Toronto (151,000) and Montreal (98,000), where they represent 3% of the city populations. In these two cities the Jews are the most highly segregated of all ethnic groups. Gini indexes of Jewish segregation rank Montreal (.90) the highest followed by Toronto (.78), and Winnipeg (.74) (Balakrishnan and Hou, 1995). About 30% of Jewish households in Toronto and Montreal were foreign-born, which means that many have come to Canada only recently (Shaffir and Weinfeld, 1981:

12–13). 'Jews are perhaps the most cosmopolitan, the most internationalist, of all Canadian minority groups' (Weinfeld, Shaffir, and Cotler, 1981: 20).

Shaffir and Weinfeld (1981: 17–20) discuss the uniqueness of the Jewish *culture* by saying that they are both an ethnic and a religious group. They have in their cultural portfolio a host of traditions and as many as three languages (Yiddish, Hebrew, and Ladino) (Davids, 1993). Brym, Gillespie, and Gillis (1993) found that density of ingroup ties and endogamy correlated highly. They are relatively affluent, predominantly of middle and upper-middle class, although that was not always the case when they lived in the East European *shtetls* or small village-towns (Weinfeld, 1993). Many also maintain close ties with Israel, and through radio, television, and newspapers maintained by Jews, they are daily reminded of Israel's problems (Taras and Weinfeld, 1993). Finally, the holocaust still looms large in their minds, especially for older Jews; it is hard for them to trust others after Hitler's onslaught (Weinfeld et al., 1981: 17–20; Weimann and Winn, 1993). Thus, Canadian Jews are often obsessed with survival.

Shaffir (1974; 1993) has described in great length the Orthodox culture of the Lubavitcher Chassidim Jews in Montreal, who continue the study of the Jewish Torah, following their traditions transplanted from Poland. They represent a very traditional, back to-the-Torah movement which lays great emphasis on distinctive dress, study of the scriptures, observance of the traditional rituals, and a general move toward more sacralism and away from secularization. Thus, religious Jewish tradition and culture is again reinforced and new boundaries of separation are strengthened (Brym et al., 1993).

Jewish culture was also transplanted to the prairies, but there is evidence of a cultural shift as well (Medjuck, 1993). Driedger (1978) found that third-generation Jewish students in Winnipeg reported high endogamy in their families (81%), one or more years of parochial education (74%), and a majority of ingroup friends (63%). However, other cultural features had declined: only 2% spoke Yiddish at home, just over one-fourth (29%) participated in Jewish organizations, and regular synagogue attendance was minimal (7%). While community practices and religious ideology remained strong, a shift such as Driedger (1989) predicted seemed to occur in some of the cultural elements such as a change from the use of Yiddish to English, and declining participation in traditional religious and voluntary organizations. The 16,000 Jews in Winnipeg, in 1991 the fourth-largest Jewish community in Canada, continue to perpetuate orthodox and conservative practices in modern synagogues, schools, and organizations. Driedger and Church (1974) found that of all ethnic groups in Winnipeg, the Jews maintained their schools and synagogues as well as any of the others. The religious Jewish reality had been successfully transferred from the east European *shtetls* to the urban prairie. From its early beginnings in the 1900s, the North End of Winnipeg was occupied by East Europeans (Jews, Ukrainians, and Poles). The North End became an enclave of urban ethnic villagers (Gans, 1962; Driedger, 1987). Ecologically it is segregated by river, railroad, and open farmland boundaries; dominated by East Europeans, the area is dotted with Jewish synagogues and Ukrainian Orthodox and Catholic institutions; culturally, the North End is more akin to the Old World with the maintenance of ethnic languages, endogamy, customs, schools, and clubs (Driedger, 1980). At first it was a transplantation of the Jews' old communities into the new urban setting, an alternation of their social reality rather than a conversion to the new.

Land seems to have been a fragile stake in the Jewish canopy for a long time. They have been a migratory people, and in many parts of Europe they were not permitted to own land. They certainly have not become agricultural-ists like the Hutterites. Jews were forced to live in urban ghettos in Europe and in *shtetls* (Tulchinsky, 1993). This resulted in forced segregation, which they transferred into voluntary segregation in Toronto, Montreal, and Win-nipeg. Seventy per cent of all Jews living in Winnipeg in 1941 were located in one part of the North End. By 1961 many had moved out of the North End and 58% formed two new segregated areas in West Kildonan and River Heights (Driedger and Church, 1974). While segregation seems to be declin-ing somewhat, Jews continue to perpetuate voluntary enclaves. The land stake in the Jewish canopy seems to be in decline, although much still exists. Some of this support seems to be transferred into zionism, a form of symbolic land identification with Jews in Israel with financial and political support and fre-quent visits to the Holy Land (Taras and Weinfeld, 1993). Jews are still among the most highly segregated in the largest cities of Toronto, Montreal, and Vancouver (Balakrishnan, 1995).

Three types of reality structures have been discussed: 1) the Native Indians who were faced with the reconstruction of a meaningful order, 2) the Hut-terites who transferred their sacred canopy to the prairies, and 3) the Jews who transformed their shared knowledge and experience into a viable urban nomos. This involved an ordering of ideology, community, culture, and land into a sacred canopy as a shield against terror. Nomos-building was required so that shared knowledge and ordered experiences could become a meaningful con-struct of reality. The Hutterites did this effectively in the country, the Jews have struggled to build in the city, but the Native Indians have been faced with almost impossible odds.

Other immigrants who entered Canada can be fitted into these three types. The Mennonites moved onto agricultural reserves in Manitoba and Saskatchewan; the Icelanders sought to reconstruct fishing communities on the shores of Lake Manitoba and Lake Winnipeg; the Ukrainians took up land in the aspen belt where both land and woods provided the environment they were used to. Like the Hutterites, these groups transferred or transplanted their former communities to a large extent. Like the Jews more recent immigrants such as the Italians and Chinese have tried to build their nomoses in the city with considerable transformation of parts of their ideology, community, culture, and territory. Other migrants to the city will face similar problems. Like the Indians, the Inuit and other food-gathering peoples will be faced with reconstruction of their sacred canopies.

SACRED ENCLAVIC COMMUNITIES

With the rural and urban sacred canopy types as the backdrop, let us demonstrate some of the empirical sacred ethnic enclaves found in Canada. While the French who represent one-fourth of the Canadian population, 80% of which are concentrated in the one territory of Quebec, can seriously think of 'nation', smaller groups must resort to smaller territorial enclaves or communities over which they may have some control. Let us first discuss rural means of developing a 'tribe' or 'Volk' as Weber phrased it, to sustain 'a people' in an ethnic 'sacred' territory or community, and then segregated urban means of doing the same in the city.

DAWSON'S SACRED RURAL COMMUNITIES

The Chicago School of the 1920s was dominant in the development of sociology in America. Canadian sociology began later than its American counterpart, and early sociologists in Canada such as C.A. Dawson, Everett Hughes, and Horace Miner were Chicago graduates. Dawson and Hughes in particular carried the Chicago tradition to Canada. Because they were both at McGill where early Canadian sociology began in the 1930s, and because they both published studies of ethnic importance, we shall begin with their contributions. Quebec, a very different ethnic milieu from the rest of Canada, served to modify their Chicago assimilationist inclinations and led them to consider ethnic pluralism more.

Dawson's *Group Settlement: Ethnic Communities in Western Canada* (1936) was the seventh volume in the nine-volume Canadian Frontiers of Settlement series, edited by historians Mackintosh and Joerg. To be a sociologist in Canada in the 1930s, to do research on ethnic groups, and to do so in western rather than eastern Canada, was rather astounding. Indeed, the short preface by editor Mackintosh clearly shows the early British bias when he refers to western minorities as 'peculiar peoples' who have 'formed "cultural islands" which have retarded the progress of assimilation', and when he says Dawson will present them as groups rather than as 'foreigners'. Few present-day scholars would dare include any of the words 'peculiar', 'retarded', 'assimilation progress', or 'foreigners' in any sentence, let alone in a preface to a book on western pluralism.

The Chicago influence clearly shows when Dawson frames his study using 'the main characteristics of sects which have been set forth with insight by Professor R.E. Park' (Dawson, 1936: xiii). The main writings of the 'sect cycle' and the sect-church continuum were actually introduced by the German sociologist Ernst Troeltsch and then adopted and applied by Park in Chicago. The sect cycle implies a secularization process of religious groups (especially Christian groups), where a new group may spring forth out of a larger church because the new believers think the old church does not observe the original intent rigorously enough. However, as this new sect practises with greater fervour and follows the Scriptures more intensely, concern with purity ages, commitment again wanes, and slowly the group becomes an established sect, then a denomination, and finally a church-like organization more concerned with structures than original beliefs and practice. This secularization process is similar to the assimilation process discussed in Chapter Two, only it applies more strictly to religious groups. In this sense, Dawson is a typical Chicago School sociologist, concerned more with the process of change and assuming that solidarity or concern with the Sacred will give way to secularization. All indicators of change are seen as the decline of ethnic identity rather than as change expressed in new forms more adapted to the new social milieu for the sake of survival.

Because Dawson (1936) was interested in the change of ethnoreligious sects, he chose to study the Doukhobors, Mennonites, Mormons, German Catholics, and French Catholics of western Canada. He and his associates made extensive studies of these five groups at the beginning of the Depression (1930–32), and the findings were published in 1936. The West had been settled by European immigrants only fifty years before. Many of these settlers were first- and second-generation immigrants, so their ethnic origins were still salient. Dawson was one of the first sociologists to study this new frontier. Many of these groups had settled in the West in rural bloc communities, and they could easily be studied as distinct segregated ethnic groups.

Dawson (1936) also chose to study five ethnoreligious groups for comparative purposes, much in the style of Max Weber. His work has not been sufficiently recognized in Canada as one of the first comparative studies. Dawson's methodology includes a combination of qualitative and quantitative means of data collection through ethnographic, survey, interview, community, and census sources. Although he describes each group in sixty to a hundred pages, these are not community studies in the sense of a scholar's having lived and done participant observation in the community in a more qualitative way.

Dawson is mainly concerned with the process of secularization; he uses the Doukhobors and Mennonites as a segregated sacred sect group baseline to see how they have changed, or become more secular. He also includes the German and French Catholics as non-sectarian religious groups, and compares the sect and church groups to see differences in secularization and assimilation. As expected, he finds that the sects have distinguishing features such as more concern with segregation, maintenance of sect institutions of their own, reluctance to associate with the outside world, and seeing themselves as distinctive and apart using different dress, languages, morals, and the like. Dawson sees the Doukhobors, Mennonites, and Mormons as more sacred groups and the German and French Catholics as more secularized.

As illustrated in Figure 7-3, Dawson carefully plotted eleven bloc settlements of the five groups and then proceeded to discuss each in detail. Generally, he outlined how each groups came to the prairies and from where, the locale in which they settled, the institutions and organizations they formed, the process of invasion of the area, how in turn the groups were invaded by others, the general social adjustments which were involved, and the resistance to secularization. This is enormously useful data because it describes these multi-ethnic groups in a very pluralist region more than fifty years ago, a treasure which can no longer be duplicated. These five groups also provide a

FIGURE 7-3 LOCATION OF THE ELEVEN ETHNO-RELIGIOUS RESERVES AND SETTLEMENTS STUDIED BY DAWSON

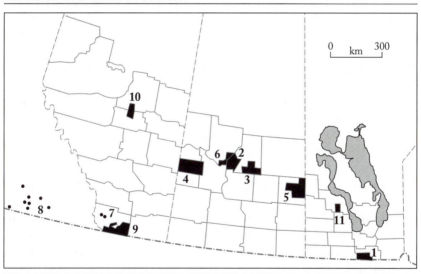

Map of the Prairie Provinces showing location of group settlements included in the present study; 1, Mennonite West Reserve (Dutch-German); 2, Rosthern Mennonite colony (Dutch-German); 3, St Peter's colony (German); 4, St Joseph's colony (German); 5, North and South colonies and Devil's Lake colony (Doukhobor) (also called Yorkton and Swan River colonies); 6, Saskatchewan (Blaine Lake and Saskatoon) colonies (Doukhobor); 7, Cowley colony (Doukhobor); 8, British Columbia colonies (Doukhobor); 9, Mormon country (Anglo-Saxon); 10, St Albert settlement (French-Canadian); 11, Ste Rose settlement (French-Canadian).

SOURCE: C.A. Dawson, *Group Settlement: Ethnic Communities in Western Canada.* Toronto: Macmillan Company, 1936, p. xviii.

baseline of religious practices, customs, traditions, and values that can be compared today to see how the means of solidarity have changed, how some groups have indeed integrated, and the extent to which community distinctiveness is still present in changed forms.

Dawson (1936: 377–80) concluded that all five rural ethnic communities were changing considerably. Their cultural traditions and the development of their community organizations served as a sacred anchor supported by ecological segregation. Outside forces, however, pressured them to adjust and readjust their economic, community, and educational life considerably. Dawson interpreted these changes as assimilation; today we would see them more as modified pluralism, because all of these communities still exist as changed vibrant rural religio-ethnic communities sixty years later.

Fortunately, E.K. Francis (1955) studied the same Mennonites in southern Manitoba in more depth twenty years later: *In Search of Utopia: The Mennonites in Manitoba*. Francis was among the first in Canada to look at modified forms of pluralism, and he published about twenty articles developing plural ethnic theory in the major sociological journals (Francis, 1947, 1948, 1950, 1954).

The Mennonites originally settled in one hundred villages on the East and West Reserves of southern Manitoba that were reserved for Mennonite rural bloc settlement. The West Reserve was also studied by Dawson and is marked in Figure 7-1, located on the west side of the Red River and on the American border; the East Reserve is on the east side of the Red River centred by Steinbach, forty miles east of Winnipeg. In 1881, seven years after the first Mennonites arrived, they represented 13% of the Manitoba population, the fourth largest ethnic group. When Francis studied these two reserves in 1945–47, there were 40,000 Mennonites in Manitoba. They were the sixth largest ethnic group, representing 5.4% of the provincial population.

Almost all Mennonites in 1955 spoke the Low German dialect at home and in the villages and towns, reserving the High German dialect for church services. Families were highly endogamous, schools on the reserves included mostly Mennonite children and teachers, and the business activity in the towns of Steinbach, Winkler, and Altona were mostly in German. Because the Mennonites selected some of the best soil for farming, they had a very good rural economic base. Their prosperity soon resulted in expanded farms and new industry in the towns and villages as well as supporting institutions, schools, and business. Since then, many have moved to cities, and four times as many are in the professions (28%), as are engaged in farming (7%) (Kauffman and Driedger, 1991). These Mennonites represent an enormous change from segregated sectarian farmers to pluralist professionals more like the urban Jews, half of them who are now living in cities, a modified example of religious pluralism.

FORMING URBAN SACRED COMMUNITIES
We were not able to find the same kinds of sacred ethnographic urban community studies that we were able to find on the rural French and Mennonites,
although William Shaffir's (1974) Lubavitcher Chassidim Jews in Montreal,
and Stebbins's (1994) study of the Franco-Calgarians would be good examples. However, a great deal of literature is available on general ethnic residential concentration of urban ethnic minorities (Driedger and Church, 1974;
Kalbach, 1987; Balakrishnan, 1987; 1995).

Recently, using Canada census data, Balakrishnan and Kralt (1987: 148)
plotted the residential concentration of six minorities in Toronto, Montreal,
and Vancouver (see Figure 7-4). They show a small area in Toronto comprising seven census tracks near the centre of the city where over half of the
Catholic Portuguese (56%) live, seven tracks where the majority of the Jews
(53%) live, and twelve tracks where the Catholic Italians (51%) live. The Jews
of highest socio-economic status live the farthest from the centre, the more
recent Portuguese immigrants of lowest status are located closest to the business centre, and the Italians in between.

In Vancouver over half of the Chinese, many of whom are Buddhist, are
segregated in Chinatown, closest to the uptown business section, while smaller
percentages of other ethnic groups are concentrated farther out. In Montreal, a
majority of the Jews (70%) are segregated in six census tracks, by far the highest concentration of any of the ethnic groups (Balakrishnan and Kralt, 1987:
138–57). These concentrations need to be examined more closely.

The 1991 census reports 247,000 Portuguese Catholics in Canada, most of
whom came after the Second World War and especially during the 1960s.
Three-fourths of them live in Ontario, and half live in Toronto (124,000)
where they represent 3% of the metropolitan population. Over half (56%) of
the Portuguese in Toronto live in seven small census tracks in the Kensington
Market area near downtown Toronto (Balakrishnan and Kralt, 1987: 143).
The Portuguese are among the most segregated ethnic groups in Toronto.
They clearly represent immigrants who have come most recently, drawn to
the southern Ontario industrial milieu. Race is not a factor, since they are
Caucasian, but social class is: most of them came from poor Portuguese-held
islands, and they have little education and few special occupational skills.
Most of them are Roman Catholic.

We are fortunate to have several intensive studies of the Portuguese in
Toronto by Grace Anderson (1974) and Anderson and Higgs (1976). Anderson writes (1974: 167):

> When the residents of metropolitan Toronto think of the Portuguese, they
> usually call to mind the colourful Kensington Market with its Portuguese
> stores spilling over onto the sidewalks. Chickens can be bought, still alive,

FIGURE 7-4   ETHNIC CONCENTRATIONS IN TORONTO AND IN VANCOUVER, 1981

SOURCE: T.R. Balakrishnan and John Kralt, 'Segregation of Visible Minorities', in Leo Driedger (ed.), *Ethnic Canada*, Copp Clark Pitman Ltd, 1987, p. 148.

from cages. Fresh fruit stores, vegetable stands, and fish shops are there in abundance. The delicious aroma of Portuguese pastries floats from the bakeries. Everywhere there is bustle and animated conversation. The groups jostle each other . . . blocking the free flow of pedestrian traffic on the crowded sidewalks. Occasionally a car attempts to make its way down the road. . . . Many visitors come to the area to see the 'Portuguese district'.

Richmond (1972) has plotted the Portuguese Catholics and other ethnic groups in Toronto on maps to show their relationships, and Balakrishnan and Kralt (1987: 148) have done so as well (see Figure 7-4). 'Between 1953 and the mid-60s, the Portuguese poured into the Kensington Market area' (Anderson and Higgs, 1976: 69). The Portuguese are located adjacent to Chinatown, and the two business areas tend to complement each other.

In terms of Raymond Breton's 'institutional completeness' of an ethnic group, the Portuguese have their own schools, churches, and voluntary associations. Anderson writes (1974: 170):

> The Portuguese in Toronto now constitute in many ways a very 'institutionally complete' ethnic group. . . . Within the Kensington Market area there are also . . . Portuguese restaurants, real estate agents, printers. Books and records from Portugal can be purchased there. Several newspapers are available . . . A radio station reports Portuguese programmes regularly. In the ethnic press various services are offered in addition to those mentioned above—taxis, driving school. . . , a Portuguese bank, and services of immigration consultants, interpreters and income tax specialists.

Two Catholic churches specialize in Portuguese services. Several centres provide social activities and social assistance. There are clubs and pool halls, as well as soccer teams with various Portuguese emphases. Religion is an important sacred cohesive factor.

The family is very important, and mutual aid is common. Relatives live within easy reach of each other. The average size of the family is five to six persons, and the average education is three to four years of schooling for those who came from the Azores Islands, where few could go to school beyond grade four (Anderson and Higgs, 1976: 71). Half of the immigrant men were farmers, so in addition to the cultural changes, life in Toronto is new to them. Most of them are happy to find blue collar jobs. Owning a home is very important to them, and often families work very hard to save for their own property, which bring status in their Portuguese circles.

The Portuguese in Toronto represent one of the many recent immigrant groups who are highly segregated in the centre of the city, who are cohesive religiously, who are of lower socio-economic status, who have developed their own institutionally complete enclaves, and who communicate at home and in much of their life in Portuguese. As a result, many of them speak a broken form of English. This urban ethnic group will retain its identity for the first several generations. We need to see what changes will take place by the third generation.

Elizabeth Bott (1957) was among the first to develop the social network perspective, beginning with the family as a small network unit. Bott (1957) suggests that as ethnics move from segregated rural communities or as rural communities become less isolated (Blau, Blum, and Schwartz, 1982: 45–62) and move to a more open urban environment, they must make sure that the family as a network remains very tightly knit. All the families she researched 'maintained relationships with external people and institutions—with a place of work, with service institutions such as school, church, doctor, clinic, shops, with voluntary associations such as clubs, evening classes, and recreational institutions. They also maintained more informal relationships with colleagues, friends, neighbors, and relatives' (Bott, 1957: 98). Such a tightly knit family can link with other selected social networks such as a network of extended relatives, an ethnic church, or school, friends, professionals and others to strengthen itself. Such a 'sacred' network of sub-networks can be sufficiently strong so that linkage with other networks will be less threatening. These networks of beliefs and values can provide guidelines and the opportunities for youth to find ingroup partners. The Jews seem to be most successful in creating such urban networks.

SUMMARY

Nomos-building is a phenomenon creating order for individuals and groups so that life makes sense. Berger's concept of 'sacred canopy' deals with four structural components: ideology, community, culture, and land—stakes that help to uphold the canopy's protective roof or shield against terror, normlessness, and meaningfulness. We have compared the Aboriginal, Hutterite, and Jewish canopies to see how they fared.

While the Jewish sacred canopy is not as secure as that of the Hutterites, it has not succumbed to the devastation of anomie faced by many Aboriginals. They appear to have created a nomos in the city, which Hutterites have not attempted, and which Aboriginals moving to the city find difficult. It appears that most other sub-groups could be fitted into one or other of these types. Other groups could at least be examined to see which type of structure and process might be most applicable.

Dawson found that religion or sectarianism in the western prairie is an important means of maintaining traditional ethnic enclaves. Francis illustrated that among rural Mennonites there is also considerable change, and that change is easier to integrate in stable communities.

To some extent, segregated ethnic enclaves are also perpetuated in cities. However, recent immigrants of lower socio-economic status, such as the

Catholic Portuguese, continue to establish ethnic enclaves that are segregated and bounded spatially, as illustrated by Anderson.

There is considerable evidence that as ethnic groups move to the city, they are exposed to many more situations where interaction with outgroup members is necessary at work, at play, at school, and in many social situations. Some assimilate but others change and adapt considerably, maintain modified forms of ethnic identity, and therefore save their ethnic identity in a modified sacred form.

PART IV

Stratification: Power, Status, Inequalities

CHAPTER 8

Class and Socio-Economic Status

Part III focused on voluntary ethnic identity, solidarity, and cohesion; Part IV will focus on differentiation of power and stratification of ethnic groups. This often leads to involuntary differentiations—inequalities—as found in Cell D of our model. Clearly, size, regional distribution, length of stay, and influence varied enormously between the various ethnic groups, and some will be in a position of dominance and more powerful than others. Scholars' views differ on the relationships between class and ethnicity, and on the extent to which ethnic identification is a drawback or a resource of social mobility. Chapter Eight focuses on the varying levels of power of the various ethnic groups and on their socio-economic status. Chapter Nine deals with voluntary and involuntary spatial segregation. Chapter Ten looks at race and its importance for stratification as biological characteristics enter into differentiation of the Canadian population.

THEORIES OF STRATIFICATION

John Porter's sociological study, *The Vertical Mosaic: An Analysis of Social Class and Power in Canada* (1965) sets the stage which many others have developed since (Clement, 1974; Grabb, 1984; Curtis et al., 1988). Class and power are his major themes, and the importance of mobility and migration. Porter addresses 'ethnicity and class' first (1965: 60–103), giving ethnicity a central and prominent place. Located in Ottawa at Carleton University, Porter was especially aware of the British-French historical power axis. Ottawa, the national capital, has for generations been the political battleground between these two ethnic blocs. The two groups, each in their respective Ontario and Quebec strongholds, watched each other suspiciously across the Ottawa River. It is not surprising that Porter saw the British-French axis as crucial, and that he was interested in exploring the power relationships and the social class differentials between the two founding peoples (Elliott and Fleras, 1992: 77–86).

Porter (1965) outlines two important theories of the function and purpose of social classes. The first he calls the functional theory of stratification, and the second the Marxian theory; the first he claims is more subjective and the second more objective, based on defined classes. The first claims that inequality is necessary; the second wants to do away with stratification, thinking that social class is unjust and unacceptable.

CLASS AS FUNCTIONAL INEQUALITY

According to Porter (1965: 16), the functional theory of stratification reflects the American conservative ideology that inequality is normal and necessary, and that people generally occupy the class positions they deserve. Kingsley Davis and W.E. Moore (1945) suggest that stratification occurs because not all jobs are equally pleasant, though all these jobs need to be done. Social inequality becomes an unconsciously evolved device by which societies ensure that the most important positions are conscientiously filled by the most qualified people (Musynski, 1995: 19f). Different jobs require different training and inherited capacity, so the more able and better trained get better, higher-status jobs than others. According to the functional inequality theorists, because of differential ability, more opportunity for training, and the will to expend the effort, some people have higher-status jobs than others.

There are many critics of this theory. The theory assumes equality of opportunity, especially education. It does not explain why there are such differential rewards between a corporate president and high ranking public servants. Nor does the theory take sufficiently into account the fact that some jobs and positions are often inherited, eliminating free competition for them. The theory also takes little account of power as a reward itself, where power compensates for monetary reward, as is the case for religious practitioners or politicians (Hunter, 1986). The factor of prestige satisfies many; university professors have relatively higher prestige than their salaries would suggest. Porter (1965: 17) claims that class is 'a product of a conservative ideology and a theory to support the status quo. Other variations all assert that social class rests on prestige, derived from occupational roles.'

THE RADICAL MARXIAN PERSPECTIVE

Rick Ogmundson (1986: 237) has called Porter's second, Marxian perspective 'radical' because it emphasizes the divergent interests in society, the conflict that will result, and the coercion that is almost inevitable if things are to change. The Marxian tradition holds that members of a particular class become quite conscious of their class identity and interests, and usually ethnicity and race are seen as part of the powerlessness of the lower classes. This class consciousness is functional because class conflict forces change. In Marxian theory society comprised owners and non-owners of the productive instruments, an inequality that results from domination and exploitation. The injustice of this inequality must be remedied (Grabb, 1984: 13–36).

'It was ironic, that Marx, a radical opponent of capitalism, should find tolerance and refuge within which to express his ideas only in England, the prime example of what he most despised' (Berlin, 1963: 181). In Marx's time in England the contrast between rich and poor was especially acute, with child labour, long working hours and weeks, and extremely poor working conditions. Marx himself lived in poverty, although he occasionally had financial help from friends. It was in England that Marx and his lifelong friend Engels helped to form the new Communist League in 1847, and in 1848—the same year that popular revolts against established monarchies occurred in France, Italy, Germany, Austria, and Hungary (Grabb, 1984: 18)—they published the *Communist Manifesto*. The crux of Marx's views is stated clearly in the beginning of the *Manifesto*: 'The history of all hitherto existing society is the history of class struggles' (Marx and Engels, 1948: 57). The first volume of *Das Kapital*, the elaboration of their theory, was published by Marx during his lifetime; volumes Two and Three were completed by Engels after Marx's death.

In short, Marx saw private property (the capitalists) and alienated labour according to his revised Hegelian dialectic, as antitheses that were in conflict. The earlier theories of the French social thinker Saint-Simon, that economic relationships were the key to explaining historical social change, prevailed in Marx's theory as well. Marx saw the macro society as a struggle between economic classes pitted against each other for power. He was appalled at the small returns labourers got for their long labour, and the disproportionate share of returns that went as profits to owners. Since the small group of bourgeois capitalists were in league with governmental power, he saw no other solution than the overthrow of these capitalists by the masses to establish a classless society in which all people would benefit more equitably from their labour.

Marx's focus on economic stratification as the major force of change led him to make short shrift of other forces such as religion, and he wrote nothing about ethnicity. He assumed that religion and ethnicity were only social manifestations of the major power struggle, as some forces such as religious leaders siding with the bourgeoisie and others like ethnic minorities representing the proletariat. According to Marxists, the key to understanding inequality lies in economic factors (Satzewich, 1995: 98–121). In addition to land, labour, and capital as resources for earning a living, Marx also added the importance of social technology and the organization of economic activity that he called the mode of production (Ogmundson, 1986: 238). Marx saw the dominant capitalist class who owned the means of production as the bourgeoisie, and those who work for wages as the proletariat. Since the bourgeoisie who owned the capital were primarily concerned with profit, they would try to exploit the workers in order to gain a greater margin of profit. Marx's theory assumes that minority groups are usually among the powerless.

WEBER'S FUNCTIONAL AND CONFLICT SYNTHESIS

Much of Max Weber's writing was in response to Marx's economic determinism; Weber thought that Marx had not placed enough emphasis on non-economic factors such as ideology, although he agreed that the relations between the propertied and non-propertied were important. However, he thought Marx tended to over-simplify matters and was too rigid on economic materialism as the major factor. Weber argued that the employer-worker relationship was not the only significant one. Other relationships such as those of creditors to debtors, producers to consumers, and questions of usury or high interest rates and just prices all entered into a more complex equation (Ogmundson, 1986: 247).

Weber also thought that the social and political bases of human inequality were at least as important as the economic base. He thought that hierarchies based on differing levels of prestige could be independent of economic factors. For example, descendants of aristocrats, confident intellectuals, or members of some ethnic groups might feel themselves superior to other social groups who merely possess money (Ogmundson, 1986: 247). A recent millionaire immigrant might not have as much social status as another citizen with little money, but who is educated and teaching at a university. Race, religion, gender, language, ethnicity, and education could all be factors that might make a difference in social rankings.

Weber thought political hierarchies based on differential power could also be independent of social or economic hierarchies. Weber disagreed with Marx's belief that economic and political power could hardly be separated, arguing instead that each should be considered separately. Whereas Marx thought in terms of one basic economic class hierarchy, Weber argued that there were at least three hierarchies, including class (the economic), status (the social), and power (the political). Weber also saw the bureaucracy as a master trend in the industrialization process that would increasingly control the lives of all, although he argued that social factors such as religion and ethnicity could act as deterrent forces to industrial dehumanization.

We maintain that in Canada ethnic and racial prestige vary considerably and are based on many factors, among them occupation and income, which are economic factors. However, social factors such as education, residence, religion, language, gender, age, race, and the like need to be taken into account as well. Historical factors including recency of immigration into Canada are also important. Some ethnic groups will have higher prestige not only because of their economic condition, but also because of different combinations of social factors.

POST-MARXIAN INDUSTRIAL ÉLITES

Like Marx, Porter was interested in social class and power, but he argued that modern industrial society no longer requires as much unskilled labour because it has become complex and varied and the labour force has become more skilled. With the development of corporations, managers rather than capitalists run these corporations, which are owned by thousands of shareholders, few of whom ever own the majority of any one stock. Thus, the stockholders or owners are not concentrated in one or in several individuals but are dispersed.

Second, large corporations have concentrated their economic power in the hands of a relatively few large firms that continue to consolidate, resulting in interlocking directorships. Porter (1965: 25) contends that ownership or non-ownership of property is no longer the major criterion for class conflict. The power has now shifted to those who make the decisions, who Porter contends are the managers or élites of these large corporations. Not only the corporations but labour unions, educational institutions, social agencies, the military, and governmental institutions are now run by managing élites. C. Wright Mills (1956) called these managers the 'power élite'. The struggle is no longer between those who employ or are employed, but between the major decision-makers in their institutional systems. This then raises the question of whether some élites are more heavily drawn from some ethnic groups than others. Porter clearly thought so and proceeded to show that the British were heavily concentrated in the decision-making roles of the economic and political power élite.

In *The Vertical Mosaic*, Porter describes Canada as a stratified mosaic with vast differentiations in social stratification. Whereas the regional mosaic discussed in Chapter Four focused on the distribution of ethnic groups, Porter's vertical mosaic has to do with vertical strata of status, prestige, and power. Some ethnic groups are much more heavily represented in the lower classes. It is here that Porter's group status and entrance status principles apply.

Charter Group Status. The British North America Act of 1867 gave the founding groups of Canada (the British and French) what has been termed by some as charter group status (Porter, 1965). The act legalized the claims of the two original migrating groups for such historically established privileges as the perpetuation of their separate languages and cultures. The Royal Commission on Bilingualism and Biculturalism (1970) continued to support and encourage the charter group status of the French, even though by 1991 those of other ethnic origins comprised at least one-third of the Canadian population. Since then the new constitution has entrenched these special rights for all. Though legally of equal status, the French have always been junior partners in the alliance with the British. Though the charter group status of the French was legally secure, they nevertheless had difficulty matching the numerical, economic, and political strength of the British. They came to rely on regional segregation and their institutions and culture as a means of counteracting British dominance.

The dominance of the charter groups has never been seriously challenged because of natural increase among the French and continuing high levels of British immigration. Also, the ethnic structure of a community in terms of its charter and non-charter groups is determined early and tends to be self-perpetuating. The French made up almost one-third of the Canadian population (although that proportion had declined to 23% by 1991), while the British have always been the largest ethnic group, although their proportion has been steadily dropping from over one-half to 28% in 1991.

At the time of Confederation, the charter groups (91% of the population) in Upper and Lower Canada and the Maritimes formed a bilingual and bicultural nation with few representatives from other countries (9%) (Porter, 1965). The French, however, have been very much junior partners in the charter alliance, the British have dominated economically and politically.

Entrance Group Status. Porter (1965) describes the position to which ethnic groups are admitted and at which they are allowed to function in the power structure of a society as entrance status. For most ethnic groups in Canada, this position is characterized by low-status occupational roles and a subjection to the processes of assimilation laid down by the charter groups. Less preferred immigrants were allowed to enter Canada but were channelled into lower-status jobs and because of their later entrance into Canada were often left with marginal farm lands (Driedger, 1989). German, Dutch, Jewish, and Scandinavian immigrants entered Canada earlier than many of the others, and they could be considered older entrance status groups. Many of these older immigrants have moved out of an entrance status into higher educational, income, and occupational status. The Jews placed great value on education and entered higher status occupations; on the average, they have a higher status than any of the other groups, including the charter groups.

Porter suggests that the idea of an ethnic mosaic, as opposed to the idea of the melting pot, impedes the process of social mobility. 'The melting pot with its radical breakdown of national ties and old forms of stratification would have endangered the conservative tradition of Canadian life, a tradition which gives ideological support to the continued high status of the British charter group' (Porter, 1965: 71). This seems to be changing, however, as many former entrance groups are gaining status educationally, occupationally, and economically, and nevertheless retain many of their ethnic characteristics (Isajiw, Sev'er, Driedger, 1993). The Jews would be an excellent example of a group that shows high upward mobility with a high level of maintenance of ethnic identity (Driedger, 1989).

The political and economic power élite, however, is still largely British. The British élite (Porter, 1965) dominates the Canadian economic system with a strong influence in urban industrial Ontario, emerging strength in Alberta, and declining strength in the Maritimes. The French dominate the political structure in Quebec, the British dominate in Ontario and the East, and other ethnic groups are becoming increasingly more politically influential in the West. Any theory of Canadian political ethnic relations must deal with these multi-dimensional regional, economic, and political status structures in order to account for the factors which will influence the Canadian mosaic and the identity of individual ethnic groups (Driedger, 1989).

CLASS AND SOCIAL MOBILITY

Porter (1975: 293–5) found ethnic occupational stratification in his study of the Canadian census and argued that ethnicity serves as a deterrent to social mobility. Porter's vertical mosaic thesis has served as a provocative hypothesis, and numerous scholars have focused their attention on the relationship of ethnicity to social mobility (Blishen, 1970; Tepperman, 1975; Reitz, 1977; Cuneo and Curtis, 1975; Darroch, 1979). Clement's study (1974) leaves little doubt that non-charter groups have not entered the positions of power extensively, and Blishen (1970) finds considerable evidence of the vertical mosaic. Many others, however, have been highly critical of the 'mobility trap' hypothesis. Among them are Tepperman (1975: 156), who concludes that the hypothesis is in many ways 'patently false', and Darroch (1979: 22), who found it 'an exaggeration of any data available to date'.

The literature on the interrelationship between class and ethnicity helps to distinguish two traditional theoretical positions: 1) that ethnicity, whatever its cultural origin, is a by-product of the class structure and hence is, in some sense, reducible to class as Marxists assume; and 2) that ethnicity may or may not be reducible to class, but that it is a drawback to social mobility as Porter believed. Marx expounded the first position and so did Oliver Cox (1948: 321–52): in his view, race or ethnic relations are merely one aspect of exploitation of labour by the capitalist class. Hence, what are considered to be attributes of ethnicity are simply attributes of the exploited class, and race or ethnic relations are in essence a form of political class conflict.

More recently a much more sophisticated, though similar, position has been taken by advocates of the 'cultural division of labour' approach. There are at least two variants of this approach. One is represented by Edna Bonacich (1972) who suggests that ethnic solidarity is a derivative of dual labour market exploitation in which the immigrants are funnelled into jobs that are less stable, offer lower wages, and preclude advancement, yet are similar to jobs performed by the indigenous population who receive better wages and have a chance of advancement and upward social mobility.

A second type of the 'cultural division of labour' thinking is Michael

Hechter's theory of 'internal colonialism'. According to Hechter, ethnic solidarity emerges as a reaction of a culturally distinct periphery against exploitation by the centre. This happens especially when there is a division of labour in which the periphery is engaged in an activity which is most advantageous for the centre, but least economically profitable for the periphery. Ethnic solidarity of the periphery is a reaction against exploitation, and the more the periphery is disadvantaged in relation to the centre, the more likely it will develop strong feelings of solidarity.

Wiley (1967) suggests that if a person chooses to move into an ethnic opportunity community rather than that of the society at large, this structure, although it may offer some possibilities for mobility, will ultimately become a mobility trap because it offers a smaller chain of minority opportunities than the mainstream structure outside the ethnic minority group. According to him, being tied to a minority sub-culture, and hence being socialized to anticipate opportunities within the confines of a minority group, places a low ceiling on a person's career and leaves no easy way into the world at large. Likewise, a psychological commitment to a minority group and its interactional style becomes in itself a mobility trap.

Gordon Darroch (1979: 1–25), reviewing the literature on the relationship between ethnicity and social class, found that three major themes emerged: 1) limited evidence of entrance of non-charter groups into positions of power; 2) evidence (which he suggests is exaggerated) that an ethnic mosaic (maintenance of identities) impedes the processes of social mobility; and 3) evidence that continued ethnic identification (lack of assimilation) can harden so that ethnic groups remain in their original low entrance class, which he seriously questions based on the data he found and could examine. Darroch's (1979: 20) review leads him to suggest 'that for some members of a given ethnic population there exist serious "mobility traps", while for others ethnic identity may be of no consequence to mobility whatsoever. Still others may be able to translate their heritage into distinct occupational opportunities.' In other words, ethnicity can be both a resource and a drawback.

Darroch (1979: 8–10) also reexamined Porter's 1931, 1941, and 1961 census data, using indexes of dissimilarity for each ethnic group. He found that in the 1931 data dissimilarity differences by ethnic group were considerable for all non-charter groups when compared to the national average. By 1961, however, these differences had almost disappeared for some groups (Germans and Eastern and Other Europeans) and had declined enormously for all but the Native Indians and Inuit. This would suggest that most non-European groups in Canada are rising considerably socio-economically, compared to the national average.

Tepperman (1975: 120–57) explicitly addresses Porter's thesis that some ethnic groups may have been locked into the ethnic statuses they held when they entered Canada, promoting immobility. He doubts that cultural separateness and economic assimilation are incompatible, saying that Canada imports immigrant talent at various levels of the occupational hierarchy. 'All immigrants but the most recent earn more than their native-born ethnic counterparts; Jews and Asiatics are the notable exception of this rule' (Tepperman, 1975: 149). He suggests that some immigrant groups enter at higher levels to begin with, that some move faster than others, that some aspire to higher education than others, and that many are willing to enter new sectors of the economy while native Canadians often are not. Tepperman's findings seem to be in direct opposition to the claims of Porter.

EMPIRICAL STUDIES OF POWER AND STATUS

The literature review has suggested a number of interesting possible relationships between social class and ethnicity, and the theories also illustrate many outcomes and interpretations, including potential for conflict.

First, we examine Frederick Armstrong's (1981; 1987) study of the rise and formation of the Ontario establishment, the most powerful Anglo-Saxon economic and political force in Canada. Raymond Breton (1980) reviews the literature on British-French charter status relations. Peter Pineo's (1977) discussion of the social standing of ethnic groupings provides a good opportunity to see how ethnic groups rank with respect to social prestige. Fourth, Jeffrey Reitz's (1990) exploration of ethnic inequality, segregation, and control of jobs in Toronto shows considerable ethnic differentiation. Finally, Wsevolod Isajiw, Aysan Sev'er, and Leo Driedger's (1993) study of Toronto adults explores the relationship between ethnic identity and social mobility. These last two empirical studies deal largely with ethnicity in Toronto, the heartland of Canadian industrial power.

FORMATION OF THE ONTARIO ESTABLISHMENT

The 1759 defeat of the French on the Plains of Abraham adjoining Quebec City opened North America to British political dominance. Only a few years later, however, the American Revolution in 1776 took a large section of the colonial empire out of British hands, leaving only Canada as a British colony (Armstrong, 1981). United Empire Loyalists who remained loyal to the crown left the United States for Upper Canada (southern Ontario) beginning in 1784. Thus, the opportunity for the establishment of a British élite began about 200 years ago.

Since southern Ontario is the heartland of Canada's industrial power, Frederick Armstrong (1987) sought to trace the historical formation of this economic power centred in York, which was renamed Toronto in 1834. By 1991 Toronto had emerged as the largest metropolitan centre in Canada with a population of 3.9 million. The census of 1842 is the first that shows the ethnic composition of southern Ontario. Of the 487,053 population, approximately one-half (247,665) were born as English Canadians and another third (159,000) were born in the British Isles. Only about five per cent were French Canadian or originated in Europe, while the remainder did not report their ethnicity, or were born in the United States. At least 90% were of British origin. Armstrong (1981: 23) suggests that with the arrival of the first United Empire Loyalists in 1784, the consolidation of the élite began. The crucial element in gaining power in Upper Canada was the imperial connection with Britain, the colonizing power in Europe. The rulers were usually not Canadian, but representatives sent from Britain to control British interests (Armstrong, 1981). The first component of power was the Family Compact of Loyalists who had held important positions in the American colonies. The second component was imperial appointees, who, because of connections in Britain, were granted important political posts that were often perpetuated and kept in the family or among friends. Others, with connections with the governor appointed from England, got influential posts as part of a patronage system. Those who had served in the military were also often in line for positions (Armstrong, 1981: 26–7). The wealthy were often favoured since they commanded respect and were influential because of their commercial success.

The defeat of the French in Quebec and the arrival of the United Empire Loyalists into new British territory meant that many political positions were available, the basis of creating a British colonial power structure. Many of these appointments were for life, and residency was not required. Plural office holding was common, as was the tendency to follow hereditary lines in appointments (Armstrong, 1981: 28). The office of Justice of the Peace was responsible for handling local and judicial cases, and the opportunity for promotion to higher courts and more responsible positions was always an attraction. With the British in power, and the vast majority of the population of British origin, these positions of power were held mostly by those of British ancestry. It should not be surprising that in the 1960s Porter still found the British heavily represented among the political and economic élite in Canada. The original British power networks have simply been perpetuated.

How did many become wealthy in this new country? The accumulation of land was a common source of wealth, and holding important political offices often helped to accomplish such acquisitions. Much land was available, and land was often paid as bonuses to officials or loyalists. In those days the landed gentry symbolized prestige. Many who held high rank in the military or in government were given special land grants to develop as they wished. Thus, the amassing of large estates was underway (Armstrong, 1981: 129). Beyond acquiring wealth through political position and land acquisitions, commerce— and later finance and manufacturing—also provided opportunities. Later, acquiring wealth through commerce was most common; some of the élite came to control vast financial empires.

In addition to public office, land, and wealth, there were secondary routes to advancements, such as family connections. The élite tended to intermarry to keep power and wealth within their family, and positions increasingly became hereditary until the oligarchy was entrenched. Armstrong (1981: 30) cites 'the Hamiltons of Niagara, Queenston, Hamilton, Kingston and London' as a good example. The city of Hamilton was named after one of them. The Hamiltons were prominent in business, fur trading, and as senators, sheriffs, and magistrates appointed by the Legislature.

Education was another form of mobility open in the early days. Much of the education was in private schools catering to the élite. Religion also played an important role as the state Church of England tried to become dominant in the colonies. The church and its leaders often got special privileges.

The relations between the British ethnic divisions were interesting to observe. The English were initially the largest group and most directly connected with the imperial power; with few exceptions all governors were English (Armstrong, 1981: 33). The Irish also formed a large group, but they were split into Catholics and Protestants, each division with its own dynamics. The Protestant Irish arrived first, were well off and well connected, and made considerable progress in their quest for power. The Irish Catholics came later, when the power structure had already been formed; they were less well educated and became influential only later. The Scottish Protestants gained a great deal of power in the governance and commerce of the colony. They were early arrivals and worked hard, so they had a great deal of influence. Many Scots gained important political positions.

Armstrong (1981: 35–6) concludes that a composite establishment of the British arose in Upper Canada with Toronto as its capital more than 200 years ago. Various individuals gained power through colonial associations, wealth, education, and the right connections with centres of power. While the British as the senior charter-group partner consolidated their power, the French, as junior charter partners, were faced with less opportunity for power dominance.

POLITICAL DOMINANCE OF CHARTER GROUPS
While the British establishment clearly developed in Ontario, to what extent do the two British and French charter groups share in the Canadian power relationships? In 1867 the British were almost twice as numerous as the French demographically. Since then the French have slipped to one-fourth, and the British to one-fourth of the single-response Canadian population so that the charter groups still represent half of all Canadians. Breton (1991: 2–5) suggests that these charter groups behaved as ethnic political communities, with governance structures and ethnic politics. A study of the two groups' political representation is in order.

Raymond Breton (1980) shows that the anglophones and francophones have lived separately in their own social circles and institutions in what he calls segmentation. Breton analyzes three dimensions (economic, political, and social) of English-French relations, showing that the French, segmented in Quebec with their dominant French language, are often pitted against the English in the rest of Canada. Using Breton's (1980: 177–328) findings, let us explore the political differences.

Breton and Roseborough (1980) found that the charter groups did dominate the political élite, as demonstrated by those who headed the various federal political ministries from 1867 to 1966, shown in Table 8-1. Non-charter groups were hardly represented at all, while the British were heavily over-represented in all categories during the entire hundred-year period. The British dominated the top policy-making and human capital ministries in particular. Among the policy-making ministries, they dominated consistently in finance, trade and commerce, and external affairs. During this time the French represented about 30% of the Canadian population, but only in the ministry of fisheries were they sufficiently represented, and they were shut out entirely in finance and trade and commerce. French representation in the ministries of human capital was even lower than their representation in policy-making ministries. It is only in the supportive and coordinative ministries that the French were slightly over-represented at 34%. Non-charter Canadians were shut out of all coordinative ministries for a century and were only briefly represented in seven of the twenty-five ministerial portfolios. Clearly the British political élite have dominated the first century of Canada's political history; the French were under-represented as junior charter partners, and others were practically unrepresented in the power élite. Unfortunately, we are not aware of any similar study of political influence since 1966.

British dominance of federal cabinet positions also shows in Table 8-2. The French were sufficiently represented during two periods (1927–30 and 1962–66), while other non-charter Canadians were shut out until 1927 and have been grossly under-represented since. The French were more fairly represented in the House of Commons, but again they were usually under-represented, although not as badly as in the cabinet. Other Canadians still remained very under-represented.

Breton and Roseborough (1980) show that, while the French were over-represented in the federal bureaucracy before 1900, for the next seventy-five years (until 1975), they were grossly under-represented. In 1946 French Canadians represented 29% of the Canadian population, but only 13% of the federal bureaucracy was French. During the last forty years this inequity has been in the process of correction. By the 1970s, when Trudeau and his strong French ministers were in power, the French were better represented. There was a concerted attempt during the Trudeau era to bring the French Canadians to parity in most of these political élite categories, and for the most part it succeeded.

TABLE 8-1   PERCENTAGE OF YEARS IN WHICH SPECIFIED MINISTRIES WERE HEADED BY REPRESENTATIVES OF ETHNIC GROUPS, 1867–1966

Ministries	English	French	Scottish	Irish	Other	N
Policy-making ministries						
Prime Minister	51	23	24	2	—	100
Finance	78	—	4	18	—	100
Agriculture	49	11	27	13	—	100
Fisheries	39	33	23	5	—	100
Mines	33	20	38	3	5	60
Northern Affairs	53	18	29	—	—	17
Trade and Commerce	69	—	26	—	5	74
Transport	40	16	18	26	—	88
National Defence	55	18	18	9	—	100
External Affairs	91	3	—	5	—	58
Total	55	15	20	9	1	797
Human capital ministries						
Interior	60	—	14	25	—	63
Indian Affairs	59	4	16	20	—	69
Veteran Affairs/						
Health and Welfare	56	23	19	4	—	79
Labour	49	5	23	15	9	66
Immigration and						
Citizenship	44	8	44	3	—	36
Total	55	9	21	14	1	313
Support ministries						
National Revenue	36	22	15	24	3	145
Receiver General	42	33	—	25	—	12
National Defence	82	—	—	18	—	28
Post Office	34	45	3	18	—	100
Public Works	30	49	16	5	—	100
Total	37	34	11	17	1	385
Co-ordinative ministries						
President of Privy						
Council	54	32	11	3	—	91
Justice	31	25	25	19	—	100
Solicitor General	17	54	26	3	—	35
Secretary of State	31	39	—	30	—	100
Total	36	34	14	16	—	326
Ministries without						
portfolio	45	14	28	13	—	135

Note: Total number of years varies by ministry, since each has not lasted the same length of time.

SOURCE: Raymond Breton and Howard Roseborough, 'Ethnic, Religious and Regional Representation in the Federal Cabinet, 1867–1966'. Unpublished manuscript, Toronto: University of Toronto, 1980.

TABLE 8-2 PERCENTAGE OF ETHNIC GROUPS REPRESENTED IN CANADIAN
CABINET BY POLITICAL PARTY IN POWER, 1867-1966

		(%)					Total
Period	Party	English	French	Scottish	Irish	Other	Years
1867–1873	Lib.-Cons.	42	23	22	13	—	86
1874–1878	Lib.	52	30	10	8	—	63
1879–1896	Lib.-Cons.	44	21	13	23	—	255
1897–1911	Lib.	46	21	17	17	—	229
1912–1917	Cons.	46	16	0	38	—	108
1917–1921	Unionist	60	6	18	16	—	73
1922–1925	Lib.	27	27	27	20	—	75
1926	Cons.	71	—	14	14	—	7
1927–1930	Lib.	33	33	18	11	6	73
1931–1935	Cons.	43	16	31	11	—	95
1936–1956	Lib.	51	23	21	4	2	303
1957–1962	Cons.	60	14	9	13	5	133
1962–1966	Lib.	44	33	20	—	3	102

SOURCE: Breton and Roseborough, 'Ethnic, Religious and Regional Representation in the Federal Cabinet, 1867–1966'. Unpublished manuscript. Toronto: University of Toronto, 1980.

With some variations the charter group political dominance is also evident in provincial politics. During the period 1961–73 in Quebec, most of the cabinet ministers were French, as expected, and there were a few ministers of British origin, with all the bureaucrats being French. In Ontario, this was reversed with eighteen British and one French minister, and all the bureaucrats were of British origin; others were not represented at all, even though they represented 31% of the Ontario population. British dominance of provincial government also continued in the West. While the British and others comprised equal numbers in the population (47%), ten ministers were British, and only four were non-charter, while all but two of the twenty-four bureaucrats were British. The same was true in British Columbia, with the other non-charter Canadians grossly under-represented.

These findings corroborate the general findings of Porter that the British élite are dominant in political Canada, that the French are junior partners, and that others are hardly represented. During the past twenty years this has changed more in favour of the French and non-charter groups, but it is happening only slowly. Laponce (1994: 179–202) clearly shows that the British, French and other ethnic groups have distinctive voting patterns. Future research is needed to update trends into the 1990s, to see whether visible

TABLE 8-3   ETHNIC ORIGIN OF NEW MEMBERS OF HOUSE OF COMMONS BY
PERIOD DURING WHICH FIRST ELECTED, 1867–1964

						%	
Period	French	English	Scottish	Irish	Other	Total	N
1867–1873	24.9	31.5	26.2	14.5	2.8	99.9	317
1874–1877	25.3	16.5	35.2	22.0	1.1	100.1	91
1878–1895	27.2	25.3	23.5	20.9	3.1	100.0	383
1896–1899	24.8	23.9	26.5	20.4	4.4	100.0	113
1900–1910	20.5	26.9	26.9	22.4	3.2	99.9	308
1911–1929	21.7	26.2	29.7	19.5	2.9	100.0	512
1930–1939	30.8	24.2	27.9	14.6	2.5	100.0	240
1940–1953	28.7	32.3	22.5	11.6	4.9	100.0	387
1954–1958	31.3	30.8	15.9	12.6	9.3	99.9	214
1959–1964	48.1	29.1	13.3	5.1	4.4	100.0	158
Total percentage of members of Parliament	27.0	27.6	24.9	16.6	3.8	99.9	
Total N	736	751	679	453	104		2,723

Note: Because of rounding of numbers, totals do not always correspond to sum of parts.

SOURCE: Ronald A. Manzer, *Canada: A Socio-Political Report*. Toronto: McGraw-Hill Ryerson, 1974.

minorities are getting political positions. Rick Ogmundson (1990, 1992a, 1992b) has been following the continued presence of the British élite and generally says the Canadian pattern is in transition, with the Canadian élites becoming less exclusive.

SOCIAL PRESTIGE OF ETHNIC GROUPS

We would expect that the British establishment, with its political power, would also translate this high profile into high social prestige rankings, Breton's second dimension of social status.

To what extent do the French, the other charter group, have a similar social standing in the eyes of Canadians, and where do the other ethnic and racial groupings rank in comparison? Are distinctions made between the different racial and religious groups as well? The relative social standing of ethnic groups in Canada should give us some idea of their chances of upward mobility and treatment in Canada. What criteria do respondents use to judge social standing? Do wealth, power, influence, heritage, colour, and length of residence influence prestige? We shall look for correlations between ethnic and occupational prestige.

Peter Pineo (1977) made one of the best studies of the relative social standing of ethnic groups in Canada by comparing the ratings of English and

French Canadians as well as English Canadians and Americans. Pineo and Porter (1967) took a national sample of 393 Canadians, asking them to sort the various ethnic groups in hierarchical order, placing the most prestigious at the top, and the less prestigious ones lower. They reported their findings, showing the differences in ranking between English and French Canadians, and compared these rankings with similar rankings made by ethnic groups in the United States. There are both similarities and important differences.

The general ranking of ethnic groups by Pineo's sample of Canadians placed the charter groups first, followed by western and northern Europeans, Mediterranean and central Europeans, and non-Caucasians at the bottom. Americans tended to rank ethnic groups in the United States in a similar way. These general rankings seem to be similar and the categories are fairly similar; however, specific groups are ranked quite differently by Canadians in English and French Canada. Americans tend to group all ethnic groups more closely together, making the differences between their prestige rankings of northern Europeans and non-Caucasians not nearly as great. Canadians tend to place the British much higher than the rest; as the British have had a greater and longer influence in Canada, this should not be a surprise.

In Table 8-4 we show the hierarchy of ethnic and racial groupings as seen by English and French Canadians using Pineo's data (1977; 1987). The differences are more obvious than the similarities. The French and English both ranked their own ethnic backgrounds at 74, and they both ranked non-Caucasians at the bottom, ranging from 24 to 35 in the bottom sixth of the hierarchy. English Canadians ranked the Japanese (35) and Chinese (33) a little higher than French Canadians did. Negroes (24) and Coloured (26) were ranked at the very bottom. Canadian Indians (28 and 33) were ranked almost at the bottom. Race seems to be an important factor in prestige and social standing.

The differences in rankings by English and French Canadians are most interesting. First, English Canadians rank English Canadians (83), the English (82), and the British (81) very high; French Canadians do not rank them nearly as high (78, 71, and 66 respectively). Others from the British Isles such as the Scots (75) and Irish (70) are also ranked highly by English Canadians; French Canadians rank them closer together in the middle (57 and 55 respectively). As expected, British origin is ranked highly; because they are the major charter group, they have socio-economic and political power, and they were also the largest group.

French Canadians rank French Canadians and English Canadians highest (78) and equal in status; the English Canadians rank themselves much higher (83), and French Canadians (56) much lower. While French Canadians see the two charter groups (French 72 and English 71) as equal partners in status, English Canadians rank French Canadians (56) and the French (60) much lower among northern Europeans. The French actually rank a bit higher than

T A B L E   8 - 4   HIERARCHY OF ETHNIC AND RACIAL GROUPS IN ENGLISH AND
FRENCH CANADA

English Canada (N = 300)		French Canada (N = 93)
English Canadians (83.1)	83	
English (82.4)	82	
British	81	
	80	
	79	
	78	
	77	French Canadians, English Canadians
	76	Catholics (77.6)
Protestants (75.3) Scots (75.2)	75	
My own ethnic background (74.4)	74	My own ethnic background (73.7)
	73	
	72	French (72.4)
	71	English (71.0)
Catholics (70.1)	70	
Irish (69.5)	69	
	68	
	67	
	66	British (66.0)
	65	
	64	
	63	
	62	
	61	
French (60.1)	60	
	59	
Dutch (58.4)	58	
Swedes (56.6)	57	Scots (56.5)
French Canadians (56.1) Swiss (55.7)	56	
Norwegians (55.3)	55	Irish (55.2) Protestants (54.8)
	54	
	53	
Danes (52.4)	52	
	51	Italians (51.3)
People of Foreign Ancestry (50.1)	50	Dutch (49.7)
Austrians (49.6) Belgians (49.1)	49	
Germans (48.7) Finns (47.6)	48	
	47	
Jews (46.1) Icelanders (45.6)	46	
	45	Belgians (45.3) Swedes (44.8)
Ukrainians (44.3)	44	Swiss (44.4)
Italians (43.1 Hungarians (42.6)	43	Jews (43.10)
Poles (42.0) Romanians (42.1)	42	
Lithuanians (41.4)	41	
Czecho-Slovaks (41.2)		
Greeks (39.9)	40	Germans (40.5) Ukrainians (40.0)

TABLE 8-4 (CONTINUED)

English Canada (N = 300)		French Canada (N = 93)
	39	People of Foreign Ancestry (38,9)
	38	Hungarians (38.4) Poles (38.0)
	37	Norwegians (38.0) Austrians (37.5)
Russians (35.8)	36	
Japanese (34.7)	35	
	34	Romanians (33.9) Greeks (33.5)
Chinese (33.1)	33	Russians (33.1) Icelanders (32.9)
	32	Canadian Indians (32.5) Czecho-Slovaks (32.4)
	31	Finns (32.3)
30		Danes (32.2)
	29	Lithuanians (29.1)
Canadian Indians (28.3)	28	Japanese (27.8)
	27	Coloureds (26.5)
Coloureds (26.3)	26	
Negroes (25.4)	25	Chinese (24.9) Negroes (23.5)

SOURCE: Peter Pineo, 'The Social Standing of Ethnic and Racial Groups',*Canadian Review of Sociology and Anthropology* 14 (1977): 147–57.

French Canadians. English Canada does not seem to see the two charter groups on the same level (Pineo, 1977).

Interestingly, Catholics (78) are ranked highest—with the French and English Canadians—by French Canadians, and fairly high (70) by English Canadians as well, although they are ranked lower than those of British origin. English Canadians rank Protestants (75) somewhat higher than Catholics; French Canadians rank Protestants much lower in the middle (55). This seems to reflect the high status that the Roman Catholic church has held in Quebec where the vast majority adhere to the Catholic church; Protestants in Quebec are a very small minority. Since about one-half of all Canadians are Catholic, the Catholics are ranked generally high by all.

English Canadians rank northern Europeans in the middle with the French (60), Dutch (58), Swedes (57), French Canadians (56), Swiss (56), Norwegians (55), Danes (52), Austrians (50), Belgians (49) and Germans (49) clustered in the fifties. French Canadians tend to rank northern Europeans in the forties. The Germans are at the bottom of the northern European pack, no doubt because of being the enemy during the two world wars (Pineo, 1977).

In the United States the Germans rank on top of the northern European cluster with the French, perhaps because there are so many Germans in the country.

Southern and eastern Europeans usually rank after northern Europeans. English Canadians rank the Ukrainians (44), Italians (43), Hungarians (43),

Poles (42), Romanians (42), Lithuanians (41), Czecho-Slovaks (41) and Greeks (40) in the forties and the lower middle. French Canadians follow this ranking with two exceptions: they rank the Italians higher (51) at the top of their northern European cluster and they rank the rest after northern Europeans, but generally lower in the thirties. Both groups rank the Russians (36 and 33) low, presumably because of the cold war. Non-Caucasians rank below the Caucasians.

The Pineo (1977) study just presented does not provide us with the answer to why Canadians ranked these groups in the manner that they did. It does not show whether prestige is related to socio-economic status, political power, size of group, racial biases and preferences, or simply because of familiarity with these groups. We need to document what importance socio-economic status plays, for example, and this we can do in the next study of ethnic groups in Canada and Toronto.

SOCIO-ECONOMIC STATUS AND MOBILITY

The information on ethnic power and status provided by Armstrong, Breton, and Pineo leads us to ask whether the Anglo-Saxons who created the industrial concentration in southern Ontario and who also are clearly considered ethnics of the highest prestige actually have more control over education, occupations, and income, the three objective indicators usually used to measure socio-economic status. Let us look first at comparative income data from the 1991 census, followed by a comparison of ethnic groups in Toronto, using the three socio-economic indicators.

NATIONAL CANADIAN ETHNIC INCOMES, 1981–1991

Using the 1981 and 1991 Canadian national census data, we have ranked twenty ethnic groups by their 1991 annual average incomes in Table 8-5. The top ten are all of European heritage, and most of them entered Canada a hundred or more years ago. The Jews rank first with average incomes of $37,146 which are more than twice as much as the $16,460 incomes of Latin Americans who rank lowest (Census Canada, 1991). The British rank seventh, a drop from second rank in 1981. The other charter group, the French, does not rank in the top half.

The French charter group ranks in twelfth place, in the second half of Table 8-5, similar to where they ranked in 1981. The last third of the twenty listed are mostly non-white, so that income clearly separates visible minorities from the rest, many of whom have also come more recently. Aboriginal peoples and recent Latin American immigrants earn half as much as Jews who rank first.

Comparing 1981 and 1991 rankings, we note that Italians have improved their rank most (from twelfth to tenth), and the British (from second to

TABLE 8-5   MEAN WAGE INCOMES OF CANADIAN EMPLOYED MALE
POPULATION AGED 20-60 BY ETHNIC GROUP, 1981–1991

Ethnic Group	ANNUAL INCOME	
	1981	1991
Jewish	$ 19,054	$ 37,146
Ukrainian	17,109	34,110
Other Single	15,510	31,927
German	16,887	31,506
Dutch	16,461	30,888
Multiple British/French	16,556	30,649
British	17,360	30,420
Multiple non British/French	16,190	29,928
Polish	17,095	29,656
Italian	15,588	29,550
Grand Mean	16,462	28,946
Other European	15,776	28,458
French	15,389	27,222
Portuguese	14,776	26,926
Chinese	14,120	26,392
South Asian	—	25,718
Other E/SE Asia	—	24,080
Black/Caribbean	14,442	23,346
Arab/West Asian	—	21,284
Aboriginal	—	18,779
Latin American C/S	—	16,460

SOURCE: The 1981 and 1991 Census of Canada Public Use Sample Tapes.

seventh) have dropped the most between 1981 and 1991. We need to look at other socio-economic indicators as well.

ETHNIC SOCIO-ECONOMIC STATUS IN TORONTO
John Porter thought the British élite clearly led the way in socio-economic and political power, and that Canadians of other ethnic backgrounds would need to play down their distinctive ethnicities if they wanted to keep up. Let us look at Toronto, the largest metropolitan centre in Canada, to gain a socio-economic perspective using education, occupation, and income indicators.

Raymond Breton and associates (1990) collected a sample of 2,338 adults of ten ethnic groups in Toronto to look at socio-economic factors. This

TABLE 8-6   ETHNIC GROUP MEANS AND SOCIO-ECONOMIC STATUS USING INDICES

Ethnic Groups	Composite SES Rank	Education (years)	Overall Income (dollars)	Occupational Status (Blishen)
			SES INDICES	
Jewish	1			
Men		14.2	12,860	51.4
Women		13.9	8,735	49.9
English	2			
Men		13.0	13,481	51.1
Women		12.6	10,017	48.7
Chinese	3			
Men		14.6	12,391	50.4
Women		13.0	10,333	46.1
German	4			
Men		12.8	13,132	46.5
Women		12.8	9,652	48.0
Ukrainian	5			
Men		12.7	12,522	45.3
Women		12.5	10,317	47.3
Italian	6			
Men		10.6	12,278	40.2
Women		11.4	8,840	43.7
West Indian	7			
Men		11.5	12,329	41.4
Women		11.4	8,800	38.9

SOURCE: Aysan Sev'er, W.W. Isajiw, and Leo Driedger, 'Anomie as Powerlessness: Sorting Ethnic Group Prestige, Class and Gender', *Canadian Ethnic Studies* 25 (1993): 84–99.

sample included the English (N of 343), Irish (78), Scottish (76), Germans (321), Ukrainians (354), Italians (351), Jews (348), Portuguese (164), Chinese (153), and West Indians (150). Breton et al. compared their educational, occupational, and income status, which varied considerably.

In Table 8-6 we have collapsed some of the Toronto data published by Sev'er, Isajiw, and Driedger (1993). We have ranked the eight ethnic groups in a composite which includes a summary of ethnic rankings on education, occupation, and income. Males and females have been controlled for comparison as well. First, we note in general that the Jewish and Majority Canadians rank on top, and the West Indians and Italians at the bottom.

Comparing the education of males on the three socio-economic status indicators, Chinese and Jews rank first, while Italians rank last. The other groups tend to be in the middle. West Indians have a fairly high educational status that is somewhat deviant from their overall socio-economic ranking. The rankings for females are quite similar to those of males.

Using Blishen occupational status scores, we find that Jews rank the highest, with the English close behind; Italians and West Indians are at the bottom. Females all rank lower than males in their respective groups, and in most cases the differences are considerable. Italian and West Indian female incomes are very low.

Sev'er et al. (1993) show that ethnic females' status compares well with males on education and least well on income. The range of differences between ethnic groups is enormous; Jews and English Canadians are on top, while the most recent immigrants such as the West Indians, and Italians are clearly at the bottom of the socio-economic hierarchy. This may be because they came from poor countries and have not yet had the opportunity to rise in status. More study is required to plot the social mobility of the various ethnic groups to see how they fare over the generations. West Indians are a visible minority.

John Porter feared that if ethnic groups did not shed their ethnic identity, their distinctiveness would keep them from competing in the job market, leaving them in lower-status occupational ghettos. Reitz (in Breton et al., 1990) explored ethnic occupational segregation in Toronto and found, for example, that Italians were usually employed as brick and stone masons (16.8 on index of concentration), barbers and hairdressers (14.4), labourers and construction workers (12.6), plasterers (11.4), and excavation workers (6.0). Jews were concentrated in medicine (10.2), fabric and textiles (8.0), law and notary work (7.9), and as physicians and surgeons (6.0). Others who ranked above a concentration of 5.0 were the Portuguese in labour and construction (9.2), the Chinese in restaurants (5.3), and the British in fire-fighting (5.0). These data do show that individuals of some ethnic groups concentrate in certain jobs more than others; the Italians and Jews especially did so, representing opposite ends of the socio-economic scale.

In his own study, Reitz (1982: 7) concludes that 'these considerations raise doubts about the extent to which the theory of majority group control can adequately explain all the important variations in allocations of occupational rewards among ethnic and racial groups. Ethnic status does not seem to correlate sufficiently with reward allocation, and it is difficult to explain many of the discrepant cases where they can hardly be attributed to conformity to the larger Canadian culture.' Reitz (1982: 9) suggests that ethnic businesses, for example, may serve the clientele of their own ingroup; as a business flourishes, however, it often expands to include customers of the larger population, thus becoming oriented to a more general market. In his analysis, Reitz (1982) concludes that Anglo-conformity in jobs is hard to document, and while this influence may apply for some groups, it clearly does not for others.

SOCIAL MOBILITY: ETHNICITY AS A RESOURCE
Isajiw and Driedger (1987) used the same sample of 2,338 adults of ten ethnic groups in Toronto that Reitz (1982 and 1990) used to explore the relationship between ethnicity and social mobility. Like van den Berghe, they assumed that ethnicity and class are two different, analytically distinct phenomena, with neither derived from the other. Isajiw and Driedger (1987) used ethnic identity scales to measure salience of ethnicity, and income, education, and occupation as socio-economic indicators to measure social class. They found that Jews, Majority Canadians, and the Chinese cluster in the top socio-economic status (SES) category; the Germans and Ukrainians rank intermediately; and the Italians, West Indians, and Portuguese cluster in the lowest category for both genders. The Majority Canadian, German, Jewish, and Chinese males attained the highest number of years of schooling (14); the Portuguese (6 years) and Italians (8 years) average the lowest number of years in formal education. The mean income range was not as great for males, but some females (West Indian) earned less than half as much as Jewish females. English-other, Jewish, and Ukrainian males earn the most, while West Indians and the Portuguese earn the least. The income extremes for both males and females tended to correlate with the high and low education clusters as well. The Chinese, Majority Canadians, and Jewish males showed the highest mean job status, while the Portuguese, Italians, and West Indians clustered in the lowest status category.

Isajiw, Sev'er, and Driedger (1993) plotted the socio-economic mobility of five groups (Italians, Ukrainians, Germans, Jews, and the British) beginning with the occupational Blishen scores of the fathers of first-generation respondents and, finally, the Blishen scores of third-generation respondents. Occupational mobility for the five groups varied considerably. The extent of mobility between the mean status of the fathers and the mean status of first-generation respondents varied considerably. It was the greatest for the Italians and Ukrainians, and the least for the Germans. The mobility from first to third generation also varied considerably; it was greatest for Italians and lowest for Jews (Isajiw, Sev'er, Driedger, 1993).

The data showed considerable variation in social mobility between ethnic groups. Isajiw, Sev'er, and Driedger (1993) also explored the direct relationship between ethnic identity and social mobility. They compared degrees of ethnic identity (ECI index) with the respondent's perception of his own social mobility (comparing his own job with the job his father had held while the respondent grew up). They found little correlation between occupational mobility and ethnic identity for the total sample, nor was there any significant correlation when they controlled for the six levels of socio-economic status (using the Blishen scale) and perceived mobility.

The percentages in Table 8-7 show that while roughly two-thirds of the very low and low respondents perceived that they held higher status jobs than

TABLE 8-7 ETHNIC ORIGIN GROUPS AND THEIR ETHNIC CULTURAL IDENTITY (ECI) USING SIX INDICATORS

	ETHNIC CULTURAL IDENTITY INDEX (ECI)						
Respondents' Occupational Status (Blishen Scale) %	0	1	2	3	4	5	Pearson's r Total
Very High	79	88	85	67	100	—	-.07
High	79	84	89	73	88	50	-.04
Medium High	71	75	78	74	71	55	.01
Medium Low	67	66	79	71	70	79	-.04
Low	68	70	66	76	73	76	-.02
Very Low	65	55	70	70	65	61	.00
TOTAL	72	73	78	72	72	68	-.02

their father, about three-fourths of the very high and high-status job holders thought they were more upwardly mobile. This does not vary by ethnic identity. Isajiw, Sev'er, and Driedger (1993) also controlled for three generations and the results were the same. These findings led them to reject Wiley and Porter's hypothesis. Isajiw, Sev'er, and Driedger (1993) concluded, first, that the eight ethnic groups do not all begin with the same degree of ethnic identity. First-generation West Indians scored highest, while the Germans scored lowest. First-generation ethnic identity ranged from high to medium depending on the group. We cannot assume that all first-generation immigrants start off with high identity scores.

Second, the eight ethnic groups did not all begin at the same socio-economic level when they arrived as first-generation immigrants. Indeed, their socio-economic status ranged from very high (the Jews) to very low (the Portuguese). Whereas first-generation Jews because of their high status had limited room for upward mobility, the Portuguese could theoretically move from lowest to highest status.

In the third place, the degree of maintenance of ethnic identity through three generations also varied greatly. Jewish identity remained high with very little change, while Italian identity changed enormously from among the highest to the lowest in three generations. Italians in Toronto were assimilating quickly, while Jews were not.

Finally, Isajiw, Sev'er, and Driedger found that socio-economic mobility also varied considerably. Since the Jews began on a very high status level when they arrived in Canada, their descendants had very little opportunity for upward mobility. The same was true for the British, who actually dropped slightly by the third generation. Italians ranked low on socio-economic status. Their opportunities for upward mobility were enormous, and they became the most mobile. These general observations show that the issues of ethnic identity and social mobility are multidimensional, multidirectional, and vary considerably by generations. Starting points vary, and the degree of change from their original identity and status positions also vary considerably.

We conclude that class and ethnicity are different phenomena, and each can be a resource or a drawback, depending on social conditions.

SUMMARY

John Porter's work, *The Vertical Mosaic*, outlined two major perspectives: the functional inequality theory, and the radical Marxist theory of social class. The functional theory of stratification, popular with many Americans, assumes that inequality is inevitable where the more able and more trained get higher-status jobs in the process of market competition. Marxists think that the social class system is unjust and unacceptable. Marx and neo-Marxists tend to think that ethnicity is only one variation of the class struggle and give ethnic and race relations little attention.

John Porter also tended to see social class as the major factor of change in the industrial Canadian society, with the majority of power allotted to the two charter groups. The British, being larger numerically, more dominant politically and economically, and having the benefits of the British colonial heritage on their side, have a great advantage over the French, who are junior partners. Ethnic groups who migrated to Canada later were relegated to entrance status, and were faced with fitting into a Canada defined and controlled by the two charter peoples. Porter's empirical studies supported his contention that the British were in the economic, political, and status power positions. Other scholars have contended that social mobility is possible, especially in the socio-economic area, and that maintenance of ethnic identity need not be a drawback for social mobility; indeed, it may be an asset.

Five empirical studies were examined to illustrate the theoretical discussion. Frederick Armstrong illustrated how the British establishment was formed in Ontario and linked with the British colonial power to attain political and economic power positions, an advantage which the French and others did not have. Thus southern Ontario has become the Canadian industrial heartland, the most powerful centre of Canada.

Raymond Breton shows that the British have always been politically dominant and that the French—although politically involved—have usually been under-represented politically. Non-charter Canadians have hardly been represented.

In Peter Pineo's study of the social standing of the various ethnic groups in

Canada, the British ranked highest, followed by northern Europeans, eastern and southern Europeans, and finally at the lowest level of prestige, non-Caucasian social minorities. This study clearly shows that the prestige of the various ethnic groups in Canada varies enormously.

Reitz's study of the education, income, and occupations of eight ethnic groups in Toronto demonstrated that the prestige rankings found by Pineo can indeed be substantiated empirically. Again the English rank on top and West Indians at the bottom, but the Chinese and Germans are higher on the socio-economic scale than in their prestige ranking. This study helps show the importance of socio-economic status in prestige rankings. Isajiw, Sev'er, and Driedger used the same Toronto sample to show the extent to which socio-economic status and ethnic identity are related. They found that identity and status vary by groups, that some groups move up faster than others, and that ethnicity and status are both independent factors which need to be considered separately.

CHAPTER 9

Apartheid: Segregation of Minorities

Anthony Richmond, in *Global Apartheid* (1994), suggests that refugees, racism, and the new world order are integrally tied up with social and spatial segregation of peoples:

> The word apartheid literally means 'aparthood' (c.f. neighbor-hood), that is, the separation of people into different areas.... From a sociological perspective, these are all actions, structures, and institutions associated with forcible isolation of people who are different. Because of the differences, they are perceived as having actually (potentially) conflicting relationships. Distancing is used to deal with the conflict. Then separation is imposed by a dominant group upon a less powerful one, the conflict is only temporarily resolved. Restitution and retribution may be delayed for generations, but the power struggle continues.... (Richmond, 1994: 206)

The principle of separation as a means of social control has a long history in Canada: witness the expulsion of the Acadians from the Maritimes in 1756, the separation of Upper and Lower Canada, the creation of Indian reserves, the formation of separate Catholic and Protestant school systems, and the separation of racial groups.

Power, status, and socio-economic factors tend to separate the rich from the poor, the educated from the illiterate, and white collar from blue collar occupational groups. While much of this differentiation seems to follow lines of socio-economic status, it is clear that recent immigrants and visible minorities are heavily represented among the have-nots. While structural functionists may see such differences as 'natural' differentiation which will always remain with us, political economy advocates see them as an on-going source of conflict which must be solved. For good or for ill, social and spatial ethnic residential segregation are means of 'apartheid'.

PERSPECTIVES ON SEGREGATION

The early Chicago sociologists were interested in the ecological segregation of humans in cities. They wanted to plot the spatial arrangements of humans by race, culture, occupation, religion, and the like. Some of these human spatial patterns where segregation happened voluntarily were influenced by political power, but other patterns occurred involuntarily because of coercion. Let us discuss two perspectives on how human ecological segregation may be studied.

DUNCANS' ZONAL SEGREGATION MODEL
Two well-known models, one developed by the Duncans (1957) and the other by Shevky and Bell (1955; Driedger, 1991), examine urban residential segregation. The Duncans' (1957) model is oriented to social class as the major factor that determines where people live in the city, based on the concentric zone theory of urban growth. The Duncans assume that the lower class residents live close to the centre where the oldest, cheapest housing is located because socio-economic status rises towards the outer zones. The Duncans predict that the higher status families such as the British, other northern Europeans, and Jews will live in the suburbs, and recent immigrants from low status, non-white racial groups will live near the centre. The Duncans used occupational mobility data as the basis for their study. Much work was devoted to social rank. The Duncans' model is based on the concentric zone model developed by Ernest Burgess in Chicago.

Burgess attempted to order and predict growth patterns of a city, using Chicago as his laboratory. He thought Chicago had grown like a tree, with concentric circles around a centre where the main business district was located. These circles grew ever larger as they expanded towards the periphery. Burgess suggested that each of these zones had a different land usage. *The Central Business District* is the innermost zone, the oldest business section; here business first began when the city was small. This concentration of business, commerce, and services meets the needs of downtown shoppers.

The Second Zone of Transition surrounds the business district and is often referred to as the slum. This zone still contains the oldest housing of the early days of the city, housing which has begun to deteriorate and which is in the immediate path of business and industrial expansion. This area tends to be heavily populated by lower income classes, by Old World immigrants, recent immigrants, racial groups, and social outcasts. Burgess called it the zone of transition because the people living there were often transient, and the housing would soon be demolished to make room for business expansion (Driedger, 1991; McGahan, 1995).

The Zone of Workingmen's Homes is the third zone moving out towards the periphery. In fact zones two to five are all residential zones, with the oldest and least desirable housing in zone two and the best housing located in zone five. *The Zone of Middle Class Dwellers*, even farther out from the centre, consists of professional, small business, managerial, and clerical people. *The Commuters' Zone* is on the outer periphery of the city, often beyond its political boundaries, and consists of satellite towns and suburbs that exist in a mutually dependent relationship with the metropolis, as 'bedroom communities'.

In their study, *The Negro Population of Chicago*, the Duncans plotted the distribution of Blacks in Chicago in 1920, 1930, 1940, and 1950, using census tract data. The Black Belt, which began between 10th and 40th streets in 1920, spread westwards and extended southwards to 70th street by 1950; it was 99% Black. The Duncans preferred to think in zonal terms and tried to fit the Black Belt phenomenon into socio-economic (income, education, occupation) patterns, directing their attention to invasion and succession trends, thinking that the larger racial patterns had resulted from these trends; more recent immigrants who were non-white and poor would replace older groups who had moved to better places. The Duncans focused on crowding, education, unemployment, home ownership, and rental costs, all of which were socio-economic factors. While the Duncans were busy looking at Blacks in Chicago in socio-economic terms, trying to fit the racial patterns into the zonal model of Burgess, Shevky, and Bell were beginning to follow the multiple nuclei perspective to predict racial and ethnic patterns.

SHEVKY AND BELL'S MULTIPLE NUCLEI MODEL

Shevky and Bell (1955), in their studies of Los Angeles and San Francisco, were able to break out of past thinking based on the zonal theory and to pursue the multiple nuclei theory proposed by Harris and Ullman (McGahan, 1995). Duncan (1955: 84–5) recognized their novel, comparative approach and the opportunities it provided for both economic and social research; however, he severely criticized their conceptual framework and their methodological measures. It is true that their methods could have been improved, but their multiple nuclei conceptual framework offered many possibilities, which others have since used with considerable success.

In 1945 Chauncey Harris and Edward Ullman had developed another theory which suggested that as a city grew it diversified considerably, and land use diversified as well (Harris and Ullman, 1965). They agreed that a city will begin with a major central business district (CBD), which is an important sector in most cities. This central district, however, develops along locational, cultural, and economic lines that the concentric zone theory often does not explain.

> For example, while wholesale and light manufacturing (2) . . . might be near the CBD, low-income residences (3) might be in various separate districts around it. A medium-income residential district (4) might abut the CBD and be bordered on its outer edge by a high-income residential area (5). Between the two might exist a secondary business district (7), and farther out might exist a completely separate residential suburb (8). Heavy manufacturing (6) might be a relatively large distance from the CBD and evolve an industrial-residential suburb (9) near it. (Spates and Macionis, 1987: 175)

Why did these more complex patterns develop? Dealing with zones seemed too rigid, especially when the specific land uses were being more carefully considered. Another reason for differentiation of land use is that the various activities are not always compatible and therefore separate themselves into nuclei some distance from each other. Residential and industrial areas become separated and this separation is reinforced by zoning laws.

Third, different racial and ethnic groups such as East Indians and Sikhs may enter a city and begin to concentrate in one area where a cluster of businesses provide specialized foods and clothing, and then become a node attracting more immigrants of the same cultural background.

Fourth, people want to separate themselves for economic and social class reasons. Some can afford only older and less expensive housing and tend to look for the cheapest residential areas. Others can afford newer or better housing and pay more attention to prestige and status, often escaping to the suburbs. Suburbanites also try to locate close to traffic beltways that will permit easy commuting to their work. Industrial suburbs may spring up close to the industries in which blue-collar workers are employed, saving transportation costs as well as traffic hassles (Driedger, 1991; McGahan, 1995).

Basically, Harris and Ullman (1945) suggested in their multiple nuclei theory that land use cannot always be predicted. Historical, cultural, and socioeconomic values will have differing impacts on cities, and the exact location of an economic or ethnic nucleus cannot be determined for all cities. The formation of these nuclei depend on a variety of factors—topographical, historical, cultural, racial, economic, and political—that do not result in the same combination for each urban area. The Burgess zonal pattern suggested inevitable predetermined patterns of location. Harris and Ullman suggest that these patterns vary depending on circumstances.

By using factor analysis, Shevky and Bell could incorporate and control for more variables. In addition to their three factors—social rank, family status, and ethnicity—Shevky and Bell (1955) developed indices of isolation and segregation that others have found useful (Driedger, 1980). Shevky and Bell (1955: 44) defined ecological isolation as 'the residential concentration of the members of a particular group with other members of the same group'.

Their segregation ratio was used to measure a second dimension of interaction, that involving the probable interaction between members of a subordinate ethnic group with members of all other subordinate groups in the metropolis. Their reasoning was that minorities within spatial enclaves or minorities in proximity to each other could band together to strengthen their specific interests when negotiating with majority groups. Shevky and Bell's approach is helpful because it shows that ethnicity is an independent influence on spatial location, and results in ethnic nuclei that do not necessarily conform to zonal or sector patterns.

DAWSON'S SEGREGATION IN MONTREAL
Charles Dawson began his studies at the University of Chicago in 1914, where he also worked with Robert Park (Shore, 1987: xiv). Like many in the Chicago School, Dawson saw the city as a social organism. When Dawson went to teach at McGill University in 1922, Montreal was exploding with activity and growth; by 1928 it had at least 1,400 industries, stockyards, and packing houses, so Dawson and his students were among the first in Canada to categorize minorities according to the Burgess concentric zone model learned in Chicago. In 1929 Dawson and Gettys (1929: 130) published some of the patterns of growth they had discovered in Montreal; these are shown in Figure 9-1.

Dawson was mostly interested in describing the general growth pattern of Montreal and the extent to which it conformed to the Chicago concentric-zone model. He made 'no attempt to account for . . . the division of the city, straight through the centre, into French and anglophone groups' (Shore, 1987: 136). Examination of Dawson and Gettys' drawing of Montreal in Figure 9-1 shows that indeed the English are clearly located in the west, segregated by Mount Royal from the French. Immigrants from other countries—Negroes, Italians, Russians, and Chinese—are concentrated near the central business section between the English and French solitudes. Dawson's students later began to examine the effects of transportation lines on population patterns, and the location of ethnic groups such as Blacks, Chinese, Italians, and recent immigrants in the city.

Mount Royal dominates Montreal ecologically, so that the concentric zone pattern could not unfold as it did in Chicago (where by the way Lake Michigan also interrupts a full circle). Thus, the second image in Figure 9-1 is skewed out of shape. This suggests that the landscape and topography tend to influence the shape of spatial urban development as it did in Los Angeles where Shevky and Bell did their first study of multiple nuclei, and in San Francisco where hills, bays and coastlines play a similar shaping role. However, Dawson did find Blacks in the second zone of transition in the oldest residential section next to downtown in zone two. Since then many other immigrants have come to Montreal, so that it has become a complex mosaic of ethnic and racial groups which resembles the multiple nuclei model (Lazar and Douglas, 1993).

ETHNIC CONCENTRATION IN WINNIPEG
One of the simplest ways of plotting ethnic concentrations is to take the Canadian census data and see to what extent persons of one or several groups tend to be concentrated in one area of the city. Driedger and Church (1974) did extensive studies of ethnic groups in Winnipeg, tracing their concentration, segregation, and isolation using 1941, 1951, 1961 and 1971 census data.

FIGURE 9-1   DAWSON'S STUDY OF SEGREGATION PATTERNS IN MONTREAL

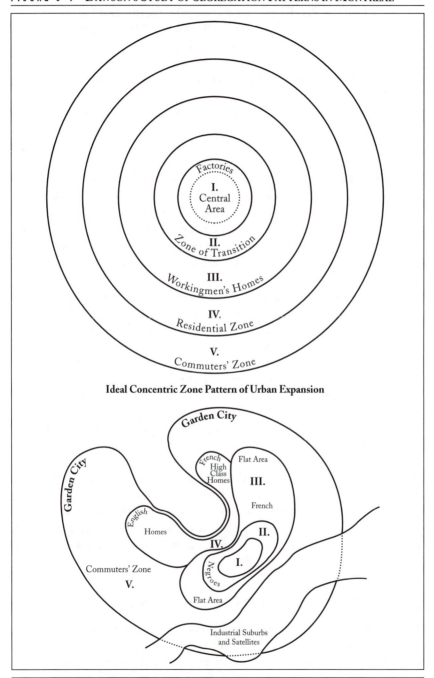

Ideal Concentric Zone Pattern of Urban Expansion

SOURCE: Dawson and Gettys, *Introduction to Sociology* (1929), p. 130.

Their studies showed that the French were concentrated in St Boniface on the east side of the Red River since the early 1800s, the East Europeans were concentrated in the North End (Jews, Ukrainians, Poles) since the late 1800s, and the British were concentrated heavily in the western and southern parts (St James, St Charles, Fort Garry) of the city. As new immigrants arrived, these concentrations have shifted with Jews and some Ukrainians moving out of the North End into the suburbs.

To illustrate some of the recent clusters of ethnic concentration in Winnipeg we present 1991 census data in Figure 9-2 showing four very interesting ethnic concentrations which represent a wide range of variations. The French are still very heavily concentrated in their original St Boniface area where they have now resided for nearly 200 years (shown in map A). A hundred years after the East Europeans settled in the Winnipeg North end, we see that many of the Polish Winnipeggers, reinforced by new recent immigrants, are still concentrated in parts of the North End (map B). These were among the early white European immigrants who have been in Winnipeg for a long time, and they are still concentrated in their original separate areas.

More recently, visible minorities have come to Winnipeg, and settled in the inner city. The Filipinos (map C) are concentrated in the west end of Winnipeg, just west of the central business district, in Burgess's zone of transition, as well as in the northwest corner near the airport which is also in commercial-industrial transition. Nine per cent of Winnipeg's population are aboriginal (map D), the largest population in any metropolitan centre in Canada, and they have moved to the city from northern reserves and areas into the very centre of the city. This is the oldest part of the city, and the least desirable housing, located near the central business district and the Canadian Pacific Railway tracks.

These four maps using 1991 census data show that these four ethnic groups are concentrated in quite different areas. Two white European groups (French and Polish) have stayed in their original respective areas for a long time, and two visible minority groups (Filipino and Aboriginal) have occupied different inner city areas more recently. Race, social class and immigrant status are important factors which separate these groups, in a multi-nuclear way as Shevky and Bell predicted.

ETHNIC RESIDENTIAL CONCENTRATIONS

To what extent have the Duncan and Shevky and Bell approaches to research on segregation been applied to Canadian cities? Stanley Lieberson and T.R. Balakrishnan have done the most work in a national context. Anthony Richmond (1972) was among the first to focus on segregation in Toronto, and

FIGURE 9-2 ETHNIC CONCENTRATION IN WINNIPEG, 1991

French in Winnipeg 1991
Based on mother tongue

Concentration Index
3+
1
0

Filipinos in Winnipeg 1991
Based on mother tongue

Concentration Index
3+
2
1
0

Polish in Winnipeg 1991
Based on mother tongue

Concentration Index
3+
1
0

Aboriginals in Winnipeg 1991
Based on mother tongue

Concentration Index
3+
2
1
0

SOURCES: Statistics Canada, *Ethnic Origin: The Nation,* Catalogue 93–315, and *Home Language and Mother Tongue, The Nation,* Catalogue 93–317.

Driedger and Church (1974) did the same in Winnipeg. How have other factors influenced residential segregation, in Canadian cities?

NATIONAL URBAN DIVERSITY

Stanley Lieberson (1970) was one of the first sociologists to study residential segregation in Canadian cities; he focused especially on language. He used a slightly modified form of the segregation index proposed by Bell (1954), and worked with census data. Comparing thirteen metropolitan centres in Canada, he found that there was a considerable correlation between residential segregation and retention of the French language. A score of 1.0 on the index means that the correlation between residential segregation and language maintenance is perfect; a score of 0.0 means that there is no correlation between the two. French language retention was highest in Quebec City (1.0), Montreal (.99), Trois-Rivières (.98), and Ottawa (.81); the concentrations of the French-speaking population in these cities was also highest; in cities where French language retention was low, such as Regina (.18), Calgary (.21), and London (.20), the French populations were also sparse. He concluded that French retention ratios will vary inversely to the degree to which French Canadians encounter people who speak only English (Lieberson, 1970: 216).

T.R. Balakrishnan and associates (1982, 1987, 1990, 1995) have done the most extensive work in Canada on comparing large numbers of ethnic groups in most of the metropolitan areas. Their work is also the most recent and uses the latest available census figures. In their first work (Balakrishnan and Jarvis, 1979: 218–27) they used 1961 and 1971 census data to compare all metropolitan centres in Canada; they found very little change (1961 to 1971) in segregation patterns. They also found that socio-economic status was predominantly sectoral, family status was zonal, and ethnic status followed neither pattern—similar to findings in the USA where ethnic groups seemed to follow multiple nuclei patterns.

Balakrishnan (1995) has now updated his work using a variety of diversity, concentration, dissimilarity and segregation indexes. Table 9-1, using an ethnic diversity index, indicates that ethnic diversity between 1961 and 1991 has not increased in the maritimes where (except for Halifax), the population is nearly homogeneously British. The same is also true for metropolitan centres east of Montreal in Quebec, where the population is homogeneously French. Montreal was much more ethnically diverse in 1961 (.45), a diversity that has increased somewhat by 1991 (.53).

Urban centres west of Montreal were already ethnically diverse in 1961, ranging from .58 to .75 (exceptions Victoria and London). By 1991 all of these centres west had become considerably more ethnically diverse, seven of them ranging in the seventies and seven in the eighties on the diversity index.

T Λ B L E 9 - 1   INDICES OF ETHNIC DIVERSITY FOR CENSUS METROPOLITAN AREAS
OF CANADA, 1961–1991

Metropolitan Area	1961	1971	1981	1991
St John's	.09	.08	.11	.08
Halifax	.45	.38	.42	.47
Saint John	.38	.34	.38	.35
Chicoutimi	—	.12	.08	.07
Quebec	.11	.13	.11	.10
Sherbrooke	—	—	—	.17
Trois-Rivières	—	—	.09	.08
Montreal	.45	.55	.54	.53
Ottawa-Hull	.63	.64	.69	.71
Oshawa	—	—	.51	.68
Toronto	.61	.64	.72	.80
Hamilton	.58	.60	.61	.74
St Catharines-Niagara	—	.68	.67	.76
Kitchener	.69	.66	.67	.75
London	.46	.46	.51	.63
Windsor	.72	.72	.75	.79
Sudbury	.74	.71	.73	.70
Thunder Bay	—	.76	.75	.83
Winnipeg	.75	.76	.79	.85
Regina	.72	.72	.74	.81
Saskatoon	.72	.74	.74	.83
Calgary	.64	.66	.67	.79
Edmonton	.75	.75	.76	.84
Vancouver	.60	.63	.67	.80
Victoria	.39	.43	.46	.59

Note: Index of ethnic diversity is defined as $1 - P_i^2$, where P_i is the proportion of the population in the i th ethnic group. Only single ethnic origin groups are included in the calculation for 1981, and 1991 indices.

Clearly the maritimes are homogeneously British, Quebec is French, and Ontario and the West multicultural. This diversity needs to be examined more closely, especially the variations in race.

CONCENTRATION OF VISIBLE MINORITIES

Visible minorities have increased from five to about ten per cent of the Canadian population between 1971 and 1991. Because of changes in the immigration act in the sixties, visible minorities are now able to compete for entrance into Canada, and those who landed in turn sponsor immediate kin to join them. Visible minorities who came as immigrants during the past two decades came mostly to Canada's cities, especially Toronto and Vancouver.

By 1991 almost one-fourth (22%) of the population of metropolitan Vancouver were visible minorities, and about one-fifth of the population of metropolitan Toronto were visible non-whites. Calgary (15%) and Edmonton (13%) ranked third and fourth, and Winnipeg (10%) approached the national average (Balakrishnan and Hou, 1995). These five metropolitan areas have the highest concentrations of visible minorities, and we would expect that patterns of residential segregation would also be highest there.

In Census Metropolitian Areas (CMAs) east of Montreal, except for Halifax (6%), only one or two per cent of their populations are non-white. CMAs in the west all have more than five per cent of their populations who are visible minorities, largely of Asian and aboriginal descent. Except for Montreal (7%), CMAs in Quebec have almost no visible minorities. Except for Toronto, Ontario CMAs have less than the Canadian average of ten per cent—closer to five per cent or less.

Balakrishnan and Hou (1995: 12) used the data in the 1991 Canada census and we have presented some of their results in fourteen metropolitan centres in Table 9-2. The British, Germans, French, and Italians, a select group of whites, are among the least concentrated (not highly clustered in a few census tracts). British scores are very low (except for Montreal where they are a small minority). Italians who have arrived in Canada more recently are the most concentrated of the whites, but generally lower than visible minorities. The Chinese, Blacks, Aboriginals, and South Asians who are considered visible minorities, all score above .50 in all of the centres. They are clearly more concentrated than whites. The Jewish Canadians, considered a religious group, are more concentrated residentially than any other group. We conclude that both race and religion are important factors which differentiate ethnic residential concentration.

While concentration of whites is low in Halifax in the east, concentration scores for visible minorities and Jews are similar to that of other centres. The Chinese are the most concentrated in Montreal (.71), Blacks in St Catharines (.75), Aboriginals (.70) in Toronto and Hamilton, and South Asians (.79) as well as Jews (.93) in Montreal. Overall, Montreal has the most segregated whites, visible minorities and Jews, and Calgary the lowest.

Balakrishnan and Hou (1995) have also presented ethnic concentration comparisons in Toronto and Montreal, in the form of Lorenz curves (Figure 9-3). The Lorenz curve is a simple way of examining concentration to see whether an ethnic group is over-represented in certain areas of the city compared to others. To plot the curve the census tracts are arranged in

TABLE 9-2   GINI INDICES OF CONCENTRATION BY ETHNIC GROUP FOR MAJOR CENSUS METROPOLITAN AREAS OF CANADA, 1991

	White Europeans				Visible Minorities				Religious
	British	German	French	South Italian	Chinese	Black	Aboriginal	South Asian	Jewish
Halifax	.05	.17	.15	.47	.68	.69	.64	.69	.81
Montreal	.47	.47	.46	.67	.71	.66	.49	.79	.93
Ottawa	33	.29	.67	.59	57	.58	52	.61	.72
Toronto	.25	.28	.28	.63	.65	.55	.70	.56	.90
Hamilton	.09	.20	.22	.43	.58	.60	.70	.59	.81
St Catharines	.06	.32	.39	.42	.64	.75	.69	.69	.80
Kitchener-Waterloo	.10	.28	.20	.39	.56	.60	.63	.48	.77
London	.03	.11	.17	.37	.59	.52	.52	.60	.83
Windsor	.06	.17	.21	.39	.61	.53	.64	.65	.73
Winnipeg	.16	.26	.53	.44	.60	.52	.67	.67	.86
Calgary	.04	.11	.19	.45	.50	.58	.56	.60	.79
Edmonton	.09	.19	.23	.59	.53	.56	.58	.65	.84
Vancouver	.17	.18	.26	.54	.63	.57	.67	.61	.73
Victoria	.05	.13	.29	.39	.54	.74	.53	.63	.55

SOURCE: T.R. Balakrishnan and Feng Hou, 'The Changing Patterns of Spatial Concentration and Residential Segregation of Ethnic Groups in Canada's Major Metropolitan Areas 1981–1991'. Paper presented at the annual meetings of the Population Association of America, San Francisco, 6–9 April 1995, p. 12 (an adaptation).

FIGURE 9-3   CONCENTRATION CURVES FOR SELECTED ETHNIC GROUPS

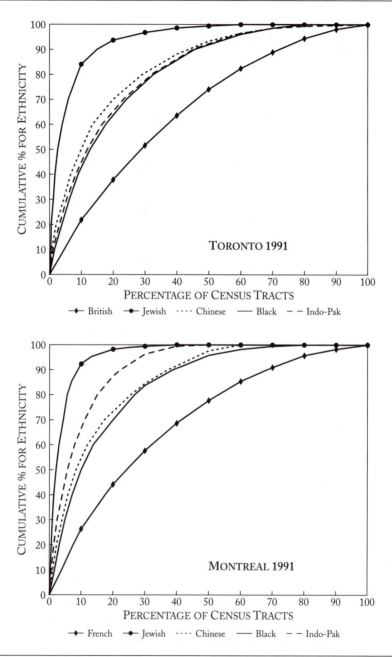

TORONTO 1991

PERCENTAGE OF CENSUS TRACTS

→ British   → Jewish   ---- Chinese   —— Black   – – Indo-Pak

MONTREAL 1991

PERCENTAGE OF CENSUS TRACTS

→ French   → Jewish   ---- Chinese   —— Black   – – Indo-Pak

SOURCE: T.R. Balakrishnan and Feng Hou, 'The Changing Patterns of Spatial Concentraion and Residential Segregation . . .', 1995.

descending order of the ethnic group population. Then the cumulative percentage of the ethnic population is plotted. The straight diagonal line from bottom left to top right represents equal distribution, or a score of zero concentration on a 0 to 1 range (Balakrishnan and Hou, 1995). The Gini index measures the proportion of the area above the diagonal between the curve and the diagonal.

For the Jewish population the indices are the highest, reaching values over .90 in the largest centres of Toronto and Montreal. For the visible minorities, including Blacks, Chinese and South Asians, the indices range around .60. The British in Toronto, and the French in Montreal, who represent white European groups, are closest to the straight diagonal of zero, with low index scores of about .20. The Lorenz curve illustrates comparative degrees of ethnic concentration already plotted in more detail in Table 9-2.

Race and social class often combine to force many visible minorities to live in deteriorated sections of the city where it is difficult to raise families because of limited resources and disorganized social environments. Early Chinese bachelors clustered together in Chinatowns to survive and protect themselves against prejudice and discrimination (Lai, 1988). Jews in Montreal, Toronto, Vancouver, and Winnipeg were and still are highly clustered together to support their Jewish institutions, family life, and distinctive religion. However, aboriginals in Canadian cities are forced to live in the inner cities because of unemployment, low incomes, and often discrimination (Winnipeg has the highest concentration). Descendants of northern Europeans usually have the greatest freedom from discrimination because they have the jobs, the means, and therefore the opportunities to live where they choose (Anderson and Frideres, 1981: 299–304).

APARTHEID: STUDIES IN SEGREGATION

To get some sense of the diversity of ethnic residential segregation in Canada, we shall examine studies of Blacks in Nova Scotia and Toronto, and Chinatowns. Blacks and Chinese were among the most concentrated and segregated using indexes (Balakrishnan and Hou, 1995). These studies will show that there are a variety of social reasons why minorities live and work spatially apart and segregated into nuclei.

BLACKS IN NOVA SCOTIA

Black studies are numerous in the United States where there are more Blacks than the entire population of Canada. There are relatively few Blacks in Canada; in fact, they comprise less than one per cent of the population. They first settled in Nova Scotia, and a large proportion are still located around Halifax. Blacks have been in Canada at least since 1628, when a young slave was brought to New France; by the mid-eighteenth century there were about 4,000 Black slaves in New France (Winks, 1971: 26). The United Empire Loyalists brought some slaves with them, but slavery was usually abandoned because it was not profitable in Canada. Slavery was practised in British North America until 1834 when all slaves within the British Empire were freed. Although the first Blacks came to Nova Scotia, more recently they have entered Toronto and Montreal in larger numbers (Calliste, 1987: 1–20).

Fortunately, Frances Henry (1973) researched thirteen Black rural and urban communities (Figure 9-4) in Nova Scotia. Interviews were conducted by a team of Black students in each of these thirteen communities, so that in her volume *Forgotten Canadians: Blacks in Nova Scotia* (1973), Henry could provide a general context of Black communities showing the rural and urban diversity of the province. Interviews in each of these communities showed that 42% of the Blacks had less than a grade school education, that their incomes were very low, that they were employed in the lower status occupations, that many were unemployed, that they were pessimistic about chances for upward mobility, and that they often reported prejudice and discrimination.

Henry and associates selected two Black communities to study ethnographically in depth. Vale Haven is a small, depressed rural community located 300 miles from Halifax in southeastern Nova Scotia. Far Town is a lower-class semi-urban Black community about ten miles from Halifax. It is also in an economically depressed area. These two ethnographic studies qualify for our ethnic community search and demonstrate the life of a visible minority in the Atlantic Region.

The small, rural, Black community of Vale Haven lies along an inland dirt road that is an extension of one of the streets of Sea View (a White coastal town). It has a small primary school, two churches, and a community hall. Vale Haven is entirely dependent upon Sea View's services, which include five grocery stores, a clothing store, a bank, a post office, a funeral parlour, two garages, a hospital, a courthouse, a pool hall, schools, and churches (Henry, 1973: 38).

In 1970 Vale Haven had a population of 294. Very little use was made of the land, except that a few residents planted gardens. A few kept a horse and cart; there were twelve cars and three or four trucks in the town. Most of the houses were ramshackle, unpainted and neglected, although two had inside plumbing and running water. One-third of the houses had no electricity. Few appliances were found, and the furniture was old and sometimes broken. A few houses had telephones, radios, and a television. Most of the people wore poor-quality clothes that were often torn (Henry, 1973: 42–3).

Many of Vale Haven's Blacks were out of work and were disillusioned about finding work. Younger people tended to leave for work outside the community, leaving the children and the elderly in Vale Haven. The Baptist church was served by a minister who came in on occasional rotation, and

FIGURE 9-4   LOCATION OF THIRTEEN BLACK COMMUNITIES IN NOVA SCOTIA

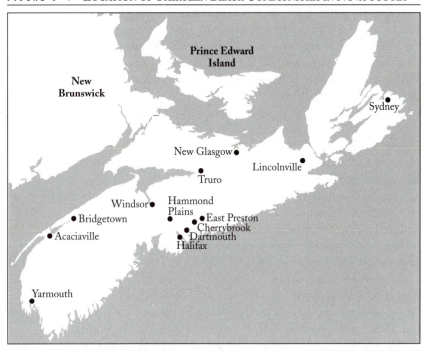

SOURCE: F. Henry, *Forgotten Canadians: The Blacks of Nova Scotia.* Don Mills, Ontario: Longman Canada, 1973, p. 17. Reprinted by permission of Harcourt Brace Jovanovich, Canada.

church attendance was small and sporadic (Henry, 1973: 40–5). Vale Haven residents went for supplies to Sea View; there was little interaction between the Blacks and Whites. Men in Vale Haven tended to meet in the evenings for joking, drinking, and storytelling, and privacy was almost non-existent. Vale Haven, a segregated rural Black community, tucked away from general Nova Scotian life and activity, is a good example of rural apartheid.

Far Town, a second Black community studied in detail by Henry, was located in a semi-urban string of houses along an unpaved road ten miles out of Halifax. Three Black communities (Far Town, New Town, and East Town) represent the densest population of Blacks in Nova Scotia, estimated to be about 3,000 in 1970. Almost all of Far Town's Blacks had radios and televisions, and one-third of them owned cars. Far Town's population of 700 comprised fifty-two households with fairly stable families (Henry, 1973: 57). Women were able to get jobs more easily than men by working as domestics in Halifax.

Support for the Baptist church in the community was declining. Politicians tended to visit the area only during election time when they needed Black votes, but did little for the community. Far Town's Blacks were in need of help but expecting little. There were few militants agitating for change among the Blacks, and the community was generally conservative, unwilling to confront the White power structures directly. Blacks and Whites were seldom in contact, even when they worked at the same place. Semi-urban Far Town was similar to Vale Haven, only larger with a few more conveniences and opportunities for work in Halifax.

These two ethnographic studies are good rural and semi-urban samples of most of the Black communities plotted in Figure 9-1. They all face a life of poverty at the periphery of White society. They are usually segregated, services are lacking, and schools, churches, and social institutions are limited. Blacks in Nova Scotia are marginalized largely because of race.

Donald Clairmont and Dennis Magill (1974) have documented the life and death of Africville, that no longer exists. 'Africville was a Black enclave within the city of Halifax, inhabited by approximately 400 people, comprising 80 families, many of whom were descended from settlers who came over a century ago' (Clairmont and Magill, 1974: 19). It was tucked into a corner of Halifax, where it was relatively invisible, and was referred to as 'shack town'. The ghetto was isolated from the rest of Halifax behind the railroad and city dump, and was surrounded on three sides by water (Bedford Basin). Most of the Black families had squatter rights; those who did not, rented.

'Slavery was never instituted by statute in Nova Scotia, yet slavery was practised in Halifax a year after the city was founded (1749) and, over the next five decades, it was not uncommon in other parts of the province' (Krauter and Davis, 1978: 41–68). At the outbreak of the American Revolution, there were approximately five hundred slaves, many of whom had come with their New England masters. Slave-holding Loyalist immigrants increased the number by approximately a thousand. There were also refugee Blacks who settled at Preston near Halifax on small lots of rocky soil and scrubby forest ranging from three to four hectares (Clairmont and Magill, 1974: 42).

The area that eventually came to be known as Africville was settled by the slaves who had settled at Preston but could not make a living because of the poor land. They came to the shore of Bedford Basin in the area that is now just below the A. Murray McKay bridge. This area was convenient for fishing and also near opportunities for wage labour. The Africville population increased tenfold between 1850 and 1964. The people had little education and very low incomes; a third of the adult population was unemployed, another third had irregular work, and the final third worked in low paid jobs as porters, domestics, labourers, clerical workers, and dockworkers. Sewerage, lighting, and other public services were conspicuously absent in Africville (Clairmont and Magill, 1974: 19). The people obtained water from improvised wells that were often in a poor state. There were no paved roads.

The Africville land seemed to be a prime site for potential industrial development. The city of Halifax owned properties near it, the railway was close by, and the shoreline was valuable for harbour development. Discussions began after 1955 about removing the Black community. After numerous studies and reports it was decided in 1974 to relocate the residents of the community (Clairmont and Magill, 1974: 180).

Once relocation was agreed on, the Halifax City Council accepted the responsibility of providing the relocatees with safe, sanitary, and decent housing. About 75% were relocated in urban renewal projects within walking distance of their former dwellings. They received better housing but they were now renters instead of landowners or owners of dwellings; only one-third owned their own homes after relocation. The lack of a regular income made it difficult to pay mortgages and service and maintenance bills. Most families of Africville were relocated in Uniacke Square; this was two-storey public housing. Clairmont and Magill (1974: 223) interviewed many relocatees. Two-thirds said they had more difficulties making ends meet in their new homes. Over half said they were able to stay in contact with their former Africville friends; but over half also thought they could no longer count on their neighbours for help. A majority felt they had lost a feeling of belonging, and that the friendliness and trustworthiness of neighbours had declined. These were the social costs of relocation. Now old Africville is a public park where formerly there was a segregated Black community.

ARRIVAL OF CARIBBEANS IN TORONTO
While the history of Blacks in Nova Scotia dates back two hundred years to slavery, the more recent immigration—after a change to the points system—opened Canada up to the arrival of Caribbeans, most of them Black. In 1967, 8,400 arrived in Canada which represented 4% of all arrivals; to a high of 28,000 arrivals in 1974 represented 13% of all immigrants that year (Anderson, 1993: 59). By 1990 this had dropped to some 14,000 arrivals, 7% of all newcomers that year (Henry, 1994). Caribbeans are highly visible, coming principally from Jamaica, Guyana, Haiti, and Trinidad and Tobago. Since many of them had to score highly on the immigrant point system, they are much better educated and skilled than rural Nova Scotia Blacks. Since they came from newly independent countries where Blacks and non-whites are large majorities, they are also much more self-assured and expect more from their host country than Blacks in Nova Scotia who came out of centuries of slavery and oppression.

In Figure 9-5, Anderson (1993: 67) has plotted a summary of Caribbeans who arrived in Canada between 1967 and 1989. Of the 301,000 who arrived during these 23 years, representing 9% of all immigrant arrivals, 36% came from Jamaica, 21% from Guyana, 17% from Haiti, 14% from Trinidad and

FIGURE 9-5   ORIGIN AND DESTINATION OF CARIBBEAN-CANADIAN
IMMIGRATION, 1967–1989

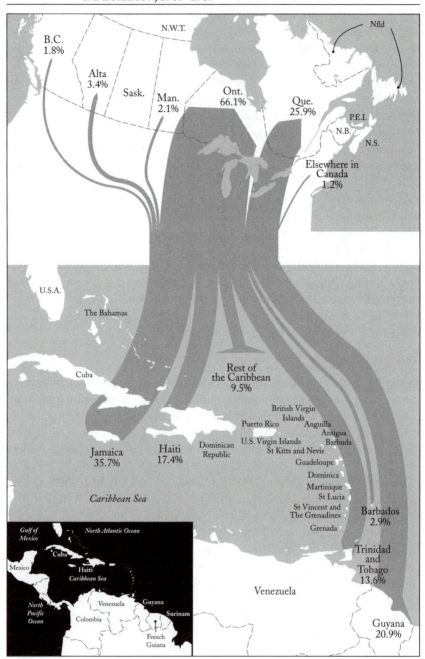

SOURCE: Wolseley W. Anderson, *Caribbean Immigrants: A Socio-Demographic Profile*. Toronto: Canadian Scholars Press, 1993, p. 67.

Tobago, and 10% from other points in the Caribbean. Two-thirds of these Caribbean immigrants arrived in Ontario (66%) from former British colonies such as Jamaica, Guyana, and Trinidad, where they learned English, and most of these arrived in Toronto (Walker, 1984: 14). Immigrants from Haiti who knew French went mostly to Montreal, representing a large portion of the 26% who went to Quebec.

These Caribbeans who settled mostly in Toronto and Montreal found jobs in 1987 in services (18%), product fabricating (16%), and clerical (12%) occupations more heavily than the average Canadian (Anderson, 1993: 103). Caribbeans were represented about average in medicine and health (3%) and entrepreneural (3%) occupations. They were under-represented in managerial, administrative, professional, and technical occupations which usually require development of social networks over a longer period of time, which new arrivals have not yet been able to build.

Recent arrivals of visible minority immigrants into Canada's large metropolitan areas, such as the Caribbeans to Toronto and Montreal since the sixties, illustrate that immigration trends have clearly changed from mostly white Europeans earlier, to largely non-white visible minorities with more diverse cultural, religious, and racial heritages, although Gatzewich (1989: 77–9) disputes that racism ceased. Our indices show that Blacks in Canadian cities are not as segregated as in the USA, but they are more highly segregated than whites of European origin. Anderson (1993: 10) outlines how the paths of Caribbeans have been different: 1) their historical paths have been different, 2) although from British colonies, their entrance status is determined more by race than by culture, and 3) the creolization process of mixing of cultures, religions, and races has prepared them well for Canadian pluralism.

Canadians must remember that historically many Caribbeans worked on the sugar cane plantations and factories as slaves where entrepreneurship and private enterprise were prohibited; where rigid dependency and authoritarian structures were total; in a caste system where whites were at the top of the pyramid and Blacks at the bottom (Anderson, 1993: 11; Henry, 1994). While these immigrants come from a variety of countries in the Caribbean, their experiences of white colonial racism have been similar (Walker, 1984: 3). Caribbeans are not all Black, they come from 29 territories, formerly controlled by four white European countries (Britain, France, Spain, Netherlands), where slaves dominated the West Indian population numerically in a highly stratified society, where colour dominated the society (Walker, 1989: 4). Maroons—disaffected Blacks from Jamaica—had been brought to Nova Scotia as early as 1795.

In Toronto and Montreal, opportunities for housing and jobs have been difficult for visible minorities like the Caribbeans, so that in April 1992 the youth of Toronto rioted (Mata, 1989). Stephen Lewis was commissioned to study the situation. His report to the government read in part:

What we are dealing with, at root and fundamentally, is anti-Black racism
... wounds of systemic discrimination throughout Southern Ontario ... It
is Blacks who are being shot, it is Black youth that are under-employed in
excessive numbers, ... it is Black kids who are disproportionately dropping
out. ... (Anderson, 1993: 125)

The 37-page Lewis report shows that while Caribbeans are among the most
highly educated newcomers, the practices of racism against Blacks and visible
minorities 'have become an escalating staple of news reports on an almost
daily basis' (Anderson, 1993: 129).

THE CHINESE: SEGREGATED CHINATOWNS
Emigration from China to Canada began in 1858 (Tan and Roy, 1985: 4).
These early Chinese immigrants were mostly men seeking to find jobs in the
British Columbia gold rush. In 1881 men were brought in from the USA and
Asia to help with the building of the Canadian Pacific Railway (Lai, 1988:
3–33). By 1885, there were 10,000 Chinese in Canada, all in British
Columbia (Wickberg, 1982: 27), more than one-fourth (2,900) in railroad
construction. When the completion of the railroad in the 1880s, thousands of
Chinese were left unemployed. While many Chinese settled in Victoria, Vancouver was to be the western terminus of the Canadian Pacific Railway (Li,
1988: 11–22). Large groups of Chinese were employed to clear the area, and
these workers became a threat to the Whites, because they were cheap labour
that took much-needed jobs. 'In 1884 the Chinese in Burrard Inlet comprised
five merchants, ten store employees, thirty cooks and laundrymen, and one
prostitute, as well as sixty sawmill hands' (Wickberg, 1982: 61). By 1886
many Chinese in the Burrard Inlet area began to raise vegetable gardens and
started truck farming; soon they supplied most of the vegetables for the Vancouver settlement. By 1886 they began to settle in the Pender area; here the
oldest and for many years the largest segregated Canadian Chinatown has
existed for a hundred years, next to the largest segregated Japantown in
Canada (Driedger, 1989: 248–50). The Chinese segregated themselves in
Chinatowns largely to protect themselves from discrimination and racism
(McEvoy, 1982: 24–42; Li, 1988; Baureiss, 1987: 1–14; Creese, 1987: 35–46;
Lai, 1987: 47–67; Yu, 1987: 114–24; Li, 1988: 102–13).

In 1941 there were 35,000 Chinese in Canada; by 1981 there were
289,000. Their number almost doubled to 58,000 in 1961, more than doubled
in 1981 to 289,000, and doubled again in 1991 to 587,000. Before the Second
World War the Chinese were centred in British Columbia; after 1945, Chinese immigrants spread across Canada. By 1981 about one-third resided in
Vancouver, another third in Toronto; the remaining third scattered mostly in
other cities across Canada (Lai, 1988: 118). The two largest Chinatowns in
1986 were located in Toronto (143,235) and Vancouver (109,370); these were
studied in some depth by David Lai (1988).

By 1991, 40% (232,000) of the 587,000 Chinese in Canada resided in Toronto, and 28% (167,000) in Vancouver, which represented two-thirds of all Chinese. Eighty-five per cent (500,000) of the 567,000 lived in the five urban centres of Toronto, Vancouver, Montreal (34,000), Edmonton (33,000), and Calgary (33,000). The predominance of Chinese in these five centres is shown in Figure 9-6. Only 70,000 lived in the remaining centres including 14,000 in Ottawa-Hull, 10,000 in Winnipeg, 5,000 in Hamilton, 3,000 each in Kitchener, Windsor, London, Saskatoon, and less than 2,000 in the rest of the centres.

In 1971 there were little more than 100,000 Chinese in Canada, a number that increased more than five-fold to 567,000 in 1991, in a short twenty years. During this 1971–91 period the Chinese population increased nine times in Toronto from 26,000 to 232,000, in Vancouver five-fold from 36,000 to 167,000, in Montreal 11,000 to 34,000, in Edmonton 5,000 to 33,000, and in Calgary 5,000 to 35,000. So all of these metropolitan centres have seen an enormous increase of Chinese populations in one generation, which makes these new immigrants more visible. Those who are afraid of 'visible minorities' unlike themselves will tend to feel threatened, especially in centres like Vancouver and Toronto where many other visible minorities are also arriving. Most of these newcomers have not been settled in the Chinatown areas, but scattered in the suburbs, where they are less visible.

While the new Chinese arrivals have located more evenly in a less segregated way in the total city, their increased population mass has also benefited the existing Chinatowns. While the older 'bachelor' Chinese were less well-to-do, Chinese newcomers are better off and are also better educated and politically sophisticated, so that they have helped enhance rehabilitation and new growth in business, schools, and institutions, many of which have continued to concentrate in Chinatowns in the centre of the city. Thus, many declining Chinatowns have found new life and have been developed and expanded. In Figure 9-7 (Lai, 1988: 127) the old Chinatown in Vancouver is shown as C and D near the newly renovated historic site of Gastown, which has also linked with a development of a historic Chinatown (Lai, 1988: 126–35). In many of these cities plans of drastic slum clearance, which would have razed many historic Chinatowns, were stopped by Chinese leaders whose lawyers persuaded city councils of the importance of a colourful Chinatown. Chinese elderly did not want to leave the community, so new housing was built for them, and in Vancouver a series of redevelopment projects were started. Development of housing projects, new parks, Chinese gardens, cultural centres and schools and institutions all created a momentum to which new businesses were also attracted. These new Chinese developments were integrated with historic Gastown and the large development when the Pan American games came to Vancouver. Thus, the redeveloped Chinatown became an important part of Vancouver's city centre, rather than a slum as

FIGURE 9-6   DISTRIBUTION OF MAJOR CHINESE COMMUNITIES IN CANADA, 1991

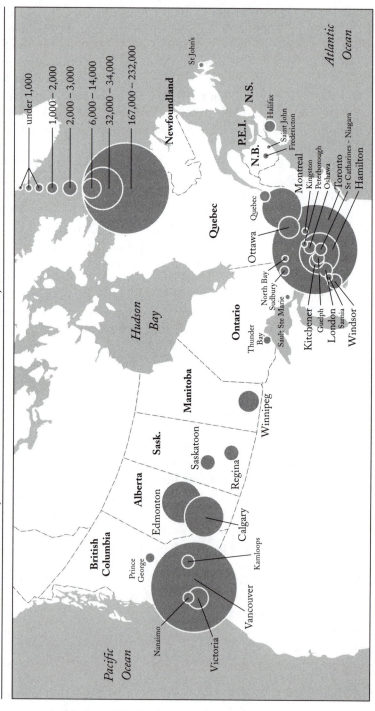

SOURCE: David C. Lai, *Chinatowns: Towns Within Cities in Canada*. Vancouver: University of British Columbia Press, 1988, p. 177 (an adaptation to include 1991 Census of Canada data from *Ethnic Origin: The Nation*, Catalogue 93–31, 93–315).

FIGURE 9-7   VANCOUVER'S CHINATOWN AND STRATHCONA DISTRICT, 1950s–1980s

SOURCE: David C. Lai, *Chinatowns: Towns Within Cities in Canada.* Vancouver: University of British Columbia Press, 1988, p. 127.

some had often thought of it. With the influx of new Chinese immigrants, who were of higher status, more integration and less segregation has occurred.

The Vancouver Chinatown comprises some eight city blocks along Pender Street close to the downtown business section, and just off Burrard Inlet. Hundreds of stores, shops, and businesses of all kinds are located in Chinatown, along with all the services that the Chinese need (Lai, 1988: 126–35). A number of Chinese newspapers are published here, and movie houses, restaurants, clubs, voluntary organizations, churches and temples, and recreational facilities are located in Chinatown (Wickberg, 1982: 254–67). The community puts on annual Chinese festivals and various attractions such as musicals, drama contests, and literary events. Chinese 'bachelors' of the early days live here, as well as many families, so that it is a living Chinese community where activity never ceases (Lai, 1988: 126–35). Since Chinatown constitutes a business section that attracts tourists, it has a viable economic base that has survived for more than a hundred years and most likely will continue for the foreseeable future.

The dissimilarity scores for the Chinese in Vancouver (.55), in Toronto (.57), and in Montreal (.67) are still quite high although much lower than they used to be, because of the differing patterns of early and later immigration. Those who still live in Chinatown are as segregated as any other ethnic group, if not more so. The Toronto Chinese community has been moving and has relocated recently, which has not happened in Vancouver (Lai, 1988: 146–9). The Vancouver Chinatown is one of the best examples of a segregated urban community near the downtown business district.

Because the first Chinese immigrants were not allowed to bring their families, Chinatowns met the special needs of the Chinese 'bachelors' who relied on each other's social support (Lai, 1988: 13–21; Tan and Roy, 1985). The many Chinese immigrants who came to Canada after the Second World War came as families; they were often professional and business people who located freely in urban suburbs, and were therefore relatively unsegregated. Many are integrating fast, and are experiencing an extensive modification of their culture. Some intermarriage is taking place, but they remain physically visible which is a brake on assimilation for many (Li, 1988).

SUMMARY

Minorities in rural and urban areas do not cluster equally in space, so sociologists have devised various methods to measure class, ethnic, racial and religious concentrations, and segregation. This 'aparthood' is often referred to as 'apartheid', where minorities are clustered into separate areas apart from others either voluntarily or involuntarily. Such segregation can be a means of control which has taken a variety of forms.

Two major perspectives in such urban-area segmentation focus on Duncan's zonal segregation model, and Shevky and Bell's multiple nuclei model. The Duncan model is based on Burgess' concentric zone model of urban growth which assumes that cities grow in concentric circles like trees, adding to their perimeter each year. Duncan assumed that the smaller older circles in the middle were inhabited by the lower class populations, while the better-off increasingly moved to the periphery. Thus, social class is a major means of differentation. Shevky and Bell based their model on Harris and Ullman's multiple nuclei model, where they found that residents cluster more randomly in class, racial, and family status nuclei, based less on predetermined spatial patterns. Dawson found that in early Montreal, groupings seemed to follow Duncan's concentric zone model.

Various measures and indices have been developed to study these complex residential patterns. Balakrishnan and associates developed indices of ethnic diversity and they found that concentration of ethnic minorities varies enormously by cities and by groups. Western Canadian cities are much more ethnically diverse than eastern ones. Visible minorities concentrate heavily in Vancouver and Toronto, and visible minorities are much more concentrated than European whites. Jews, however, who are a religious minority, are most segregated even though they are white. Dissimilarity indices, which measure spatial separation of minorities from larger British and French charter groups, show again that visible minorities are more segregated into their own groupings away from charter groups.

Our several studies of Blacks and Chinese in Canada show that there is much evidence of apartheid. Blacks who came to Nova Scotia two hundred years ago were set apart, so that even today they are still segregated in rural Black areas or on the periphery of cities. Caribbeans who have come recently, many of whom are Black, have concentrated mostly in Toronto and Montreal, where they are also segregated, although not as severely as Blacks in the United States. This involves residential, occupational, and social segregation which creates conflict.

Chinese men who came to work in mines and helped build the railroads in Canada, were segregated in workcamps, and again separated themselves in Chinatowns in urban centres for protection against prejudice and discrimination. While immigration laws severely restricted Chinese immigration large numbers of Chinese families have recently come to Canada. These Chinese newcomers are more educated and occupationally specialized so that they are able to compete better with the general population. They increasingly live amongst other Canadians, so that Chinese segregation patterns are diminishing. So far we have shown that social class and residential segregation are major factors in the life patterns of Canada's minorities. A third factor—race—we will explore in the next chapter.

CHAPTER 10

Race and Historic Racism

While power and socio-economic status are important forms of stratification of ethnic groups in Canada, physical or biological characteristics such as race provide another means of social stratification. Stratification by race is a fairly recent phenomenon perpetuated especially during the last several hundred years by white Europeans and their ancestors. Racial stratification has been particularly severe in the United States, where slavery occurred for centuries, but it is also present in Canada and will likely become more important as increasing numbers of immigrants from the Third World enter Canada.

Recently, Pierre van den Berghe (1981) has tried to develop a sociobiological theory of ethnicity and race which again brings physical and biological features into the heart of the ethnicity discussion:

> . . . The view of ethnicity and 'race' does clash with the two dominant ideologies of industrial societies—liberalism and socialism. Ethnicity and 'race', I will argue, are extensions of kinship, and, therefore, the feelings of ethnocentrism and racism associated with group membership are extensions of nepotism between kinsmen. . . . If my argument is correct, then it follows that ethnocentrism and racism, too, are deeply rooted in our biology and can be expected to persist. . . . In liberal ideology ethnocentrism and racism are archaic, irrational residues of preindustrial societies, which can be expected to yield to univeralism under conditions of 'modernization'. In socialist tradition, these phenomena are seen as the product of the capitalist mode of production and as misguided forms of 'false consciousness' designed to wither away after the advent of socialism. Both ideological traditions have been equally at a loss to explain the persistence, indeed, the resurgence, of ethnic and racial sentiments. . . . (van den Berghe, 1981: xi)

Van den Berghe (1981: 1–3) argues that in the second half of the nineteenth century, social Darwinists such as Herbert Spencer and William Sumner tended to perpetuate genetic determinism, which influenced sociology until the 1920s. However, the pendulum began to swing toward an environmental-ist direction when Franz Boas and Robert Park emphasized the opposite view of cultural relativism that was expounded by liberals like Adorno, Myrdal, Warner, Allport, Frazier, Klineberg, and Dollard, and which held sway until the 1960s. The liberals played down racial distinctions, which often went hand in hand with the assimilationist ideology and the optimistic notion of a melting pot. Robert Park and many of the Chicago School tended to see little difference between race and ethnicity and used the terms interchangeably. They expected both to disappear by assimilation.

Since the sixties, however, heritage roots, ethnic identity, and 'Black is Beautiful' sent scholars looking for black culture, black soul, and black roots clearly based on physical, biological distinctions of the 12% of Americans who were black. Thus, Pierre van den Berghe (1981) began to develop a the-ory of socio-biology that takes both the social environment and the biolo-gical inheritance seriously. He sees race as a special marker of ethnicity, upon which 'dominance orders', 'hierarchies', and 'pecking orders' are based. Racism thus becomes a cultural invention, and ethnicity and class (including race) become two alternative and competing principles of sociality (van den Berghe, 1981: 58, 257).

The meaning of the concept of race has evolved and changed over time. Explorers and traders were finding people who looked and behaved somewhat differently, so they became interested in common and distinctive features and invariably began to wonder about the origin of these differences in colour and physical characteristics. At first 'the race of mankind' had been used, generally distinguishing *Homo sapiens* from other animals, but now increasingly people were faced with classifying the varieties of human beings into categories or races. So 'race' today is defined as an arbitrary biological grouping of people on the basis of physical traits.

The concept 'racism' has been defined by Banton (1967: 19) as 'the doctrine that behavior is determined by stable inherited characteristics deriving from separate racial stocks, having distinctive attributes and usually considered to stand to one another in relations of superiority and inferiority.' As white Euro-peans increasingly came into contact with peoples around the world, and as the theory of evolution developed, there were many attempts at arranging the vari-eties of *Homo sapiens* into distinctive groupings. Had some of these humans developed into superior beings? There was often the tendency to identify Europeans as superior and others inferior, especially because white Europeans at the time had a relatively well-developed technology. Racists today believe that some people are inferior or superior biologically; as a result, they often treat people of other races negatively.

While 'racism' is a negative concept, based on the belief that some races are inferior to others, the concept of inequality (subtitle of this book) is an attempt at ranking people more objectively on the basis of opportunities to compete in the social, economic, and political spheres of our society. It is assumed that humans have roughly the same abilities, but for many reasons they do not all have the same opportunity to fulfil their potential. In this sense inequality is a part of the social structure of a society, rather than a form of biological determinism. While biological features are difficult to change, social structures can be changed, although not easily.

CLASSIFICATION OF HUMANS

The Swedish botanist Carl Linnaeus (1701–78) developed an orderly nomenclature for plants, which soon encouraged biologists similarly to classify organic forms of life. Today it is generally accepted that contemporary mankind belongs to the same *Homo sapiens* species, and that there is no basic biological or genetic difference between the various human populations. Physical features, however, do vary, and as early as 1745 Linnaeus proposed that mankind be classified into four main races: European, Asiatic, African, and American Indian (Hughes and Kallen, 1974: 6). In 1781 the German physiologist Johann Blumenbach proposed a classification of humans based on head and skull shape, forming five races: Caucasian (European), Negro, Mongol, Malayan, and American Indian. There have been many attempts at ordering the complex array of characteristics of humans, as these examples suggest.

During the eighteenth and nineteenth centuries, classification of peoples around the world became popular among physical anthropologists who wished to compare the differences that they encountered. Since evolution was becoming more accepted, many of them attempted to arrange races in a hierarchical order from primitive to highly civilized types. The genetic discoveries of Gregor Mendel (1822–4) revolutionized and encouraged further interest in classification (Hughes and Kallen, 1974: 8). Slowly the story of human development began to unfold.

Many criteria have been used in the various classifications, and the American physical anthropologist Earnest Hooten expanded the list of physical criteria in his formation of three primary divisions of humans: Caucasian, Mongoloid, and Negroid. Once he had outlined these three major groupings, he subdivided them into intermediate types to account for the complex variations. Table 10-1 outlines Hooten's (1946) three primary divisions; these have been used fairly extensively in the discussion of race today.

Hooten (1946) used seven criteria including skin colour, eye colour, hair type, nose shape, lip shape, and amount of body hair in the formation of his Caucasoid, Mongoloid, and Negroid racial types. The Caucasoids have the fairest or lightest colour skins and eyes, while the Negroids are the darkest, with the Mongoloids falling in between. The nose and lip shapes of the

TABLE 10-1   HOOTEN'S CRITERIA TO DISTINGUISH PRIMARY DIVISIONS OF
HUMANS

Criteria	Caucasoid (White)	Mongoloid (Yellow)	Negroid (Black)
Skin Colour	White, pink or 'ruddy' to light brown	Yellow or yellow-brown	Dark brown to black
Eye Colour	All lighter shades, but never black	Medium brown to dark brown	Dark brown to black
Hair Type	Straight to wavy, occasionally curled	Straight (coarse in texture), and circular in cross-section	Woolly to frizzy; oval in cross-section
Nose Shape	Usually high-bridged and narrow	Low root, short tip, medium width at nostrils	Usually low, depressed, broad tip and nostrils
Lip Shape	Thickness, medium to thin; little or no lip eversion	Medium thickness; variable eversion	Usually thick with obvious eversion
Cheek-bone Region	Not prominent	Projecting forwards and laterally; may be covered by fat pad	Variable, but usually more obvious than in Caucasoid
Body Hair (including beard)	Medium to heavy; very variable	Usually less than Caucasoid or Negroid	Medium to scanty

SOURCE: Modified from Hooten's *Up From the Ape* (1946) by Hughes and Kallen (1974: 9).

Caucasoids are the narrowest, while the Negroids have the broadest and thickest. The Mongoloids have the straightest and coarsest hair texture, while the Negroids have the woolliest hair. The Mongoloids also have the most visible cheek-bones, while these are least prominent among Caucasoids. Caucasoids have the most hair on the body, and Negroids the least.

Classifying *Homo sapiens* into three types makes it quickly apparent that there is a wide range of variation within each of the three types. Many have questioned whether such classification is still useful, but it does appear that Europeans in particular have made much of skin colour and some of the other differential characteristics, so that we are forced to examine the differences and reasons for placing values on such physical characteristics.

Another major problem with this classification is that large numbers of the world's population do not fit the scheme, such as the East Indians of south Asia, the aboriginal Native Indians of the two Americas, and most of the Pacific Polynesians and Melanesians. The South Asians from the subcontinent of India represent roughly one-fifth of the population of the world and they seem to fit the Caucasian type in most respects, except that their skin colour is considerably darker. They are classified as Caucasian, but since skin colour is often considered so important by other whites, they are often treated as coloured or visible minorities (Ujimoto and Hirabayashi, 1980). The Aboriginals of North and South America (originally two of the six peopled continents) seem to fit between the Caucasoid and Mongoloid types, but are usually classified as Mongoloid. The peoples of the Pacific islands, having somewhat darker skins than the Mongoloids, seem to fit best between the Mongoloid and Negroid categories. It is for reasons such as these that many scholars have created more than three racial types, but Hooten suggested that we begin with these three basic types, and then subdivide into more groups as considered necessary.

In summary, the division of the peoples of the world into useful categories or races is difficult, and since all *Homo sapiens* are fundamentally similar, many people suggest that we abandon attempts at classifying humans into races according to their physical characteristics. However, it is a social fact that humans are often stratified and treated differently because of their physical differences, so that we are forced to deal with racial types and inequalities.

GENETIC AND SKELETAL VARIATIONS
Physical anthropologists have also analyzed the skeletal characteristics and blood types of the three primary divisions that we have discussed. We can only introduce their work here. There is considerable evidence that *Homo sapiens* evolved over thousands of years, and in the selection process minor skeletal differences evolved in different regions. When skulls are examined, the Europeans brow ridges are more developed than those of the other two groups. The Caucasoids have a straighter facial profile with small brows and a prominent chin, whereas Asian cheekbones and jaws are more prominent, and African jaws protrude more, with smaller chins and narrower palates (Hughes and Kallen, 1974: 14). Europeans have high, narrow nasal aperatures, and Asians have versions in between. The body bones of Europeans are thickly constructed with larger joints, while the African bone structure is longer and more slender. Asians again have intermediate versions. Although the human skeletal structures are basically the same, there are minor variations which again tend to fall into three primary divisions.

Blood types tend to follow a similar pattern of variation which seems to have emerged from the three major geographical 'breeding grounds' of Africa, Asia, and Europe (Hughes and Kallen, 1974: 15). Of the ABO blood group system, Europeans and Africans show moderate evidence of A_2 genes, while in Asians it is virtually absent. B type genes are infrequent among Europeans, frequent among Asians, and intermediate among Africans. The Rh (or Rhesus) factor is high among Europeans, but virtually absent among Asians (Hughes and Kallen, 1974: 16). On the other hand, the sickle-cell tendency is high among Africans, but low for the others. Much more could be said about these differences, but it is sufficient to say that there are variations which can be classified into three basic divisions of mankind according to physical characteristics, skeletal types, and blood types. Although *Homo sapiens'* physical evolution seems to have come from one basic source, more recently smaller variations have occurred in the various regions of the world, accounting for differences in skin colour and some variations in skeletal and blood types.

VISIBLE MINORITIES AS SOCIAL REALITY
Because such a large majority of immigrants came to Canada from Europe, especially from northern Europe, these less pigmented 'whites' set a standard for the visible norm. Thus non-whites, largely from Asia and Africa, look different physically. A hierarchy of values has developed in which lighter-skinned humans are more valued. Differences are even made between northern and southern Europeans; even among Blacks, those with lighter coloured skins are valued more. The 'Black is beautiful' call that began in the 1960s has made being Black more acceptable, but the value hierarchy based on skin colour tends to continue.

Thus, in this chapter, rather than using Hooten's technical three categories, we will use references to Europeans, Asians, and Africans, as well as the terms whites and non-whites which are in more common usage today. While Anthony Richmond of York University in Toronto published *Readings in Race and Ethnic Relations* in 1972, it included contributions by American scholars on race mostly outside of Canada because very little Canadian research on race existed. So when Ujimoto and Hirabayashi held conferences at the 1977 and 1978 Learned Societies' meetings focusing on Asians in Canada, these papers were among the first to deal more seriously with research on Canada's racial minorities. Victor Ujimoto and Gordon Hirabayashi (1980) published these papers in *Visible Minorities and Multiculturalism: Asians in Canada*, which included contributions dealing with Chinese, Japanese, Koreans, Vietnamese, and Filipinos. Since then the concept of 'visible minorities' has gained acceptance to include those who are of mongoloid and negroid races. At that time they included 'multiculturalism' in their title which was becoming more popular. Increasingly, the term 'visible minorities' is gaining acceptance. In some ways, this category is very general and undefined, based largely on skin colour so that often Arabs and many others are included, depending on how tightly the definition is drawn to include only northern European-origin Canadians.

Since then 'visible minorities' in Canada have doubled to roughly ten per cent, more problems related to race have emerged, and more research and publication has occurred. These works used bolder titles including words like 'racism' (Bolaria and Li, 1988; James, 1990, 1992; McKague, 1991; Satzewich, 1992; Henry, Tator, Mattis, Rees, 1995), 'oppression' (Bolaria and Li, 1988), and 'Apartheid' (Richmond, 1994) in their titles.

RACISM IN HISTORICAL PERSPECTIVE

If the concept of race is difficult to define, and since it is difficult to classify the many differentiations of humans into racial categories, why do we continue to try? It is because humans need to simplify and order the universe to be able to comprehend it. But more importantly, whites of European Caucasian origin have judged—and continue to judge—others on the basis of skin colour. Racial attitudes and behaviour based on physical characteristics are a fact in North America, and we are forced to deal with the phenomenon of racism. Many North Americans believe that human behaviour is determined by stable, inherited characteristics deriving from separate racial stocks with distinctive attributes that can be ranked as superior or inferior. This is racism.

Aboriginals in North America were slaughtered or placed on reserves. Blacks in America were forced to become slaves; the Japanese in Canada and the United States during the Second World War were forcibly transferred into the interior. Blacks and coloureds in South Africa lived in ghettos and needed passes to enter white territories. These are but a few examples of racism. Let us explore how such thinking developed over time.

WHITE EUROPEAN DOMINANCE

Prior to the sixteenth century, the white Europeans represented only one-sixth of the total world population. However, when the Protestant Reformation began in the 1500s—the same time that Europeans explorers began to discover the rest of the world—ideas, inventions, and technology developed to enhance European power and dominance in the world (van den Berghe, 1981). As European industry flourished, Europe's population exploded and new settlements were established; soon Europeans became one-third of the world's population (Driedger, 1989).

Europeans had traded with the Chinese, South Asians, and others for centuries, facilitated by Arab and other middle entrepreneurs who brought spices and goods across the lands and deserts. After Columbus, however, Europeans soon made direct contacts with the East via the sea. Asians looked physically different; their features were very different. Europeans now had direct contact with these 'different' peoples. As they sought to find a direct passage to the East going west, the Spaniards and Portuguese found South and Central Aboriginals; the British, French, and Dutch found more Aboriginals in North America. Some, such as the Maya, Aztec, and Inca, had developed great civilizations, but others were in the food-gathering stages. Again, they looked different physically. The same was true of the darker peoples on the coasts of Africa. One dominant impression these new experiences left was that other peoples of the world are not white. Skin colour became an easy way of differentiating between white Europeans and others (van den Berghe, 1981).

As these white invaders, who had fairly recently been barbarians themselves, explored the world, many of them were both awed by some of the great and old civilizations that they had found, and hard-pressed to seek ways of justifying their presence there. Since European technology permitted extensive sea travel, technological advances, white physical appearance, and a sense of a superior 'white image' soon appeared around the world. It was only a matter of time before 'white is more beautiful' became popular with the Europeans, first no doubt unconsciously, and later justified by various ideologies.

COLONIALISM

The patterns of contact varied. In some parts of the world, trading relationships developed, in others exploitation was extensive, and in still other areas pioneer settlers came to possess the land. Trading had taken place overland for centuries, but now the white Europeans made contacts with the Chinese, South Asians, Aboriginals in the Americas, and Blacks in Africa (van den Berghe, 1981: 85–110). Since the Asians had highly developed civilizations, the Europeans desired their finely crafted cloth, their spices, and many other articles of trade. Europeans created small port enclaves on the coastlines of China, India, Indonesia, and elsewhere to establish trading communities. Raw materials such as furs were also desired, so forts were established across North America where the fur trade flourished. In all of these trading relationships Europeans were a small minority, but they possessed sufficient technological superiority to protect themselves and maintain their white bases amidst peoples of many varieties of colour.

While the temptation to exploit these newly encountered peoples was always present, the great Mayan, Aztec, and Inca civilizations of Latin America provided special opportunities for exploitation (van den Berghe, 1981: 85–90). In the 1530s, gold was found by the Spanish among the Inca in what is now Peru. Small groups of powerful Spanish and Portuguese subjugated, often exploited, and sometimes enslaved aboriginals to work in mines. Many European men, away from their families, exploited Native women, and many married them and created families.

Pioneer settlement was a third form of white European contact when North Europeans settled in North America. The French and British created communities on the American and Canadian east coasts and soon began to differentiate between white Europeans and aboriginals. Most of these aboriginals were food gatherers, less technologically advanced, and skin colour or differentiation by physical features became an important means of social differentiation.

IMMIGRATION AND RACE

IMMIGRATION POLICIES

There is no doubt as to who came to the Americas first, and it is well known that many aboriginals had developed civilizations which rivalled white European development. Aboriginals, the first immigrants to the America, came at least 12,000 years ago. These early *Homo sapiens* possessed the land now called Canada, the United States of America, Mexico, and Central America twenty-five times as long as any Europeans have lived here. In Canada most of the aboriginals were food gatherers, although food producing had begun among the Hurons and Iroquois in southern Ontario, and large scale fishing, chiefdoms, and a distinctive art had developed on the northwest coast. In Mexico, Central America, and Peru some of the great civilizations of the Aztec and Inca still flourished when Europeans invaded and exploited their land.

After 1600 British, French, Spanish, and Dutch colonies were established in what is now Canada and the United States. Most of these came as families settling permanently, and they needed the land that the aboriginals used for hunting. At first their needs were limited, but slowly white agriculturalists began to crowd out Native food gatherers. As Indians were increasingly pushed westward, the number of whites and their dominance and power increased, leading to conflicts with the Iroquois, the Hurons, and later the Métis battles that took place in 1870 and 1885 at Fort Garry and Batoche (Stanley, 1969). Treaties were signed, and Riel was hanged. The last stand of Indians and Métis had taken place; the white traders and agriculturalists had triumphed.

The white European industrial dominance over coloured Africans and Asians as preindustrial suppliers and servants was a common pattern which emerged around the world (van den Berghe, 1981: 111–36). Most countries of Europe created colonies that supplied raw materials for the European industrial revolution. These colonial arrangements always benefited the whites, and in some places took such brutal forms as slavery, especially in colonial America when Blacks were brought mainly from Africa to work in the cotton fields of the Deep South. White dominance had taken the most blatantly inhumane course—the buying and selling of humans as commodities. Ideologies such as the Christian religion of love, professed by many, had to be adjusted in order to present a sense of consistency (van den Berghe, 1981: 111–15). The doctrine that Blacks were less than human, or subhumans, followed. Others argued that God had created some to be dominant and others to be subservient. Still others exploited their fellow humans at will, without thought of morality or justice for all. Always, European whites were the masters, and coloured phenotypes were the servants. We propose that these are some of the historical reasons for the white preoccupation with race.

Europeans have remained 90% of the Canadian population into the nineteen-nineties. Barely one hundred years ago, the two charter groups laid the foundations of the Canadian confederation, so that white Europeans became the legal and dominant force in the shaping of the dominion. For the most part, Canadian immigration policy preferred north European immigrants and allowed very few non-Europeans to enter. There were exceptions, however, when Chinese were brought in to build the railroad in British Columbia in the 1880s, or when labourers were needed in mines and factories in the North or southern Ontario. An informal agreement was made with Japan so that few Japanese entered after the initial ones came during the turn of the century. Often head taxes were imposed to discourage 'the yellow hordes of Asia' from entering.

The new point system introduced in the early 1970s was important in Canadian immigration policy. Immigration became possible in three ways: citizens of Canada willing to take responsibility for their care and maintenance could sponsor their parents, brothers, or sisters and have them enter Canada under the category 'Sponsored Dependants' (Richmond, 1994: 117–30). Since most Canadians are of northern European ancestry, this opportunity heavily favoured further white European immigration. However, a category for 'Independent' applicants permitted entrance if they could score fifty out of a possible one hundred points. This category permitted anyone in the world to compete to enter Canada, especially if they had sufficient educational, occupational, and language skills. The 'Nominated' category is an intermediate version that requires applicants to score some points independently, but prior settlement arrangements and having a relative in Canada can boost the chances of entrance (Richmond, 1994: 117–30).

Since the advent of the point system, the change in the leading source countries of immigrants is quite evident. In 1951 the ten countries that contributed the largest number of immigrants to Canada were all European except for the United States. By 1995, most of the ten top contributors were from Asia and the Caribbean. A large proportion of these immigrants was highly visible; many brought with them different religions and cultures, as well as racial differences. Since Canada is a large country with a relatively sparse population, and since the world pressures for living space are increasing, many people expect Canada to take in more refugees and immigrants who have been left homeless. Some, like the Tamils and Sikhs, have come by boat illegally. Thus, we can expect that in the future more non-whites will enter Canada and that the proportion of Asians, Africans, and other visible minorities will increase. It is interesting to note that during economic downturns, there are usually pressures from labour unions and others to restrict immigration, based on the argument that there are not enough jobs for everyone. This conflict of interest can lead to changes of laws to restrict immigrants. These changes, some of them very recent, have been part of the changing dynamics of Canada's immigration history.

RACIAL DEMOGRAPHIC CHARACTERISTICS
While the proportion of Canadians of Asian and African racial origin was only about three per cent in 1971, by 1991 it had increased to nearly 10%. This increase in visible minorities, nearly 2.5 million of the total in 1991, was largely due to a change in immigration policy. Whereas Canadian immigration policy clearly preferred northern Europeans until the early 1970s, now the new point system gives immigrants from the Third World a better chance to compete. Many more visible minorities have arrived in the past decade, so let us compare the non-white minorities with those in the American population.

The 1991 census does not show racial divisions in Canada very well, but Table 10-2 shows that roughly 90% of the Canadian population could be classified as European, 6% as Asian, 2% as aboriginal, and 1% as African or Black. The rest were of multiple or mixed origins, terms which require some interpretation. The census takers indicated that, of the Europeans who married others, most married other non-charter Europeans. The aboriginals who married non-Indians could be classified as Métis. Most likely the Pacific Islanders would be heavily Asian, and the Latin Americans heavily white.

With so few non-whites in Canada, we could hardly expect that Asians or Africans would be a majority in any region of Canada. The 587,000 Chinese represent 2% of the Canadian population. However, the aboriginal peoples in 1991 were a majority in the Northwest Territories, representing over half of the residents there. In addition to being a majority in the North, aboriginals are much more concentrated in the five most westerly provinces. In fact, about 7% of the populations of Manitoba and Saskatchewan are aboriginals. There are, however, relatively few aboriginal peoples east of Ontario, living in the five most easterly provinces.

While the 471,000 aboriginals represent about one-fifth of all visible minorities in Canada, the Chinese represent one-fifth as well, and are heavily concentrated in Ontario and British Columbia. Three-fourths of all of Canada's Chinese live in Ontario and British Columbia, mostly in Toronto and Vancouver, where the two largest Canadian Chinatowns are also located. The Chinese have been a part of British Columbia history ever since they came to the west coast a hundred years ago, while the Chinese in Ontario have concentrated in Toronto somewhat more recently.

The South Asian Indo-Pakistani visible minority of 325,000 is unique in that they are usually technically classified as Caucasian. They fit most of the

TABLE 10-2 CANADIAN AND AMERICAN VISIBLE AND NON-VISIBLE RACIAL
POPULATIONS

Racial/Ethnic Groupings	Canada 1991 N	%	USA 1990 N	%
Non-Visible Caucasian	24,493,000	91	189,000,000	76
Europeans	15,904,000	59		
British				
French				
Other Europeans				
Multiple Responses[a]	7,794,000	29		
Canadian[a]	765,000	3		
Visible Minorities	2,507,000	9		24
Asian	1,608,000	6	7,000,000	3
Chinese	587,000			
Indo-Pakistani	325,000			
Filipino	157,000			
Arab	144,000			
Indo-Chinese	117,000			
West Asian	82,000			
Pacific Islands	7,000			
Aboriginal	471,000	2		
Native Indian	361,000			
Inuit	110,000			
African	251,000	1	31,000,000	12
Black	225,000			
African	26,000			
South American	178,000		22,000,000	9
Total National Populations	27,000,000	100%	249,000,000	100%

Note
[a]We expect that 9 out of 10 in the multiple and Canadian response categories were non-visible Europeans; that means that about 3% could be of visible minorities, which should be added to the 9%.

SOURCES: Statistics Canada, *Ethnic Origins*, Census of Canada 1991, 20 per cent Data Base. Ottawa: Statistics Canada, 1993; John R. Weeks, *Population: An Introduction to Concepts and Issues*, 5th ed. Belmont, CA: Wadsworth, 1994, pp. 280–4.

Caucasian criteria except skin colour. We discuss them here because they are a visible minority, and whites tend to make much of different phenotypes. Similar to the Chinese, three-fourths of all Indo-Pakistanis live in Ontario and British Columbia, again mostly in Toronto and Vancouver. Interestingly, 80% of all East Indians in Vancouver are Sikhs from the Punjab. The Indo-Pakistanis represent the third largest visible minority in Canada after the Chinese and aboriginals (see Table 10-2).

African and Black origin Canadians (250,000) represent the fourth largest visible minority in Canada. The African racial group in any case is very small, about one per cent of the Canadian population. Well over half of the Africans are located in Ontario, mostly in Toronto. In 1971 about one-third of Canada's Blacks resided in Nova Scotia, especially in Halifax, but by 1991 that has changed.

The Japanese are similar to the Chinese in that they are Asians racially, and are most heavily located in Ontario and British Columbia; indeed, they were a part of early British Columbia society. A Japantown existed in Vancouver until the Second World War. During the 1940s, however, they were forcibly evacuated into the Canadian interior and today the Japanese total only 49,000, three-fourths of which are scattered in two provinces.

The Indo-Chinese entered Canada mainly during the decade of the 1970s. They represent a multi-ethnic category of Vietnamese, Cambodians, Laotians, Filipinos, and Thais. They speak many languages, represent many traditions, and do not exhibit the same solidarity as the groups discussed so far. Many of them came as boat refugees. One-third of them located in Quebec, and another third in Ontario. In these two provinces, they are concentrated in the cities of Montreal and Toronto respectively. They add a smaller part to the Canadian Asian racial group.

Thus, Canada's non-white minorities represent less than 10% of the total population, and over half of these are Asian racially. They are represented largely by Chinese and the Aboriginals (Driedger, 1986: 450). Figure 10-1 shows visible minorities in Canada are distributed proportionately. Of those listed in the table, the Chinese (24%) are the largest group, Blacks (20%) the second largest, followed by South Asians (19%), West Asians and Arabs (11%), Filipinos (7%), Southeast Asians including Vietnamese (5%), Latin Americans (5%) and others. Figure 10-1 does not include aboriginals which would add another 1.7%, which Samuals (1992) who designed this figure did not include. If aboriginals are included, this would raise the proportion of visible minorities in Canada to around ten per cent in 1991.

In contrast to the small non-white population in Canada, there are much larger proportions of non-whites (24%) in the United States population of 250 million in 1990 (Weeks, 1994: 280–5). Of these 62 million visible minorities, 12% of the American population are Afro-Americans (Weeks, 1994: 280–2). These 31 million Blacks are more than the total Canadian population of 27 million. Thus, it is not surprising that Americans are often very preoccupied with the question of race. While in the past, American Blacks lived mainly in the Deep South, they have recently moved in large numbers into urban areas, including many northern cities. In 1990 Blacks still represented large percentages of the populations in the southern states of Mississippi, South Carolina, and North Carolina. Although there are many Black tenant farmers in the Deep South, their families are beginning to move to the southern cities (Pinkney, 1975: 39–53).

Blacks have also moved into many northern American cities. More than

FIGURE 10-1   ETHNICITY OF RACIAL MINORITIES, 1991

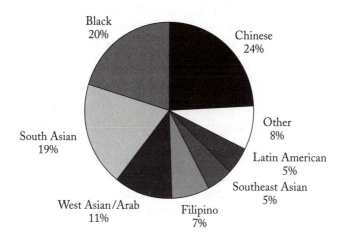

SOURCE: T.J. Samuals, *Visible Minorities in Canada: A Projection.* Toronto: Race Relations Advisory Council on Advertising, Canadian Advertising Foundation, 1992.

seventy per cent of the population of the District of Columbia (mostly metropolitan Washington) is Black. Many other northern cities such as Newark, Baltimore, Philadelphia, Cleveland, Detroit, and Chicago are over half Black or are nearing a Black majority. Many of these cities have Black mayors. In many of these cities there are ghettos that are almost exclusively Black (Lieberson and Waters, 1990). There are no comparable areas or cities in Canada where people of African or Asian race make up such large numbers, nor such potentially powerful political blocs.

There are also 31 million Americans of other races, representing about 13% of their total population (Weeks, 1994: 275–82). Seven million or 3% are Asians. While Canada's proportion of Asians is somewhat larger (6%), the aboriginals make up one-fifth of this category. Not so in the United States: two million American Indians represent less than one per cent of the total population. Since the American population is roughly ten times the Canadian population, the United States should have five million aboriginals, if they were to have a proportionate number compared to Canada. Thus, while Canadians are more preoccupied with aboriginals as a racial group, Americans tend to be much more aware and concerned with their Blacks, of which Canada has very few.

But there are also other Canadian and American racial differences. There are 22 million people in the United States of Spanish origin, representing 9% of their population. They are considered white racially, but are fairly visible physically (Weeks, 1994: 282). Most of these Spanish-speaking people are hispanics from Mexico, who represent a racial mixture of Europeans from Spain and Central and South American aboriginals. Like Canada's South Asians, these Spanish origin peoples are classified as whites, but their darker skin colour makes them more visible and tends to attract prejudice and discrimination.

In summary, a much larger percentage of the American population are from the African (12%) and Asian (3%) races. Along with the visible hispanic minority (9%) they make up one-fourth of the total American population. In Canada, the non-Caucasian racial percentage is much smaller (less than 10%). Therefore we would expect Americans to be more preoccupied with racial categories, problems, and issues. This tends to be true, except that the more open immigration policy of Canada has brought many more visible minorities into Canada, so that Canadians are now becoming increasingly conscious of racial and physical differences, especially in larger cities such as Toronto and Vancouver.

SOCIO-ECONOMIC INEQUALITY

Sociologists often place individuals or groups into socio-economic categories and rank them according to high and low status. Occupation, education, and income are the most commonly used indicators of social and economic status (SES). Since the non-white percentage of Canada's population is small, and since none of the groups is large, objective data on socio-economic inequality tend to be limited.

In Table 8-5 we ranked twenty ethnic groups, showing which ethnic groups ranked above the Canadian mean income of $28,946 in 1991, and which ranked below the mean. We found that all visible minorities ranked in the bottom third of the rankings on income. In Table 10-3 we use the three indicators of education, occupation, and income which are usually used as objective measures of socio-economic status, comparing non-visible (white European) and visible (non-white Asians and Africans).

We have ranked eight non-visible minorities and find the Jewish Canadians on top of the category, ranking the highest on education (mean 14.7 years), white collar occupational status (56.4%), and income ($37,146). They rank first on a composite ranking of the three indicators combined. The British and French charter groups who were the first Europeans to arrive, rank second and third. The other northern and eastern European entrance groups who followed rank in the middle, and the Italians and Portuguese who have arrived more recently, rank seventh and eighth in the non-visible category. The Portuguese who rank last, compared to the Jews, who rank first, have half as much education (mean 7.9 years), one sixth as many in white-collar occupations (7.7%), and earn two-thirds as much ($26,346) as the Jews.

TABLE 10-3   SOCIO-ECONOMIC STATUS BY VISIBLE MINORITY STATUS[a] AND
ETHNIC ORIGINS,[a] CANADA, 1986 AND 1991

Ethnic Groups	Composite SES Rank[b]	Rank[c]	Years of Education (Mean)	White-Collar Occupations[d] (Per cent)	Income 1991
Non-Visible Minority					
Jewish	1	1	14.7	56.4	$37,146
British	2	2	14.0	42.7	29,928
French	3	3	13.5	41.7	27,222
Dutch	4	6	12.4	31.5	30,888
German	5	7	12.4	28.9	31,506
Ukrainian	6	10	11.1	19.0	34,110
Italian	7	12	9.0	15.2	29,550
Portuguese	8	13	7.9	7.7	26,926
Visible Minority					
West Asian	1	4	14.2	43.2	21,284
South Asian	2	5	14.2	36.4	25,718
Chinese	3	8	14.9	34.3	26,392
Southeast Asian	4	9	13.4	29.0	24,080
Black	5	11	13.3	22.9	23,346

Notes

[a] Single ethnic origin responses only, for males of designated groups age 25–64.

[b] Sum of the three ranks divided by three, for each of the non-visible and visible categories.

[c] Sum of the three ranks divided by three, combining both non-visible and visible categories.

[d] Includes managerial and administrative occupations as well as occupations in the natural sciences, engineering, mathematics, social sciences, teaching, medicine and health, and artistic, literary and related occupations.

SOURCES: Monica Boyd, 'Gender, Visible Minority, and Immigrant Earnings Inequality' in Vic Satzewich (ed.), *Deconstructing a Nation: Immigration, Multiculturalism and Racism in '90s Canada.* Halifax: Fernwood Publishing, 1992, pp. 300–2; The 1991 Census of Canada Public Use Sample Tapes.

There are significant SES differences amongst non-visible minorities. Comparing five visible minority groups in the second category, we see that the West Asians (Arabs in the Near East, etc.) rank highest in that category on white-collar occupations (43.2%), are tied for first in education (mean 14.2 years), and last in income ($21,284) for an overall ranking of first in the visible minority category. Blacks rank last in education (mean 13.3 years), white-collar occupations (22.9%) and second last in income ($23,346).

Having looked at each of the two non-visible and visible categories separately, we need to compare all thirteen groups to see where each ranks overall, using a composite rank score for all three socio-economic indicators. While the Jews, British, and French rank in the top three overall, the West Asians and South Asians (East Indians, etc.) rank fourth and fifth, and the Chinese and Southeast Asians (Vietnamese, etc.) eighth and ninth. Overall, it is the non-visible Italians and Portuguese who rank last. Using these objective socio-economic criteria, we find that visible minorities by no means all rank lower in socio-economic status. Visible minorities rank especially high on education, because most of them have arrived since the point immigration system established in the 1960s, where they had to have higher education to qualify for entrance into Canada, so they have an educational advantage. With more education, the visible minorities have also been able to get into higher status white-collar occupations on average, than the lower third of the non-visible category. However, this has not translated into comparably higher incomes, which suggests that other factors, such as discrimination, operate.

HISTORIC RACISM

The many racial groups in Canada in their many settings cannot be dealt with in depth here. However, two selected types of problems (Black slavery and Japanese internment) will show generally the extent of racial stratification and some of its problems.

SLAVERY OF BLACKS

The slave trade became an important part of the American economy and social structure and became a caste system unparalleled in North America. The stratification of 31 million Blacks who are a sizeable population in many southern states and many large cities of the United States is continuing evidence of inequality based on racial strata (Weeks, 1994: 280–4). To a lesser extent, slavery also became a part of the early social structures of Canada. In 1628 a British ship brought a Black child, the first known Black resident of Canada, to New France (Hill, 1981: 3). Although the laws of France forbade slavery, Louis XIV gave his limited approval to slavery because there was a shortage of workers and servants. By 1709 full permission was given, and the long-standing practice of slavery in New France continued.

The British had brought slaves to the New World as early as 1562, selling them to the Spanish-American settlements, and the first shipload of twenty African slaves to reach British North America was landed at Jamestown, Virginia, in 1619 (Hill, 1981: 5). A century later, when the French territory of Acadia was ceded to the British by the Treaty of Utrecht, New England settlers moved north, bringing their slaves to build Halifax in 1749. When the French were defeated by the British in 1759, the French slave system of Quebec passed smoothly into the British regime (Hill, 1981: 6). Many British officers, prominent citizens, and, on occasion, clergymen owned slaves, and the slave trade was brisk.

The French were not too anxious to promote slavery because they felt that it did not pay and that free labour was more productive. 'Nonethless, slavery was given a legal formulation in New France between 1689 and 1709' (Winks, 1971: 3). By 1759, there were about 4000 slaves in New France, both Indian and Black.

> With the Treaty of Paris in 1763, France ceded the whole of its North American territory east of the Mississippi River to Great Britain. One side effect of this was to strengthen the institution of slavery legally and religiously. Not only did the British officials and Protestant sects support slavery, but governmental authorities encouraged the immigration of slave owners (like the New England Loyalists) and their slaves into the country. (Krauter and Davis, 1978: 48)

When the British Empire Loyalists fled to Canada during the rebellion of the American colonies after 1776, they also brought their slaves to Nova Scotia, and Upper and Lower Canada (Walker, 1992: 1–93). Mohawk and Iroquois Indians who had fought with the British also moved north into Canada, some of them bringing with them Black slaves whom they owned. Some Black Loyalists received land grants. These Blacks later formed Black settlements in Nova Scotia, the Niagara Peninsula, York (now Toronto), Kingston and Prescott. Members of the Legislative Council of Lieutenant-Governor John Graves Simcoe in Upper Canada and members of his Executive Cabinet owned slaves, even though Simcoe himself worked hard to abolish slavery (Hill, 1981: 16). Legislation to restrict slavery in 1790 preceded the historic 1803 decision that slavery was inconsistent with democracy. Few slaves were left in Canada when the British Imperial Act of 1834 abolished slavery throughout the empire (Walker, 1992: 331–59).

There were also free Blacks who entered Nova Scotia. 'Free Blacks had been promised treatment equal to that of their white peers; the British pledge of one-hundred-acre grants of land to each Black failed to materialize. Most Blacks received no land at all; if anything was given them it was mainly barren one-acre lots on the edge of white loyalist townships where they were segregated from the main population' (Krauter and Davis, 1978: 42). This meant that from the beginning free Blacks did not receive the same chances as whites to improve themselves economically, and they were segregated, as they are in Nova Scotia to this day. 'In every instance where acreage was granted to both Black and white settlers, Blacks received less. For example, while Blacks were given one-acre lots in Digby, Whites were granted from one-hundred- to four-hundred-acre lots throughout the Annapolis County' (Krauter and Davis, 1978: 42). Although freed in Canada, most Blacks had to go back to work for Whites as servants or workers, which kept them from developing their own economic independence. 'Blacks in Nova Scotia had become so disillusioned by 1792 that 1200 of them accepted an offer by the Sierra Leone Company and sailed to Africa' (Krauter and Davis, 1978: 43; Walker, 1992: 94–114).

While the slavery of Blacks and the lack of allocation of free land to free Blacks kept them in subjugation, they also were kept in their segregated places by limited education, employment, and housing. Blacks did not enjoy educational opportunities equal to other Nova Scotians, and by the 1850s segregated Black schools were operating in both Nova Scotia and Ontario (Winks, 1969: 164–91). Educational opportunities for Blacks were grossly inadequate: teachers were poorly qualified to teach and were underpaid, and student attendance was irregular (Clairmont, 1965). Many Black students left school by the sixth or seventh grade; the high school drop-out rate was very high, so very few Blacks entered university. This raised the likelihood of poor job opportunities and perpetuated the poverty cycle.

Many Blacks who came to Canada became farm labourers, and when the railroads came, many worked on rail construction gangs. When the Maritimes became less competitive economically as forests and fish declined, many Blacks became unemployed with little hope of finding jobs. 'More recently, Blacks have occupied the lowest rungs of the urban employment ladder. In 1941, almost half the employed Black males of Montreal were railway porters, while four-fifths of the Black females were domestics' (Potter, 1961: 49; Calliste, 1988: 36–52). 'A federal government survey of Black workers of the civil service shows that Blacks in Nova Scotia are systematically discriminated against at all levels of employment' (Head, 1975: 86; James, 1992: 58–72).

Our review of Blacks in Nova Scotia earlier showed that many of them are rural, and that their houses are substandard with a minimum of heating and plumbing (Henry, 1973). Elsewhere, Blacks live mostly in cities; the census shows large numbers in Montreal and Toronto. While in Nova Scotia both rural and urban Blacks are segregated, this is not the case in the larger cities in Ontario and Quebec (Anderson, 1993: 67). Table 10-3 showed that the income of West Indians is much lower than most other ethnic groups. As as result, they often cannot afford good housing and have to live closer to the centre of the city, where housing is older and less adequate (James, 1990).

More recently, however, with the change in Canada's new immigration point system, many more West Indian Blacks have come to Canada from the Caribbean, and they have come especially to urban areas such as Toronto (Anderson, 1993: 69). Hill (1960), Ramcharan (1982), and Anderson (1993) have studied Black and West Indian communities in Toronto and their social institutions. Recently four Toronto sociologists: Breton, Kalbach, Isajiw, and

Reitz (1990), studied a number of ethnic groups in Toronto. Race relations in Toronto are especially interesting. In 1871 96% of the population were of British origin, and this has declined to roughly one-half by 1991 (Kalbach, 1980). People of many other origins have entered Toronto so that it is now one of Canada's most multiethnic and multiracial cities. Kalbach (1980) shows that in 1971 there were at least 28,000 Blacks in Toronto, although the 1981 census was not able to find that many. Anderson (1993: 66–7) reports that two-thirds of the 28,000 Caribbean Blacks who arrived in 1974 came to Ontario; the same proportion of 14,000 who came in 1989 also settled in Ontario. Kalbach's (1980: 14) measures of discrimination show that in 1971 Jews, Italians, Chinese, and Blacks were in many ways less similar to the British than many of the other groups considered. Reitz (1981: 28) found that the West Indians were among the lowest in job status, job security, and mean income of eight groups compared in Toronto.

The recent influx of multiracial groups into Toronto has resulted in racial incidents; as a result, a task force was set up to study the adequacy of the school system to cope with these problems. The task force found that:

> principals and teachers tended to be defensive about the possibility that there were incidents of conflict and confrontation that could be attributed to racist attitudes. Racism in children's lives in Metro Toronto poses a serious challenge not only to the education system but to the future community. (Pitman, 1978: 183–4)

These findings suggest that Blacks and other racial minorities find it difficult to compete in our society; with the history of racism in Canada, it is not surprising. These problems will be discussed again in Chapter Eleven (James, 1990; Anderson, 1993; Christianson and Weinfeld, 1993; Dei, 1993; Henry and Tator, 1994; Henry et al., 1995).

JAPANESE INTERNMENT

In our discussion of the slavery of Blacks, we have suggested that Canadian society has been and still is structured to promote racial inequalities. Lest some think that this happened long ago, the evacuation of Japanese from the Pacific coast to the Canadian interior during the Second World War is a second illustration of structured inequalities in our economic and political systems.

A small number of Japanese began to settle in Canada around 1884, and by 1894 about 1,000 had entered Canada. They had been good fishermen in Japan and found it relatively natural to continue their trade on the Canadian west coast. Indeed, they were able to compete so well that other Canadian fishermen soon saw them as a threat. Cries to stop Japanese immigration increased until, in 1908, Japan and Canada signed a 'gentlemen's agreement' which effectively limited Japanese immigration to less than 1,000 per year. In 1908 alone, 7,985

Japanese entered Canada (Nakamura, 1975: 301). Citizens in British Columbia had previously pressured governments to restrict immigration of Asians in general, especially excluding the Chinese. Political and labour leaders marched into Chinatown in 1907, causing a riot and thousands of dollars of damage. They were stopped by the Japanese from entering the Japanese quarter on Powell Street. Even prior to 1941, discrimination against Asians was commonplace, with many legal restrictions and injustices.

To protect themselves, Chinese and Japanese Canadians established segregated areas where they did their business and where they lived and built their social institutions (Sugiman and Nisheo, 1983; Kobayashi, 1987). The largest Chinatown in Canada is still in Vancouver. Prior to the bombing of Pearl Harbor, the majority of Canada's Japanese lived in two large communities: 2,151 lived in Steveston, a fishing community on the coast south of Vancouver, and 8,427 lived in Vancouver (Nakamura, 1975: 309). In Steveston, the Japanese were the majority. They owned a fleet of fishing boats, and their various organizations processed and marketed their catch. They had a thriving segregated community where they used their own language and supported their schools, clubs, and religious and social organizations. The same was true on Powell Street in the heart of Vancouver, where Japantown was a growing bustling enclave like many Chinatowns we know today (Broadfoot, 1977).

In 1941, 21,175 of the 23,149 Japanese in Canada were located on the British Columbia coast. A small minority, less than 8%, was scattered throughout the rest of Canada. Ten years later, in 1952, only 12% remained on the West coast and the majority had been sent inland, 4,527 to the eastern Canadian provinces (Nakamura, 1975: 330). Three-fourths of these Japanese Canadians in 1941 were Canadian-born. Many families had lived in Canada for several generations (Sunahara, 1980: 93–120).

The evacuation and relocation caused significant changes; it wiped out many of the hard-won economic gains that the Japanese had built up over the years. Most had to start all over again, because before the war they had well over 200 different Japanese organizations, few of which remained after the war. Kin associations, a traditional Japanese heritage, ceased to function; fathers were separated from families, and families were disbanded; Japanese-language schools and newspapers were closed down. The life, culture, customs, and traditions that were symbolized by Vancouver's Powell Street were over (Nakamura, 1975: 330). The evacuation took nine months; the Japanese were sent to road camp projects and old mining towns such as Tashme, Slocan, and New Denver in British Columbia, and to sugarbeet projects in the prairies. Some were deported to Japan. The property of the Japanese, such as fishing boats, houses, businesses, and public buildings, was confiscated and often sold for a fraction of its value. Some Japanese have returned to the coast, but many have not. Only a block of Japanese businesses and shops remains on

Vancouver's Powell Street today, a remanant of the former thriving Japantown (Petrie, 1982: 11–46).

The destruction of the Japanese communities of the west coast through evacuation and deportation during the Second World War was possible because of the racial hatred and pressures of west-coast Canadians and politicians who themselves were open to condone and/or vote for discriminatory legislation (Kobayashi, 1992). Sunahara (1980: 94) lists four major reasons. Mackenzie King and the federal government often sympathized with or yielded to the American government, which may have influenced other Canadian politicians. West-coast labour unions were threatened by the Japanese and pressured politicians to eliminate the Japanese fishermen from the industry, which evacuation did for them. In general, the anti-Asian bias was so strong that very few people objected to the injustices which escalated in evacuation, confiscation, internment, and deportation (Broadfoot, 1977). War hysteria added to the problem. Minority communities were destroyed, social institutions were wiped out, and the Japanese culture was greatly weakened as a result of racism in Canada.

Ujimoto (1983: 141) suggests that the Japanese experience can be understood in terms of Daniels and Kitano's (1970: 5) minority-majority model which involves two categories:

> By the 'two category' system, they mean 'a system of stratification that is divided into two broad categories: the white and the non-white'. In this system of analysis, it is assumed that the white group is superior to the other group. Although it is recognized that there are other systems of stratification, our analysis of Japanese Canadian historical data indicates that the prejudice, discrimination and concomitant segregation in internment camps inflicted on the Japanese Canadians can be adequately assessed in terms of the simple two category system. . . . It becomes evident how the social and political structures were manipulated, often by legislative means, in order to perpetuate the two category system of stratification. (Ujimoto, 1983: 141)

In Table 10-4, we present Daniels and Kitano's (1970: 11) four basic stages of racial separation, which begin as three ordinary solutions, and follow into a fourth drastic extraordinary solution. Research (Berger, 1981; Ujimoto and Hirabayashi, 1980; Ujimoto, 1983) shows that the first stage of prejudice—avoidance and stereotyping—was common in British Columbia before the First World War. There was fertile ground for more serious actions against minorities such as the Japanese, Chinese, and East Indians. Japanese successes in fishing, farming, and lumbering became a serious threat to many who found it hard to compete. The anti-Japanese feelings and the eventual culmination of these feelings in the Vancouver Race Riots of 1907 probably best

TABLE 10·4 THE FOUR STAGES OF MAINTAINING THE TWO-CATEGORY SYSTEM OF STRATIFICATION

Stages	Beliefs	Action Effects	Primary Mechanisms
Ordinary 1 solutions	Prejudice	Avoidance	Stereotyping, informally patterned rules governing interaction
2	Discrimination	Deprivation	More formal rules, norms, agreements; laws
3	Segregation	Insulation	If the out-group is perceived as stepping over the line, there may be lynchings and other warnings
Extraordinary solutions 4	A. Apartheid concentration	Isolation	A major trigger such as war is necessary; outgroup perceived as a real threat or danger to the existence of the host culture. Ordinary mechanisms (e.g., Stages 1, 2, and 3) have failed.
	B. Expulsion, exile	Exclusion	
	C. Extermination	Genocide	

SOURCE: Roger Daniels and Harry H.L. Kitano, *American Racism: Exploration of the Nature of Prejudice* (Englewood Cliffs, NJ: 1970) by permission of Roger Daniels and Harry H.L. Kitano, copyright assignees.

characterize the first stage of the two category system of stratification' (Ujimoto, 1983: 144).

It was almost inevitable that the second stage of discrimination—overt action—would move toward deprivation and that more formal rules and laws would follow to restrict this form of economic threat. Many believed that the Japanese would deprive them of the majority of jobs and take away their employment opportunities, so that the political power of the majority would need to stem the Japanese tide. 'The Japanese were believed to constitute a threat to the economic and cultural supremacy of British Protestants and thus a significant threat to the distribution of power' (Baar, 1978: 336). By 1908 the gentlemen's agreement with Japan limited Japanese immigration to a trickle. Under the second stage of discrimination, laws had been put into effect to restrict the Japanese minority influence.

Daniels and Kitano (1970: 11) suggest that there would be a sequential escalation through the four stages, and indeed, this did happen in British Columbia. Stage three was the segregation and insulation through mass evacuation of Japanese Canadians from 'protected areas' of British Columbia into interior camps and work projects; it effectively removed the economic threat under the guise of political threat. 'Former mining towns or "ghost towns" in the province were renovated to house the evacuees in Greenwood (1,177 evacuees), Kaslo (964), Sandon (933), New Denver (1,505) and Slocan (4,814)' (Ujimoto, 1983: 138). Complete insulation from the rest of society was accomplished by confiscating radios, cameras, and automobiles; freedom of movement was restricted, and letters were censored. During the internment, higher education was not available, thus restricting social mobility; institutionalized discrimination had taken place.

Daniels and Kitano's (1970) fourth extraordinary stage followed. Subtypes A, concentration and apartheid through isolation, and B, exclusion through expulsion and exile, also took place. In the case of Japanese Canadians, Canada called this exile 'repatriation'. The Second World War was the trigger for this extraordinary action. Through an Order-in-Council in December, 1945 (after the war had ended), Canada still tried to deport Japanese Canadians (Ujimoto, 1983: 140). Arrangements were made to deport 800 in January of 1946, but because many prominent Canadians opposed the deportation, it did not take place. Some Japanese, however, were deported earlier. Since then Canada and its Japanese have agreed to a redress settlement in 1988 as partial compensation for injustices suffered (Kobayashi, 1992: 1–19).

These two examples of Black and Japanese minorities show that Daniels and Kitano's (1970) four-stage model took place in both the United States and Canada. Canadians are often not aware of the lengths to which we have gone to stratify ethnic minorities in the past. We find it hard to believe that analogies to the Indian caste system and apartheid in South Africa could happen here. These two cases show that they have happened in Canada.

SUMMARY

What is unique about humans is that they are so much the same throughout the world. However, visual differences do exist, so that *Homo sapiens* are most often classified into groupings of Caucasians, Mongoloids, and Negroids, based on such characteristics as skin colour, facial features, and head and body forms. These physical, genetic, and skeletal differences are attributed largely to evolutionary variations.

If these differences are minor compared to human similarities, then why do we attempt a discussion on racial inequalities? Historically, whites from Europe have developed a sense of white superiority and dominance over Asians and Africans that has resulted in colonialism, invasion, exploitation, and slavery. The belief in racial superiority has led to racism, which still exists in many parts of the world.

In Canada's history there are many examples of the social structure's promotion of injustices, slavery, and deportation. Aboriginals were slaughtered, Europeans invaded aboriginal lands without compensation, treaties were made and broken, and many Native claims are not settled while industry and technology continue to exploit their rights. Blacks were bought and sold and slavery was accepted; even today many people complain that those who are not white find it difficult to compete. The Japanese during the Second World War were freely evacuated, their property confiscated, and their communities destroyed without adequate compensation.

Racial inequalities are a reality in Canada, even though many Canadians claim that all humans are physically equal. Social stratification in Canada means that the political and socio-economic power clearly remains in the hands of European whites. Because of strong recent immigration from the Third World, more non-whites have arrived, but they still remain a small proportion of the total population. In Part Five we will explore the extent to which conflict and social injustice prevail because of inequality and stratification, and the provisions made for human rights in Canada.

PART V

In Search of Human Rights and Freedoms

CHAPTER 11

Racism: Prejudice and Discrimination

Chapter Eleven reviews the total effects of ethnic and race relations on Canadian attitudes and behaviour. Chapter Twelve reviews the rights and freedoms outlined by the American, United Nations, and Canadian charters. The two chapters together are a search for human freedoms in Canada and for the extent to which human rights are feasible.

Let us begin with the ideology of democratic racism and explore the extent to which multiculturalism is indeed viable. We shall examine whether Canadians prefer the mosaic to the melting pot, and whether they are comfortable with a diversity of minorities. We shall also examine how minorities are, or are not, positively accepted in Canadian society. These general attitudes will provide a background for understanding the perceptual ethnic hierarchies that exist and the extent to which there are negative attitudes of prejudice and discriminatory behaviour based on negative ethnic stereotypes.

DEMOCRATIC RACISM

Frances Henry and Carol Tator (1994: 1) present the ideology of 'democratic racism', which resists equal access to opportunities in Canada.

> The conflict between the ideology of democratic liberalism and the racist ideology present in the collective belief system of the dominant culture of Canada creates a fundamental dissonance. Although lip service is paid to the need to ensure equality in a pluralistic society, in reality individuals, organizations and institutions are far more committed to maintaining the status quo in order to stabilize or increase their power.
>
> This paper identifies the concept of 'democratic racism', an ideology that permits and justifies the maintenance of two apparent conflicts of values. One set consists of a commitment to a democratic society motivated by egalitarian values of fairness, justice and equality. In conflict with these liberal values, a second set of attitudes and behaviours includes negative feelings about people of colour that carry the potential for differential

treatment or discrimination. In its simplest form, democratic racism reduces this conflict between egalitarian and non-egalitarian values.

Henry, Tator, Mattis, and Rees (1995) expound on these basic premises in *The Colour of Democracy: Racism in Canadian Society*.

In the United Kingdom, Henry and Tator (1994: 5–9) describe democratic racists as 'distancing themselves from the crude ideas of biological inferiority and superiority', and 'defining a national British culture which is homogeneous and white' (Henry et al., 1995: 17–19). Mechanisms of inclusion and exclusion, who belongs and who does not, have been set in motion to protect the 'authentic' against the 'alien' characteristics of culture related to the national weakness and decline (Gilroy, 1987: 45–6; Richmond, 1994: 155–69).

Recently Gaertner and Dovidic (1986: 208) have explored 'aversive racism' in the United States. Their findings are based on social psychological research which suggests that some Americans are prejudiced but do not act out their beliefs in actual discriminatory behaviour. They may avoid racial minorities or, if contact is unavoidable, assume a demeanour of formal politeness (Elliott and Fleras, 1992: 59). Others who are liberals may have a strong social conscience, believe in fairness and equality for all, but offer a superficial favourableness which does little to change things. They may pride themselves in being open-minded and prejudice-free, but feel ambivalent about how things are changing (Henry and Tator, 1994: 6–7).

Henry and Tator (1994: 9) suggest that democratic racism applies to Canada, which may combine the British and American versions of 'new racism', 'aversive racism', and 'symbolic racism' because it involves value conflict:

> 'Democratic racism', therefore, is defined as an ideology in which two conflicting sets of values are made congruent to each other. Commitments to democratic principles, with their egalitarian notions of justice, equality, and fairness, are valued positively. These are in conflict, however, with those attitudes and behaviours that include negative feelings about minority groups and the potential for differential treatment or discrimination against them.

As a consequence there is a lack of support for policies and practices which ameliorate existing racial problems. Interventions are seen as conflicting with liberal nations of democracy, so democratic racists are reluctant to change basic structures (Henry, Tator, Mattis, Rees, 1995: 17).

Table 11-1 lists the thirteen expressions Henry and Tator (1994: 9–12; Henry et al., 1995: 21–9) discuss as evidence of democratic racism. Some believe racism cannot exist in a democratic society, but discrimination happens to all. Others believe that immigration policies are at fault, or that minorities don't want to adapt, or that these are cultural problems. Others feel new immigrants lack skills to succeed, that multicultural policies are

T𝐀BL𝐄 11-1   V<small>ALUES AND</small> M<small>YTHS</small> A<small>SSOCIATED WITH</small> D<small>EMOCRATIC</small> R<small>ACISM</small>

Expressions by Canadians

1. Racism cannot exist within a democratic society.
2. Discrimination is a problem faced by all from time to time.
3. Racism is a consequence of immigration and increased diversity.
4. Minority groups refuse to fit in and adapt.
5. These are cultural not racial problems.
6. Non-whites lack the skills to succeed.
7. Multicultural policies are sufficient.
8. Education will change ignorance and attitudes of people.
9. Race is a problem for non-whites mostly.
10. What we need to do is treat everyone equally.
11. Individual rights are primary, including free speech.
12. Smear and innuendo are used to undermine anti-racism initiatives.
13. Anti-racism initiatives are racism in reverse.

<small>SOURCE:</small> Frances Henry and Carol Tator, 'The Ideology of Racism—"Democratic Racism"', *Canadian Ethnic Studies* 26 (1994): 9-12.

sufficient, and that more education is the answer. Still others say it is a problem for non-whites, that fair treatment will solve the problems, and that individual rights and free speech must remain paramount. Deeper forms of racism resist action by innuendo opposing anti-racism initiatives, claiming that such action is racism in reverse. Let us examine some empirical studies that explore the extent of racist attitudes and behaviour (Henry et al., 1995: 21–9).

ATTITUDES TOWARD PLURALISM

Since charter Canadians are clearly dominant in Canada numerically, it is important to study what is happening to other minorities and their place in Canada. We shall examine whether Canadians prefer the melting pot over the mosaic, what their attitudes are toward pluralism and multiculturalism, and whether they feel at ease with the growing numbers of visible non-charter minorities.

M<small>OSAIC AND</small> M<small>ELTING</small> P<small>OT</small> P<small>REFERENCES</small>

Reginald Bibby (1987a: 161) asked his 1985 national sample of Canadians whether they preferred the mosaic or melting-pot models. He found that well over one-half (56%) preferred the mosaic, and that over one-fourth (27%) opted for the melting-pot model. These preferences varied by region, age, and education of the respondent.

Preference for the model of the mosaic was strongest in the prairies, Ontario, and Quebec (58%), and weaker in British Columbia (53%) and the Atlantic region (49%). Interestingly, the melting pot, in which all groups would lose their ethnic identity, was least preferred by Canadians in Quebec (16%) and Ontario (29%). The mosaic has considerable support from the most populous regions, the central provinces, where charter group strength also lies. To what extent does this support include the rights of minorities and positive attitudes toward minorities?

Younger Canadians aged 18 to 34 (61%) also support the mosaic more than those over 55 (54%), while the reverse is true for the melting-pot model. Not nearly as many young Canadians (20%) support the melting-pot model as do older Canadians (33%). The trend in the future is clearly toward the mosaic. Respondents with university degrees (70%) also favour the mosaic, while very few (17%) favour the melting-pot model. The better educated people will likely have more influence in shaping the direction toward the mosaic as well. The social climate definitely favours diversity and pluralism; will this also translate into acceptance of diverse racial and ethnic minorities?

In 1991, the multicultural and citizenship branch of the Government of Canada commissioned the Angus Reid organization to undertake a national poll on the extent to which Canadians favoured diversity in Canada. Some of these results are presented in Table 11-2 (Angus Reid, 1991: 4–5). We note that a large majority of Canadians favoured a federal governmental policy that promotes and ensures equality, eliminates racial discrimination in education, health care and justice systems, helps police to improve their services, and assists new immigrants to acquire skills to integrate. Indeed over half to three-fourths of the respondents gave their strongest support (7 on a 7 point scale), to the top eleven items.

Eight out of ten also favoured proactive moves such as developing helpful school materials that recognize that diversity is acceptable, and helping organizations reflect Canadian diversity.

There was less enthusiasm for funding festivals and special events, and helping minorities preserve their heritages, with roughly six out of ten favouring such action. Very strong support (7 on scale) dropped to below one-third for items 12 and 13. The questions usually included both 'ethnic' and 'racial' designations, and most respondents seemed to favour strong support for both categories.

FEELING AT EASE WITH VISIBLE MINORITIES

The multicultural attitudes of Canadians suggest that there is considerable goodwill toward a variety of ethnic expressions, although a minority has negative attitudes toward pluralization. To what extent do Canadians feel at ease with visible minorities? Reginald Bibby (1995: 57, 59) asked the 'at ease'

TABLE 11-2   CANADIAN ATTITUDES TOWARD IMMIGRATION, ETHNIC AND
RACIAL DIVERSITY, ANGUS REID POLL, 1991

Canadian Federal Policy Should:	General Disagreement	Neither Agree nor Disagree	General Agreement
	(Percentages)		
1. Promote equality among all Canadians regardless of racial or ethnic origin	4	5	91
2. Ensure equal access to jobs regardless of ethnic or racial background	4	6	90
3. Eliminate racial discrimination through public education	5	7	88
4. Eliminate racism in health care, the justice and education systems	6	7	87
5. Help police to improve their ability to deal with different ethnic/racial groups.	6	7	87
6. Help citizens who are immigrants to acquire skills/ knowledge to integrate	6	9	85
7. Have people from different ethnic/racial groups live in the same country	5	11	84
8. Help everyone deal with ethnic, cultural, and racial diversity	6	7	83
9. Develop school materials to teach children and teachers about other cultures/life	11	9	80
10. Recognize that cultural/racial diversity is fundamental to Canadian society	10	14	76
11. Ensure that organizations reflect the cultural and racial diversity of Canadians	9	12	79
12. Fund festivals and special events celebrating different cultures	26	16	58
13. Help ethnic and racial minorities maintain their cultural heritages in Canada	25	17	58

SOURCE: Angus Reid Group, 'Multiculturalism and Canadians: National Attitude Study 1991'. Ottawa: Multiculturalism and Citizenship Canada, 1991, pp. 4–5.

questions of Canadians in his national samples in 1975, 1980, 1985, 1990, and 1995.

Bibby found that in 1975 a majority of Canadians (ranging from 84 to 91%) felt at ease with Jews, Canadian Indians, Orientals, and Blacks. In 1995 feelings of ease had increased slightly to 85–94% (Bibby, 1995: 57). There is some difference in attitudes toward the five visible minority groups, with only 6% feeling uneasy with Jews and 15% uneasy with East Indians. The differences also varied very little regionally, although in 1995 Quebeckers (22%), and British Columbians (19%) felt most uneasy with Asians, and Quebec (14%) and Prairie (11%) residents most uneasy with aboriginals (Bibby, 1995: 58). More educated respondents again were more at ease with these minorities than were those respondents with less than a high school education; but degree of ease did not vary by gender or age. The percentages are so high that very few 'ill at ease' respondents remained; however, there were roughly ten per cent, depending on the group. From Bibby's work we conclude that there is enough comfort with visible minorities that we would expect considerable goodwill on the part of most people in Canada, but there is always a small minority who are uncomfortable.

The Angus Reid Group did a national poll in 1991 asking their respondents 'How comfortable would you feel being around recent immigrants?' listing thirteen groups. On a seven point scale zero meant not comfortable, and seven very comfortable. Table 11-3 plots their responses. Seven or eight out of ten respondents felt very comfortable with the six white European groups listed, and almost none felt uncomfortable around these groups. Two-thirds still felt very comfortable with Chinese, Jews and West Indian Blacks, but more placed themselves in the middle between comfort and discomfort, although still very few claimed they were very uncomfortable in the presence of these groups.

Only a minority felt comfortable around Arabs, Muslims, Indo-Pakistanis and Sikhs which would clearly be visible religious and ethnic minorities. Ten to twenty per cent felt uncomfortable around these four groups, and more than one-third, uncertain about their feelings, checked the middle range of the scale (3,4,5). These data show that discomfort clearly increased as respondents moved from feelings about white European Christian groups to other minorities.

INDICATORS OF RACISM

'Somewhere in Canada, a fellow leans across a beer-laden table to ask his comrades, "Why does it take a Ukrainian three days to fill the salt shaker?" The punch line ("The salt is forced through the little holes") reflects the "dumb" jokes' (Mackie, 1985: 219). Ethnic jokes are but one way of keeping

TABLE 11-3 DEGREE OF COMFORT CANADIANS FEEL AROUND A VARIETY OF
RECENT IMMIGRANTS IN CANADA, 1991

Feel Comfortable Around:	Not Comfortable 1,2	3,4,5	Very Comfortable 6,7
British	3	14	83
Italians	2	11	77
French	5	11	74
Ukrainians	3	14	73
Germans	4	14	72
Portuguese	3	17	70
Chinese	5	16	69
Jews	4	22	64
West Indian Blacks	8	31	61
Arabs	11	37	52
Muslims	11	40	50
Indo-Pakistanis	13	39	48
Sikhs	17	40	43

SOURCE: Angus Reid Group, 'Multiculturalism and Canadians: National Attitude Study 1991'. Ottawa: Multiculturalism and Citizenship Canada, pp. 7–8.

minorities 'in their place', away from the status and prestige of the majority. Let us discuss common forms of racism such as social distance, stereotypes, prejudice, and discrimination, and the extent to which they exist in Canada to see how well Canadians have been able to follow their ideals of rights and freedoms for all.

SOCIAL DISTANCE
Our discussion so far suggests that some Canadians place themselves closer to some groups than to others. The Anglocelts, for instance, express a sense of nearness to the French and a sense of distance from Doukhobors and Hutterites. This suggests that we could order ethnic groups along a nearness-farness continuum, or a social distance scale. The farness end of the scale represents racism.

According to Levine et al. (1976), Simmel's utilization of the metaphor distance constitutes a pervasive feature of his sociology as a whole. They summarize Simmel's meanings as 1) ecological attachment and mobility, 2) emotional involvement and detachment, and 3) the extent to which persons share similar qualities and sentiments. Simmel himself thought that distance could be expressed in many ways. Recent work on social distance has attempted to sort out the many meanings of the concept and to devise ways of measuring it (Driedger and Peters, 1977: 161). Westie (1959) includes the dimensions of residential distance, positional distance, interpersonal physical distance, and interpersonal interaction distance. Banton (1960) distinguishes four forms of social distance (attitudinal, positional, qualitative, and ecological). Kadushin (1962) speaks of normative distance, interactive distance, cultural or valuational distance, and personal distance. Laumann (1965) seeks to measure subjective social distance and objective social distance. It is apparent that the widely used metaphor 'distance' must be adapted to specific study situations.

Bogardus (1959) expands Park's personal dimension of social distance and chooses to use 'the degree of sympathetic understanding that functions between person and person, between person and group, and between group and group as his measure of social distance. Sympathy refers to feeling reactions of a favourable responsive type, and understanding involves that knowledge of a person which also leads to favourably responsive behaviour. . . .' Bogardus selects one component of Simmel's notion of social distance and substitutes an operational continuum for Park's informal observations. Krech, Crutchfield, and Ballachey (1962: 154) note that 'with appropriate modifications, the scale can be adapted to measure attitudes toward any category of persons.' We wish to use the Bogardus scale to measure the associational component—the social distance of personal relationships.

While the Bogardus social distance scale has been used in scores of studies in countries around the world, very little use has been made of the scale for social distance research in Canada. However, Driedger and Peters (1977) did a revealing study of students in nine Winnipeg high schools.

We see (Table 11-4) that a sample of 2,328 high school students in Winnipeg are much more willing to marry persons of European origin than of non-European origin. They appear to make racial distinctions between whites and non-whites in their marriage preferences (Driedger and Mezoff, 1981: 7). It is also clear that nearness differentiations made within the European category are great. Three times as many high school students are willing to marry Americans as are willing to marry Jews. In fact, the Jews are classified more like non-Europeans; only one-fifth to one-fourth of the sample were willing to consider them as eligible partners.

Bogardus's instrument is a seven-point scale indicating nearness at the low end and farness at the top. Looking at the farness (6 and 7) end of the scale, we find that a small proportion of the students wishes to debar certain groups and permit only visits to Canada. About fifty students (2%) were in favour of excluding the Dutch and the Blacks (the least restricted group), while 200 students (11%) wished to restrict the Jews. The restrictions of the Jews by

TABLE 11-4   The Degree of Distance Winnipeg High School Students Prefer to Maintain from Others

| Ethnic Groups[a] | Social Distance Scale (Bogardus) Willingness to: | | | | | | |
	Marry	Have as Close Friend	Have as Neighbour	Work with on Job	Have as Acquaintance	Have as Visitor Only	Debar From Nation
				(Percentages)			
European origin							
American	75	14	5	2	2	2	2
British	65	20	6	4	2	3	1
Scandinavian	56	24	8	6	3	2	1
Dutch	53	25	11	5	4	1[b]	1
Polish	51	26	9	6	4	2	2
Ukrainian	50	28	9	6	4	2	2
French	50	24	9	6	6	2	5
German	48	25	11	7	6	3	2
Italian	44	28	10	7	6	3	3
Russian	41	27	11	7	6	3	5
Jewish	28	34	12	7	9	4	7
Non-European Origin							
Negro (Black)	29	49	11	6	3	1	1
Mexican (Hispanic)	29	37	14	8	6	4	1
Japanese	26	44	14	7	6	2	2
Filipino	26	40	13	9	6	4	2
Chinese	25	45	13	7	5	2	2
West Indian	23	43	13	9	8	3	3
Indo-Pakistani	23	42	13	10	8	3	2
Aboriginal	22	41	10	10	10	3	4
Eskimo (Inuit)	19	45	13	10	8	3	2

Notes

[a] Ingroup evaluations were deleted (e.g., the British in the sample did not evaluate their own group).   [b] The Ns in any one cell never dropped below 20.

SOURCE: Leo Driedger and Richard Mezoff, 'Ethnic Prejudice and Discrimination in Winnipeg High Schools', *Canadian Journal of Sociology* 6 (1981): 1–17.

11% of the sample appears to be clear ethnic or religious prejudice; let us examine these negative attitudes more closely.

ETHNIC STEREOTYPES

Walter Lippmann was the first to use the concept 'stereotype' in his book, *Public Opinion* (1922). Since then, stereotype has become a major concept in the vocabulary of the social sciences. Canadian research on ethnic stereotypes has been extensive (Anderson and Frideres, 1981; Taylor, 1981; Mackie, 1985). More study of the complexity of stereotypes is needed; there are virtually no analyses of autostereotypes (how people or groups stereotype themselves) and there are few evaluations of the reciprocity of ethnic stereotypes (Taylor, 1981; Driedger and Clifton, 1984). This is particularly important in the Canadian context because the preservation of ethnic identities that may precede the development of ethnic stereotypes is now enshrined in a federal policy on multiculturalism.

In his discussion of stereotypes, Lippmann assumes that his readers are familiar with the concept as it is used in the printing industry. In this context, a stereotype is a plate made by moulding a matrix of a printing surface to be used in casting a metal type face. That is, a stereotype is a uniform matrix of type which is moulded so that the printing is standard and unchanging. The printer's stereotype was obviously in Lippmann's mind when he coined the concept of social stereotypes:

> The problem of the acquisition of meaning of things, or of forming habits of simple comprehension, is thus the problem of introducing: 1) definiteness and distinction and 2) consistency or stability of meaning into what is otherwise vague and wavering. In the great booming, buzzing confusion of the outer world we pick out what our culture has already defined for us, and we tend to perceive that which we have picked out in the form stereotyped for us by our culture. (Lippmann, 1922: 81)

Lippmann continues his images of the printer's stereotype using phrases such as these: 'stereotyped ideas accumulated and hardened', 'series of images', 'stereotyped shapes', 'habit of molding', 'substitution of American for European stereotypes', 'to see all things freshly and in detail, rather than as types and generalities', 'uniformities', and 'economizing attention' (Lippmann, 1922: 79–94).

Anderson and Frideres (1981: 57–78) reviewed the conceptualization of stereotypes by such American scholars as Simpson and Yinger, who characterize the concept as a highly exaggerated picture, the invention of supposed traits, and the formation of incomplete images leaving little room for change or individual variation. This raises additional questions of myth versus reality, and the problem of evaluating the content of stereotypes (Anderson and Frideres,

1981). Canadian studies have dealt extensively with stereotypes of English- and French-speaking groups. Lambert et al. (1960) found that English speakers were more favourably evaluated than speakers of French. These studies show that stereotypes vary by group, situation, and time. There has been considerably less research on 'other' ethnic groups in Canada and their stereotypes, although Driedger and Clifton (1984) explore this new field.

Taylor (1981: 161) lists two important functions of stereotyping. First, stereotypes involve categorization; when little is known about a group, there is a tendency to 'fill in' missing information. There may also be too much information, and therefore a need to simplify it. What is included and left out in the process of selecting information leaves much room for misinformation, bias, and prejudice. On the other hand, while the self is bombarded by stimuli, it is continually shaping and forming its own self-image. Emotions are an important part of this image and, depending on past experiences, may involve negative or positive tendencies and preferences. In the process of perception and cognition, most people are inclined to rate themselves positively, and often may not give enough credit to others.

These examples suggest that cognitive and affective dimensions of social interaction are involved in the formation of stereotypes. People form a *gestalt* which may be fairly accurate or very biased and inaccurate. The assumption that when we know the facts about another person or group, we will act on those facts is not necessarily true. Reason does not always prevail: emotions often impose positive and negative evaluations. When images of others become rigid, like the printer's stereotype, and when they produce the same reaction automatically without further examination, then we have a social stereotype.

Edwards (1985) developed four dimensions which include *content*, the traits which make up the stereotypes; *uniformity*, the degree of agreement of these traits; *direction*, the favourableness or unfavourableness of these traits; and *intensity*, the degree of favourableness or unfavourableness of responses to these traits.

Content can be seen as the matrix in the printer's stereotype. It is the linotype grid, the raw materials from which clusters of meaning spring. For example, Jews can be seen as shrewd, industrious, grasping, intelligent, and ambitious (Cauthen, Robinson, and Kraus, 1971).

Uniformity is a second important dimension of stereotypes in which the printer clamps the matrix into a rigid form. Common images that are held by many individuals and groups may emerge from the matrix. There may not be perfect agreement as to which traits apply to certain ethnic groups, but we expect clusters to emerge. We expect that uniformity is determined by cultural factors. Thus, it is reasonable to assume that ethnic stereotypes will vary. Most ethnic groups in Canada have come from different cultural contexts, and they have brought to Canada various traditions and attitudes. Two questions arise: first, will all of these groups have uniform images of themselves, or will there be more internal variation in some than in others? Second, how uniformly will others view specific groups? Fairly uniform images of some groups may already have been moulded in their mother countries and may be transplanted and perpetuated in Canada. When Germans, for example, are viewed as being aggressive, when this assessment is common in many groups, then we have evidence of a uniform attitude toward Germans. If Germans view themselves as aggressive as well, then the autostereotype and the stereotypical view of others is uniform.

Direction of stereotypes can be either positive or negative as Taylor (1981) stresses. Moreover, he suggests that 'stereotypes can be an important mechanism for recognizing and expressing ethnicity, and to the extent that they are accurate reflections, and refer to positive attributes of the stereotyped group, stereotypes can play a constructive role in intergroup relations' (1981: 163). Actually, ethnocentrism is a stereotype if the ingroup evaluates itself fairly rigidly, and if it does not change its attitudes when new evidence requires re-evaluation. There may be a tendency for individuals to evaluate themselves more positively than others may evaluate them. The gap between ingroup evaluations and the evaluations of others may be either positive or negative. The ingroup may evaluate itself positively, a tendency that is often labelled ethnocentrism, and it may be evaluated negatively by others, a tendency that is often labelled prejudice.

Taylor (1981: 163–4) argues that in ethnic relations it is important that (1) the stereotype an ingroup has of itself and that others have of it match, and (2) that these stereotypes are positive and not negative. If this is true, then the assumption inherent in the policy of multiculturalism would assume that positive relations would result in each group's retaining its own cultural distinctiveness. We expect that ingroup evaluations will be generally positive, but we also expect that there will be significant variations on some of the scales. While autostereotypes are expected to be positive, each group is expected to evaluate itself significantly higher on some attributes than others.

Intensity, Edwards's fourth dimension, has to do with the degree of favourableness or unfavourableness of a response. Thus, the dimension implies both the direction and the degree of a response.

When autostereotyping is positive and outgroup stereotyping is negative, the gap between the two evaluations may be so great that expectations from both sides will not conform to reality. There can also be counter stereotyping. Deroche and Deroche (1991: 69) found that on television black police were portrayed as more level-headed and correct than their co-workers. When the expectations of both sides coincide, then the stereotype can satisfy the desires of both groups involved, and ethnicity, for example, can take a constructive

TABLE 11-5 INGROUP AND OUTGROUP HIGH SCHOOL STUDENT EVALUATIONS OF JEWS

Scales	Jewish Self-Identity	Outgroup Evaluations			F-ratios
		French	German	Ukrainian	
A. Positive Autostereotype (4 is neutral)					
Unintellectual – Intellectual	6.21	4.90[a]	4.06[a]	5.14[a]	27.47[b]
Bad – Good	6.07	4.65[a]	4.35[a]	4.27[a]	54.57[b]
Worthless – Valuable	6.04	4.33[a]	4.10[a]	4.32[a]	54.81[b]
Boring – Interesting	5.98	4.18[a]	4.19[a]	4.10[a]	44.30[b]
Unfriendly – Friendly	5.91	4.47[a]	4.15[a]	4.02[a]	38.27[b]
Cruel – Kind	5.90	4.68a	4.43[a]	4.29[a]	39.42[b]
B. Ingroup and Outgroup Consensus					
Delicate – Rugged	4.03	4.16	4.14	3.96	0.92
Calm – Excitable	4.69	4.36	4.59	4.70	1.45
Submissive – Domineering	4.78	4.37	4.69	4.62	2.56
Cooperative – Competitive	4.69	4.80	5.08	5.09	2.64
Rational – Emotional	5.07	4.79	5.04	4.65	3.15[a]
Irreligious – Religious	5.57	5.77	5.94	6.04	3.72[b]
Poor – Wealthy	5.52	5.45	5.71	5.87	3.91[b]
Quiet – Talkative	5.68	5.24	5.77	5.82	5.16[b]
C. Negative Outgroup Stereotype					
Materialist – Humanistic	4.67	3.52[a]	3.33[a]	3.61[a]	21.11[b]
Dishonest – Honest	5.43	3.87[a]	3.48[a]	3.72[a]	46.24[b]
Traditional – Progressive	4.51	3.46[a]	3.90	3.65[a]	8.46[b]

Notes: [a] $p > .05$ [b] $p > .01$

SOURCE: Leo Driedger and Rodney Clifton, 'Ethnic Stereotypes: Images of Ethnocentrism, Reciprocity or Dissimilarity?' *Canadian Review of Sociology and Anthropology* 21 (1984): 287–301.

rather than a destructive form. Negative evaluations of a group, if they do not reflect reality, indicate prejudice. It is at this point that stereotypes and prejudice become synonymous. Too often the distinction between stereotype and prejudice becomes blurred and stereotypes merely become negative attitudes (Driedger, 1989: 346).

Table 11-5 presents the findings of Driedger and Clifton (1984) derived from their Winnipeg high school sample. Individual semantic differential scales comparing Jewish and non-Jewish students indicate stereotypes that range from positive to negative. The Jewish autostereotype of the intellectual, good, valuable, interesting, friendly, and kind Jew in Part A is positive, but students from the other three groups evaluate Jews much less positively.

Part B indicates considerable ingroup and outgroup consensus that Jews are excitable, domineering, competitive, emotional, religious, wealthy, and talkative. If Jews and the three other groups are indeed different in beliefs, values, customs, and culture, then these differences do not seem to have an effect upon the consensual stereotype. Is this a stereotype that is a fair assessment of Jews by all and that is accepted by all?

As illustrated in Part C, only three scales indicate the negative stereotype of Jews held by respondents of the three other groups. These are the only three scales in which the ratings fell below the neutral point, indicating slight negative tendencies to form a traditional stereotype of materialism and dishonesty. Jewish students do not agree with the other three groups' stereotypes of them—especially on the dishonest and materialist variables—and rate themselves more positively. The data in Part C suggest that dissimilarity may breed negative evaluations. It is important to note, however, that these are only three of seventeen scales; the other fourteen scales are not negative.

Overall, the results of the Driedger and Clifton research (1984) indicate that students have more positive self-identities than their evaluations of others, that they have neutral or slightly positive evaluations of students from other ethnic groups, and that generally the more positive the students' self-identities are, the more positive their evaluations of other groups will be. Let us turn next to a discussion of prejudice or negative attitudes.

ETHNIC PREJUDICE

Allport (1954) suggests that prejudice refers to attitudes while discrimination refers to action. Both phenomena are subject to irrational emotions that often lead to attitudes and behaviours inconsistent with the values of freedom and equality legitimized by a democratic society. Francis (1976: 268–70) defines prejudice as illegitimate categorization and discrimination as illegitimate differential treatment. Illegitimate forms of categorization and differential treatment have preoccupied many scholars of ethnic prejudice and discrimination (Francis, 1976; Hagan, 1977; Mackie, 1985; Henry et al., 1995). Since all humans need to classify their experiences, this process of categorization involves valuations which may or may not be legitimate, depending on the norms of a particular society. In democracies, where freedom and equality are highly valued, there are many discrepancies between ideal and real attitudes and behaviour.

But the problem is more complex because actions and attitudes that are considered legitimate for all may be based on a society's expectations of what should happen to minorities or immigrants in that society. Assimilationists would expect that all people should fuse in a cultural 'melting pot', while pluralists would deem differentiation and a multitude of sub-identities as the legitimate right of minorities. A question arises about the rights of members of a society to extend their political and religious diversity to ethnic pluralism. In Canada such a legal right has been extended to the two founding peoples (the British and the French), but the extent to which a distinctive identity is the right of others in a multicultural society is problematic. In the United States, multiculturalism appears to be less 'legitimate' than in Canada, although pluralism seems to be on the rise there. In most societies some groups have more rights than others (officially or unofficially), even though the equality of all may be the official ideal.

Hagan (1977: 168) suggests that *differential treatment* can be a predisposition to discrimination. All humans have to categorize their experiences, but some categories may promote the norms of a society more clearly than others. Canadians, for example, hold to the ideal of the right to equal treatment in a democratic society. In reality, not all people are treated equally and differentiation that does not provide equal distribution of opportunities or rewards can be seen as discriminatory.

Francis (1976: 269–70) adds the dimension of functional and dysfunctional differentiation, which further complicates the matter. 'Foreigners are admitted on the, at least tacit, assumption that relations with their hosts will be governed by particularistic norms specified by the terms of their admission. Thus, participation in the host society is, on principle, contractual and valid until further notice' (Francis, 1976: 269). The situation is different when a newcomer is expected to settle permanently in a modern state:

> Although he is not a member upon arrival, he is a prospective member supposed to acquire, in due course, all the qualifications necessary for regular membership. Whereas the hosts expect him to comply with the conditions under which he has been admitted as a prospective member, the ethnic in turn expects that, upon assuming his obligations, he will be granted all the benefits the host society has to offer to its charter members in accordance with generally accepted 'universalist' rules. We conclude that under certain conditions the differential treatment of ethnics may be not only functional but also legitimate, and that this is, as a rule, recognized by both the natives and the ethnics themselves. (Francis, 1976: 269)

The definition of prejudice should be confined to attitudes of illegitimate differentiation between members of a democratic society that are due solely to ethnicity and that prevent the victims from competing with other aspirants on equal terms. It is difficult to determine how much differentiation is illegitimate; we need to sort out legitimate and illegitimate differential attitudes to citizens' rights.

Prejudicial treatment is viewed by Hagan (1977: 170) as a negative predisposition to behaviour that could lead to discrimination. Francis (1976: 264) says, 'Prejudice is a legal term referring to the anticipation of judicial decision without due process.' Prejudice is a prejudgement insofar as preconceived opinions have been assumed to be true before having been put to the test. What makes identifying prejudice difficult is that prejudice is made of the same stuff as categorization (which we are all involved in), but that prejudice is based on invalid negative attitudes.

We need to see whether some people are more prone to evaluate others negatively, and then infer whether this connotes a disposition to prejudice that may, in turn, lead to discrimination. Unfortunately, there is not always a constant relationship between opinions, attitudes, and discrimination, but this assumed cause-and-effect relationship is only one of numerous types of problems in finding prejudice.

DISCRIMINATION: ILLEGITIMATE TREATMENT

Discrimination is related to illegitimate behaviour. Hagan (1977: 170–1) suggests that *denial of desire* can be a form of discrimination if we assume that all persons should be allowed equal preference and the freedom to choose. 'Restrictions on immigration and naturalization have been common, yet once ethnics have been admitted to potential regular membership, their differential treatment is relatively soon recognized as illegitimate' (Francis, 1976: 272). Lately, these egalitarian democratic principles may also be expanded to broader spheres of social life such as club membership or intermarriage. This raises the question of how open or closed a society or community may be with regard to access to its institutions and places of social, economic, and political life.

Many ethnic minorities such as the Hutterites choose to be segregated and do not wish to avail themselves of what an open society has to offer. Those who seek greater freedom and equality, however, are presumed to be discriminated against if they are denied such opportunities as jobs, open housing, or access to leisure and institutional activities. It should be possible to measure how open respondents perceive our society to be and whether opportunities are equal, as Canadian society says they are supposed to be. Discrimination comes about only when we deny to individuals or groups of people equality of treatment that they may wish.

Hagan (1977: 17) denotes *disadvantaged treatment* as a clear form of discrimination. Discrimination occurs when the object of prejudice is placed at

TABLE 11-6   TYPE OF DISCRIMINATION REPORTED BY HIGH SCHOOL STUDENTS
BY ETHNIC GROUPS

Form of Discrimination	Jews (N=290)	Poles (227)	Italians (65)	French (396)	Ukrainians (517)
	(Percentages)				
Total[a]	68	51	46	45	36
Ethnic jokes	50	45	37	33	30
Verbal abuse	53	17	19	21	13
Language ridicule	27	15	30	29	13
Hate literature	19	2	6	4	3
Physical attack	21	2	3	4	3
Vandalism	13	1	2	1	2

Note
[a]The percentages in this row represent the proportion of students in each category who reported at least one type of discrimination, or reported discriminations in a given place.

SOURCE: Leo Driedger and Richard Mezoff, 'Ethnic Prejudice and Discrimination in Winnipeg High Schools', *Canadian Journal of Sociology* 6 (1981): 1-17.

some disadvantage not merited by his own misconduct. Discrimination may be defined as the effective injurious treatment of persons on grounds rationally irrelevant to the situation (Driedger, 1989: 351).

The definition of disadvantage and the level of disadvantage induced are important to studies of prejudice and discrimination. Freedom to compete for the rewards of society and equal opportunity to attain these rewards have already been designated as 'rights' in a democratic society. When members of groups are abused verbally, this presumably would be disadvantageous over time to their attaining respect and status, which, in turn, are important for equal competition. However, are ethnic jokes sufficiently disadvantageous in a high school setting to result in discriminatory disadvantage? Different minorities could interpret such a mild form of negative language usage differently. Jokes may mean different things to different people, depending on the intention of the speaker, and the context of the situation. While the disadvantage of ethnic jokes is difficult to discern, more severe forms of action such as receiving hate literature, being vandalized, or being attacked physically can certainly be designated as discriminatory disadvantage. Thus we are forced to examine a wide range of disadvantageous action. Severe forms will be relatively easy to designate as discrimination; we will need to see how well we can interpret milder forms of disadvantage and whether these represent discrimination or not.

TABLE 11-6 (CONTINUED)

Form of Discrimination	Germans (333)	Scandinavians (78)	British (502)	Total (N=2408)
		(Percentages)		
Total[a]	33	19	18	35.5
Ethnic jokes	23	9	8	27.5
Verbal abuse	19	8	4	18.3
Language ridicule	13	4	8	15.7
Hate literature	5	0	2	5.0
Physical attack	3	1	2	4.7
Vandalism	3	1	0	2.7

The four denotations of prejudice and discrimination (differential, prejudicial, disadvantageous treatment, and denial of desire) form a useful continuum. The differentiation end represents only predisposition to prejudice, while the disadvantageous treatment end represents blatant forms of discrimination.

Driedger and Mezoff (1981: 1–17) asked students to report whether they had been discriminated against in various situations, and what types of discrimination were involved. In Table 11-6 we see that about one-third (35.5%) of the high school students in the sample reported discrimination at some time in a given place. Table 11-6 reports six types, ranging from ethnic jokes (a fairly minor form of disadvantage) to vandalism (a serious form of destruction). The six types of discrimination form a type of Guttman scale: about one-fourth (27.5%) of the respondents reported discrimination in the form of ethnic jokes; about one-fifth (18.3 percent) reported verbal abuse; one-sixth (15.7 percent) reported language ridicule; and 3 to 5% were victims of hate literature.

More than two-thirds (68%) of the Jewish students perceived discrimination; about one-half of the Polish (51%), Italian (46%), and French (45%) students also perceived discrimination; about one-third of the Ukrainian (36%) and German (33%) students reported discrimination; less than one-fifth of the Scandinavians (19%) and British (18%) reported disadvantageous treatment. The data in Table 11-6 also show that most discrimination seems to take the form of jokes, ridicule, and verbal abuse. Except for the Jews, most of the students did not report severe attacks, hate literature, or vandalism. Driedger and Mezoff (1981) concluded that evidence in four distinct areas—

differential treatment, prejudicial treatment, denial of desire, and disadvanta-geous treatment (as described in Hagan)—shows that prejudice and discrim-ination occur among students in Winnipeg.

Differential treatment was clearly shown by the fact that three times as many students were willing to marry northern Europeans as non-Europeans and Jews. More than ten per cent of the students wished to debar Jews or restrict them to visits to Canada.

A majority of students agreed that openness in leisure activity, semantic expression, public places, and public communication was desirable. However, Driedger and Mezoff (1981) again found that a minority who could not agree to equal treatment and openness of parties, sports, restaurants, clubs, oral expressions, and communication.

Denial of the desire for equality took place mostly in the school. The Jews, Italians, Poles, and Germans perceived the greatest discrimination in the classroom and in textbooks. Less than 10% of the students, however, reported being denied open access to all types of places.

Wilson Head (1981) conducted a study of racial minorities in Toronto related to discrimination in housing, employment, and community services and found that 90% of Blacks and 72% of South Asians felt 'some' or a 'great deal of' discrimination; in contrast, only 35% of European respondents reported discrimination. Henry and Ginzberg (1984) in *Who Gets the Work?* in Toronto matched Black and White job seekers applying for jobs advertised in a major newspaper, and found that Whites received three times as many job offers. They also found that telephone callers with accents, especially South Asian and Caribbean, were more often screened out when they inquired about job vacancies (Henry and Ginzberg, 1984). In a follow-up study of employers who advertised jobs, Billingsley and Musynski (1985) found that 28% of the respondents felt that racial minorities did not have the ability to meet their performance criteria. Jain (1988) concluded that visible minorities face pay and employment discrimination. Ponting and Wanner (1983: 57–76) found that Blacks in Calgary encountered similar discrimination in areas of employment and housing, results also reported by Christiansen and Weinfeld (1993: 26–44) and Henry (1989). Similar problems were found among black students in school by Dei (1993: 45–65) and, as a black teacher, Dei (1993: 38–51) outlines challenges which teachers face in anti-racist teaching (Tuzlak, 1989: 103–19).

NATIONAL PERCEIVED DISCRIMINATION 1980–95

Reginald Bibby (1995) has been taking national samples every five years between 1980 and 1995, asking 'Do you feel that racial and cultural groups in your community are discriminated against?' Table 11-7 shows that while in 1980 about one-half felt that some groups were discriminated against, by 1995

T A B L E 11-7 NATIONAL PERCEIVED DISCRIMINATION, 1980–1995

Region and Year		Do you feel that any racial or cultural groups in your community are discriminated against?	
		Yes	No
		(Percentages)	
National	1995	67	33
	1990	59	41
	1985	54	46
	1980	55	45
B.C.	1995	67	33
	1980	71	29
Prairies	1995	64	36
	1980	55	45
Ontario	1995	63	37
	1980	49	51
Quebec	1995	75	25
	1980	65	35
Atlantic	1995	58	42
	1980	32	68

SOURCE: Reginald Bibby, *The Bibby Report: Social Trends Canadian Style.* Toronto: Stoddart Publishing, 1995, pp. 52–4.

two-thirds thought so. Since 1980, the percentage who think discrimination is getting worse has averaged about 15%; those who think it is better has risen from 15 to 20%, and those who think it is about the same has decreased from 45 to 33% (Bibby, 1995: 52).

In 1995 Quebeckers (75%) are most likely to report discrimination and residents of the Atlantic region (58%) least likely. Residents in all regions except British Columbia are reporting increases in discrimination since 1980 with exceptionally high increases in Ontario and the Atlantic region. One-fourth of British Columbians think it is getting worse (much more than the others), while one-fourth of Quebeckers (the highest), think it is getting better now. Acknowledgement that discrimination exists varies little by ethnic group.

One measure of the acceptance of each other is approval of intergroup marriage. There has been a gradual increase in the approval of marriage between different Canadians, ranging from a low of 57% in 1975 approving of marriage between Whites and Blacks, to 81% in 1995 (Bibby, 1995: 54), very similar to that of intermarriage of Whites and East Indians/Pakistanis. In 1995 most respondents (80–84%) approve of Whites marrying East

Indians, Blacks, Asians, and Aboriginals. There was more readiness to inter-marry between the religious groups in 1975 (78–86% range) and this has increased by 1995 (89–92% range). Still, 10–20% are opposed to some forms of intermarriage, depending on type.

DIFFERENTIAL AND UNFAIR TREATMENT

Our discussion of stereotype, prejudice, and discrimination strongly suggests that the symbolic status we attribute to groups varies along at least three dimensions. In Canada we treat people differently on the basis of ethnicity, race, and religion. Canadians are not all of equal status; although our ideals (as seen in the Charter of Rights and Freedoms) say that all people must be treated with respect and equality, for a variety of reasons this seldom happens. Let us summarize by reviewing these three symbolic status indicators.

ETHNIC ORIGIN

In Chapter Eight we found that the British score among the highest on socio-economic status, with higher levels of income, education, and occupa-tional status than most people in Canada. These indicators are highly valued in a technological, industrial society, and present a model of success to which many aspire. Because the British are numerically the largest ethnic group (as well as one of the two founding charter peoples) and are politically most pow-erful, they are a considerable force to be reckoned with when studying status and prestige as illustrated in our model (Cell B) in Chapter Two.

The French, the other charter group, have been settled in Canada even longer than the British. They have consolidated their strength spatially in Quebec, and they are numerically the second largest ethnic group. They, too, have extensive political influence. The Canadian Charter of Rights and Free-doms has provided special status and privileges to both charter groups, raising their languages to official status and guaranteeing the survival of their respec-tive cultures. These privileges have been more entrenched during the past sev-eral decades. The Canadian constitution symbolically, as well as legally, places the two charter groups above all others in Canada.

On the other hand, the aboriginals of Canada have been placed symboli-cally at the bottom of our hierarchy of status and privilege because of treaties that place them in a subservient position. Historically, large stretches of land were surrendered for a minimal return. Aboriginals were shunted onto special reserves, making it difficult to compete in the Canadian mainstream. The Indian Act and federal agencies still relate to them in paternal ways, giving them little control over their destiny. In non-treated territories, Canada has not yet dealt with Indian and Inuit land claims, and there is considerable pro-crastination in settling these rights. Furthermore, only limited aboriginal rights have been entrenched in the Canadian Constitution because the aboriginals represent less than two per cent of our population and are very weak economically and politically.

RACE AND RACISM

While ethnic origin has been solidified into high (charter group) and low (aboriginal) ethnic status polarities, race and skin colour also enter the equation of stereotypes, prejudice, and discrimination. In Chapter Ten we clearly showed Canada's socio-economic racial differentiations. Whites, largely of European origin, tend to rank high, while aboriginals, Blacks, and some Asians who are visible minorities rank low. Whites are an overwhelming majority in Canada, and the proportion of visible minorities is small compared to comparable proportions in the United States.

To some extent it is surprising that such large numbers of Canadians feel relatively comfortable with East Indians, aboriginals, Blacks, Asians and Jews (Table 11-3). It is not surprising to see (Table 11-4) that Canadians of European origin (all white) were much more preferred for marriage partners than were non-Europeans of Asian and African racial origin. Ramcharan's (1982) findings on racism toward non-whites documents some of the discrimination against West Indians, Chinese, Japanese, East Indians, Filipinos, and Arabs.

Ramcharan (1982: 88) proposes that discriminatory behaviour in Canada can be analyzed from two perspectives—the colour-class and the stranger theses:

> With regard to the colour-class thesis, the supposition is that the majority groups in the society identify nonwhites with the lowest social class mainly because of the historical relationships between whites and nonwhites. The Stranger thesis sees the nonwhite immigrants as archetypal stranger both in appearance and behaviour, and react to them with distrust, antipathy, and a resultant negative attitude. (Ramcharan, 1982: 88)

Ramcharan suggests that for many people both of these perspectives may be operating. As a result, non-whites may be seen as both outsiders and strangers, marginal to society but also relegated to an inferior socio-economic status. What remains to be seen is whether the duality has been institutionalized in Canada, and whether these attitudes can still be changed.

Recently there has been a much larger influx of non-white immigrants so that colour and racial factors are creating larger visible minority sectors, especially in some of the larger cities such as Toronto, Montreal, and Vancouver. A very large proportion of recent immigrants entering Canada come to Toronto; many of these are non-whites. Studies by Frances Henry (1978: 383; 1996) show that the Black presence in Toronto is resulting in more racism. Toronto discriminates in employment and access to housing four to eight times as often for Blacks as whites (James, 1995: 135–46). Ramcharan's (1982: 89) study of West Indians in Toronto shows that 58% reported discrimination in housing, 38% in access to housing, and 16% in hotels, bars, and relations with the police. The Ontario Human Rights Commission reports that in 1977 over half of their complaints were from visible minorities. Since then Toronto has commissioned the Task Force on Race Relations to look into the problem.

Ramcharan (1982: 90) suggests that there are also differences among visible minorities; his suggestion is supported by the Toronto Task Force:

> The report believes, however, that it was not a phenomenon of institutional racism but rather of 'culture shock' with the white majority being unable to adjust to the fact that Toronto had become a multicultural entity. . . . It notes that the Asian migrant is usually a professional and skilled worker, and as a result has not started at the bottom of the stratification system as was expected. The immigrants' sudden emergence above the expected level shocked and surprised many majority group members who were born here and have not risen to the upper echelons of the economic system. (Pitman, 1978: 38–41)

Ramcharan (1982: 90) suggests this shows the combination of the stranger and colour-class theses. Some visible minorities are discriminated against because their cultural traditions are considered inferior, and others are discriminated against because higher-status visible immigrants have not accepted an ascribed low entrance status.

Frances Henry classifies racism in three categories: 'Individual racism refers to conscious prejudice; institutional racism is that which is carried out by an individual because of others who are prejudiced; and structural racism has its base in the inequalities rooted in the operations of society at large' (Henry, 1978: 385).

Henry (1978: 392; Henry et al., 1995: 92, 93) found that roughly half of her sample in Toronto expressed some degree of racism; approximately 16% were considered very racist, 35% somewhat racist, 30% somewhat liberal, and 19% very liberal. She found that younger Torontonians were less racist, and that the more educated also were less racist, which confirms Bibby's (1987: 160) national findings. Again we must ask, what affirmative action should be initiated?

RELIGION AND ANTI-SEMITISM

In addition to ethnic origin and race, religion is also a means of differentiating status. John Berry et al. (1977) found that both Angloceltic and French Canadians placed Doukhobors, Hutterites and Mennonites at the bottom of the distance scale. These religious minorities ranked lower than visible minorities.

Reginald Bibby found that his national samples felt about as at ease with Jews as with East Indians, Canadian Indians, Blacks, and Asians. Driedger's Winnipeg high school students placed Jews roughly at a par with the non-European origin category with respect to social distance (Table 11-4). Only one-fourth were willing to marry Jews, 7% wanted them only as visitors to Canada. Lambert and Curtis (1984: 30–46) compared four samples of Canadians and found that opposition to mixed racial and religious marriages declined between 1968 and 1983. These data suggest that many Canadians place considerable distance between themselves and some religious minorities.

Howard Palmer (1982) found that during the Second World War, German-speaking Canadians were associated with the enemy; this association led to the 1940 burning of two Mennonite churches in Vauxhall, Alberta. Similar reports can be found with regard to Jehovah's Witnesses. In Chapter Twelve we shall discuss the Jewish holocaust, the attitudes of Canadians toward the Jews, and the degree of prejudice and discrimination based on anti-Semitism in Canada (Elliott and Fleras, 1992: 51).

In Winnipeg, Driedger and Mezoff (1981: 11–15) found that Jewish high school students reported the greatest discrimination. About half of the Jewish and Polish students reported being subjected to ethnic jokes. Twenty Jewish students interpreted some of the joking as malicious. Verbal abuse, a more serious form of negative expression, was reported by about one-sixth (18.3%) of the total sample of students. In contrast, half of the Jews reported verbal abuse. 'Dirty Jews' was reported by thirty-one Jewish students as the most common verbal abuse, followed by reference to 'cheap and rich Jews' (eleven), and 'bloody Jews' (four). Less than five per cent also reported more serious forms of discrimination, such as receiving hate literature, physical attack, and vandalism. Over half of such discrimination was reported by the Jewish students. One-fifth of the Jewish students had received hate literature; a similar proportion also reported physical attacks, but it was not always clear whether they were assaulted because they were Jewish. Their reports included the following comments: 'I was hit', 'attacked at school', 'beat up because I was Jewish', 'kids threw sticks and leaves at one', 'physical attack in younger years', 'fights in high school', 'got into a fight', 'attacked in Grade 5', 'kicked and punched in school', 'boys came to private school to pick fights', 'attacked in school halls', 'attacked by drunks', 'pushed down in park', 'beaten up by Protestants', and 'gang bullied me'. Vandalism was reported by 13% of the Jewish students in the following places: 'at the Jewish cemetery', 'house broken into', 'against religious property', 'family plot in cemeteries', 'swastikas on the walls of synagogues', '"Dirty Jew" written on garage door', and 'Jewish school broken into'. There is little doubt that the hate literature, physical attacks, and vandalism reported and confirmed by citation of places and events are forms of discriminatory abuse.

Canadians clearly differentiate between others on the basis of ethnicity, race, and religion. Canadians make and use symbolic differentiations as a basis of discrimination. There is considerable evidence that prejudice and discrimination do exist, even though more thorough documentation would be desirable. John Porter was keenly aware of the potential for disadvantage, and favoured less stress on ethnic differentiation so that all could compete in the labour market on the same basis. With the increase of a more pluralist ethnic, racial, and religious mosaic, it is also essential that Canadians increasingly accept variety and diversity as the norm. As long as expectations of ethnic minority assimilation and amalgamation survive, minorities will be viewed as inferior and second class citizens. Affirmative action to fight discrimination and racism again seems appropriate.

SUMMARY

With stratification and increased pluralism come a variety of attitudes and behaviours. Some Canadians are 'much more equal' than others, and there is considerable evidence of social distance in the form of ethnic stereotypes, prejudice, and discrimination.

The charter groups have received special privileges in the Canadian Constitution to preserve their languages and culture. The British and French also reinforce their higher status and privilege by supporting their charter status and ranking others in lesser positions. The majority in Canada now supports bilingualism, although this support is greater in Quebec, where the French are a large majority, than in the West, where the ethnic mosaic is more diversified. Generally the prestige of the charter Canadians is set and is increasingly recognized.

Attitudes toward a plural society are also growing, with a majority favouring the mosaic over the melting pot. Attitudes of Canadians show that immigrants are welcome, and that they may retain their cultures. There is considerable recognition that such pluralism may not be easy, with a sizeable minority who would rather dispense with multiculturalism. A huge majority claim that they feel relatively at ease with visible minorities, an openness which offers hope for Canada's multicultural future.

However, there is also considerable social distance or racism in the form of stereotyping, prejudice, and discrimination. Two to three times as many Canadians would rather marry European-origin than non-European-origin Canadians. Negative stereotypes of Jews persist, and there is considerable evidence that visible minorities are also subject to abuse by a minority of Canadians who do not wish them well. Aboriginals are continually shunted to the periphery and given inferior opportunities and status. In large cities there is evidence of racism based on skin colour, especially as visible minorities try to compete for jobs and better housing. There are also religious differentiations, focused mainly on anti-Semitism.

Canada is becoming an increasingly pluralist society, and there is progress in the acceptance of multiculturalism and diversity of colour, race, and beliefs. A sizeable minority, however, neither accepts ethnic diversity nor complies with the ideals of minority rights and freedoms. This is especially evident in repeated incidents of racism and anti-Semitism. It will not be easy to build a pluralist ethnic, racial, and religious society. Attitudes and behaviour do not easily conform to ideal norms set on paper. A just society based on equality and freedom seems always a step away.

CHAPTER 12

The Quest for Human Rights

While multiethnicity is normal in civilized societies, the ideal of one ethnically unitary state, perpetuated by British and French nationalism until the 1920s, was rarely approached in practice. The unitary national state simplified the wielding of power by a majority because such nationalism seeks to justify the power relations discussed in Part IV. The settlement and invasion of the Americas by Europeans since the early 1500s was fraught with numerous wars between the British, French, Spanish, and Portuguese. These nations wished to extend their power as colonizers of weaker peoples and to entrench their own political dominance and economic advantage.

Karl Marx's main concern was with these macro political-economy power issues, and he hoped for a 'classless society' in which all people could survive under more equal relations. Unfortunately, he spent little time spelling out the fine points of how such relations on a micro level might work. Max Weber focused more on multi-dimensional factors of human relations that operated on the micro level. His concern for individuals and their needs allowed him to consider economic and political factors, and also the religious and value systems that often motivate humans in a variety of directions.

In Chapter Twelve we will look at the rights and freedoms of all humans, irrespective of majority or minority power positions. We shall first discuss three charters of rights: the Constitution of the United States of America, the United Nations Universal Declaration of Human Rights, and the Canadian Charter of Rights and Freedoms adopted in the Canadian Constitution in 1982. The first document deals with individual rights, and the second and third include both individual and collective rights. Later in the chapter, we shall discuss collective rights and the injustices that have been perpetuated by the expulsion of the Acadians, Métis aspirations for a new nation in the West, the Jewish holocaust during the Second World War, and still-unsettled Indian land claims.

INDIVIDUAL RIGHTS AND FREEDOMS

THE AMERICAN BILL OF RIGHTS

The two Americas were settled mainly by the Spaniards, Portuguese, British, and French. The Spanish and Portuguese explorers who settled Central and South America came from homelands where Roman Catholicism was the state religion. They propagated their religion in Latin America, and all these countries are now also dominantly Roman Catholic. The state religion was considered an integral part of power politics, when the aboriginals were conquered and subdued. Catholicism replaced aboriginal religions, although in greatly modified forms.

North American settlement, however, did not follow the pattern established in Latin America. The thirteen American colonies on the east coast began in a more heterogeneous manner. Jamestown, the first permanent English settlement in North America, was established in 1607 in what is now Virginia. One year later in 1608, Champlain established the first French settlement on the St Lawrence River at Quebec. The Pilgrim Fathers, a group of separatists from the Church of England who founded Plymouth Colony near Boston, came to America in 1620 on the *Mayflower*. In 1624, the Dutch West Indies Company established the colony of New Amsterdam, which in 1664 was surrendered to the English and renamed New York. In 1681 William Penn, an English Quaker who had earlier been jailed for his writings on religious freedom and his defence of the doctrine of toleration, received a grant of territory later to be named Pennsylvania after him. These varied settlements were founded because refugees and settlers left their European states for more freedom and tolerance, particularly of religious beliefs.

It is not surprising that when the American Constitution was drafted and signed in 1787, shortly after independence from British rule, it guaranteed freedom of religion, speech, and assembly. Many of the new settlers were dissenters who could not freely practise their beliefs in the normal context of European state religions. They came from a variety of situations with a variety of aspirations that could prosper only under norms of freedom and toleration.

The First Amendment of the Constitution of the United States of America reads:

> Congress shall make no law respecting an establishment of religion, or prohibiting the free exercise thereof; or abridging the freedom of speech or of the press; or of the right of the people peaceably to assemble, and to petition the government for a redress of grievances.

Congress's first concern was that there should not be an official state religion, and that all people should have the right to practise their religions freely. Freedom of speech and of the press were important for maintaining and propagating Americans' beliefs, and the ability to meet and assemble as the people saw fit was an important part of these freedoms. The Constitution was ratified by the states only after the promise of amendments that related directly to human rights. The first ten amendments, known as the Bill of Rights, were passed in 1791.

After the bloody Civil War between the North and the South, seventy-five years later, the Thirteenth, Fourteenth, and Fifteenth Amendments abolished slavery, conferred citizenship on former slaves, and established the principle that the state cannot deprive any person of life, liberty and/or property, without due process of law. Section One of the Thirteenth Amendment reads:

> Neither Slavery, nor involuntary servitude, except as a punishment for crime whereof the party shall have been duly convicted, shall exist within the United States, or any place subject to their jurisdiction.

Section One of the Fifteenth Amendment reads:

> The right of citizens of the United States to vote shall not be denied or abridged by the United States or by any State on account of race, color, or previous condition of servitude.

Although religious rights were entrenched 200 years ago, it was almost a century later, after a civil war, that equality of race was entrenched. To this day, problems of racial inequality exist.

It was not until 1920 that women received the right to vote under Section One of the Nineteenth Amendment, which reads:

> The right of citizens of the United States to vote shall not be denied or abridged by the United States on account of sex.

These are not, however, articles or amendments that relate directly to ethnicity except the Fifteenth Amendment's guarantee of voting to all races. All these articles protect individual rights; none deal with group rights. Individual religions, races, or ethnic groups are not provided any specific rights. The United States is one of the first modern states to entrench human rights and freedoms by restricting state powers. It has been a struggle, but in the process America has been held up by many as the land of liberty and freedom. The drive for religious freedom was an important part of this historical quest and played an important part in setting these standards.

The western world has been profoundly influenced by Judeo-Christian religious ideology. Although secularization has ensured that this ideology is no longer as dominant as it was in Europe during the Middle Ages, a large majority of North Americans claim to be Christian. Christianity is an ideology that grew out of the Jewish religion, which is based on the law and the prophets. Prophets such as Amos proclaimed the concept of justice based on the fundamental tenet that all human beings are of equal worth. Justice implies that there are standards for the treatment of human beings, and that these must be applied fairly in accordance with principles based on what is 'right'. The prophets proclaimed these standards and appealed to Israel to comply.

The Christian religion grew out of this Jewish tradition, confirmed the law and the prophets, and extended the ideology to embrace and promote 'love' (see, for instance, Matthew 5, the Sermon on the Mount). Again the worth of every human being was stressed and was extended to include even the enemy. The 'brotherhood of man' applied to all people, nations, and races. Everyone was considered worthy of love. It was a message not only for the Jews, but for Gentiles as well.

Western political ideology (especially in the democracies) is based on principles quite in line with Western religious ideology. While in Britain freedom was at first mainly for the élite, slowly freedom for all citizens was recognized and affirmed. The French call for 'liberty, equality and fraternity' was also intended for the masses. The conclusion of Abraham Lincoln's Gettysburg Address (19 November 1863)—calling for government for, by, and of the people—perhaps summarized this ideology best, giving notice that all citizens have the franchise and deserve a voice in the affairs of the nation. Enshrined in the Constitution and its subsequent Amendments, freedom of speech, freedom of assembly, and the pursuit of life, liberty, and happiness were legal rights upheld by the law.

While North American religious and political ideologies generally aim in the same direction, our economic ideologies often pull in opposite directions. Laissez-faire capitalism had as its basic tenets freedom of individual enterprise, ownership of private property, rights to inheritance, and the need for competition under minimal government interference. Capitalism tends to embrace some of the individual freedoms of Christianity and democracy, but it is much less open to the group and social responsibilities of our religious and political ideologies. Early capitalism tended to promote individual rights and often sacrificed the welfare of others, usually the workers and the masses.

Since then capitalism in Canada has been greatly modified to accommodate more social needs. This seems to have come about because of socialist philosophies that advocated greater emphasis on state control of some of the basic economic industries. These philosophies hold that the basic and common needs of education, welfare, health, transportation, and communication should be operated or controlled by the government for the benefit of all. Thus we have a modified socio-capitalist economy that tries to hold together individual freedoms and collective responsibility. Access to economic management and control, however, lies mostly in the hands of those of northern European (especially British) origin. Not all Canadians have an equal chance to compete within the economic structure.

Thus, we are faced with individual, institutional, and structural inequalities in the social order that need to be addressed. Kallen (1995: 13–40) points out that despite a proliferation of human rights legislation, racism persists. Some people call for the restructuring of our social institutions so that schools, churches, governments, and the workplace articulate and promote equal human rights, the only foundation upon which legislation can be justly based and enforced. Since the 1960s such restructuring related to the equal freedom of Blacks in the United States has been a major issue.

THE UNITED NATIONS UNIVERSAL DECLARATION OF HUMAN RIGHTS
The Universal Declaration of Human Rights was unanimously adopted in 1948 by the General Assembly of the United Nations (Kallen, 1995: 286–91). The Declaration's main objective is to promote and encourage respect for human rights and freedoms. Thirty articles proclaim the personal, civil, political, economic, social, and cultural rights of humans. It goes considerably farther than the American Constitution's guarantee of individual rights. It is amazing that the nations of the world were able to agree on such far-reaching freedoms for all world citizens.

Article One declares that 'all humans are born free and equal in dignity and rights' and should act 'towards each other in a spirit of brotherhood'. Article Two states that these 'freedoms are set forth without distinction of any kind, such as race, color, sex, language, religion, political . . . national or social . . . origin'. Article Two clearly declares that racial, ethnic, and religious equality must be respected. In Article Three the right to 'life, liberty and security of person' is articulated and Article Four says that 'no one shall be held in slavery or servitude'. These four articles cover the basic rights of all humans.

The remaining articles continue to spell out rights related to freedom from torture, recognition before the law, and protection by the law. No one shall be subjected to arbitrary arrest and detention; everyone shall have equality in a fair hearing in the case of criminal charges, and shall be tried under the presumption of innocence. Privacy, family, home, honour and reputation must be protected by law. There should be rights to freedom of movement, and all people should have the right to asylum when persecuted.

Articles Fifteen through Thirty each elaborate briefly on a series of rights and freedoms including the right to nationality, the right to marry and to found a family, the right to own property, freedom of opinion and expression, freedom of assembly and participation in government, and the right to social security which includes work, rest and leisure, health, education, and the cultural life of a community. Social and international order are noted as being necessary to make these rights possible. The articles also declare the nations' duty to help create communities in which such rights and freedoms are possible. The list of rights and freedoms is so extensive that few societies are able to fulfil all these obligations, especially in Third World countries where capacity to provide educational, work, and economic opportunities is limited. Presumably the rights and freedoms are spelled out in detail as a goal to which all nations may aspire.

While these rights and freedoms are all related and relevant to ethnic relations, Articles Two, Four, Seven, Sixteen, and Eighteen are more specifically focused on race, ethnicity, and religion (Kallen, 1995: 287–9). Article Two clearly states that the rights and freedoms are universal:

> Everyone is entitled to all the rights and freedoms set forth in this Declaration, without distinction of any kind, such as race, sex, language, religion, political or other opinion, national or social origin, property, birth or other status.

The foundation for freedoms clearly extends to persons of any race, language, religion, or national origin. Article Four is clear on slavery:

> No one shall be held in slavery or servitude, slavery and slave trade shall be prohibited in all their forms.

This goes farther than the American Bill of Rights did originally. Although the United States waited seventy-eight years after the first states ratified the Constitution before they outlawed slavery, they ratified the Thirteenth Amendment in 1865, eighty-three years before the United Nations Declaration. The definition of slavery might be subject to interpretation. While ownership of persons might not be direct, they could still be subject to circumstances such as those in which Black South Africans recently lived, which amounted to informal forms of slavery where a white minority subjugates a Black majority.

Article Seven addresses the issue of equality before the law.

> All are equal before the law and are entitled without discrimination to equal protection of the law. All are entitled to equal protection against any discrimination in violation of this Declaration and against any incitement to such discrimination.

We know, of course, that not all accused have equal access to a fair hearing or legal help; some can afford it better than others. The fact that a highly disproportionate number of aboriginals are found in Canadian prisons indicates inequality; the same is true for Afro-Americans in the United States. These Natives may be less knowledgeable about legal matters, may not have the means to secure bail, and may be more vigorously pursued by the police because of their visibility. This kind of discrimination can be subtle.

The first part of Article Sixteen clearly mentions ethnicity and the rights to marriage and a family:

1) Men and women of full age, without any limitation due to race, nationality or religion, have the rights to marry and to found a family. They are entitled to equal rights as to marriage, during marriage and at its dissolution . . .

Marriage to a partner who wishes to perpetuate similar beliefs and values is important for ethnic identity. Thus, no one should be forced to marriage outside these restrictions. On the other hand, persons are also free to marry across racial, national, and religious lines if they wish to do so. Thus, both freedom to maintain ethnic solidarity and to move beyond it are assured (Kallen, 1995: 288).

Article Eighteen deals with freedom in religion:

Everyone has the right to freedom of thought, conscience and religion; this right includes freedom to change his religion or belief, and freedom, either alone or in community with others and in public or private, to manifest his religion or belief in teaching, practice, worship and observance.

For minorities such as Jews, Hutterites, Mennonites, Doukhobors, and others, ethnicity and religion are closely intertwined; their religion must be safeguarded to protect their ethnicity. However, this freedom is also important for larger groups: the French, Italians, and Poles are usually Roman Catholics; the British are largely Anglican, United Church, or Presbyterian. Religious freedom for minorities is crucial in India, Pakistan, Northern Ireland, the Arab countries, Israel, and most Latin American countries where the majority belongs to one religion.

The freedoms stated in the American Constitution and its Amendments are confined to individual rights, and that is also largely the case for the rights stated in the United Nations Declaration. However, the Universal Declaration of Human Rights does provide more social context to support individual rights. Article Twelve speaks against family and home interference. Article Thirteen deals with freedom of residence and movement, and Article Twenty supports the right of peaceful assembly. Both documents speak to social group supports. Article Twenty supports the right to take part in government, and Articles Twenty-Two through Twenty-Nine all support rights to associations such as social security, work, leisure, health services, education, community, and international order. Thus, the United Nations Declaration protects the social context and supports much more freedom in a greater holistic fashion.

Evelyn Kallen (1982: 12–19) has evaluated the United Nations Declaration and suggests that it supports individual rights, but offers little support for ethnic collectivities living within the boundaries of a nation. Kallen (1995: 9–12) suggests that if multiculturalism in Canada is to mean anything, rights will have to reach beyond individual levels, to subnational ethnic collectivities. For example the Québécois, the Dene Nation, and the Inuit of Nunavut will be dealt with as peoples who deserve special rights within the nation-state.

THE CANADIAN CHARTER OF RIGHTS AND FREEDOMS

Whereas the United States was concerned with protecting individual rights and freedoms 200 years ago, the British North America (BNA) Act of 1867, created in Britain, made no specific reference to human rights. Aside from provisions to protect the English and French languages, and the rights to Protestants and Catholics to have their own denominational schools, the BNA Act did not address human rights. This seems to have been a reflection of the dominance of two colonial powers that shaped the Canadian nation. Aside from the aboriginals in Canada, the two charter European founding peoples represented more than 90% of the population in 1867.

The BNA Act virtually ignored Canada's aboriginals, and recognized almost no rights for them.

> For almost a century after the British Emancipation Act of 1833, which marked the official demise of slavery in Canada, the trend at the federal, provincial and municipal levels of Canadian government was to enact discriminatory legislation. Among the most pernicious pieces of legislation was the Indian Act, whereby Indians were virtually denied all of their fundamental rights; but many other discriminatory laws impeded the rightful participation of Asians, Blacks and other ethnic minorities from anything like full participation in Canadian society. (Kallen, 1982: 43)

Questions of human rights and discrimination began to be considered seriously only after the Second World War, most likely in reaction to the atrocities of the Nazis and the concerns of the increasingly numerous immigrant population who considered themselves other than charter Canadians.

Legal rights, some of which are formally stated (charter status and treaty status) and others of which are assumed (entrance status), have evolved during the last 130 years. The British North America Act of 1867 gave the founding groups of Canada charter group status (Porter, 1965). The Act legalized the claims of the two groups to such historical privileges as the perpetuation of their separate languages and cultures. Though legally of equal status, the French have always been junior partners in their alliance with the English, especially where British political, economic, educational, and demographic influences have been dominant outside Quebec.

The presence of two major European linguistic and cultural groups from the beginning of Confederation has in some ways set a precedent for the recognition of more than one ethnic presence. Most nations assume one dominant culture to which others must conform, although all nations do have a variety of subgroups (French and Flemish in Belgium; German, French, and Italian in Switzerland; English, Scottish, Irish, and Welsh in Great Britain; etc.). Even in the new Constitution two official languages are recognized and legally entrenched. French Canadians in Quebec have moulded their curricula to emphasize their long 350-year history, and the British have done the same in the rest of Canada. The two often interpret the same events quite differently to cast their respective histories in the best light. In the process, minority languages and heritages were often legislated against by both the British (e.g., the Manitoba School Question) and the French (e.g., Bill 101). Canada is seeking to correct some of these injustices and inequalities, and to recognize the contributions of non-charter Canadians now that multiculturalism within a bilingual framework has been recognized.

While the legal rights and special privileges of the charter groups became a part of the social structure early in Canada's history, the structure created by treaties with Canadian Indians often placed aboriginals in underprivileged positions. About one-half of Canada's aboriginals were forced onto reserves to free land for white European settlers and to provide a more convenient administrative arrangement of control. Indians on the prairies in particular did not yet have a concept of private property and the value of land, which aboriginals on the west coast, for example, had developed. Thus, most west coast aboriginals have not yet signed treaties, while prairie Indians signed away their lands for a pittance in Treaties 1–11. These reserves, often in marginal regions, have been mostly non-competitive in today's industrial society. As a result large numbers of young and unskilled aboriginals leave the reserves in search of jobs and many are coming to Canada's cities. In the meantime, new questions arise as to whether the treaties still apply, how they should be interpreted, and what land rights can be negotiated where treaties have not been made. A wide range of interpretations can be given to the present plight of Canada's 'first peoples', what rights they have, and what they deserve in the future.

Now that the rights of the charter groups and some of the rights of half of our aboriginal people have been partly clarified, we turn to the rights of the one-third of Canada's population who are neither British, French, nor aboriginal. This proportion of the population has been growing steadily and is trying to find its place in a multicultural society. Advocates of pluralism often complain that the contributions of these groups have not been sufficiently recognized and taught.

In the past decade a point system of desired traits has resulted in an increase of immigrants from the Third World, including Asians, South Americans, Africans, and other visible minorities, often of other religions and non-European cultures. Many of these new immigrants are also well educated, and thus increasingly demand equal rights and just treatment. How can we integrate their contribution into our social system so that their voices may be heard as equals?

Canada passed its Charter of Rights and Freedoms in 1982, when it became a part of the new Canadian Constitution that replaced the BNA Act

(Kallen, 1995: 292–8). Article 2 lists four fundamental freedoms: '(a) freedom of conscience and religion; (b) freedom of thought, belief, opinion, . . . the press and other media of communication; (c) freedom of peaceable assembly; and (d) freedom of association' (Constitution Act, 1982, Appendix 1). Articles 2 through 15 have to do with individual rights. Article 3 deals with the right to vote, and Article 6 with the right to mobility inside and outside Canada. Articles 7 through 14 provide legal rights: the right to life, liberty, and security, and freedom from unreasonable seizure, arbitrary imprisonment, and cruel punishment (Driedger, 1989: 372–3).

Article 15 specifically spells out individual equality of rights:

1) Every individual is equal before and under the law and has the right to the equal protection and equal benefits of the law without discrimination and, in particular, without discrimination based on race, national or ethnic origin, colour, religion, sex, age or mental or physical disability.

This is the first of the three documents to include ethnic origin. The traits protected from discrimination, including ethnicity, are again mentioned in subsection two. Thus, the multicultural nature of Canada is recognized beyond racial and religious variations.

Articles 16 through 35 deal with collective rights, which are also found only in the Canadian Constitution. Articles 16 through 22 deal with the two official languages, English and French. Article 16 declares English and French the official languages of Canada, and Article 17 states that the official languages may be used in the Canadian parliament and in the New Brunswick legislature. Article 18 says that statutes and records must be in both official languages, Article 19 says the same applies to the courts, and Article 20 says that the public may communicate in both languages when dealing with government services. Articles 21 and 22 solidify these rights as preeminent. Thus, the languages of the original European charter peoples have been entrenched (Driedger, 1989: 373).

Article 23 spells out minority language educational rights. In Quebec, for example, minorities such as the British or others, when of a sufficient number, have the right to learn in English; the same applies to the French minorities in the rest of Canada.

Article 25 deals with aboriginal and treaty rights:

The guarantee in this Charter of certain rights and freedoms shall not be construed so as to abrogate or derogate from any aboriginal, treaty or other rights or freedoms that pertain to the aboriginal peoples of Canada including:
(a) any rights of freedoms that have been recognized by the Royal Proclamation of 1763; and
(b) any rights or freedoms that may be acquired by the aboriginal peoples of Canada by way of land claims settlement.

Article 35 reinforces the treaty rights of the aboriginal peoples of Canada:

(1) The existing aboriginal treaty rights of the aboriginal peoples of Canada are hereby recognized and affirmed.
(2) In this Act, 'Aboriginal peoples of Canada' includes the Indian, Inuit and Métis peoples of Canada.

The meeting of aboriginal peoples and the governments has not, however, been able to clarify numerous issues that apply to the contemporary scene. Three official meetings held in the mid-eighties have not been able to resolve the differences; therefore, the aboriginal peoples are still unsatisfied with the wording.

The rights of the non-charter and non-aboriginal one-third of Canadians have been recognized, as outlined in Article 27:

This Charter shall be interpreted in a manner consistent with the preservation, and enhancement of the multicultural heritage of Canadians.

This ethnic segment of Canada has been growing most rapidly, and although it has gained recognition in the Constitution, there are no specific guarantees to any particular group. The Manitoba School Question in the early 1900s would likely not have happened had we had rights of non-charter groups spelled out more clearly. Bill 101 which declares French as dominant in Quebec is again a more recent issue which needs clarification.

Our discussion of these three declarations of rights and freedoms shows the common search for individual rights and freedoms, and the willingness in Canada to begin to consider group rights, are still not clearly entrenched, and multicultural rights are only recognized, but not elaborated.

TYPOLOGY OF HUMAN RIGHTS

Evelyn Kallen (1995: 10) presents and summarizes these human rights (Table 12-1). She moves from micro individual rights to more macro group rights, and then spells out the principles, violations and claims of cultural, national and aboriginal rights. Kallen's typology helps sort some of the important categories Chapters 8 to 12 have dealt with: 1) *Individual rights* to life, freedom, opportunity, and dignity, 2) *Group or category* rights to life, freedom, opportunity, and dignity, 3) *Collective cultural rights* to ethnocultural distinctiveness, design for living, language, religion, institutions and customs, 4) *Collective national rights* to self-determination, ancestral territory, nation, and 5) *Collective Aboriginal rights* to land, occupancy and use. All individuals are covered by the first, religious groups by the second, ethnic groups by the third, Québécois by the fourth and aboriginals by the fifth.

Individual rights can be violated by neglect, diminuation, oppression and finally homicide. Group rights can be violated by inequality, defamation,

TABLE 12-1   A TYPOLOGY OF HUMAN RIGHTS PRINCIPLES, VIOLATIONS,
AND CLAIMS

Principles	Violations	Claims
Fundamental Human Rights		
Individual		Individual claims
Right to life	homicide	
Freedom (self-determination)	oppression	
Equal opportunity	neglect	
Dignity of person	diminution	
Group or Category		
Right to life	genocide	
Freedom (group autonomy)	group oppression	
Equal opportunity	group inequity	
Group dignity	group defamation	
Collective Cultural Rights		Collective claims
Distinctive ethnocultural design for living (language, religion, institutions, customs)	cultural discrimination (deculturation/ cultural genocide)	
Collective National Rights		Nationhood claims
Self-determination as a distinctive nation within own ancestral/territorial bounds	national discrimination (denial of nationhood status)	
Collective Aboriginal Rights		Aboriginal rights claims
Right and title to aboriginal lands based on collective use and occupancy by aboriginal ethnic group 'from time immemorial'	land entitlement discrimination	

SOURCE: Evelyn Kallen, *Ethnicity and Human Rights in Canada*, 2nd ed., 1995, p. 10.

oppression and—worst of all—genocide, typified by the Jewish holocaust and more recently the atrocities in Rwanda and Bosnia-Herzegovina. Decultura-tion, discrimination, and cultural genocide can be inflicted by those who are dominant, illustrated by European treatment of Canada's aboriginals (Kallen, 1995: 10). Collective rights could be violated, if Quebeckers decided to separate and the rest of Canada denied them nationhood status; so far a majority have not called for such separation. Aboriginal rights can be violated when land settlements have not been made, as they have not in half of Canada. Let us examine some of these collective violations of human rights.

ETHNICITY AND COLLECTIVE RIGHTS

The three declarations of human rights we have reviewed focus largely on individual rights, although the Canadian Charter of Rights and Freedoms does spell out the rights of the majority charter groups, and recognizes some aboriginal and multicultural rights. In Chapter Nine we highlighted examples of racial atrocities by showing how Blacks were enslaved and the Japanese were interned in North America. Here we wish to add the expulsion of the Acadians, the demise of the Métis nation, the settling of aboriginal land claims, and the Jewish holocaust to further portray the need for minority rights. Canadians are not sufficiently aware of their own sordid history, and what they have done to many minorities in the past.

EXPULSION OF THE ACADIANS

In his book *Fragile Freedoms* (1981), Thomas Berger describes the descent of many minority groups, and we are indebted to his concise portrayal of the expulsion of the Acadians in 1755 from the earliest European settlement in Canada.

The nation states of Britain and France were traditionally and ethnically well defined by the time Columbus discovered America in 1492. They had their own internal ethnic struggles earlier, and by 1500 diversity was anathema to the rulers of these nation-states. They were more preoccupied with consolidating their sovereignty in the newly discovered lands (where power relations led to much conflict and many wars) than worrying about rights for minorities in the path of their conquests. Ever since, the central issue of Canadian history has been the working out of relations between these two societies (Berger, 1981: xiv). The final conquest of New France by the British led to a series of attempts to assimilate the people of Quebec. The struggle of French Canadians epitomizes the struggle of minorities everywhere. Confederation in 1867 was the accommodation of these two communities.

The Sieur de Monts' French expedition first wintered at the mouth of the St Croix River in 1604–05. In 1605 they moved to Port Royal on the Annapolis River on the south shore of the Bay of Fundy where they established the Order of Good Cheer. Later known as Acadia, this was the first permanent European settlement in North America north of Florida. In 1608 Champlain started the new settlement in Quebec and the centre of French activities shifted to the St Lawrence.

Although Champlain abandoned the new Acadia, others continued to build the French settlement. Argall, governor of Virginia, looted and burned their buildings in 1613. In 1671 King James I of England granted the whole of Acadia to the Earl of Stirling, making it part of New Scotland, or Nova Scotia (Berger, 1981: 4–5). In 1627 the Earl seized the small French community at

Port Royal; by a later British and French treaty, Acadia reverted to the French and several hundred new French settlers came to the Port Royal area. The boundaries of Acadia were never well defined (Dinwoodie, 1986: 15–20), but it became a centre of English-French conflict:

> It lay as a wedge between the expanding empires of New France on the St Lawrence and of New England on the Atlantic seaboard farther to the south. France and England were in constant conflict over Acadia. In just over a century, Port Royal changed hands nine times, six times by force of arms, three times by treaty. (Berger, 1981: 6)

By 1701, when the Acadians had lived around the Bay of Fundy for almost a century, they numbered 1,134; their relations with the aboriginals were harmonious, and they felt more attached to North America than to the whims of the European powers. 'In 1713, by the Treaty of Utrecht, the colony passed permanently into the hands of the British. . . . There were now 2,500 Acadians . . .' (Berger, 1981: 8). While the treaty provided that they could emigrate to French soil, they were unwilling to give up their fertile farms and abandon what had been their home for over a century. Thus, the British were faced with attempting to rule a people whose language, religion, and cultural heritage were those of their major European enemy.

The Acadians were peaceful until the British insisted that they take an oath of allegiance to the King of England. The Acadians—with their roots in the French tradition and remembering that their territory had changed hands many times—could not pledge allegiance to the British crown. Increasingly, the British were nervous about having the Acadians on their territory, and felt that they needed to secure Halifax and Nova Scotia from a potential uprising of these French-speaking Acadians. Colonel John Winslow, a British officer, wrote in his journal:

> We are now hatching the noble and great project of banishing the French neutrals from the Province. . . . If we accomplish this expulsion, it will have been one of the greatest deeds the English in America have ever achieved, for among other considerations, the part of the country which they occupy is one of the best soil in the world, and, in this event, we might place some good farmers on their homesteads. (Berger, 1981: 12).

In 1755 the governor ordered the Acadians to take an oath of allegiance to the king; when they refused, they were ordered to be dispersed among the British colonies on the continent. The order added that if the Acadians resisted, force should be used and their houses and farms were to be destroyed. They forfeited their lands, tenements, cattle, and other livestock to the Crown after the men had been locked up under guard in the church and their families herded into ships of transport (Berger, 1981: 14, 15). Many families were dispersed, never to be reunited; the British burned their barns and houses and turned their cattle loose. 'Altogether, the British forcibly removed and transported around 6,000 Acadians in 1755, and perhaps 2,000 more in the following years, out of a total population of about 10,000. Some Acadians took refuge in the forests, just as their ancestors had when Argall destroyed Port Royal a century and a half before' (Berger, 1981: 14). Longfellow's narrative poem, 'Evangeline, A Tale of Acadie', describes the woes and sorrows of two Acadian lovers separated in the expulsion.

A few Acadians from Port Royal went to Ile St Jean (now Prince Edward Island) which was under French control; however, by 1758 the British occupied the island and the Acadians were again deported—many of them drowned at sea. When Louisbourg fell in 1758, the British were masters of Acadia and the whole region of the St Lawrence (Daigle, 1982). After the 1755 deportation of Acadians from Port Royal, some returned; by 1764 Acadians were once again allowed to own land in Nova Scotia. Most of them, however, re-established themselves on new land on the east coast of New Brunswick; more than a third of the province now speaks French. When the British Empire Loyalists arrived in southern New Brunswick, some Acadians had to move further north. Until recently, there has been little communication between the Protestant British Loyalists in the south, and the Catholic Acadians in the north of the province.

Although the British North America Act provided for parochial schools in Quebec, this was not the case in New Brunswick. In 1871, four years after Confederation, New Brunswick passed the Common Schools Act, denying funds to denominational schools (Berger, 1981: 20). The Acadians challenged the law in the courts but they were unsuccessful. By 1969, the New Brunswick Legislature did pass a law making it a bilingual province. This bilingualism has also been entrenched in the Charter of Rights and Freedoms in the new Constitution of Canada in 1982. Despite much persecution, deportation, explusion, and sorrow, the French Acadians have survived in New Brunswick and Nova Scotia, as a people who are neither Québécois, nor French, but Acadian. Much too late, some of their minority group rights have been entrenched.

THE MÉTIS NATION OF THE PRAIRIES

The Hudson's Bay Company began trading in the great Canadian northwest in 1670 by waiting for furs at their posts located on the shores of Hudson Bay. As La Vérendrye, born in Trois-Rivières, explored the prairie interior in the 1740s for the French fur traders operating out of Quebec, the British also increasingly began to follow the rivers westward in search of furs. Many of the French traders, or voyageurs, of the Northwest Trading Company wintered among the Indians and returned with their furs to Montreal the next summer.

These traders often took Indian wives, so that by 1775 the 'half-breeds' (as they were often called), or Métis, emerged as a new people, bridging the white and Indian populations (Flanagan, 1991).

The buffalo hunt lay at the heart of the new Métis culture as pemmican, the staple food of the canoe brigades, emerged as a major commodity. The voyageurs did not have time to hunt the buffalo, and the Montreal-based fur trade became increasingly dependent on a supply of pemmican. As the demand grew, the Métis began to organize elaborate expeditions westward on horseback to hunt buffalo. While the men hunted, the women skinned the animals and cut the meat to dry in the sun.

> In 1820, 540 carts left Red River to carry buffalo meat back from the plains. The expedition of 1840 included 403 horses, 536 draught oxen, 1,240 carts and horses, 740 guns and 1,600 men, women and children. When they returned, they had killed 2,500 buffalo and loaded 800 carts with pemmican, dried meat and buffalo hide. (Berger, 1981: 32).

The buffalo hunt was a large organization with an elected president, councillors, guides, and captains, each of whom was in command of ten hunters. This organization made the Métis the strongest military force in the West. For fifty years the Métis prospered in their settlement at the forks of the Assiniboine and Red rivers, where they lived in cabins on their long river lots (similar to Quebec lots), raising gardens and cattle (McMillan, 1995: 312–13). This way of life lasted until the last buffalo were destroyed by about 1885, when the railroad also arrived on the prairies. The Métis spoke French, were Roman Catholic, and were inclined to follow the life of their aboriginal mothers' people, who considered the prairies their homeland. A new people had been born because of aboriginal European contacts.

'In 1811, the Hudson's Bay Company granted 116,000 square miles of its territory, centred on the junction of the Red and Assiniboine rivers, to Thomas Douglas, the young Earl of Selkirk' (Berger, 1981: 28). Selkirk wanted to establish an agricultural colony for impoverished Scots, but the Hudson's Bay Company wanted this settlement located precisely at the confluence of the two rivers to thwart and interrupt the canoe route of the Northwest Company's fur trade and line of communication. This settlement would also control the pemmican trade.

> In January, 1814, Miles Macdonnell, governor of the Selkirk colony, prohibited the export of pemmican and forbade the Northwest Company to occupy forts within the new District of Assiniboia, as the lands granted to Selkirk had been called, In June, 1815, the Nor'Westers and the Métis arrested Macdonnell and ran the settlers out of the Red River—although in the fall they returned. (Berger, 1981: 30)

Now the British-French wars begun in the Atlantic region and Acadia had also reached the prairies. The French and the British began to see this as another struggle for sovereignty. First, Fort Gibraltar, the Nor'Westers' fort at the forks was burned; next Semple and twenty settlers were killed at the Battle of Seven Oaks. The Métis saw this as an invasion by agricultural settlers of their pemmican industry. The Selkirk white settlement soon folded.

In 1867, the Confederation of Canada involved only small segments of what is now southern Ontario and Quebec, Nova Scotia, and New Brunswick. The vast territory west and north of the Great Lakes was an unorganized, unsurveyed territory used for fur trading. The Métis buffalo culture and trade dominated the plains area. By 1871, when the census was taken, there were '5,420 French-speaking half-breeds, 4,080 English-speaking half-breeds and 1,600 white settlers' in the Red River settlement surrounding present-day Winnipeg (Stanley, 1960: 13). Only three years after the 1867 Confederation, the Red River settlement entered Canadian history with the transfer of the rights to the vast northwest territories from the Hudson's Bay Company to the Canadian government. The plan was to make the transfer between Ottawa and the British without consulting the Red River residents. The inhabitants of the Red River settlement were incensed that the transfer of the Northwest territory would take place without any consultation with the Red River inhabitants involved (Driedger, 1989).

The 10,000 inhabitants of the Red River settlement had developed strong transportation ties between themselves and St Paul, Minnesota. 'In 1865 on one trip alone, Norbert Welsh travelled with a train of 300 carts; and by 1869 some 2,500 Red River carts lunged and screeched their ungreased way behind the ponderous ox-teams that hauled them along the road to St Paul' (Stanley, 1969: 37). In 1859 merchants of St Paul launched the first steamboat north to Fort Garry. The United States seemed close by, and Canada and Britain seemed far away. All this was happening when Canada was a new-born nation, greatly preoccupied with holding together the French and English cultures in Upper and Lower Canada.

While more and more settlers came, the Métis, who were a majority, wondered whether the influx of white settlers would swamp their aboriginal and Métis way of life. They were particularly concerned about the fur trade. This was the Red River settlement into which Louis Riel came in 1868. His French-Canadian mother was a daughter of the first white woman in western Canada and his father was a French Métis leader. Riel was born in the settlement and was sent to Montreal to train for the Catholic priesthood; when he returned, he became one of the leaders of the settlement. When in 1869 the Canadian government sent a team of surveyors to stake the land in preparation for the federal takeover from the Hudson's Bay Company (which would severely interrupt the Métis riverfront strip system), the Métis under the leadership of Riel stopped them (Stanley, 1969). They also stopped the new Lieutenant-Governor McDougall, sent from the East, from taking his post at Fort Garry.

These events resulted in a Métis provisional government headed by Riel, which outlined a series of points it wished to negotiate with the government before the area would become a new province (Stanley, 1969). The settlement requests included the right to elect their own legislature, magistrates, and sheriffs; a free homestead for each family; a rail connection with the East; the right to use English and French languages in the courts and legislature; and the right to be represented in the Canadian government (Stanley, 1969). Canada agreed to most of their requests and Manitoba became the fifth province of Canada in 1870, but not before an army from the East was sent to deal with Riel and his provisional government (Driedger, 1971: 294). Riel fled to the United States uncertain about the army's intentions. As a refugee he was thrice elected to the Ottawa Parliament by his constituents, but he was never able to take his seat because of Scottish resentment against him in Ontario. Although he should have become the first Manitoba Premier, he was exiled and never given amnesty. Power politics and nation-state dominance again missed a chance for Canada's first Métis premier elected by the people from the Red River settlement. Once more, multiculturalism was not given a chance.

Many Métis of the Red River community left after 1870 and settled in the Duck Lake area on the South Saskatchewan River. Fifteen years later the Métis called on Riel to help them gain rights for their new settlement, but in 1885 the federal government once more sent troops, this time via the CPR, the new railroad, to crush the Métis and Louis Riel. Riel was hanged for treason in that same year. His grave is located in St Boniface, now Winnipeg. Two chances for the recognition of a Métis nation had been crushed, because easterners saw these French Métis uprisings as a threat, rather than as an opportunity for aboriginal and Métis representation of the majority of the northwest region. 'Macdonald refused to recognize in them the people of a New Nation. "If they are Indians," Macdonald said, "they go with the tribe; if they are half breeds, they are white"' (Berger, 1981: 52). The categories into which people were fitted were still limited: either white or Indian racially, or French or British ethnically.

A century later, in Section 35 of the 1982 Charter of Rights and Freedoms, the Métis people are listed with Indian and Inuit people as 'aboriginal peoples of Canada'. There is a great deal of confusion as to whether they all received their land claims or scrip; many claim they did not. In any case, had their leader Riel become the father of Manitoba and its first premier, as many now think he should have, most Métis would likely have stayed and settled in the Fort Garry area and Manitoba would now be a much different multicultural province. Since then, both Manitoba and Saskatchewan have erected monuments on their provincial legislative grounds honouring Riel, but a century too late.

SETTLING INDIAN LAND CLAIMS

Chapter Three provided some of the demographic data to show where the aboriginal (Inuit, Métis, Non-Status Indian, and Status Indian) populations are located. Of the 532,060 aboriginals in 1991, 3.8% were Inuit, two-thirds of whom were located in the Territories; 22.5% were Métis, two-thirds of whom were located on the prairies; 21.6% were Non-Status Indians, almost two-thirds of whom were located in Ontario and British Columbia; and over half (52.1%) were located on the prairies and northern Ontario. Aboriginals are a majority (51.2%) in the Northwest Territories, and the largest number are located on the prairies with well over half of their population in the four most westerly provinces in 1991. Treaties have not been made with almost half of these aboriginals, and there are problems with the treaties made with some of the Status Indians. Thus, numerous aboriginal land claims have not yet been settled.

In Figure 7-1 we saw that treaties have not been made (except for the James Bay area) in the five most easterly provinces (Quebec and the Maritimes), in most of British Columbia, and the Yukon (Ponting, 1986; Frideres, 1993). The earliest treaties, known as the Robinson Huron and Robinson Superior treaties, were made in northern Ontario in 1850. The Williams treaties were made a little further to the south of Ontario in 1923. Minor treaties, known as the Douglas treaties (1850–54), were also made in parts of Vancouver Island (Frideres, 1993: 32).

The eleven major treaties, known as Treaties 1–11, were made in the West, beginning in 1871 at the forks of the Red and Assiniboine rivers, the heart of the Métis region (Dickason, 1992: 273–89). Treaty 1 was signed in Fort Garry, the stone fort north of Winnipeg, one year after Manitoba became a province. The Métis Nation had been dislodged from their power base, European settlers were about to enter the territory en masse, and the Indians and Métis had to be dealt with to make room for the white Europeans. As the white settlers moved westward from the forks, more treaties were signed as needed. They were signed in 1874 in southern Saskatchewan, in 1876 and 1877 in southern Alberta, then the last treaty was signed in 1921 in the Mackenzie valley region reaching into the Northwest Territories (Frideres, 1993). These later treaties were signed as mining interests moved up the Mackenzie River.

The paternalism conveyed in the wording of these treaties shows the colonialist stance of a majority power dealing with 'poor uncivilized aboriginals who need to be cared for':

And with a view to show the satisfaction of Her Majesty with the behaviour and good conduct of Her Indians parties to this treaty, She hereby, through Her Commissioner, makes them a present of three dollars for each Indian man, woman and child belonging to the bands here represented.

And further, Her Majesty agrees to maintain a school on each reserve hereby made whenever the Indians of the reserve should desire it. (Treaty No. 1: 10)

In essence, since they are 'good children', she is taking all their land and will, out of her gracious spirit, 'give them a present': three dollars each annually and a reserve. Treaties 1–11 vary somewhat, but each family of five Métis received 160 acres on the reserve in the early treaties. However, reserves have not been established in the Northwest Territories as they were farther to the south.

Since Treaty 11 was signed in 1921, numerous attempts have been made to deal with aboriginal land claims; however, there have been many difficulties (Frideres, 1993: 66–121). The Department of Indian Affairs and Northern Development has plotted eleven major areas of aboriginal land claims presented in Figure 12-1. Claim 1 deals with Indians in the Yukon. Claims 2–5 made by Inuit, Indian, and Métis organizations cover all of the Northwest Territories. Treaties 8 and 3 and 4, and the Nunavut Treaty made in 1993 deals with Claim 5. Claims 6 and 7 by the Inuit and Innu associations cover most of Labrador, where no treaties had been made. The James Bay agreements with the Inuit and Cree deal with Claim 8. Claims 9 and 10 deal with the rest of Quebec, where again no treaties have been made. Claim 11, the Nisga'a claim in British Columbia, is but a small claim in the whole of British Columbia where except for the small Douglas treaties, no treaties have been made either.

Only about half of the Canadian territory is covered by aboriginal treaty. Land claims currently under review involve mostly northern territory, where it should be relatively easier to come to treaty agreement and a resolution of native land rights. However, settlement involves large sums of money, and increasingly, aboriginals are asking for sovereignty or some say in how these lands should be used and administered (Asch, 1984). Many of these claims are in territories where the federal government has jurisdiction, which also makes the process easier, since few whites have moved into these regions and would have to be displaced. Claims 6, 7, 8, 9, and 1, however, are located in three provincial regions. This involves provincial governments and further complicates matters (Frideres, 1993: 108–21). This is the case in British Columbia, which has historically not recognized the right of aboriginals to claim land. Even more difficult will be the settlement of treaty claims in Quebec, and the southern parts of the four maritime provinces, where white settlement has a long history, but where treaties have still not been made. Many of these areas are urban, with dense populations.

FIGURE 12-1   COMPREHENSIVE CLAIMS: AREAS CLAIMED BY ABORIGINAL ASSOCIATIONS

1   Council for Yukon Indians (CYI)
2a Inuvialuit Settlement Region
2b Land areas selected by Inuvialuit pursuant to Inuvialuit Final Agreement
3   Dene Nation
4   Métis Association of the Northwest Territories (MANWT)
5   Tunngavik Federation of Nunavut (TFN)
6   Labrador Inuit Association (LIA)
7   Naskapi-Montagnais Innu Association (NMIA)
8   James Bay "Territory" — James Bay and Northern Quebec Agreement (Grand Council of the Cree of Quebec and the Northern Quebec Inuit Association; Naskapis of Schefferville)
9   Conseil Attikamek-Montagnais (CAM)
10 Offshore Islands
11 B.C. Claims

SOURCE: James S. Frideres, *Native Peoples in Canada: Contemporary Conflicts*, 2nd ed. Scarborough, ON: Prentice-Hall, 1993, p. 79.

While we may be inclined to criticize those of the past for not attending to the rights and freedoms of the Acadians and Métis, we today still have much difficulty in dealing with aboriginal land claims. So far these claims have been dealt with only haphazardly. The fact that few treaties have been made on either coast, can again be attributed to the early power politics of nation-state colonialists who had little concern for minority rights and freedoms. To our credit, we have recognized aboriginal land rights in the western interior by signing Treaties 1–11, but these treaties are fraught with many difficulties, ambiguities, and problems. Much still remains to be done, and we are not moving very quickly in resolving these injustices, although the Nunavut settlement in the eastern Northwest Territories in 1993 is an important agreement.

THE JEWISH HOLOCAUST

The furore over Salman Rushdie's *The Satanic Verses* raises the question of the extent to which rights and freedoms are respected in the world today. The extermination of six million Jews by the Nazis during the Second World War was an event that showed that the freedoms we have are fragile, and that they continue to be attacked by those who consider themselves 'civilized'. The Jewish holocaust happened in the land that spawned Einstein, Beethoven, Mozart, Freud, and Marx. How could modern people who claim to hold to ideologies of Christianity and democracy allow such atrocities to happen? The roots of such holocausts continue to linger, as illustrated by several Canadian examples.

Levitt and Shaffir (1986) have documented the Christie Pits riot that occurred in Toronto in 1933, between Jews and Gentiles. On the evening of August 16, 1933, a riot occurred after a semi-final series of the Toronto Amateur Softball Association championship between Harbord (with mostly Jewish members) and St Peter's (a Gentile team). A number of factors led up to the riot. Toronto's eastern beaches and parks were a favourite picnic area for thousands of Jewish immigrants and their families. Their customs, cuisine, and language were different from those of the residents near these beaches, who were concerned about the increasing presence of Jews.

Life was not easy for Toronto's Jews in 1933: they were barred from certain jobs, they were not welcome in some recreation and social circles, and on occasion they were beaten up (Levitt and Shaffir, 1986: 3–4). Discrimination seemed routine, and swastika signs (which symbolized suffering, torture, and death to these Jews) were increasingly found in the parks. When a Swastika Club was formed and displayed the swastika, Jewish youths countered by organizing parades on the beaches' boardwalks. Mayor Stewart of Toronto tried to crack down on these Nazi groups and the display of their symbols, but without avail.

The riot began immediately after the game in the park. A huge swastika was unfurled with shouts of 'Heil Hitler', and a group of Jewish youths stormed the swastika group. There had already been several clashes at the game, but until this point police had been able to restore order. The fighting lasted for several hours and scores of people were injured. Later twenty-two members of the Pit Gang that unfurled the swastika were questioned. Three were taken into custody, but none were charged (Levitt and Shaffir, 1986: 17–18). The riot showed that anti-Jewish feelings often lay close to the surface, and that there was always a potential for violence. This riot occurred just as Hitler was beginning his political drive in Germany leading to the holocaust taking six million Jewish lives.

In a more modern example, David Elliott (1985: 78–89) has tried to document some of the intellectual roots of the Keegstra affair, and concludes that some anti-Semitism has its roots in the early Social Credit movement in Canada. Criminal charges were laid against James Keegstra, a high school social studies teacher (and former mayor) in Eckville, Alberta, because he taught that the holocaust was a myth and that the Jews were conspiring to rule the world (Elliott, 1985: 78). Keegstra was also a member of the national Social Credit Party Executive, which was unwilling to censure him. The Keegstra affair became a national issue. Elliott claims Major C.H. Douglas, the founder of the Social Credit Party, believed that Canada was menaced by a Jewish conspiracy to acquire key positions in the economic and political fields. 'The full scope of Douglas's anti-Semitic paranoia was found in his *Brief for the Prosecution* published in 1945' (Elliott, 1985: 82).

Keegstra lived in southern Alberta during the Aberhart and Manning Social Credit administrations and his parents were ardent Social Credit supporters. Keegstra immersed himself in the writings of Douglas, and was generally influenced by anti-communist and anti-Semitic writings. Keegstra taught his beliefs of an all-powerful Jewish conspiracy in the Eckville High School for fourteen years. Elliott (1985: 86) claims that although Aberhart denounced anti-Semitism publicly, there were anti-Semitic undertones in many of his speeches. Later Premier Manning clearly purged his Social Credit Party of anti-Semitic people. The Keegstra affair shows the extent to which anti-Semitism is present in individuals, and the extent to which it can invade legitimate Canadian institutions. The Zundel affair is another (Weimann and Winn, 1993: 97–111).

Yaacov Glickman and Alan Bardikoff (1982) published a book on the degree to which Canadian history and social science textbooks inform and sensitize Canadian students to the events of the holocaust. They examined seventy-two textbooks authorized for use in Canada's secondary schools, and found inadequate treatment of the Jewish holocaust. They did a content analysis of the texts, using a panel of eight judges. They used seven criteria including inclusion, validity, balance, comprehensiveness, concreteness, unity, and realism in their evaluation of published presentations of the holocaust. They found that 29% of the text books excluded the subject matter entirely, and 42% were judged to have treated it inadequately; only 4% were judged to have presented it well. These twenty-two texts were rated as being poor on validity (43%), comprehensiveness (71%), balance (65%), concreteness (53%), and unity (57%) (Glickman and Bardikoff, 1982: 17).

While the Jewish holocaust—the destruction of one-third of a people—occurred in Europe more than fifty years ago, we still cringe at the extent to which modern Nazis were willing to go to follow their Aryan ideology. It is clear that the holocaust has affected Canada directly, because the Christie Pits riots and Keegstra affair demonstrate that anti-Semitic tendencies continue in our midst. Elderly Jews who experienced and escaped the European holocaust will always fear the danger of similar threats in the future (Driedger and Chappell, 1987). The rights and freedoms of minorities are indeed fragile, to which the Jews can attest from several millennia's experience.

SUMMARY

We began by saying that nation-states in the past tried to establish unitary ethnic sovereign states that, nevertheless, always included numerous minorities that were often ignored or forced into assimilation. The polyethnic or pluralist ethnic view is also concerned with the rights and freedoms of minorities, so that the rights of all can be perpetuated. In Canada's past there are many examples of how collective minority rights have been trampled upon.

First, we examined three bills, declarations, or charters—sets of standards or norms which might guide us in establishing rights and freedoms. As early as 200 years ago, the American Constitution declared the free exercise of religion as a right of all. Eighty years later they recognized the equality of race and abolished slavery. The United Nations extended these rights to freedoms of language, religion, politics, national origin, and property. Most recently, the Canadian Charter of Rights and Freedoms, although belatedly, also extended these individual rights in Canada. In addition, the two charter groups were given certain group rights, and the rights of aboriginals and others of the multicultural community were also recognized.

We reviewed the fate of four tragic communities whose rights and freedoms were stripped in Canada in the past. The Acadians were forcibly expelled from their homeland in Acadia and were scattered throughout North America because they were French. The Métis Nation formed on the prairies and was twice routed by armies from the East when Riel, their leader, should have become a part of the prairie political establishment. Treaties have been made with aboriginals, but to this day half of their territory has not yet been settled by treaties. And the tragedy of the Jewish holocaust is unforgotten, yet Jews continue to be mistreated in Canada, and their rights and freedoms are often restricted.

While our standards and norms for minority rights and freedoms have evolved, these rights have been grossly neglected and misused in the past, and much more will is needed in the present to correct injustices. How these injustices are dealt with will depend greatly on the change of perspective discussed in Chapter Two. If we want a unitary state with a homogeneous language, culture, and institutions, then obviously assimilation is the way to proceed as was attempted in the past. Many minorities will then be forced to comply to the majority culture; some will need to change too quickly with disorganizational results, while still others will resist so that there will be conflict. The French in Quebec have always resisted assimilation and will continue to fight for their identity; so will the aboriginals, religious groups like the Jews, Mennonites, and Hutterites, and recent immigrants.

For a long time Canadian immigration policy has worked against a unitary melting pot and the population has become increasingly more heterogeneous. Northern European immigrants no longer dominate the top ten largest groups that enter Canada. With recent heavy Asian immigration, Canada's population is becoming more heterogeneous, so a pluralist policy makes a great deal of sense and is more compatible with Canada's democratic and religious ideology. As immigrants adjust with succeeding generations, modified forms of pluralism or assimilation seem logical as the various groups adjust to form a Canadian whole. Some groups will be given more opportunity to participate than others, and visible minorities should be given equal opportunities to participate. Many laws in the past were passed to keep some groups segregated and in inferior places, which again is not compatible with our Charter of Rights and Freedoms. Building a modern industrial pluralist Canada will not be easy because the regions vary considerably with respect to cultural, religious, racial, and national aspirations.

Quebec has always wanted to be a nation with aspirations for increased sovereignty in determining French-Canadian interests. Discussions on the Meech Lake Accord illustrate the differences of opinion on how special Quebec is. To what extent this uniqueness will be entrenched in the constitution remains to be seen. Like the Québécois, many groups, such as the Jews, Mennonites, Hutterites, and others with less demographic and political power also wish to construct unique 'sacred realities'. We discussed the identities of Quebec and other minorities in Chapters Six and Seven, illustrating the various micro and macro levels of socio-cultural and symbolic identity to which many ethnic groups in Canada aspire. Segregated rural ethnic enclaves use very different means of constructing solidarity than urbanites who increasingly turn to social networks and symbolic means of identification. In Part Three we devoted three chapters to the complexity of ethnic solidarity and identification consistent with Weber's multidimensional and comparative analysis.

While pluralists more than assimilationists tend to look for ethnic and racial diversity and identity, there is also much evidence that there is considerable socio-economic and racial stratification. There is much social inequality: some groups are more powerful than others, and many minorities are 'less equal' than others. While some people would call for the elimination of social ethnic distinction so all people would have a better chance to compete in the labour market, others look for greater tolerance toward ethnic, racial, and religious diversity, so everyone can compete without prejudice or discrimination based on colour, race, creed, or gender. It is true that diversity also poses more risks for conflict, but heterogeneous populations can also create more variety and interest for a more dynamic society.

There is much evidence of social distance, sterotypes, prejudice, and discrimination in Canada. However, the United Nations' and Canadian charters of rights and freedoms clearly show the way that a majority of Canadians would like to go. Canada is a pluralist multi-ethnic society, and there is much evidence that more and more Canadians are willing to accept and work for equality, justice, and opportunity for all.

REFERENCES

Akbari, Ather H.
1989 'Economics of Immigration and Racial Discrimination: A Literature Survey (1970–1989)'. Ottawa: Policy and Research, Multiculturalism and Citizenship.

Allport, Gordon
1954 *The Nature of Prejudice*. New York: Doubleday.

Anderson, Alan B.
1972 'Assimilation in the Bloc Settlements of North-Central Saskatchewan: Comparative Study of Identity Change Among Seven Ethno-Religious Groups in a Canadian Prairie Region'. Ph.D. dissertation in Sociology, University of Saskatchewan, Saskatoon.

Anderson, Alan B.
1980 'The Survival of Ethnolinguistic Minorities: Canadian and Comparative Research' in Howard Giles et al. (eds), *Language and Ethnic Relations*. New York: Pergamon Press, pp. 67–85.

Anderson, Alan B. and Leo Driedger
1980 'The Mennonite Family: Culture and Kin in Rural Saskatchewan' in K. Ishwaran (ed.), *Canadian Families: Ethnic Variations*. Toronto: McGraw-Hill Ryerson.

Anderson, Alan B. and J.S. Frideres
1981 *Ethnicity in Canada: Theoretical Perspectives*. Toronto: Butterworths.

Anderson, Grace
1974 *Networks of Contact: The Portuguese and Toronto*. Waterloo, Ontario: Wilfrid Laurier University Press.

Anderson, Grace and David Higgs
1976 *A Future to Inherit: The Portuguese Communities of Canada*. Toronto: McClelland and Stewart.

Anderson, Wolseley W.
1993 *Caribbean Immigrants: A Socio-Demographic Profile*. Toronto: Canadian Scholars' Press.

Angus Reid Group
1991 'Multiculturalism and Canadians: National Attitude Survey 1991'. Ottawa: Multiculturalism and Citizenship Canada.

Armstrong, Frederick H.
1981 'Ethnicity in the Formation of the Family Compact: A Case Study in the Growth of the Canadian Establishment' in Jorgen Dahlie and Tessa Fernando (eds), *Ethnicity, Power and Politics in Canada*. Toronto: Methuen.

Asch, Michael
1984 *Home and Native Land: Aboriginal Rights and the Canadian Constitution*. Toronto: Methuen.

Axworthy, Thomas S. and Pierre Elliott Trudeau
1992 *Towards a Just Society: The Trudeau Years*. Toronto: Penguin Books.

Baar, Ellen
1978 'Issei, Nisei and Sansei' in Daniel Glenday, Hubert Guidon, and Alan Turowetz (eds), *Modernization and the Canadian State*. Macmillan of Canada.

Badets, Jane and Tina W.L. Chiu
1994 *Canada's Changing Immigrant Population*, Catalogue 96–311E. Ottawa: Statistics Canada and Prentice-Hall.
Balakrishnan, T.R.
1982 'Changing Patterns of Ethnic Residential Segregation in the Metropolitan Areas of Canada'. *Canadian Review of Sociology and Anthropology* 19: 92–110.
Balakrishnan, T.R. and George K. Jarvis
1979 'Changing Patterns of Spatial Differentiation in Canada, 1961–1971'. *Canadian Review of Sociology and Anthropology* 16: 218–27.
Balakrishnan, T.R. and John Kralt
1987 'Segregation of Visible Minorities in Toronto, Montreal and Vancouver' in Leo Driedger (ed.), *Ethnic Canada: Identities and Inequalities*. Toronto: Copp Clark Pitman.
Balakrishnan, T.R. and K. Selvanathan
1990 'Ethnic Residential Segregation in Metropolitan Canada' in Shiva Halli, Frank Trovato and Leo Driedger (eds), *Ethnic Demography*. Ottawa: Carleton University Press.
Balakrishnan, T.R. and Feng Hou
1995 'The Changing Patterns of Spatial Concentration and Residential Segregation of Ethnic Groups in Canada's Major Metropolitan Areas 1981–1991'. Paper presented at the Population Association of America meetings in San Francisco, 6–10 April 1995.
Banton, Michael
1960 'Social Distance: A New Appreciation'. *Sociological Review* 8: 169–83.
Banton, Michael
1967 *Race Relations*. London: Tavistock.
Baureiss, Gunter
1987 'Chinese Immigration, Chinese Stereotypes, and Chinese Labour'. *Canadian Ethnic Studies* 19: 15–34.
Beavis, Mary Ann
1995 *Housing and Ethnicity: Literature Review and Select Annotated Bibliography*. Winnipeg: Institute of Urban Studies, University of Winnipeg.
Bell, David and Lorne Tepperman
1979 *The Roots of Disunity: A Look at Canadian Political Culture*. Toronto: McClelland and Stewart.
Bellah, Robert N.
1973 *Emile Durkheim on Morality and Society*. Chicago: University of Chicago Press.
Bendix, Reinhard
1977 *Max Weber: An Intellectual Portrait*. Berkeley, California: University of California Press.
Berger, Peter L.
1967 *The Sacred Canopy: Elements of a Sociological Theory of Religion*. Garden City, NY: Doubleday and Company.
Berger, Thomas R.
1981 *Fragile Freedoms: Human Rights and Dissent in Canada*. Toronto: Clarke, Irwin (now Stoddart Publishing).

Berlin, Isaiah
1963 *Karl Marx: His Life and Environment.* Oxford: Oxford University Press.
Berry, John W.
1990 'Psychology of Acculturation' in J. Berman (ed.), *Nebraska Symposium on Motivation* 37: 201–34. Lincoln: University of Nebraska Press.
Berry, J.W. and G.J.S. Wilde
1972 *Social Psychology: The Canadian Context.* Toronto: McClelland and Stewart.
Berry, J.W., R. Kalin and D.M. Taylor
1977 *Multiculturalism and Ethnic Attitudes in Canada.* Ottawa: Minister of Supply and Services.
Berry, J.W., U. Kim, S. Power, M. Young, and D. Mok
1987 'Comparative Studies of Acculturation Stress'. *International Migration Review* 21: 491–511.
Berry, J.W. and J.A. Laponce
1994 *Ethnicity and Culture in Canada: The Research Landscape.* Toronto: University of Toronto Press.
Bibby, Reginald W.
1987a 'Bilingualism and Multiculturalism: A National Reading' in Leo Driedger (ed.), *Ethnic Canada: Identities and Inequalities.* Toronto: Copp Clark Pitman, pp. 158–69.
Bibby, Reginald W.
1987b *Fragmented Gods: The Poverty and Potential of Religion in Canada.* Toronto: Irwin Publishing.
Bibby, Reginald W.
1995 *The Bibby Report: Social Trends Canadian Style.* Toronto: Stoddart Publishing.
Billingsley, B. and L. Musynski
1985 *No Discrimination Here.* Toronto: Social Planning Council of Metro Toronto and the Urban Alliance on Race Relations.
Blau, Peter M., Jerry C. Blum, and Joseph E. Schwartz
1982 'Heterogeneity and Intermarriage'. *American Sociological Review* 47: 45–61.
Blishen, Bernard R.
1970 'Social Class and Opportunity in Canada'. *Canadian Review of Sociology and Anthropology* 7: 110–27.
Bogardus, Emory S.
1959 *Social Distance.* Los Angeles: Antioch Press.
Bolaria, B. Singh
1995 *Social Issues and Contradictions in Canadian Society*, 2nd ed. Toronto: Harcourt Brace Canada.
Bolaria, B. Singh and Peter S. Li
1988 *Racial Oppression in Canada*, 2nd ed. Toronto: Garamond Press.
Bonacich, Edna
1972 'A Therapy of Ethnic Antagonism: The Split Labour Market'. *American Sociological Review* 37: 547–59.
Bott, Elizabeth
1957 *Family and Social Network*, 2nd ed. New York: Free Press.

Bourhis, R.Y.
1983 'Language Attitudes and Self Reports of French-English Language Usage in Quebec'. *Journal of Multilingual and Multicultural Development* 4: 163–79.

Bourhis, R.Y.
1994 'Ethnic and Language Attitudes in Quebec' in John Berry and J.A. Laponce (eds), *Ethnicity and Culture in Canada: The Research Landscape.* Toronto: University of Toronto Press.

Bourhis, R.Y. and D. Lepicq
1993 'Quebec French and Language Issues in Quebec' in R. Posner and J.N. Green (eds), *Trends in Romance Linguistics and Philology, Volume 5: Bilingualism and Linguistic Conflict in Romance.* The Hague and Berlin: Mouton de Gruyter.

Boyd, Monica
1992 'Gender, Visible Minority, and Immigrant Earnings Inequality: Reassessing an Employment Equity Premise' in Vic Satzewich (ed.), *Reconstructing a Nation.* Halifax: Fernwood Publishing.

Boyd, Monica, John Goyder, Frank E. Jones, Hugh A. McRoberts, Peter Pineo, and John Porter
1981 'Status Attainment in Canada: Findings of the Canadian Mobility Study'. *Canadian Review of Sociology and Anthropology* 18: 657–73.

Breton, Raymond
1964 'Institutional Completeness of Ethnic Communities and Personal Relations to Immigrants'. *American Journal of Sociology* 70: 193–205.

Breton, Raymond
1984 'The Production and Allocation of Symbolic Resources: An Analysis of the Linguistic and Ethnocultural Fields in Canada'. *Canadian Review of Sociology and Anthropology* 21: 123–44.

Breton, Raymond
1991 *The Governance of Ethnic Communities: Political Structures and Processes in Canada.* New York: Greenwood Press.

Breton, Raymond, Jeffrey Reitz, and Victor Valentine
1980 *Cultural Boundaries and the Cohesion of Canada.* Montreal: The Institute of Research and Public Policy.

Breton, Raymond and Howard Roseborough
1980 'Ethnic, Religious and Regional Representation in the Federal Cabinet, 1869–1966'. Unpublished manuscript. Toronto: University of Toronto.

Breton, Raymond and Pierre Savard
1982 *The Quebec and Acadian Diaspora in North America.* Toronto: The Multicultural Society of Ontario.

Breton, Raymond, Wsevolod W. Isajiw, Warren W. Kalbach, and Jeffrey G. Reitz
1990 *Ethnic Identity and Equality: Varieties of Experience in a Canadian City.* Toronto: University of Toronto Press.

Broadfoot, Barry
1977 *Years of Sorrow, Years of Shame: The Story of the Japanese in World War II.* Toronto: Doubleday Canada.

Brym, Robert
1993 'The Distribution of Anti-Semitism in Canada in 1984' in Robert Brym et al. (eds), *The Jews in Canada*. Toronto: Oxford University Press.
Brym, Robert, Michael Gillespie, and A.R. Gillis
1993 'Anomie, Opportunity, and the Density of Ethnic Ties: Another View of Jewish Outmarriage in Canada' in Robert Brym et al. (eds), *The Jews in Canada*. Toronto: Oxford University Press.
Brym, Robert and Rhonda Lenton
1993 'The Distribution of Anti-Semitism in Canada in 1984' in Robert Brym et al. (eds), *The Jews in Canada*. Toronto: Oxford University Press.
Brym, Robert, William Shaffir, and Morton Weinfeld
1993 *The Jews in Canada*. Toronto: Oxford University Press.
Burch, Thomas K.
1990 'Family Structure and Ethnicity' in Shiva Halli, Frank Trovato, and Leo Driedger (eds), *Ethnic Demography*. Ottawa: Carleton University Press.
Burnet, Jean
1979 'Myths and Multiculturalism'. *Canadian Journal of Education* 4: 43–58.
Burnet, Jean
1988 *'Coming Canadians': An Introduction to a History of Canada's Peoples*. Toronto: McClelland and Stewart.
Caldwell, Gary and Daniel Fournier
1987 'The Quebec Question: A Matter of Population'. *Canadian Journal of Sociology* 12: 16–41.
Calliste, Agnes
1987 'Sleeping Car Porters in Canada: An Ethnically Submerged Labour Market'. *Canadian Ethnic Studies* 19: 1–20.
Calliste, Agnes
1988 'Blacks on Canadian Railroads'. *Canadian Ethnic Studies* 20: 36–52.
Cameron, Duncan
1992 'A Constitution for English Canada' in Daniel Drache and Roberto Perin (eds), *Negotiating With a Sovereign Quebec*. Toronto: James Lorimer.
Cardinal, Harold
1977 *The Rebirth of Canada's Indians*. Edmonton: Hurtig Publishers.
Cauthen, N.R., I.E. Robinson and H.H. Kraus
1971 'Stereotypes: A Review of the Literature 1926–1968'. *The Journal of Social Psychology* 84: 103–25.
Census of Canada
1981 Catalogue 92–910, 92–912.
Chorney, Harold
1992 'Dividing the Debt: More than Bean Counting' in Daniel Drache and Roberto Perin (eds), *Negotiating With a Sovereign Quebec*. Toronto: James Lorimer.
Christianson, Carole P. and Morton Weinfeld
1993 'The Black Family in Canada: A Preliminary Exploration of Family Patterns and Inequality'. *Canadian Ethnic Studies* 25: 26–44.

Citizenship and Immigration Canada
1992 Immigration Statistics 1992, Catalogue MP22–1/1992. Ottawa: Public Works and Government Services.
Clairmont, Denis H. et al.
1965 *A Socio-Economic Study and Recommendations: Sunnyville, Lincolnville and Upper Big Tracadie, Guysborough County.* Halifax: Institute of Public Affairs, Dalhousie University.
Clairmont, Donald H. and Dennis W. Magill
1974 *The Life and Death of a Canadian Black Community.* Toronto: McClelland and Stewart.
Clark, S.D.
1968 *The Developing Canadian Community.* Toronto: University of Toronto Press.
Clement, Wallace
1975 *The Canadian Corporate Elite: An Analysis of Economic Power.* Ottawa: McClelland and Stewart.
Comeau, Larry and Leo Driedger
1978 'Opening and Closing in an Open Society'. *Social Forces* 57: 600–20.
Coons, W.H., Donald W. Taylor, and Marc-Adelard Tremblay
1977 *The Individual, Language and Society in Canada.* Ottawa: The Canada Council.
Coser, Lewis
1956 *The Functions of Social Conflict.* New York: The Free Press.
Cox, Oliver C.
1948 *Caste, Class and Race: A Study in Social Dynamics.* Garden City, NY: Doubleday.
Crean, Susan and Marcel Rioux
1983 *Two Nations: An Essay on the Culture and Politics of Canada and Quebec in a World of American Pre-eminence.* Toronto: James Lorimer.
Creese, Gillian
1987 'Organizing Against Racism in the Workplace: Chinese Workers in Vancouver Before the Second World War'. *Canadian Ethnic Studies* 19: 35–46.
Cummins, Jim
1994 'Heritage Language Learning and Teaching' in J.W. Berry and J.A. Laponce (eds), *Ethnicity and Culture in Canada: The Research Landscape.* Toronto: University of Toronto Press.
Cuneo, Carl J. and James E. Curtis
1975 'Social Ascription in the Educational and Occupational Status Attainment of Urban Canadians'. *Canadian Review of Sociology and Anthropology* 12: 6–24.
Curtis, James, Edward Grabb, Neil Guppy and Sid Gilbert
1988 *Social Inequality in Canada: Patterns, Problems, Policies.* Scarborough, ON: Prentice-Hall.
Dahrendorf, Rolf
1959 *Class and Class Conflict in Industrial Society.* Palo Alto, California: Stanford University Press.
Dahlie, Jurgen and Tessa Fernando, eds.
1981 *Ethnicity, Power and Politics in Canada.* Toronto: Methuen.

Daigle, Jean-Guy
1982 'The Acadians: A People in Search of a Country' in Raymond Breton and Pierre Savard (eds), *The Quebec and Acadian Diaspora in North America*. Toronto: The Multicultural History Society of Ontario.

Daniels, Roger and Harry H.L. Kitano
1970 *American Racism: Exploration of the Nature of Prejudice*. Englewood Cliffs: Prentice-Hall.

Darroch, Gordon A.
1979 'Another Look at Ethnicity: Stratification and Social Mobility in Canada'. *Canadian Journal of Sociology* 4: 1–25.

Dashefsky, Arnold
1972 'And the Search Goes on: Religio-Ethnic Identity and Identification in the Study of Ethnicity'. *Sociological Analysis* 33: 239–45.

Dashefsky, Arnold
1975 'Theoretical Frameworks in the Study of Ethnic Identity'. *Ethnicity* 2: 1–15.

Dashefsky, Arnold
1975 *Ethnic Identity in Society*. Chicago: Rand McNally.

Davids, Leo
1993 'Yiddish in Canada: Picture and Prospects' in Robert Brym et al. (eds), *The Jews in Canada*. Toronto: Oxford University Press.

Davis, Alan
1992 *Antisemitism in Canada: History and Interpretation*. Waterloo, ON: Wilfrid Laurier University Press.

Davis, Kingsley
1950 *Human Society*. New York: The Free Press.

Davis, Kingsley and W.E. Moore
1945 'Some Principles of Stratification'. *American Sociological Review* 10: 242–49.

Dawson, C.A.
1936 *Group Settlement: Ethnic Communities in Western Canada*. Toronto: Macmillan of Canada.

Dawson, Charles A. and W.E. Gettys
1929 *Introduction to Sociology*. New York: Ronald Press.

Deffontaines, Pierre
1965 'The Rang: Pattern of Rural Settlement in French Canada' in Marcel Rioux and Yves Martin (eds), *French-Canadian Society*, Volume 1. Ottawa: Carleton Library.

Dei, George J. Sefa
1993 'Narrative Discourses of Black/African-Canadian Parents and the Canadian Public School System'. *Canadian Ethnic Studies* 25: 45–65.

Denis, Wilfrid B.
1995 'The Meech Lake Shuffle: French and English Language Rights in Canada' in Singh Bolaria (ed.), *Social Issues and Contradictions in Canadian Society*, 2nd ed. Toronto: Harcourt Brace Canada.

Department of Employment and Immigration Canada
1985 *Annual Report to Parliament on Future Immigration Levels*. Ottawa: Minister of Supply and Services Canada.

Department of Employment and Immigration
1989 *Immigration to Canada: A Statistical Overview*. Ottawa: Employment and Immigration Canada, pp. 8, 25, 31, 47.
Department of Indian Affairs and Native Development
1987 *Indian Register*, 1961–87. Ottawa: Minister of Supply and Services.
Department of Indian Affairs and Development
1992 *Basic Departmental Data — 1991*. Ottawa: Minister of Supply and Services.
Department of Manpower and Immigration
1974 *A Report of the Canadian Immigration and Population Study*. Ottawa: Information Canada, Table 3.3, p. 84.
Deroche, Constance and John Deroche
1991 'Black and White: Racial Construction in Television Police Dramas'. *Canadian Ethnic Studies* 23: 69–91.
deVries, John
1988 *The Integration of Ethno-Cultural Communities Into Canadian Society: A Selected Bibliography*. Ottawa: Policy and Research, Multiculturalism and Citizenship.
deVries, John
1990 'Language and Ethnicity: Canadian Aspects' in Peter Li (ed.), *Race and Ethnic Relations in Canada*. Toronto: Oxford University Press.
deVries, John and Laverne Lewycky
1985 'Data Book on Canadian Official Language Minorities, Second Edition'. Ottawa: Centre for Research on Ethnic Minorities, Etc., Carleton University.
deVries, John and Frank Vallee
1980 *Language Use in Canada*. Ottawa: Ministry of Supply and Services.
Dickason, Olive Patricia
1992 *Canada's First Nations: A History of Founding Peoples From Earliest Time*. Toronto: McClelland and Stewart.
Dinwoodie, Catriona
1986 'Where is Acadia?' *British Journal of Canadian Studies* 1: 15–30.
Dion, Leon
1975 'French as an Adopted Language in Quebec' in P. Migus (ed.), *Sounds Canadian: Languages and Culture in Multi-Ethnic Society*. Toronto: Peter Martin Associates.
Donner, Arthur and Fred Lazar
1992 'The Case for a Single Currency and a Reformed Central Bank' in D. Drache and R. Perin (eds), *Negotiating With a Sovereign Quebec*. Toronto: Lorimer.
Drache, Daniel and Roberto Perin
1992 *Negotiating With a Sovereign Quebec*. Toronto: James Lorimer.
Driedger, Leo
1972 'Native Rebellion and Mennonite Invasion: An Examination of Two Canadian River Valleys'. *Mennonite Quarterly Review* 46: 290–300.
Driedger, Leo
1974 'Doctrinal Belief: A Major Factor in the Differential Perception of Social Issues'. *Sociological Quarterly* 15: 66–80.

Driedger, Leo
1975 'In Search of Cultural Identity Factors: A Comparison of Ethnic Minority Students in Manitoba'. *Canadian Review of Sociology and Anthropology* 12: 150–62.
Driedger, Leo
1976 'Ethnic Self-Identity: A Comparison of Ingroup Evaluations'. *Sociometry* 39: 131–41.
Driedger, Leo
1977 'Structural, Social and Individual Factors in Language Maintenance in Canada' in W.H. Coons, Donald W. Taylor and Marc-Adelard Tremblay (eds), *The Individual, Language and Society in Canada*. Ottawa: The Canada Council.
Driedger, Leo
1977 'The Anabaptist Identification Ladder: Plain-Urban Continuity in Diversity'. *Mennonite Quarterly Review* 51: 278–91.
Driedger, Leo
1977 'Toward a Perspective on Canadian Pluralism: Ethnic Identity in Winnipeg'. *Canadian Journal of Sociology* 2: 77–95.
Driedger, Leo
1978 'Ethnic Boundaries: A Comparison of Two Urban Neighbourhoods'. *Sociology and Social Research* 62: 193–211.
Driedger, Leo
1978 *The Canadian Ethnic Mosaic: A Quest for Identity*. Toronto: McClelland and Stewart.
Driedger, Leo
1980 'Jewish Identity: Maintenance of Urban Religious and Ethnic Boundaries'. *Ethnic and Racial Studies* 3: 67–81.
Driedger, Leo
1980 'Nomos-Building on the Prairies: Construction of Indian, Hutterite and Jewish Sacred Canopies'. *Canadian Journal of Sociology* 5: 341–56.
Driedger, Leo
1982 'Ethnic Boundaries: A Comparison of Two Urban Neighborhoods' in George A. Theodorson (ed.), *Urban Patterns: Studies in Human Ecology*. University Park, PA: Pennsylvania State University Press, pp. 207–17.
Driedger, Leo
1982 'Individual Freedom vs. Community Control: An Adaptation of Erikson's Ontogeny of Ritualization'. *Journal for the Scientific Study of Religion* 21: 226–41.
Driedger, Leo
1984 'Multicultural Regionalism: Toward Understanding the Canadian West' in Tony Rasporich (ed.), *Making of the Modern West: Western Canada Since 1945*. Calgary: University of Calgary Press, pp. 167–82.
Driedger, Leo
1986 'Community Conflict: The Eldorado Invasion of Warman'. *Canadian Review of Sociology and Anthropology* 23: 247–69.
Driedger, Leo
1986 'Inequalities of Race' in K. Ishwaren (ed.), *Sociology: An Introduction*. Don Mills, ON: Addison-Wesley.

Driedger, Leo
1987 *Ethnic Canada: Identities and Inequalities.* Toronto: Copp Clark Pitman.
Driedger, Leo
1989 *The Ethnic Factor: Identity in Diversity.* Toronto: McGraw-Hill Ryerson.
Driedger, Leo
1991 *The Urban Factor: Sociology of Canadian Cities.* Toronto: Oxford University Press.
Driedger, Leo
1997 'Hutterites' in Paul R. Magocsi (ed.), *The Peoples of Canada: An Encyclopedia for the Century.* Toronto: University of Toronto Press.
Driedger, Leo and Glenn Church
1974 'Residential Segregation and Institutional Completeness: A Comparison of Ethnic Minorities'. *Canadian Review of Sociology and Anthropology* 11: 30–52.
Driedger, Leo and Jacob Peters
1976 'Ethnic Identity of Students of Mennonite and German Heritage' in Stewart Crysdale and Les Wheatcraft (eds), *Religion in Canadian Society.* Toronto: Macmillan of Canada.
Driedger, Leo and Jacob Peters
1977 'Identity and Social Distance: Towards Understanding Simmel's "The Stranger"'. *Canadian Review of Sociology and Anthropology* 14: 158–73.
Driedger, Leo and Richard Mezoff
1981 'Ethnic Prejudice and Discrimination in Winnipeg High Schools'. *Canadian Journal of Sociology* 6: 1–17.
Driedger, Leo, Charlene Thacker, and Raymond Currie
1982 'Ethnic Identification: Variations in Regional and National Preferences'. *Canadian Ethnic Studies* 14: 57–68.
Driedger, Leo and Calvin Redekop
1983 'Sociology of Mennonites: State of the Art and Science'. *Journal of Mennonite Studies* 1: 33–63.
Driedger, Leo and Rodney Clifton
1984 'Ethnic Stereotypes: Images of Ethnocentrism, Reciprocity or Dissimilarity?' *Canadian Review of Sociology and Anthropology* 21: 287–301.
Driedger, Leo and Peter Hengstenberg
1986 'Non-Official Multilingualism: Factors Affecting Language Competence, Use and Maintenance'. *Canadian Ethnic Studies* 60: 374–86.
Driedger, Leo and Neena Chappell
1987 *Aging and Ethnicity: Toward an Interface.* Toronto: Butterworths.
Driedger, Leo and Donald B. Kraybill
1994 *Mennonite Peacemaking: From Quietism to Activism.* Scottdale, PA: Herald Press.
Duncan, Otis Dudley
1955 'Review of Social Area Analysis'. *American Journal of Sociology* 61: 84–5.
Duncan, Otis Dudley and Beverly Duncan
1957 *The Negro Population of Chicago: A Study of Residential Segregation.* Chicago: University of Chicago Press.
Durkheim, Emile
1897, 1981 *Suicide.* John A. Spaulding and George Simpson, transl. Glencoe, IL: Free Press.

Durkheim, Emile
1912, 1945 *The Elmentary Forms of Religious Life*. New York: The Free Press.
Edwards, John
1985 *Language, Society and Identity*. London: Basil Blackwell.
Edwards, John and Lori Doucette
1987 'Ethnic Salience, Identity and Symbolic Ethnicity'. *Canadian Ethnic Studies* 19: 53–62.
Elliott, David R.
1985 'Anti-Semitism and the Social Credit Movement: The Intellectual Roots of the Keegstra Affair'. *Canadian Ethnic Studies* 17: 78–89.
Elliott, Jean Leonard and Augie Fleras
1992 *Unequal Relations: An Introduction to Race and Ethnic Dynamics in Canada*. Scarborough, ON: Prentice-Hall Canada.
Erickson, Erik
1968 *Identity: Youth in Crisis*. New York: Norton.
Fairbairn, Kenneth J. and Hafiza Khatun
1989 'Residential Segregation and the Intra-Urban Migration of South Asians in Edmonton'. *Canadian Ethnic Studies* 21: 45–64.
Fathi, Asghar and Brian L. Kinsley
1968 'The Changing Identity of Jewish Youth in Canada'. Paper presented at the Canadian Sociology and Anthropology Association meetings.
Flanagan, Thomas
1991 *Métis Lands in Manitoba*. Calgary: University of Calgary.
Fleras, Augie and Jean Leonard Elliott
1992 *Multiculturalism in Canada: The Challenge of Diversity*. Toronto: Nelson Canada.
Fournier, Pierre
1991 *A Meech Lake Post–Mortem*. Montreal: McGill-Queen's University Press.
Francis, E.K.
1947 'The Nature of the Ethnic Group'. *American Sociological Review* 52: 393–400.
Francis, E.K.
1948 'The Russian Mennonites: From Religious to Ethnic Group'. *American Journal of Sociology* 54: 101–06.
Francis, E.K.
1950 'The Russian Mennonites: From Religious Group to Ethnic Group'. *American Journal of Sociology* 50: 101–07.
Francis, E.K.
1954 'Variables in the Formation of So-Called Minority Groups'. *American Journal of Sociology* 60: 6–14.
Francis, E.K.
1955 *In Search of Utopia: The Mennonites in Manitoba*. Altona, MB: D.W. Friesen Publishers.
Francis, E.K.
1965 *Ethnos and Demos*. Berlin: Duncher and Humblot.
Francis, E.K.
1976 *Interethnic Relations: An Essay in Sociological Theory*. New York: Elsevier.

Frazier, E. Franklin
1949 *The Negro in the United States*. Chicago: University of Chicago Press.
Frideres, James S.
1993 *Native People in Canada: Contemporary Conflicts*, 3rd ed. Scarborough, ON: Prentice-Hall Canada.
Frideres, James S. and Sheldon Goldenberg
1977 'Hyphenated Canadians: Comparative Analysis of Ethnic, Regional and National Identification of Western Canadian University Students'. *Journal of Ethnic Studies* 5: 91–100.
Friesen, John W.
1993 *When Cultures Clash: Case Studies in Multiculturalism*, 2nd ed. Calgary: Detselig Enterprises.
Fromm, Erich
1956 'Introduction' in T.B. Bottomore and Maximillien Rubel (eds), *Karl Marx*. New York: McGraw-Hill.
Gaertner, S.L. and J.F. Dovidic
1986 'The Aversive Forms of Racism' in S.L. Gaertner and J.F. Dovidic (eds), *Prejudice, Discrimination and Racism*. New York: Academic Press.
Gagnon, Alain-G.
1993 *Quebec: State and Society*, 2nd ed. Scarborough, ON: Nelson Canada.
Gagnon, M.
1974 'Quelques Facteurs Déterminant l'Attitude vis-à-vis l'Anglais, Langue Seconde' in R. Darnell (ed.), *Linguistic Diversity in Canadian Society*. Volume II. Edmonton: Linguistic Research Inc.
Gans, Herbert
1962 *The Urban Villagers*. Glencoe, IL: Free Press.
Gans, Herbert
1979 'Symbolic Ethnicity: The Future of Ethnic Groups and Cultures in America'. *Ethnic and Racial Studies* 2: 1–20.
Gardner, R.C. and P.C. Smythe
1975 'Motivation and Second Language Acquisition'. *Canadian Modern Language Review* 21: 218–30.
Gardner, Robert C.
1977 'Social Factors in Second Language Acquisition and Bilinguality' in W.H. Coons et al. (eds), *The Individual, Language and Society in Canada*. Ottawa: The Canada Council.
Gilroy, P.
1987 *There Ain't No Black in the Union Jack*. Chicago: University of Chicago Press.
Glazer, Nathan and Daniel P. Moynihan
1963 *Beyond the Melting Pot*. Cambridge, MA: Massachusetts Institute of Technology.
Glickman, Yaacov and Alan Bardikoff
1982 *The Treatment of the Holocaust in Canadian History and Social Science Textbooks*. Downsview, ON: League for Human Rights of B'nai Brith.
Gold, Gerald L.
1975 *St Pascal: Changing Leadership and Social Organization in a Quebec Town*. Toronto: Holt, Rinehart and Winston.

Gordon, Milton M.
1964 *Assimilation in American Life*. New York: Oxford University Press.
Grabb, Edward G.
1984 *Social Inequality: Classical and Contemporary Theorists*. Toronto: Holt, Rinehart and Winston.
Greeley, Andrew
1989 *Religious Change in America*. Cambridge: Harvard University Press.
Grindstaff, Carl F. and Frank Trovato
1994 'Canada's Population in the World Context' in Frank Trovato and Carl Grindstaff (eds), *Perspectives on Canada's Population: An Introduction to Concepts and Issues*. Toronto: Oxford University Press.
Gross, Leonard
1980 *The Golden Years of the Hutterites*. Scottdale, PA: Herald Press.
Guindon, Hubert
1988 *Quebec Society: Tradition, Modernity, and Nationhood*. Toronto: University of Toronto Press.
Hagan, John
1977 'Finding "Discrimination": A Question of Meaning'. *Ethnicity* 4: 167–76.
Halli, Shiva S., Frank Trovato, and Leo Driedger
1990 *Ethnic Demography: Canadian Immigrant, Racial and Cultural Variations*. Ottawa: Carleton University Press.
Hamm, Peter M.
1987 *Continuity and Change*. Waterloo, ON: Wilfrid Laurier University Press.
Harris, Chauncey and Edward L. Ullman
1945 'The Nature of Cities'. *Annuals* 242: 7–17.
Harrison, Brian and Louise Marmen
1994 *Languages in Canada*, Catalogue 96–313E. Ottawa: Statistics Canada.
Head, Wilson
1975 *The Black Presence in the Canadian Mosaic*. Toronto: Human Rights Commission.
Head, Wilson
1981 *Adaptation of Immigrants: Perceptions of Ethnic and Racial Discrimination*. North York, ON: York University.
Hechter, Michael
1978 'Group Formation and the Cultural Division of Labor'. *American Journal of Sociology* 84: 293–318.
Henripin, Jacques
1974 'Immigration and Language Imbalance'. *Canadian Immigration and Population Study*. Ottawa: Information Canada.
Henripin, Jacques
1993 'Population Trends and Policies in Quebec' in Alain-G. Gagnon (ed.), *Quebec: State and Society*, 2nd ed. Scarborough, ON: Nelson Canada.
Henry, Frances
1973 *Forgotten Canadians: The Blacks of Nova Scotia*. Toronto: Longman Canada.
Henry, Frances
1989 'Housing and Racial Discrimination in Canada: A Preliminary Assessment of Current Initiatives and Information'. Ottawa: Policy and Research, Multiculturalism and Citizenship.

Henry, Frances
1994 *The Caribbean Diaspora in Toronto: Learning to Live with Racism.* Toronto: University of Toronto Press.
Henry, Frances and E. Ginzberg
1984 *Who Gets the Work? A Test of Racial Discrimination in Employment.* Toronto: Urban Alliance on Race Relations.
Henry, Frances and Carol Tator
1994 'The Ideology of Racism—"Democratic Racism" '. *Canadian Ethnic Studies* 26: 1–14.
Henry, Frances, Carol Tator, Winston Mattis, and Tim Rees
1995 *The Colour of Democracy: Racism in Canadian Society.* Toronto: Harcourt Brace Canada.
Herbert, E.
1989 *Ethnic Groups in Canada: Adaptations and Transitions.* Scarborough, ON: Nelson Canada.
Herberg, Will
1955 *Protestant, Catholic, Jew.* New York: Doubleday.
Hill, Daniel G.
1981 *The Freedom-Seekers: Blacks in Early Canada.* Agincourt, ON: Book Society of Canada.
Hofer, John
1988 *The History of the Hutterites,* rev. ed. Altona, MB: D.W. Friesen Publishers.
Hooten, E.A.
1946 *Up From the Ape,* rev. ed. New York: Macmillan.
Hostetler, John A.
1974 *Hutterite Society.* Baltimore: Johns Hopkins University Press.
Hughes, David R. and Evelyn Kallen
1974 *The Anatomy of Racism: Canadian Dimensions.* Montreal: Harvest House.
Hughes, Everett C.
1943 *French Canada in Transition.* Chicago: University of Chicago Press.
Hughes, Everett and Helen M. Hughes
1952 *Where Peoples Meet: Racial and Ethnic Frontiers.* Glencoe, IL: Free Press.
Hunter, Alfred
1986 *Class Tells: On Social Inequality in Canada.* Toronto: Butterworths.
Isajiw, Wsevolod W.
1978 'Olga in Wonderland: Ethnicity in Technological Society' in Leo Driedger (ed.), *The Canadian Ethnic Mosaic.* Toronto: McClelland and Stewart.
Isajiw, Wsevolod W.
1981 'Ethnic Identity Retention'. Research Paper No. 125. Toronto: Centre for Urban and Community Studies.
Isajiw, Wsevolod W.
1990 'Ethnic Identity Retention' in Breton et al. (eds), *Ethnic Identity and Inequality.* Toronto: University of Toronto Press.
Isajiw, Wsevolod W. and Leo Driedger
1987 'Ethnic Identity: Resource or Drawback for Social Mobility'. Paper presented at the American Sociological Association meetings held in Chicago, August 17–21.

Isajiw, Wsevolod W., Aysan Sev'er and Leo Driedger
1993 'Ethnic Identity and Social Mobility: A Test of the "Drawback Model" and Resources'. *Canadian Journal of Sociology* 18: 177–96.
Ishwaren, K.
1980 *Canadian Families: Ethnic Variations.* Toronto: McGraw-Hill Ryerson.
Jackson, John D.
1975 *Community and Conflict: A Study of French-English Relations in Ontario.* Montreal: Holt, Rinehart and Winston.
Jackson, John D.
1977 'The Functions of Language in Canada: On the Political Economy of Language' in W.H. Coons et al. (eds), *The Individual, Languages and Society in Canada.* Ottawa: The Canada Council.
Jain, Harish C.
1988 'Employment Discrimination Against Visible Minorities and Employment Equity'. Hamilton: Faculty of Business, McMaster University.
James, Carl E.
1990 *Making It: Black Youth, Racism and Career Aspirations in a Big City.* Oakville, ON: Mosaic Press.
James, Carl E.
1992 *Seeing Ourselves: Exploring Race, Ethnicity and Culture.* Toronto: Thompson Educational Publishing.
Joy, Richard J.
1972 *Languages in Conflict.* Toronto: McClelland and Stewart.
Joy, Richard J.
1992 *Canada's Official Languages: The Progress of Bilingualism.* Toronto: University of Toronto Press.
Juteau, Danielle
1992 'The Sociology of Ethno-National Relations in Quebec' in Vic Satzewich (ed.), *Deconstructing a Nation.* Halifax, Fernwood Publishing.
Juteau-Lee, D. and Jean Lapointe
1977 'School Conflict in a Multi-Ethnic Community: A Case Study' in R.R. Carlton, L.A. Colley, and N.J. McKinnon (eds), *Education in a Changing Society.* Toronto: Gage Publishing.
Kadushin, Charles
1962 'Social Distance Between Client and Professional'. *American Journal of Sociology* 67: 517–31.
Kalbach, Warren E.
1980 'Historical and Generational Perspectives of Ethnic Residential Segregation in Toronto, Canada: 1851–1971'. Research Paper No. 118, Centre for Urban and Community Studies. Toronto: University of Toronto.
Kalbach, Warren E.
1987 'Growth and Distribution of Canada's Ethnic Population, 1871–1981' in Leo Driedger (ed.), *Ethnic Canada: Identities and Inequalities.* Toronto: Copp Clark Pitman, pp. 82–110.
Kalbach, Warren E.
1990 'A Demographic Overview of Racial and Ethnic Groups in Canada' in Peter Li (ed.), *Race and Ethnic Relations in Canada.* Toronto: Oxford University Press.

Kalbach, Warren E. and Mary Richard
1990 'Ethno-Religious Identity and Acculturation' in Shiva Halli, Frank Trovato, and Leo Driedger (eds), *Ethnic Demography*. Ottawa: Carleton University Press.

Kallen, Evelyn
1977 *Spanning the Generations: A Study in Jewish Identity*. Don Mills, ON: Longmans.

Kallen, Evelyn
1982 *Ethnicity and Human Rights in Canada*. Toronto: Gage Publishing.

Kallen, Evelyn
1995 *Ethnicity and Human Rights in Canada*, 2nd ed. Toronto: Oxford University Press.

Kallen, Horace M.
1924 *Culture and Democracy in the United States*. New York: Liveright.

Kauffman, J. Howard and Leland Harder
1975 *Anabaptists: Four Centuries Later*. Scottdale, PA: Herald Press.

Kauffman, J. Howard and Leo Driedger
1991 *The Mennonite Mosaic: Identity and Modernization*. Scottdale, PA: Herald Press.

Keyfitz, Nathan
1965 'Population Problems' in Marcel Rioux and Yves Martin (eds), *French-Canadian Society*, Volume I. Ottawa: Carleton Library.

Khubchandoni, Lachman M.
1976 'Language Factor in Census' in A. Verdoodt and R. Kjolseth (eds), *Language in Sociology*. Louvain: Editions Peeters, pp. 93–123.

Kobayashi, Audrey
1987 'From Tyranny to Justice: The Uprooting of the Japanese Canadians in 1941'. *Tribune Juive* 5: 28–35.

Krauter, Joseph F. and Morris Davis
1978 *Minority Canadians: Ethnic Groups*. Toronto: Methuen.

Krech, David, Richard S. Crutchfield, and Egerton L. Ballachey
1962 *The Individual in Society: A Textbook of Social Psychology*. New York: McGraw-Hill.

Krotki, Karol J. and Colin Reid
1994 'Demography of Canadian Population by Ethnic Group' in John Berry and J. Laponce, *Ethnicity and Culture in Canada*. Toronto: University of Toronto Press.

Lachapelle, R.
1979 *La Situation démolinguistique au Canada: évolution passée et prospective*. Montreal: Institute for Research on Public Policy.

Lai, David Chuenyan
1987 'The Issue of Discrimination in Education in Victoria, 1901–1923'. *Canadian Ethnic Studies* 19: 47–67.

Lai, David Chuenyan
1988 *Chinatowns: Towns Within Cities in Canada*. Vancouver: University of British Columbia Press.

Lambert, Ronald D, and James E. Curtis
1984 'Québécois and English Canadian Opposition to Racial and Religious Intermarriage, 1968–1983'. *Canadian Ethnic Studies* 16: 31–46.

Lambert, W.E., R.C. Hodgson, R.C. Gardner, and S. Fillenbaum
1960 'Evaluation Reactions to Spoken Languages'. *Journal of Abnormal and Social Psychology* 60: 44–51.
Laponce, J.A.
1994 'Ethnicity and Voting Studies in Canada: Primary and Secondary Sources 1970–1991' in John Berry and J.A. Laponce, *Ethnicity and Culture in Canada*. Toronto: University of Toronto Press.
Laumann, E.O.
1965 'Subjective Social Distance and Urban Occupational Stratification'. *American Journal of Sociology* 71: 26–36.
Lazar, Barry and Tamsin Douglas
1993 *Guide to Ethnic Montreal*, rev. ed. Montreal: Vehicule Press.
Lazerwitz, Bernard
1970 'An Approach to the Components and Consequences of Religio-Ethnic Indentification'. Unpublished manuscript.
Levine, Donald N., Ellwood B. Carter and Eleanor Miller Gorman
1976 'Simmel's Influence on American Sociology'. *American Journal of Sociology* 81: 813–45.
Levinson, B.M.
1962 'Yeshiva College Sub-Cultural Scale: An Experimental Attempt to Devise a Scale of the Internalization of Jewish Traditional Values'. *Journal of Genetic Psychology* 101: 375–99.
Levitt, Cyril and William Shaffir
1986 'The Christie Pits Riot: A Case Study in the Dynamics of Ethnic Violence'. Hamilton: McMaster University.
Levitt, Cyril and William Shaffir
1993 'The Swastika as Dramatic Symbol: A Case-Study of Ethnic Violence in Canada' in Brym et al. (eds), *The Jews in Canada*. Toronto: Oxford University Press.
Lewin, Kurt
1948 *Resolving Social Conflicts*. New York: Harper and Brothers.
Li, Peter S.
1987 'The Economic Cost of Racism to Chinese-Canadians'. *Canadian Ethnic Studies* 19: 102–13.
Li, Peter S.
1988 *The Chinese in Canada*. Toronto: Oxford University Press.
Li, Peter S. and Wilfrid B. Denis
1983 'Minority Enclave and Majority Language: The Case of a French Town in Western Canada'. *Canadian Ethnic Studies* 15: 18–32.
Li, Peter S. and B. Singh Bolaria
1993 *Contemporary Sociology: Critical Perspectives*. Mississauga, ON: Copp Clark Pitman.
Lieberson, Stanley
1966 'Bilingualism in Montreal: A Demographic Analysis'. *American Journal of Sociology* 71: 10–25.
Lieberson, Stanley
1970 'Residence and Language Maintenance in a Multilingual Society'. *South African Journal of Sociology* 1: 14–23.

Lieberson, Stanley and Mary Waters

1990 *From Many Strands: Ethnic and Racial Groups in Contemporary America*. New York: Russell Gage Foundation.

Lippmann, W.

1922 *Public Opinion*. New York: Harcourt Brace.

Mackie, Marlene

1978 'Ethnicity and Nationality: How Much Do They Matter to Western Canadians?' *Canadian Ethnic Studies* 10: 118–29.

Mackie, Marlene

1985 'Stereotypes, Prejudice, and Discrimination' in Rita Bienvenue and Jay Goldstein (eds), *Ethnicity and Ethnic Relations in Canada*. Toronto: Butterworths.

Mackie, Marlene and Merlin Brinkerhof

1984 'Measuring Ethnic Salience'. *Canadian Ethnic Studies* 16: 114–31.

Makabe, Tomoko

1978 'Ethnic Identity and Social Mobility: The Case of the Second Generation Japanese in Metropolitan Toronto'. *Canadian Ethnic Studies* 10: 106–23.

Makabe, Tomoko

1981 'Theory of the Split Labor Market: A Comparison of the Japanese Experience in Brazil and Canada'. *Social Forces* 59: 786–809.

Malinowski, Bronislaw

1945 *The Dynamics of Culture Change*, Phyllis M. Kaberry (ed.). New Haven: Yale University Press.

Manzer, Ronald A.

1974 *Canada: A Socio-Political Report*. Toronto: McGraw-Hill Ryerson.

Marchi, Sergio

1996 *A Broader Vision: Immigration Plan*, 1996 Annual Report to Parliament. Ottawa: Citizenship and Immigration Canada.

Marx, Karl

1867 *Das Kapital*. Volume I. Hamburg.

Marx, Karl

1963 *Early Writings*. London: Watts.

Marx, Karl and Friedrich Engels

1841–48 *Marx-Engels Gesamtausgabe*, I(MEGA). Volumes I–VI.

Marx, Karl and Friedrich Engels

1948 *Communist Manifesto*. London: George Allen and Unwin.

Mata, Fernando G.

1989 'The Black Youth of Toronto: Exploration of Issues'. Ottawa: Policy and Research, Multi-culturalism and Citizenship.

Matthews, Ralph

1980 'The Significance and Explanation of Regional Divisions in Canada: Toward a Canadian Sociology'. *Journal of Canadian Studies* 15: 43–61.

McEvoy, F.J.

1982 ' "A Symbol of Racial Discrimination": The Chinese Immigration Act and Canada's Relations With China, 1942–1947'. *Canadian Ethnic Studies* 14: 24–42.

McGahan, Peter

1995 *Urban Sociology in Canada*, 3rd ed. Toronto: Harcourt Brace Canada.

McKague, Ormond
1991 *Racism in Canada*. Saskatoon: Fifth House Publishers.
McMillan, Alan D.
1995 *Native Peoples and Cultures of Canada*, 2nd ed. Vancouver: Douglas and McIntyre.
McNeill, William H.
1986 *Poly-Ethnicity and National Unity in World History*. Toronto: University of Toronto Press.
McRoberts, Kenneth
1990 'Quebec: Province, Nation, or "Distinct Society"?' in Whittington and Williams (eds), *Canadian Politics in the 1990s*, 3rd ed.
Medjuck, Sheva
1993 'Jewish Survival in Small Communities in Canada' in Robert Brym et al. (eds), *The Jews in Canada*. Toronto: Oxford University Press.
Mills, C. Wright
1956 *The Power Elite*. New York: Oxford University Press.
Milner, Henry
1978 *Politics in the New Quebec*. Toronto: McClelland and Stewart.
Miner, Horace
1939 *St Denis: A French-Canadian Parish*. Chicago: University of Chicago Press.
Mol, Hans
1985 *Faith and Fragility: Religion and Identity in Canada*. Burlington, ON: Trinity Press.
Musynski, Alicja
1995 'Social Stratification: Class and Gender Inequality' in Singh Bolaria (ed.), *Social Issues and Contraditions in Canadian Society*, 2nd ed. Toronto: Harcourt Brace Canada.
Nagel, Joan
1984 'The Ethnic Revolution: Emergence of Ethnic Nationalism'. *Sociology and Social Research* 69: 417–34.
Nakamura, Mark
1975 'The Japanese' in Norman Sheffe (ed.), *Many Cultures, Many Heritages*. Toronto: McGraw-Hill Ryerson.
Newman, William M.
1973 *American Pluralism: A Study of Minority Groups and Social Theory*. New York: Harper and Row.
Nisbet, Robert A.
1974 *The Sociology of Emile Durkheim*. New York: Oxford University Press.
O'Bryan, K.G., Jeffrey G. Reitz, and O. Kuplowska
1976 *Non-Official Languages: A Study in Canadian Multiculturalism*. Ottawa: Department of the Secretary of State.
Odum, Howard W.
1936 *Southern Regions of the United States*. Chapel Hill: University of North Carolina Press.
Ogmundson, Rick
1986 'Social Inequality' in Robert Hagedorn (ed.), *Sociology*. Toronto: Holt, Rinehart and Winston.

Ogmundson, Rick
1990 'Perspectives on the Class and Ethnic Origins of Canadian Elites'. *Canadian Journal of Sociology* 15: 165–77.
Ogmundson, Rick
1992 'Perspectives on the Class and Ethnic Origins of Canadian Elites: A Reply to Clement and Rich'. *Canadian Journal of Sociology* 17: 313–21.
Ogmundson, Rick and J. McLaughlin
1992 'Trends in the Ethnic Origins of Canadian Elites: The Decline of the Brits?' *Canadian Review of Sociology and Anthropology* 29: 227–42.
Palmer, Howard
1982 'Ethnic Relations in Wartime: Nationalism and European Minorities in Alberta During the Second World War'. *Canadian Ethnic Studies* 14: 1–23.
Parel, Anthony
1988 'The Meech Lake Accord and Indo-Canadians'. *Canadian Ethnic Studies* 20: 129–37.
Park, Robert
1922 *The Immigrant Press and Its Control*. New York: Harper.
Park, Robert
1928 'Human Migration and the Marginal Man'. *American Journal of Sociology* 33: 881–93.
Park, Robert
1950 *Race and Culture*. Everett C. Hughes (ed.). Glencoe, IL: The Free Press.
Park, Robert
1967 'The City: Suggestions for the Investigation of Human Behavior in the Urban Environment' in Robert Park and Ernest W. Burgess (eds), *The City*. Chicago: University of Chicago Press.
Parsons, John
1985 'John Cabot' in *The Canadian Encyclopedia*. Edmonton: Hurtig Publishers.
Pendakur, Ravi
1990 *Speaking in Tongues: Heritage Language Maintenance and Transfer in Canada*. Ottawa: Policy and Research Multiculturalism and Citizenship.
Persons, Stow
1987 *Ethnic Studies at Chicago, 1905–45*. Urbana: University of Illinois Press.
Peter, Karl A.
1987 *The Dynamics of Hutterite Society: An Analytical Approach*. Edmonton: University of Alberta Press.
Petrie, Anne
1982 *A Guidebook to Ethnic Vancouver*. Surrey, BC: Hancock House.
Pineo, Peter
1977 'The Social Standing of Ethnic and Racial Groups'. *Canadian Review of Sociology and Anthropology* 14: 47–57.
Pineo, Peter and John Porter
1967 'Occupational Prestige in Canada'. *Canadian Review of Sociology and Anthropology* 14: 24–40.
Pinkney, Alphonso
1975 *Black Americans*, 2nd ed. Toronto: Prentice-Hall.

Pitman, W.
1978 *Report on Race Relations in Metropolitan Toronto: The Pitman Report.* Toronto: Metropolitan Toronto Council.

Ponting, J. Rick
1986 *Arduous Journey: Canadian Indians and Decolonization.* Toronto: McClelland and Stewart.

Ponting, J. Rick and Richard A. Wanner
1983 'Blacks in Calgary: A Social and Attitudinal Profile'. *Canadian Ethnic Studies* 15: 57–76.

Porter, John
1965 *The Vertical Mosaic.* Toronto: University of Toronto Press.

Porter, John
1975 'Ethnic Pluralism in Canadian Perspective' in N. Glazer and D.P. Moynihan (eds), *Ethnicity, Theory and Experience.* Cambridge, MA: Harvard University Press.

Porter, John
1975 'Plenary Address'. Annual meeting of the Canadian Sociology and Anthropology Association, Edmonton.

Potter, Harold H.
1961 'Negroes in Canada'. *Race* 3: 49.

Price, John
1979 *Indians of Canada: Cultural Dynamics.* Toronto: Prentice-Hall.

Ramcharan, Subhas
1982 *Racism: Nonwhites in Canada.* Toronto: Butterworths.

Raushenbush, Winifred
1979 *Robert E. Park: Biography of a Sociologist.* Durham, NC: Duke University Press.

Redfield, Robert
1953 'The Folk Society'. *American Journal of Sociology* 52: 293–308.

Reitz, Jeffrey G.
1977 'Analysis of Changing Group Inequalities in a Changing Occupational Structure' in P. Krishnan (ed.), *Mathematical Models in Sociology.* Sociological Review Monograph, No. 24. Keele, Staffordshire: University of Keele.

Reitz, Jeffrey G.
1980 *The Survival of Ethnic Groups.* Toronto: McGraw-Hill Ryerson.

Reitz, Jeffrey G.
1982 'Ethnic Group Control of Jobs'. Research Paper No. 133. Toronto: Centre for Urban and Community Studies, University of Toronto.

Reitz, Jeffrey G., Liviana Calzavara, and Donna Dasko
1981 'Ethnic Inequality and Segregation in Jobs'. Research Paper No. 123. Centre for Urban and Community Studies, University of Toronto.

Reitz, Jeffrey G. and Raymond Breton
1994 *The Illusion of Difference: Realities of Ethnicity in Canada and the United States.* Toronto: C.D. Howe Institute.

Richard, Madeline A.
1991 *Ethnic Groups and Marital Choices: Ethnic History and Marital Assimilation in Canada, 1871 and 1971.* Vancouver: University of British Columbia Press.

Richmond, Anthony H.
1972 *Ethnic Residential Segregation in Metropolitan Toronto*. Toronto: Institute for Behavioral Research, York University.

Richmond, Anthony H.
1972 *Readings in Race and Ethnic Relations*. Toronto: Pergamon Press.

Richmond, Anthony H.
1994 *Global Apartheid: Refugees, Racism, and the New World Order*. Toronto: Oxford University Press.

Richmond, Anthony H. and Warren E. Kalbach
1980 *Factors in the Adjustment of Immigrant and Their Descendants*. Ottawa: Minister of Supply and Services.

Riesman, David
1950 *The Lonely Crowd*. New Haven, Connecticut: Yale University Press.

Rioux, Marcel
1971 *Quebec in Question*. Toronto: James Lewis and Samuel.

Rioux, Marcel
1973 'The Development of Ideologies in Quebec' in Gerald Gold and Marc-Adelard Tremblay (eds), *Communities and Cultures in French Canada*. Toronto: Holt, Rinehart and Winston.

Rioux, Marcel and Yves Martin
1964 *French-Canadian Society*, Volume I. Ottawa: Carleton Library.

Rothman, Jack
1960 'In-Group Identification and Out-Group Association: A Theoretical and Experimental Study'. *Journal of Jewish Communal Service* 37: 81–93.

Royal Commission on Bilingualism and Biculturalism
1965 *A Preliminary Report*. Ottawa: Queen's Printer.

Royal Commission on Bilingualism and Biculturalism
1970 *The Cultural Contributions of Other Ethnic Groups*. Volume IV. Ottawa: Queen's Printer.

Russel, P.
1993 *Constitutional Odyssey*. Toronto: University of Toronto Press.

Ryan, John
1977 *The Agricultural Economy of Manitoba Hutterite Colonies*. Ottawa: McClelland and Stewart.

Samuals, T.J.
1992 *Visible Minorities in Canada: A Projection*. Toronto: Advertising Foundation.

Sapir, Edward
1949 *Language*. New York: Harcourt Brace World.

Satzewich, Victor Nicholas
1992 *Deconstructing a Nation: Immigration, Multiculturalism and Racism in '90s Canada*. Halifax: Fernwood Publishing.

Satzewich, Victor Nicholas
1995 'Social Stratification: Class and Racial Inequality' in Singh Bolaria (ed.), *Social Issues and Contraditions in Canadian Society*, 2nd ed. Toronto: Harcourt Brace Canada.

Saywell, John T.
1968 'Introduction' in Pierre Trudeau, *Federalism and the French Canadians*. Toronto: Macmillan Canada.
Secretary of State
1972 *Revised Handbook of Selected Ethnic Organization in Canada*. Canadian Citizenship Branch, Ottawa.
Segalman, Ralph
1967 'Jewish Identity Scales: A Report'. *Jewish Social Studies* 29: 92–111.
Sev'er, Aysan, W.W. Isajiw, and Leo Driedger
1993 'Anomie as Powerlessness: Sorting Ethnic Group Prestige, Class and Gender'. *Canadian Ethnic Studies* 25: 86–99.
Shaffir, William
1974 *Life in a Religious Community: The Lubavitcher Chassidim in Montreal*. Toronto: Holt, Rinehart and Winston.
Shaffir, William
1993 'The Hassidic Community of Tash' in Robert Brym et al. (eds), *The Jews in Canada*. Toronto: Oxford University Press.
Shaffir, William and Morton Weinfeld
1981 'Canada and the Jews: An Introduction' in Morton Weinfeld et al. (eds), *The Canadian Jewish Mosaic*. Toronto: John Wiley and Sons.
Shevky, Eshref and Wendell Bell
1955 *Social Area Analysis*. Stanford: University of Stanford Press.
Shibutani, Tamotsu and Kian M. Kwan
1967 *Ethnic Stratification: A Comparative Approach*. New York: Macmillan.
Shore, Marlene
1987 *The Science of Social Redemption: McGill, the Chicago School, and the Origins of Social Research in Canada*. Toronto: University of Toronto Press.
Simeon, Richard
1979 'Regionalism and Canadian Political Institutions' in Richard Schultz et al. (eds), *The Canadian Political Process*. Toronto: Holt, Rinehart and Winston.
Simeon, Richard and David J. Elkins
1979 'Regional Political Cultures in Canada' in Richard Schultz et al. (eds), *The Canadian Political Process*. Toronto: Holt, Rinehart and Winston.
Simmel, Georg
1950 *The Sociology of Georg Simmel*, Kurt Wolff (ed.). Glencoe, IL: The Free Press.
Simmel, Georg
1955 *Conflict and the Web of Group Affiliations*. Glencoe, IL: The Free Press.
Smith, Miriam
1992 'Quebec-Canada Association: Divergent Paths to a Common Economic Agenda' in Daniel Drache and Roberto Perin (eds), *Negotiating With a Sovereign Quebec*. Toronto: James Lorimer.
Spates, James L. and John J. Macionis
1987 *The Sociology of Cities*, 2nd ed. Belmont, CA: Wadsworth.
Stafford, James
1992 'The Impact of the New Immigration Policy on Racism in Canada' in Vic

Satzewich (ed.), *Deconstructing a Nation: Immigration, Multiculturalism and Racism in '90s Canada*. Halifax: Fernwood Publishing.

Stanley, F.G.
1960 *The Birth of Western Canada: A History of the Riel Rebellions*. Toronto: University of Toronto Press.

Stanley, F.G.
1969 *Louis Riel: Rebel of the Western Frontier or Victim of Politics and Prejudice?* Toronto: Copp Clark Publishing.

Statistics Canada
1983 *1981 Census of Canada: 20 Percent Data Base*. Ottawa: Supply and Services.

Statistics Canada
1984 *Canada's Native People*. Ottawa: Statistics Canada.

Statistics Canada
1984 *1981 Census of Canada, Catalogue 92–911*. Ottawa: Minister of Supply and Services. Table 1.

Statistics Canada
1985 *Languages in Canada*. Ottawa: Minister of Supply and Services Canada.

Statistics Canada
1993 *Home Language and Mother Tongue: The Nation*, Catalogue 93–317.

Statistics Canada
1993 *Ethnic Origin: The Nation*, Catalogue 93–315. Ottawa: Statistics Canada.

Statistics Canada
1994 *Profile of Urban and Rural Areas*, Part B. Ottawa: Statistics Canada.

Stebbins, Robert A.
1994 *The Franco-Calgarians: French Language, Leisure, and Linguistic Life-Style in an Anglophone City*. Toronto: University of Toronto Press.

Stephenson, Peter H.
1991 *The Hutterian People: Ritual, Rebirth and the Evolution of Communal Life*. Lanham, NY: University Press of America.

Sugiman, Pamela and H.K. Nishio
1993 'Socialization and Cultural Duality Among Aging Japanese Canadians'. *Canadian Ethnic Studies* 15: 17–35.

Sunahara, M. Ann
1980 'Federal Policy and the Japanese Canadians: The Decision to Evacuate, 1942' in K.V. Ujimoto and G. Hirabayashi (eds), *Visible Minorities and Multiculturalism: Asians in Canada*. Toronto: Butterworths.

Tan, Jin and Patricia E. Roy
1985 *The Chinese in Canada*. Ottawa: Canadian Historical Association.

Taras, David and Morton Weinfeld
1993 'Continuity and Criticism: North American Jews and Israel' in Robert Brym et al. (eds), *The Jews in Canada*. Toronto: Oxford University Press.

Taylor, D.M.
1981 'Stereotypes and Intergroup Relations' in R.C. Gardner and R. Kalin (eds), *A Canadian Social Psychology of Ethnic Relations*. Toronto: Methuen.

Taylor, D.M. and R.C. Gardner
1970 'Bicultural Communications: A Study of Communicational Efficiency and

Person Perception' in J.W. Berry and G.J.S. Wilde (eds), *Social Psychology: The Canadian Context*. Toronto: McClelland and Stewart.

Taylor, D.M. and R. Sigal

1982 'Defining "Québécois": The Role of Ethnic Heritage, Language, and Political Orientation'. *Canadian Ethnic Studies* 14: 59–70.

Taylor, K.W.

1991 'Racism in Canadian Immigration Policy'. *Canadian Ethnic Studies* 23: 1–20.

Tepperman, Lorne

1975 *Social Mobility in Canada*. Toronto: University of Toronto Press.

Thomas, William I.

1921 *Old World Traits Transplanted*. New York: Harper.

Thomas, William I. and Florian Znaniecki

1918–20 *The Polish Peasant in Europe and America*, Volumes I–IV. Boston: The Gorham Press.

Tilly, Charles

1967 'Anthropology on the Town'. *Habitat* 10: 20–5.

Toennies, Ferdinand

1957 *Community and Society*, translated by Charles P. Loomis. East Lansing, MI: Michigan State University Press.

Trudeau, Pierre

1962 'The Conflict of Nationalism in Canada'. *Cité Libre*, April.

Trudeau, Pierre

1968 *Federalism and the French Canadians*. Toronto: The Macmillan Company.

Trudel, Marcel

1985 'Jacques Cartier' in *The Canadian Encyclopedia*. Edmonton: Hurtig Publishers.

Tulchinsky, Gerald

1993 'The Contours of Canadian Jewish History' in Robert Brym et al. (eds), *The Jews in Canada*. Toronto: Oxford University Press.

Turpel, Mary Ellen

1992 'Does the Road to Quebec Sovereignty Run Through Aboriginal Territory?' in Daniel Drache and Roberto Perin (eds), *Negotiating With a Sovereign Quebec*. Toronto: James Lorimer.

Tuzlak, Aysan Sev'er

1989 'Joint Effects of Race and Confidence on Perceptions and Influence: Implications for Blacks in Decision-Making Positions'. *Canadian Ethnic Studies* 21: 103–19.

Ujimoto, K. Victor

1983 'Institutional Controls and Their Impact on Japanese Canadian Social Relations, 1877–1977' in Peter S. Li and B. Singh Bolaria (eds), *Racial Minorities in Multicultural Canada*. Toronto: Garamond Press.

Ujimoto, K. Victor and Gordon Hirabayashi

1980 *Visible Minorities and Multiculturalism: Asians in Canada*. Toronto: Butterworths.

Vallee, Frank G.

1969 'Regionalism and Ethnicity: The French-Canadian Case' in B.Y. Gard (ed.), *Perspectives on Regions and Regionalism*. Edmonton: University of Alberta Press.

Vallee, Frank G.
1981   'The Sociology of John Porter: Ethnicity as Anachronism'. *Canadian Review of Sociology and Anthropology* 8: 639–50.
Vallee, Frank G. and Albert Dufour
1974   'The Bilingual Belt: A Garrotte for the French?' *Laurentian University Review* 6, 2.
Vallee, Frank G. and John deVries
1975   *Data Book for the Conference on Individual, Language and Society*. Ottawa: The Canada Council.
Vallee, Frank G. and John deVries
1978   'Issues and Trends in Bilingualism in Canada' in J.A. Fishman (ed.), *Advances in the Study of Societal Multilingualism*. The Hague: Mouton.
van den Berghe, Pierre L.
1981   *The Ethnic Phenomenon*. New York: Elsevier.
Wade, Mason
1968   *The French Canadians*, Volumes I and II. Toronto: Macmillan of Canada.
Walker, James W. St.G.
1984   *The West Indians in Canada*. Ottawa: Canadian Historical Association.
Walker, James W. St.G.
1992   *The Black Loyalists: The Search for a Promised Land in Nova Scotia and Sierra Leone 1783–1870*. Toronto: University of Toronto Press.
Wallace, Samuel E.
1981   'Regional Sociology: The South'. *Sociological Spectrum* 14: 429–42.
Weber, Max
1894   Speech made at the Evangelisch-Soziale Kongress in the biography written by Marianne Weber.
Weber, Max
1904, 1958 *The Protestant Ethic and the Spirit of Capitalism*, translated by Talcott Parsons. New York: Scribner.
Weber, Max
1978   *Economy and Society*, Volumes I and II. Guenther Roth and Claus Wittich (eds). Berkeley, CA: University of California Press.
Weeks, John R.
1994   *Population: An Introduction to Concepts and Issues*, 5th ed. Belmont, CA: Wadsworth Publishing.
Weiman, Gabriel and Conrad Winn
1993   'Hate on Trial: The Zundel Affair, The Media, Public Opinion in Canada' in Brym et al. (eds), *The Jews in Canada*. Toronto: Oxford University Press.
Weinfeld, Morton
1985   'Myth and Reality in the Canadian Mosaic: "Affective Ethnicity"' in Rita Bienvenue and Jay Goldstein (eds), *Ethnicity and Ethnic Relations*. Toronto: Butterworths.
Weinfeld, Morton
1993   'The Ethnic Sub-Economy: Explication and Analysis of a Case Study of the Jews of Montreal' in Brym et al. (eds), *The Jews in Canada*. Toronto: Oxford University Press.

Weinfeld, Morton
1994 'Ethnic Assimilation and the Retention of Ethnic Cultures' in John Berry and J.A. Laponce (eds), *Ethnicity and Culture in Canada*. Toronto: University of Toronto Press.
Weinfeld, Morton, William Shaffir, and I. Cotler
1981 *The Canadian Jewish Mosaic*. Toronto: John Wiley.
Westie, Frank R.
1959 'Social Distance Scales: A Tool for the Study of Stratification'. *Sociology and Social Research* 43: 251–58.
Wickberg, Edgar (ed.)
1982 *From China to Canada: A History of the Chinese Communities in Canada*. Toronto: McClelland and Stewart.
Wiley, Norbert F.
1967 'The Ethnic Mobility Trap and Stratification Theory'. *Social Problems* 15: 147–59.
Winks, Robin W.
1969 'Negro School Segregation in Ontario and Nova Scotia'. *Canadian Historical Review* 50: 164–91.
Winks, Robin W.
1971 *The Blacks in Canada: A History*. Montreal: McGill-Queen's University Press.
Wirth, Louis
1928 *The Ghetto*. Chicago: University of Chicago Press.
Wylie, Ruth C.
1961 *The Self Concept*. Lincoln: University of Nebraska Press.
Young, Donald R.
1971 'Introduction to the Republished Edition' in W.I. Thomas, *Old World Traits Transplanted*. Montclair, NJ: Patterson Smith.
Yu, Miriam
1987 'Human Rights, Discrimination, and Coping Behavior of the Chinese in Canada'. *Canadian Ethnic Studies* 19: 114–21.
Yuzyk, Paul
1975 'Canada as a Multi-Cultural Society'. Paper presented at the Conference on Multiculturalism and Third World Immigrants, University of Alberta, Edmonton, September 3–6.
Zarbaugh, Harvey
1929 *The Gold Coast and the Slum*. Chicago: University of Chicago Press.

Aberhart, William, 306
Aboriginal people, 17, 42, 60, 65–8,
82–4, 240, 245; and assimilation, 28,
32; average incomes of, 198; census
1991, 242; collective rights, 294–5;
land claims, 3, 36, 43, 97, 278,
302–5; reality structure, 168; on
reserves, 292; residential concentrations of, 216, 219; rural population,
64, 67; sacred canopies of, 155–61,
176; socio-economic status, 278;
special demographic type, 68; treaty
rights, 293–4; in Winnipeg, 212–13.
See also Treaties 1–11
Acadia, 112
Acadians, expulsion of, 296–8
Act of Union (1840), 103
Adorno, Theodor, 233
affirmative action, 56
Africans: census 1991, 243–4;
immigrants, 242
Africville, Nova Scotia, 222–3
Alabama, 19
Algonkin linguistic group, 156
Algonquian language families, 84
alienation, 14, 152
Allport, Gordon, 233, 271
amalgamation, theory of, 25, 29–31, 38
American Bill of Rights, 285–8
American Civil War, 286
Americanization Studies, 19–20
American Journal of Sociology, 114
American Revolution, 29, 188, 222
American South, 75–6
American Sociological Review, The, 114
Anderson, Alan B., 137–8, 140, 267
Anderson, Grace, 173–4
Anderson, Wolseley W., 223, 225,
250–1
Anglo-conformity, 26, 29, 31, 41, 103,
105; in jobs, 201; model, 30
Anglo-Ontarians, in Tecumseh, 117
Angus Reid Group, 261, 263

anomie, 14, 152–4, 160
anti-Asian groups, 56
anti-Semitism, 283; groups, 56; and
Keegstra affair, 306; and religion,
280–2
apartheid, 219–31, 238
aparthood, 230
Arctic cultural area, 84
Argall, 296, 298
Armstrong, Frederick, 188, 190, 198,
204
Asian immigrants, 54–5, 59, 73–4, 242;
and assimilation, 28; socio-economic
status, 248. *See also* South Asians
Aspen Belt, 133
assimilation, 19–20, 148; and Chinese,
230; cultural, 31; Durham on, 103;
seven forms of, 31–2, 40; theory of,
19, 25–9, 35, 38
Assimilation in American Life (Gordon),
31
Athapascan language families, 84, 156
Atlantic Canada: anglophone and
anglocultural, 88–9; foreign-born
immigrants, 63
autostereotypes, 267, 269
aversive racism, in United States, 259
Azores Islands, 175

Balakrishnan, T.R., 42, 173, 175, 212,
214, 216, 231
Ballachey, Egerton L., 265
Banton, Michael, 233, 265
Bardikoff, Alan, 306
Battle of Seven Oaks, 300
Bedford Basin, 222
bedroom communities, 208
behaviourist view, of ethnic identity,
130
Bell, Wendell, 207–8, 210, 212, 214,
231
Bendix, Reinhard, 9
Berger, Peter, 154–6, 176

mana, 152
Manitoba, 94
Manitoba School Question, 292, 294
Manning, Premier, 306
Marchand, Jean, 119–20
marginality, 132; in civilized societies, 2
marginal person, 46–7, 49
markers of identification, 100
Maroons, 225
marriage, 279; approval of intergroup,
    277–8; United Nations Universal
    Declaration of Human Rights, 290
Martin, Yves, 115
Marx, Karl, 10, 26, 38, 182–3, 204, 284;
    on ethnicity, 4, 186; and industrial
    change, 11; materialism and strati-
    fication, 12–14; and production,
    12–13; view of conflict, 37
Marxism: and the labour market, 43–4;
    theory of social class, 181–2; and
    value systems, 10
mass migration, into the West, 95
master-servant relationship, and racism,
    241
materialism, 10, 12–13
Matthews, Ralph, 76
Mattis, Winston, 259
mechanical solidarity, concept of, 15
medicine bundles, 160
Meech Lake Accord (1987), 9, 122–3,
    126
melting pot, 38, 97; model, 260–1; and
    New York, 33; theory, 26–8
Mendel, Gregor, 5, 234
Mennonites, 22, 138, 168, 170–2;
    churches, 281
Métis, 160; buffalo culture, 300; census
    1991, 66; nation, 298–302
Mezoff, Richard, 275–6, 281
micro sociological interactionist
    approach, 131–3
middlemen minorities (MM), 47–9
Mid-South Sociological Society, 75
migration: into the West, 95; popula-
    tion growth, 52; to Toronto, 47
Mills, C. Wright, 184

Miner, Horace, 23, 114–16, 118, 127,
    169
minority-majority model, 30, 253–4
mobility trap hypothesis, 186, 187
mode of production, 182
modified assimilation theory, 25, 31–3,
    35, 38, 40, 105, 147
modified pluralism, 47, 120;
    Mennonites, 172; theory, 25, 33–4,
    35, 38, 147
Mol, Hans, 35, 153
Moncton, French language in, 89
Mongoloid, racial type, 234–5
monoethnicity, in northern Europe, 2
monoethnic nationalism, 30
Montreal, 42, 64; Blacks in, 220;
    Chinese in, 227, 230; ethnic
    diversity in, 214–19; ethnocultural
    identity in, 141; immigrants in, 73,
    74, 225; Jewish community, 165–7;
    residential minority concentrations,
    173; segregation in, 210
Moore, W.E., 181
morality, and rules of conduct, 16
Mormons, 22, 170–1
mosaic model, 97, 260–1
Moynihan, Daniel P., 31, 33–4, 35–6,
    131, 165
Mulroney, Brian, 122
multicultural belt, 89, 92
multiculturalism, 79, 267, 282, 283; in
    Bilingual Belt, 90–1; in Canada, 35,
    36, 41, 108, 145; and language
    maintenance, 92; in Ontario, 93;
    policy, 55; in Quebec, 87–8, 105; in
    US, 272; in the West, 96
multicultural pluralist model, 105
multiethnicity, 2–3
multiple nuclei model, 208, 231
multiple responses (MR), in the West,
    95
Musynski, Alicja, 276
Myrdal, 233

Nagel, Joan, 3
nationalism, 2, 4, 29

DATE DUE

OCT 19 2005			
NOV 0 8 2007			